INTERPRETING THE BIBLE

INTERPRETING THE BIBLE

by

A. BERKELEY MICKELSEN

Professor of New Testament Interpretation
Bethel Theological Seminary
St. Paul, Minnesota

Wm. B. Eerdmans Publishing Company
Grand Rapids, Michigan

First printing, December 1963
Second printing, December 1966
Third printing, March 1970
Fourth printing, July 1972
Fifth printing, October 1974
Sixth printing, September 1976

ISBN 0-8028-3192-3

Library of Congress catalog card number, 63-17785

To those whose support made Graduate School Studies possible

My parents

ANNA HANSEN MICKELSEN (D. 1959)

ANTON MICKELSEN

My dear friends

CLARA AND CLARENCE W. HYDE

". . . as good stewards of God's varied grace" (I Pet. 4:10).

PREFACE

Since the close of World War II there has been a rapidly growing interest in the theological science of hermeneutics. This revival of interest in the methodology of interpreting the Scriptures is found among diverse groups of Christians. It is prominent in the various branches of Protestantism. It is clear among the various Roman Catholic orders and in the Greek orthodox communion. Christians not only want to communicate to the men of today, but they want to know the biblical basis for what they have to say.

This serious interest in hermeneutics has helped to show why Christians differ with each other. Different principles and procedures yield different results, and even the same basic principles may be applied differently. Such an understanding of differences, however, is necessary to helping others and to being helped by them in one's own interpretative endeavors.

The same serious interest in interpretation has also brought into focus agreements among various interpreters. When interpreters from various groups have worked together to unfold the meaning of a passage, agreement on many significant conclusions has been reached. Thus hermeneutics is a potent unifying force in the Christian church.

The most impelling motive for learning to interpret the scriptures correctly is the necessity to understand clearly for ourselves exactly what we are trying to communicate to others. The need to communicate all of the gospel message is urgent: "Woe to me if I do not preach the gospel" (I Cor. 9:16); but double is the woe to one who, though he claims to be preaching the gospel, does in fact not do so because he has misinterpreted the written record that presents the gospel. It is my earnest desire that every reader of this book shall proclaim the

vii

truth of God with new urgency, and with greater understanding.

The principles found in this book will help the reader to understand that much of the variety in interpretation is good and that it represents a creativity for which the Christian church may be grateful. The principles will also show that much of the variety is caused by a failure to follow sound methodology in interpretation. The purpose of this book is (i) to show that the student of the Bible must have a proper method of interpretation to get at the full meaning of the Bible; (ii) to discuss the many elements of such interpretations; and thus (iii) to guide the serious reader into a correct understanding of the Scriptures.

A book of this kind makes one aware of how much he owes to others. My teachers and students, and a great number of writers on biblical interpretation have all contributed to this volume. Others have contributed in a very specific way.

I am greatly indebted to my wife, Alvera Johnson Mickelsen, for editing the first draft of the manuscript and for helping in many other ways. I am also indebted to Clifton J. Orlebeke for his pertinent criticisms and his editing of the entire manuscript to give it evenness and consistency of expression. Any deficiencies in arrangement or manner of presentation are my sole responsibility.

To the Alumni Association of Wheaton College I offer my thanks and tribute for their support of research in the various areas of the humanities, biological sciences, physical sciences, and social sciences. I was the recipient of the Alumni Research grant for the 1961-62 school year. This grant freed me from all teaching responsibilities during that year so that I could devote my whole time to research and writing. Without such help, I could not have written this volume.

I would like to thank Professor Merrill C. Tenney, Dean of the Graduate School, Wheaton College, for his many indications of help and support. In the second semester of the 1960-61 school year he took over one of my courses so that more time was available to me for research. Such unselfish giving is a beautiful expression of Christian love in action. In addition I would like to acknowledge my indebtedness to Professors Otto A. Piper, Amos Niven Wilder, and Warren Young for their help in providing bibliographical information. Finally, for his painstaking work on the subject index, I express my thanks to Mr. Warren A. Harbeck, who was my graduate assistant during the past academic year.

Part of this volume I used in the spring of 1963 as the McElwain Lectures at Gordon Divinity School, Beverly Farms, Massachusetts. I was happy indeed to discuss with Gordon faculty members and students many of the subjects here presented.

A. Berkeley Mickelsen

CONTENTS

INTRODUCTION

CONCLUSION

INTRODUCTION

I Source of the Interpreter's Principles

IMPORTANCE OF INTERPRETATION

The term "hermeneutics" designates both the science and art of interpretation. The Greek verb *hermēneuō* means "to interpret or explain." The Greek noun *hermēneia* means "interpretation," "explanation."[1] In both the Greek counterpart and the contemporary technical term, interpretation has to do with meaning. Interpretation as a discipline is important because meaning has to do with the core of a man's thinking.

The need for interpretation is not peculiar to the Scriptures. Any document, ancient or modern, must be interpreted. The decisions of the Supreme Court are actually interpretations of the Constitution of the United States. Philosophers often debate what Plato, Aristotle, or Kant meant by certain phrases or assertions. The archaeologist who carefully analyzes a religious writing from the Dead Sea Scrolls often finds statements that puzzle him, and he must use all the principles and skills he knows to reach even a tentative conclusion of meaning.

Whatever the documents, the interpreter must be careful not to distort the meaning. Such care is required especially in the interpretation of the Scriptures, for they involve not only history, proverbs, peoples, and institutions, but the very message or revelation of God. Timothy was commanded to exercise great care in handling this authoritative message: "Make every effort to present [render] yourself approved [by test] to God, a workman who does not need to be ashamed, rightly handling

---

[1] Henry George Liddell and Robert Scott, *A Greek-English Lexicon*, 9th ed. (1940), I, 690.

3

the message of truth" (II Tim. 2:15).[2] To handle the message
of truth rightly demands sound principles of interpretation.

Some Christians fear that an emphasis upon such principles
ignores the illumination of the Holy Spirit. This fear has some
foundation. Many have approached the Bible in a mechanical,
rationalistic fashion. Fleeing from the extreme of mystical
pietism, they have rushed into the error of regarding man's
intellect as self-sufficient. They have thought that man, strictly
by his own intellectual efforts, could search out and make
known the true and deep meanings of Scripture. On the opposite side, there have been some sincere people who have
thought that the witness of the Spirit in the heart of the believer enables him automatically to know the correct meaning
of every phrase, or verse, or passage. True, the illumination of
the Spirit is essential, but such illumination can be hindered by
wrong approaches to the Scripture. The Christian must skill-
fully use sound principles in his efforts to uncover meaning.
Paul speaks forcefully on this point: "Now we are not, as the
many, adulterating [i.e., lit. falsifying in the process of selling]
the message of God, but as out of pure motives, certainly as
from God, before God, in Christ we are speaking" (II Cor.
2:17).[3] The interpreter must have pure motives. He must speak as
one sent from God. He must present his conclusions before God.
He must do all this with an awareness that he is bound to Christ.

2 The Greek word *orthotomeō* (rightly handling) only occurs here and in
Prov. 3:6; 11:5 (LXX). In Proverbs the Greek word *hodous* (ways) is found
with the verb. There the figure is one of cutting a path in a straight
direction. Walter Bauer suggests here, "guiding the word of truth along a
straight path," *Greek-English Lexicon of the New Testament* (1957), p. 584.
But the context here does not involve a builder of roads or a guide, but
rather a workman. Hence, R. St. John Parry suggests that the figure may
be of a stone mason who cuts stones fair and straight to fit into their places
in a building, *The Pastoral Epistles, ad loc.* Moulton and Milligan argue
that *orthotomeō* is analogous to *kainotomeō*. Since the latter word means
"to make a new or strange assertion," the former word would mean "to
teach the word aright," *Vocabulary of the Greek Testament*, pp. 456-57.
Spicq agrees with this emphasis when he says that Timothy is "to set forth
[the message of truth] correctly and exactly as he understands it," *Les Épistres
Pastorales*, p. 353. The Vulgate, often criticized when it misses the mark,
certainly has an excellent translation of *orthotomounta* by its rendering *recte
tractantem*—"handling rightly" (correctly, accurately). The passage urges
a careful handling of the various elements in the message of truth as one
puts them together and proclaims that message.

3 The participle (*kapēleuontes*) which is translated above as "adulterating"
means *to trade in, peddle, huckster something;* Bauer, *op. cit.*, p. 404. Since
the tradesmen engaged in many tricks, the word often had a bad connotation. Windisch (*TWNT*, III, 608-09) points out that Paul's usage combines
two ideas: the offering or presenting of the message of God for money and
the falsifying of the word by additions. He concludes by saying: "*kapēleuein*

BASIC OBJECTIVE OF INTERPRETERS

Simply stated, the task of interpreters of the Bible is *to find out the meaning of a statement (command, question) for the author and for the first hearers or readers, and thereupon to transmit that meaning to modern readers.* The interpreter will observe whether a given statement tends to be understood by a modern reader identically, similarly, or differently from the sense intended by the ancient writer, and will adjust his explanation accordingly.

It is evident that all biblical interpretation has two dimensions. The first is concerned with discovering the original meaning of a statement, while the second takes account of changes in meaning which contemporary readers may attach to the same words. Much attention has recently been paid to the second dimension, and properly so. From the first century A.D. through the Middle Ages, the gulf between the New Testament world and later generations was not great. From the Renaissance to the nineteenth century, however, the gulf widened, and today modern man can scarcely appreciate many features of the ancient world and its outlook which are simply assumed by the biblical authors.

Modern man belongs to an age of technology and to the culture which accompanies it. His environment is different, and his concepts are often correspondingly different. For instance, he tends to think of society individualistically, while the biblical writer emphasizes group unity. The modern reader understands little of family solidarity, of the ancient pantheon of pagan deities, and of the tensions peculiar to a society composed of aristocrats, freedmen, and slaves. Hence he does not grasp fully Paul's discussions of racial solidarity, of meat offered to idols, and of the attitude and reaction of a slave. He understands *something,* but seldom realizes how much of the total meaning eludes him.

VALID AND INVALID PRINCIPLES

Principles of hermeneutics are precepts which express or describe the various ways followed by interpreters to get at

ton logon tou theou is thereby a drastic expression for a monstrous misuse which is carried on with the Holy Word. Paul for that reason on his part immediately sets forth in comparison the correct deportment, his deportment: unselfishness, subjection to God's own word, responsible self-consciousness in relation to God, subjection to Christ." The abbreviation *TWNT,* as used above, refers to G. Friedrich and G. Kittel, *Theologisches Wörterbuch zum Neuen Testament* (8 vols.; 1933 and ff.) .

meaning. They are statements of procedure. These principles may be *adopted* (i.e., consciously learned), *adapted* (i.e., consciously changed), or simply *appropriated* from one's habits of thinking (i.e., unconscious acceptance of what the person regards as axiomatic or the natural way to treat any particular kind of subject matter). These principles of hermeneutics are *valid* or *invalid* depending on whether or not they really unfold the meaning a statement had for the author and the first hearers or readers. They are *valid* or *invalid* depending on whether or not readers get the *idea* that the original author intended to convey. The difference between valid and invalid principles or procedures may be illustrated as follows.

(a) One valid principle for determining the meaning of a word is to study the context of the word plus the usage or meanings which the word is known to have in other contexts. To do this, one must have specific examples of the various meanings of the word, and these examples must be drawn from the same period of history as the writing being studied. On the other hand, an invalid principle is the rule that one may use etymology to determine the meaning of later occurrences of a word. Etymology is the science of tracing the meaning of a word back to its root. The etymologist asks: what did this particular word mean in its earliest form? When a word may be broken up into two or three parts, the root meaning of each part may be considered. But etymological meaning without clear-cut examples of actual usage contemporary with the given example is worthless. Such procedure may sound profound, but in reality etymological meaning may lead the interpreter far from the true meaning of a word in a particular context. For example the English word "enthusiasm" has a Latin and Greek derivation and means etymologically "the fact of being possessed by a god." As late as 1807 it is used in the sense of "possession by a god, supernatural inspiration, prophetic or poetic ecstacy."[4] But now this etymological meaning is no longer used. The word simply means "rapturous intensity of feeling on behalf of a person, cause, etc.; passionate eagerness in any pursuit."[5] To take an example of the word "enthusiasm" from a work written in the twentieth century and to give it the meaning "possessed by a god" would be to misinterpret it completely. In the twentieth century there are no examples of the word which reflect the etymological meaning.

(b) For a second and more sophisticated example of valid and invalid hermeneutic principles, we may begin by consider-

---

4 *The Oxford Universal Dictionary on Historical Principles* (1955), p. 617.
5 *Ibid.*

ing a valuable discussion by Rudolf Bultmann. Bultmann has a chapter on "The Nature of History (A)" in which he discusses the problem of hermeneutics and the question of historical knowledge.[6] He rightly insists that "each interpretation is guided by a certain interest, by a certain putting of the question."[7] Why is a man interested in a particular document? What question or purpose makes him consider the text? This interest and purpose Bultmann calls a *pre-understanding*. A document from the past may be interpreted from the standpoint of an historian. Or the interest may be that of a psychologist. Another reader may turn to a document because of his interest in aesthetics. Finally, Bultmann suggests that one may view a document from an existential perspective—seeking to understand history not in its empirical course but as the sphere of life within which the human being moves, within which human life gains and develops its possibilities.[8]

This is, of course, Bultmann's own framework or perspective. Yet any technical framework only makes possible a more unified interest. Certainly an historian could be interested in aesthetics and could also consider an ancient document from the standpoint of men looking for meaning to existence. Most people who approach the Scriptures have a rather complex "pre-understanding." But all of the various elements in this pre-understanding do affect the results. Bultmann himself is no mere existentialist in his approach to the biblical literature. He claims to be the kind of historian who holds to an unbreakable chain of cause and effect in history. This view of history is also held by philosophers known as logical positivists.

> The historical method includes the presupposition that history is a unity in the sense of a closed continuum of effects in which individual events are connected by the succession of cause and effect. . . . This closedness means that the continuum of historical happenings cannot be rent by the interference of supernatural transcendent powers and that, therefore, there is no "miracle" in this sense of the word.[9]

Here it becomes clear that "pre-understanding" and "presupposition" are related as a part to a whole. A presupposition is one particular part of a total pre-understanding.

Bultmann himself illustrates the fact that presuppositions tend to control the interpreter in his investigation. He readily

---

[6] Rudolf Bultmann, *The Presence of Eternity* (1957), pp. 110-22.
[7] *Ibid.*, p. 113.
[8] *Ibid.*, pp. 114-115.
[9] Rudolf Bultmann, "Is Exegesis Without Presuppositions Possible?" in *Existence and Faith* (1960), pp. 291-292.

admits that the Old Testament speaks of the interference by God in history. But he claims that since historical science cannot demonstrate such an interference, the Old Testament merely records that there were those who believed in such an interference. The interpreter cannot say that God has not acted in history. If a man wants to see an act of God in an historical event, he may do so. But history will always record this event in terms of immanent historical causes.[10] Hence a Christian may believe that God led some Israelites out of Egypt. Yet since there are no accounts outside of the Bible "of a company of slaves that escaped from Egyptian slavery and that was established as a racial and religious community by a man named Moses,"[11] one must depend upon evidence which is circumstantial. The people known as *Habiru* or *Apiru* led a seminomadic life. It is likely that the Hebrews of the Old Testament were a part of these peoples since their migration to Egypt and their manner of life seen in Genesis and Exodus is very similar. History indicates the "perennial tendency of nomadic and seminomadic groups to infiltrate into the sown lands of Egypt and Palestine."[12] Thus for Bultmann, history is limited to cause and effect relationships in a time-space framework. The possibility of God breaking through into these relationships is automatically ruled out by an empirical definition of what is possible. This view is widespread among many who would not classify themselves as sharing Bultmann's existentialistic demythologizing approach to scriptural materials.

There is no neutral ground in this controversy. If God did break through into history[13] as the Bible records, then he is not only active in history, but he acts freely and purposefully above and beyond history. He then becomes the Cause of all other causes and effects, and at the same time he may act in, with, alongside of, and apart from any secondary causes or effects. Instead of Bultmann's *closed continuum,* such an interpreter would have a *controlled continuum.* Nothing is haphazard or erratic. God has established laws, but he is not a prisoner of his own laws. Bultmann has a universe with a lid on. Unfortunately one gets the uncomfortable feeling that not only is man shut up to existence under this lid but so is God.

Hence orthodoxy, insisting on a controlled continuum, is

---

10 *Ibid.,* p. 292.

11 Cf. J. Coert Rylaarsdam, "Exodus," *The Interpreter's Bible,* ed. George Arthur Buttrick *et al.,* I, 836.

12 *Ibid.*

13 See H. H. Farmer, "The Bible: Its Significance and Authority," *The Interpreter's Bible,* I, 5-7.

actually asserting the freedom of God. That God is free to act becomes clear in the miracles of Jesus. As we examine these carefully, certain characteristics emerge. There are other accounts in ancient times of miracles, but there are vast differences between these and the biblical accounts. Grundmann makes some wise observations on this point:

> As a doer of miracles Jesus does not stand alone in his time. The Hellenistic and Jewish environment is full of miraculous events and miracles of the gods, and miraculous deeds. The miracles of Jesus are to be differentiated in a threefold manner from the miracles of his time: *a.* The NT miracles of Jesus have nothing to do with magic or magical means and proceedings as do the majority of the miracles outside of the New Testament. *b.* The miracles are called forth through the powerfully fulfilled word of Jesus which has nothing to do with magical formuli . . . The miracles of Jesus are a part of the breaking through of the reign of God, which Jesus brought with his person in proclamation and action. They are the reign of God which overcomes and represses the Satanic-demonic sphere of influence. The miracles of Jesus are, as his entire history, eschatological events. . . . In this situation the basic distinction to all other miraculous events appears although the miracles of Jesus may exhibit a number of parallels. Therein the history of Jesus is eschatological history so that with him the reign of God breaks through. *c.* The miracles have as a supposition the faith of the authors and of those who receive the miracles. They are accomplished thus in a thoroughly personal relationship. Jesus can do no miracles in Nazareth because faith is lacking (Matt. 13:58 & parallels). The disciples were not able to heal the boy because they lacked faith (Matt. 17:19-20; Mark 9:28-29). By this, magic is removed in this supposition: not the knowledge of magical means or formuli, but on the contrary, the personal relation between God and Jesus on the one hand, between Jesus and men on the other, accomplishes the miracle without magical compulsion or force.[14]

Miracles then become a sample of what will happen when God's power is fully expressed and when his rule becomes total. The idea of a controlled continuum in which God may act according to his purposes for men is a motif that occurs frequently in Scripture. The idea of a closed continuum is invalid because it tries to make a norm that controls God. But God will not be regulated in this fashion. The Scriptures assert God's freedom: "Who knows the mind of the Lord, or who has become his advisor, who has instructed him" (Isa. 40:13LXX, cf. Rom. 11:34). Obviously the Scriptures know nothing of a God who adheres to the norm of a closed continuum.

[14] Walter Grundmann, *"Dunamai / dunamis," TWNT,* II, 302-03.

AREAS OF STUDY FROM WHICH PRINCIPLES ARE DRAWN

Every interpreter, whether he is aware of it or not, draws his principles from certain areas of study. It is important, therefore, to survey these areas and to discuss briefly the relevant principles derived from them.

Language

Language is one of the most important areas from which principles are drawn. The Bible is written in three languages: Hebrew, Aramaic, and Greek. The better an interpreter knows these languages, the easier will be his task. But what about those who do not know these languages? They should know all they can *about* the languages. With such knowledge they can adapt some of the principles which should be applied to the original text to the English translation (or German, French, Spanish, etc., as the case may be).[15]

Hebrew and Aramaic. Both Hebrew and Aramaic are part of the Semitic language family. Semitic languages were spoken over a wide territory. Snaith points out that "the Semitic languages may be roughly grouped over four geographical areas: (a) *Eastern*—Akkadian (the modern name for Assyrian and Babylonian) ; (b) *Western*— Hebrew and the languages of ancient Palestine and Trans-Jordan; (c) *Northern*—the various Aramaic dialects, including the later Syriac; (d) *Southern*—Arabic and Ethiopic."[16] All of the Old Testament was written in Hebrew except for two words of Aramaic in Genesis 31:47, a verse of Aramaic in Jeremiah 10:11, a large section of Aramaic in Daniel 2:4-7:28, and two Aramaic sections of Ezra consisting mostly of letters (Ezra 4:8-6:18; 7:12-26). These quantitative comparisons do not, however, convey accurately the influence of each of these languages. Hebrew, as one of the languages of ancient Palestine, dominated a relatively small territory. Aramaic, on the other hand, had a long history and developed to cover a large territory. Albright points out that in the late Bronze Age (about 1550-1200 B.C.) there are many references to the Semitic nomads of the Syrian Desert who were then called the Ahlamu. These were scattered from the Persian Gulf to the Upper Euphrates Basin.[17] Tiglath-pileser I (1116-1078 B.C.) clarifies who these Ahlamu were

---

[15] Norman H. Snaith, "The Language of the Old Testament," *The Interpreter's Bible*, I, 220.

[16] *Ibid.*

[17] William F. Albright, "The Old Testament World," *The Interpreter's Bible*, I, 263.

by calling them specifically in his inscriptions "the Aramaean Ahlamu," that is, the Aramaean Bedouin.[18] When the Hittite and Egyptian powers collapsed early in the twelfth century B.C. these Aramaeans occupied much of Syria. But Aramaic itself, as Albright sees it, developed as the local speech of some district of the Middle or Upper Euphrates basin. From here it spread among the seminomadic population in the oases around the fringes of the Syrian desert. In the spread of Aramaic the original Aramaean tribal groups were re-enforced by Arab tribes. As time went on Aramaic reached out to more and more tribes. Finally "Aramaic became the principal language of all Mesopotamia, Syria, and Palestine, and the secondary language of the entire Persian Empire."[19]

A history like this leads us to view the whole history of the Hebrew language as a fight against its first cousin, Aramaic.[20] The Aramaeans in their advance were nomadic and possessed no urban culture of their own. When they came into eastern Syria and northwestern Mesopotamia they adopted the Syro-Hittite culture found in these territories. As an oral language, Aramaic goes back into the middle and late bronze age and antedates Hebrew. The written form developed when these wandering people settled in urban communities. This written form may be recovered archaeologically by going down through the various strata which remain from these settled communities.

When the Israelites came into Palestine, they may have spoken a dialect similar to Aramaic. When Jacob departed from Haran, he made a covenant with Laban by a heap of stones. Laban gave the spot an Aramaic name while Jacob spoke in Hebrew (Gen. 31:48). Since Laban and Jacob lived together for quite some time, it is obvious that they understood each other. We do not know how extensive were the differences between Hebrew and Aramaic, or how the language of Jacob's descendants developed during the sojourn in Egypt, or whether the popular speech of the Israelites when they returned to Palestine was the same as their formal literary writing. When the people of Israel settled down in Canaan, the Aramaic language was still a rival. Snaith shows indications of Aramaic in the book of Judges.[21] By the time of Hezekiah, however, there was a marked difference between Hebrew and Aramaic (II Kings 18:26; Isa. 36:11) so that the average person

18 *Ibid.*
19 *Ibid.*
20 Cf. Snaith, p. 223.
21 *Ibid.*

in Jerusalem could understand little or nothing of Aramaic. It must be noted that only oral speech was involved in the discussion between the messengers of Sennacherib and those of Hezekiah. Those who could read and write Hebrew may not have found the written form of Aramaic so difficult.

After 721 B.C. the Aramaic influence on Judah increased. Assyria moved deportees into the Northern kingdom. With the Babylonian captivity of Judah, the Jews were confronted with Aramaic both in their captivity and in their return to Palestine. After the captivity, Hebrew was used among the educated people because to them it was a religious and literary language. But the common people used Aramaic. By the time of Jesus, Aramaic had been the dominant language for hundreds of years.

In the Talmuds both Hebrew and Aramaic are found. Throughout the centuries the Rabbis fought to keep alive the knowledge of Hebrew. During the Renaissance Hebrew again became an active tool in the hands of Christian scholars. Since the formation of Israel in 1948, Hebrew has become a modern, living language.

Biblical Hebrew, like all Semitic languages, has a tri-literal or three consonantal verb root. Prefixes and suffixes of various kinds are added both to verbs and nouns. Throughout its active use Hebrew was a consonantal language. This means that when the language was written no vowels were used. The Hebrew read from right to left. When he saw consonants, he mentally added the vowels which went with the consonants to form syllables. If two words had the same consonants, he distinguished meanings by the context. Take for example the following two English sentences: (1) My brother is strngr than I. (2) My brother felt like a strngr when he returned to the place of his birth. The context makes it clear that in the first sentence the word is "stronger" and in the second sentence the word is "stranger." But sometimes ambiguities can occur. For example, the English consonants "frm" are found in a number of English words such as "firm," "form," "frame," "farm," "from," etc. In Hebrew, to help overcome some of these difficulties, certain consonants served as a partial expression of vowels. But since the Hebrews were used to working without vowels, they felt no need to designate specifically the vowel sounds. Yet during the centuries when the language was no longer spoken (well over two thousand years) those who copied the Hebrew writings feared that the correct pronunciation would be lost and the ambiguities would multiply. So in the sixth and seventh centuries A.D. vowel signs or points began to be used to indicate which vowel should be supplied. In the present Hebrew text these points are placed under the letters and over the letters. Similar marks are placed within letters to show that consonants should be doubled or that certain consonants should have a harder or softer sound: *b* and *v*, *k* and *ch* (weak), *p* and *ph*, *t* and *th* (in thin), *go* and *age*, *day* and *this*. The first of these pairs is hard and the second is soft.

The Hebrew and Aramaic languages may be studied and classified in a threefold way: (1) Accidence—the forms of words; (2) Lexicography—the meaning of words; (3) Syntax— the relationship of words, phrases, and clauses. The first and third subjects are covered in the standard Hebrew and Aramaic grammars,[22] while the second is treated in the Hebrew and Aramaic lexicons. Hence if the student uses these sources correctly, he is in effect applying those *principles* of biblical interpretation which derive from the languages themselves.

Greek. The Greek language has a magnificent history. It has been a living language continuously for 3000 years, beginning in the second millennium B.C. and passing through four distinguishable periods. The classical period extends from Homer (about 1000 B.C.) to Aristotle (died 322 B.C.), followed by the "Koine" period, which lasted to A.D. 529 when Justinian closed the academy of Plato at Athens and prohibited the teaching of Greek philosophy. The Byzantine period ends with the capture of Constantinople by the Turks (A.D. 1453), and is succeeded by the modern period, which extends to the present day.[23]

Although the interpreter of the New Testament is interested primarily in the "Koine" period (322 B.C. to A.D. 529), he does not ignore the meaning of words in classical Greek. He knows that the "Koine" simplifies classical Greek in its use of particles, its syntactical constructions, its failure to change moods after secondary tenses, and the like. Yet he cannot afford to ignore the indispensable background of usage established by the classical writers.

Moreover, although the biblical interpreter is primarily interested in the "Koine" of the New Testament, he does not ignore other authors and writings of the same period. These include the Septuagint; the writers of literary "Koine" such as Polybius, Diodorus, Strabo; a Stoic philosopher such as Epictetus; the Jewish theologian, Philo; and the Jewish historian, Josephus. He is aware that the Greek fathers of the

---

[22] See Chapter 6.

[23] Bruce M. Metzger, "The Language of the New Testament," *The Interpreter's Bible*, VII, 44.

church also wrote in "Koine" Greek. All those mentioned above belonged to the educated level of society. In addition, there are abundant materials written on papyrus and ostraca which show us how the common man in the lower classes of society expressed himself. These are also valuable to the interpreter.

Greek, like Hebrew, may be analyzed and classified under the headings of: (1) Accidence—the forms of words; (2) Lexicography—the meanings of words; (3) Syntax—the relationship of words, phrases, and clauses. Greek is inflected even more highly than Hebrew or Aramaic, and hence is capable of great precision. Its fuller range of possibilities permits thought to be expressed in richer and deeper nuances, offering a real challenge to those who want to find the exact meaning of a word in a particular context. Here the interpreter is helped by excellent lexical tools.[24] In the relationship of words, phrases, and clauses, the interpreter who knows Greek can study the flow of thought very accurately. The person who does not know Greek must depend upon a good commentary. Unfortunately, the commentator often gives only one choice of meaning and proceeds to show why this is correct, or he may show a number of possibilities and confuse the reader who does not know the basis for choosing one over the others.

Principles which rest on the best procedures in accidence, lexicography, and syntax are essential for the interpreter of the Greek New Testament. The conscientious interpreter must analyze language to draw out its meaning but must steadfastly resist any procedure that "reads in" meaning. The true linguist is impatient with historical, philosophical, or theological ventriloquists who project their ideas upon the author.

Textual Criticism. Textual criticism is the science of determining as closely as possible what the original author wrote. Valid principles of textual criticism are those that have stood the test of usage and criticism. Westcott and Hort did a monumental job in their day of showing what was involved in textual criticism.[25] They dealt with the need, method, and application of principles of textual criticism. They pointed out that the "textus receptus" (received text) is a late, polished text which deviates frequently from the original writings, and

24 See Chapter 6.
25 Brooke Westcott and F. J. A. Hort, *The New Testament in the Original Greek: Introduction; Appendix* (Cambridge and London: Macmillan and Co., 1881). The Introduction consists of 324 pages, the Appendix of 188 pages. These 512 pages are a strong protest against any haphazard approach to N.T. textual criticism.

that the King James version, which is based on this text, contains similar faults. Burgon and Miller[26] opposed Westcott and Hort and defended the "textus receptus," but in the years that followed, the defenders of the "textus receptus" became fewer and fewer. Westcott and Hort's principles won out. Yet their theory has also been modified by now, as is inevitable and necessary when new data and materials continually become available. At the present time the New Testament scholar has at his disposal 78 catalogued papyrus manuscripts, 247 capital letter manuscripts, 2,623 manuscripts in a cursive hand, and 1,968 lectionary manuscripts.[27]

The biblical interpreter cannot, of course, expect that all textual problems have now received definitive solution. He must be careful to consult the most competent scholars and to employ valid principles when he must exercise his own option. But in general, the interpreter can be quite sure of a text that closely reproduces the original writing. Basic works in textual criticism will help the student to understand this important area.[28]

In Old Testament studies, the Dead Sea Scrolls brought about a major breakthrough in textual criticism. One-fourth of the manuscripts found in the Dead Sea caves consists of books or fragments of books in the Old Testament.[29] During the first ten years after the discoveries at Qumran complete copies or fragments were found of every book in the Old Testament except Esther. Ten or more copies were found of Deuteronomy, Isaiah, the Minor Prophets, and the Psalms.[30] The manuscripts from Qumran were written between 200 B.C. and A.D. 100; manuscripts from Murabba'at south of Qumran and another unidentified area come from the first century A.D. and from the second century about A.D. 135, the time of the second Jew-

---

[26] John W. Burgon and Edward Miller, *The Traditional Text of the Holy Gospels* (1896).

[27] Kurt Aland, *Kurzgefasste Liste der griechischen Handschriften des Neuen Testaments,* Vol. I: *Gesamtübersicht* (1961).

[28] See Vincent Taylor, *The Text of the New Testament* (1961). Jean Duplacy, *Où en est la critique Textuelle du Nouveau Testament?* (1957). Kurt Aland, *Kurzgefasste Liste der griechischen Handschriften des Neuen Testaments,* Vol. II: *Einzelübersichten.* Kurt Aland and H. Riesenfeld, *Vollständige Konkordanz des griechischen Neuen Testaments,* Unter Zugrundlegung aller moderne kritischen Textausgaben und des textus receptus, Vol. III. Kurt Aland, *Das Neue Testament auf Papyrus,* Vol. IV. Vols. II, III, IV are to be published.

[29] J. T. Milik, *Ten Years of Discovery in the Wilderness of Judea* (1959), p. 23.

[30] *Ibid.*

ish revolt.[31] By studying the forms of the letters in these manuscripts, scholars have worked out further the development of the square script.[32] Paleography (study of the forms of writing) has proved a useful tool in dating.

As a result of the Dead Sea Scrolls, scholars are seeing again that the Septuagint (the Greek translation of the O.T. made from 250 to 150 B.C.) may point to earlier readings than those found in the Massoretic text (developed from the second to ninth centuries A.D.). In the near future better texts of the Old Testament will be produced and the methods of Old Testament textual criticism will achieve greater precision and confidence in clearing up those passages where the meaning has been obscure because of errors or changes by those who copied the text. New handbooks on Old Testament textual criticism will also be forthcoming. Ernst Würthwein's *The Text of the Old Testament* (1957) represents the development of Old Testament textual criticism up to the time when Kittel-Kahle's *Biblia Hebraica* served as a standard Hebrew text. It covers the transmission of the Hebrew text, the translations made from the Hebrew text in ancient times, and the methodology of Old Testament textual criticism. The newer handbooks, like all previous works in textual criticism, must show how one goes from quantities of unsifted materials to the text chosen by the interpreter as being of the best quality according to his discriminating judgment.

The interpreter must work out his interpretation of any passage from the best text, i.e., the text closest to the original writing. If he does not know Greek, Hebrew, or Aramaic, then he should check a good commentary which goes into sufficient detail to tell the reader that different readings make a difference in meaning. Brief commentaries cannot say much, but they can point out the various possibilities of translation.[33] Those who know the biblical languages should know textual criticism well enough so that on crucial passages they can tell why they prefer one reading over another.

Interest in Semantics. Professor Barr defines "semantics" as

---

31 *Ibid.*, pp. 19, 98, 135.

32 *Ibid.*, p. 135.

33 See G. T. Thompson, "Romans," *The New Bible Commentary*, ed. F. Davidson, A. M. Stibbs, and E. F. Kevan, p. 948, where Prof. Thompson comments on Rom. 5:1. On such seemingly small details as punctuation see A. B. Mickelsen, "Romans," *The Wycliffe Bible Commentary*, ed. Charles Pfeiffer and E. F. Harrison, p. 1209. The passage discussed here is Rom. 9:5. On Rom. 5:1, see p. 1196. On the various locations of the final doxology in Romans (in various manuscripts) see p. 1180.

"the study of signification in language."[34] He points out that semantics is a branch both of logic and of linguistics. Semantics in the area of biblical linguistics is concerned with "the way in which the meaning of biblical language is understood."[35] Semantics thus defined is almost synonymous with hermeneutics. Linguistic semantics, however, stresses how the elements of language must be fitted together, what meaning is conveyed separately by the elements, and what is the total meaning of these elements when analyzed in natural units of thought,[36] while hermeneutics is a broader term covering these aspects plus other factors involved in interpretation. Scholars from diverse backgrounds are giving semantics careful attention.

History

Since the Bible contains much historical data, we also must utilize principles which help to clarify this material. Sennacherib's invasions into Palestine (the crucial one in 701 B.C.) certainly receive extensive treatment in the Biblical record (cf. II Kings 18-20; II Chron. 32; Isa. 36-39). But to get a total picture we must also make use of all of the extra-biblical sources available.[37] This means that a valid procedure must be followed to compile the evidence, note chronological sequences, and evaluate the various facets in the historical picture. Consequently, methodology in historical research is important for the interpreter.

Philosophy

Interpreters are always influenced in their approach by phil-

[34] James Barr, *The Semantics of Biblical Language* (1961), p. 1.
[35] *Ibid.*
[36] Prof. Barr's book illustrates this in its chapter titles: I, The Importance of the Problem; II, The Current Contrast of Greek and Hebrew Thought; III, Problems of Method; IV, Verbs, Action, and Time; V, Other Arguments from Morphological and Syntactic Phenomena; VI, Etymologies and Related Arguments; VII, "Faith" and "Truth"—An Examination of Some Linguistic Arguments; VIII, Some Principles of Kittel's Theological Dictionary; IX, Language and the Idea of "Biblical Theology"; X, Languages and the Study of Theology. The purpose of the book is "to survey and to criticize certain lines on which modern theological thinking has been assessing and using the linguistic material in the Bible" (p. 4). This book is an evaluation of the principles and procedures used by theologians which are taken from the area of language and linguistics. Prof. Barr insists that these principles and procedures be valid ones. In the process of his evaluation he uncovers a number of invalid principles and procedures.
[37] See William F. Albright, "The Old Testament World," *Interpreter's Bible*, I, 265-66. Samuel J. Schultz, *The Old Testament Speaks*, pp. 213-214.

osophical presuppositions. Bultmann shows how some may approach exegesis with idealistic conceptions, and others with psychological conceptions. In place of these Bultmann advocates existentialistic presuppositions.[38] Still other interpreters approach the Bible from the viewpoint of realism, or from a complex combination such as a synthesis of logical positivism, existentialism, and analytical philosophy.[39]

Many interpreters do not recognize or analyze their own philosophical assumptions. But this is dangerous, since philosophical assumptions must be tested to see if they are valid in philosophy and further if they are valid for use outside of philosophy.

Consequently, the interpreter must always keep in mind philosophy as a source for principles of interpretation. The more the interpreter realizes what is controlling his thinking, the better his chance of evaluating all assumptions that control thought. He asks himself: "Should such an idea influence me on this particular subject?" Such self-questioning is necessary for good interpretation.

Theology

Ever since the Reformation, various schools of theology have divided the Christian world. There are Thomists, Calvinists, Arminians, Lutherans, and many smaller movements. Each has the loyalty of some small or large segment of Christendom. Most of these schools of thought see themselves as logically presenting the whole of biblical teaching.

At the same time, the leaders of these schools have never contended that their theologies were inspired of God. They know that error creeps into the best theological formulations. Sometimes this error consists in omitting part of what is found in Scripture. Sometimes the error is one of misplaced emphasis. More frequently, perhaps, error creeps in by the subtle process of extension. Since the Scriptures make this assertion, it seems natural to infer that such a statement coupled with others would lead to this further conclusion. Then this further conclusion leads to still another. Soon one is far removed from the simple, clear-cut biblical assertion. Because valid and invalid propositions often lie side by side in theological formulations, it is easy for us to allow our views in theology to control our

---

[38] Rudolf Bultmann, *Jesus Christ and Mythology*, See Chap. IV: "Modern Biblical Interpretation and Existentialist Philosophy," pp. 45-59.

[39] See, e.g., William F. Zuurdeeg, *An Analytical Philosophy of Religion* (1958).

interpretation and exegesis rather than to let our interpretation and exegesis control our theology. Theological principles which affect the interpreter must be examined as objectively as philosophical principles.

If the interpreter is convinced that his influencing framework is the right one and should influence him in his interpretation, then he must be prepared to establish the correctness of this controlling framework. He must not only know its basic premises, but he must be able to show that none of these premises is in the least bit contrary to the major emphases and assertions of Scripture. This will make the interpreter aware of the factors influencing his thinking.

PRINCIPLES VERSUS MECHANICAL RULES

The interpreter should realize that principles are not fixed formulas. The mechanical rule approach to hermeneutics builds mistaken ideas from the start. Finding a correct interpretation cannot be achieved in the way that a druggist fills a prescription. The druggist mixes ingredients in the exact proportions demanded by the physician. Everything is precise. But synthesizing or analyzing thought is not like synthesizing or analyzing chemicals. Ideas are imponderable: they cannot be weighed, measured, or counted. Hence they cannot be exposed to light by following set formulas. The interpreter uses the valid principles which are relevant to his particular task, but he must do so with imagination, sympathy, and judgment. He must recognize that ideas belong to persons, and that the personal factor inevitably introduces an element of subjectivity.

BIBLIOGRAPHY

Albright, William F., "The Old Testament World," *The Interpreter's Bible,* I (1951).
Barr, James, *The Semantics of Biblical Language* (1961).
Bultmann, Rudolf, "Is Exegesis Without Presuppositions Possible?" *Existence and Faith,* ed. Schubert M. Ogden (1960).
———, *The Presence of Eternity. History and Eschatology* (1957).
Farmer, H. H., "The Bible: Its Significance and Authority," *The Interpreter's Bible,* I (1951).
Grundmann, Walter, *"dunamis, dunamai," Theologisches Wörterbuch zum Neuen Testament,* II (1935).
Metzger, Bruce M., "The Language of the New Testament," *The Interpreter's Bible,* VII (1951).
Snaith, Norman H., "The Language of the Old Testament," *The Interpreter's Bible,* I (1951).
Taylor, Vincent, *The Text of the New Testament* (1961).
Würthwein, Ernst, *The Text of the Old Testament,* tr. Peter R. Ackroyd (1957).

II Lessons from the Past

Interpretation is not something new. Throughout the ages men have used certain principles with which to interpret the Scriptures. Many excellent books have been written about the history of interpretation.[1] The purpose of this chapter, however, is to see what lessons can be drawn from the procedures of the past and what have been the major trends in past epochs. When necessary, we may criticize some of the methods employed, even though we deeply appreciate the achievements of these men of past years. In fact, history shows that erroneous principles have often spoiled the exegetical work of fine men, some of whom were great saints. This should be a warning to us against carelessness in interpretation. There is less excuse for us because we can profit by the lessons of the past. It should also remind us that the use of correct procedures must be founded upon a dedication to God, a consecration to the task, and a love for men which unites all that we are and know. Christians now, as in the past, must be totally involved not

---

[1] Milton S. Terry, *Biblical Hermeneutics* (n.d.), Part III: "History of Biblical Interpretation," pp. 603-738. Robert M. Grant, *The Bible in the Church* (1948). F. W. Farrar, *History of Interpretation*, Bampton Lectures (1885). James D. Wood, *The Interpretation of the Bible: An Historical Introduction* (1958). There is also a trilogy in *The Interpreter's Bible* which shows how interpreters have approached the Bible. Robert M. Grant, "History of the Interpretation of the Bible: I, Ancient Period," *The Interpreter's Bible*, I, 106-114. John T. McNeill, "History of the Interpretation of the Bible: II, Medieval and Reformation Period," *The Interpreter's Bible*, I, 115-126. Samuel Terrien, "History of the Interpretation of the Bible: III, Modern Period," *The Interpreter's Bible*, I, 127-141.

only in the task of bidding men to be reconciled to God in Jesus Christ but also in showing what this reconciliation means.

JEWISH INTERPRETATION

Beginnings

Work of Ezra. In post-exilic Judaism Ezra was a prominent figure. He is called a ready scribe *(sopher mahiyr)* in Ezra 7:6. He is called Ezra the priest and the scribe in Ezra 7:11, 12, 21; Nehemiah 8:9; 12:26, and Ezra the scribe in Nehemiah 8:1, 4, 13; 12:36. This language must not be taken anachronistically. The term in the time of Ezra did not have the connotation of pedantic concern with minutiae, as it did in Jesus' day. Rather, Ezra was one who was learned. He was to teach the law of Moses, the law of God. Instruction demands interpretation and explanation.

Those Associated with Ezra. In Nehemiah 8 Ezra reads from the law of Moses to a large assembly of people from early morning until midday (vs. 3). He is helped in this endeavor by a group of men (vs. 7) some of whom are stated to be Levites (see 9:4, 5). If we assume that the men mentioned in Nehemiah 8:7 are Levites, it follows that this verse together with verse 9 speaks of a branch of Levites as "the Levites that taught the people." The fact of divisions of work for the Levites is indicated in II Chronicles 34:13, "And of the Levites there were scribes *(sopherim)* and officers and porters." This group could speak truth, as in Nehemiah 8, or could write falsehood, as seen in Jeremiah 8:8. The ones with Ezra were dedicated to the truth. Their role in interpretation is made explicit in Nehemiah 8:7-8:

> And they gave understanding to the people in the law, and the people [stood] in their place. And they read aloud in the book, in the law of God making it distinct [expounding extemporaneously] and setting forth the understanding [i.e. the meaning], and they gave understanding in the reading.[2]

This was a complex operation because of the bilingual situation. As Bowman points out: "The original Hebrew text was doubtless translated aloud as Aramaic, the common speech of postexilic Palestine."[3] In place of the above translation "making it distinct and setting forth the understanding" Bow-

---

[2] See Raymond A. Bowman, "The Book of Ezra and the Book of Nehemiah," *Interpreter's Bible*, III, 737.

[3] *Ibid.*

man would render the phrase "translating at sight and giving understanding."[4] Hence in the postexilic period the interpreter of the Old Testament had to translate the original Hebrew text into Aramaic and then explain the meaning. Note how interpretation is joined with oral discourse. The Rabbis see in this passage the beginning of the Targums—the Aramaic explanations of the Hebrew text. " 'Originally the Law was given to Israel in Hebrew writing and the holy language. It was again given to them in the days of Ezra in the Assyrian [i.e. Aramaic] writing and the Aramaic language' (Babylonian Talmud: Sanhedrin 21b; Nedarim 37b; cf. Megillah 3a; Jerusalem Megillah 74d)."[5] Since this bilingual situation prevailed from this time on, the need for translation and explanation would have continued. There is reason to believe that a group of men in Israel had the task of handing down (copying) the sacred writings and also giving to the common man a translation and explanation of the Scriptures. No doubt when these men became indifferent to God it showed in their unfolding of the meaning of Scripture. We know that Judaism rose and fell between the time of Ezra and the time of Christ. The exile may have cured Israel of idolatry, but it did not prevent apathy, formalism, indifference to human need, and social and political corruption. When the Jews were oppressed, the word of God became meaningful, and they were willing to die for their faith. When oppression ceased, the Jewish people usually settled down to seeking as much political independence as possible under varying degrees of foreign domination.

The Qumran Community. Some Jews felt that the complexities of life in Palestine and the political and social forces hostile to the Jewish religious heritage made it impossible for them to serve God as they should. They could not really keep His law. They could not find enough opportunity to study the Old Testament Scriptures. Corporate worship was difficult. Some of the people with these persuasions withdrew to ascetic communities where they felt that they could live in conformity to the law of God. In times of great oppression others joined their group. Sometimes persecution blotted out all or part of the ascetic community, but after a while it would rise again with its teaching, ceremonial washings, prayer, and meditation. Qumran was one such community. Here the Scriptures were copied. Commentaries were written as well as manuals on community life and various tractates. In the commentaries interpretation is frequently carried out without reference to context.

4 *Ibid.*
5 *Ibid.*

Milik and Burrows point out that in the commentaries on Habakkuk, Micah, and the Psalms, the biblical material is explained in terms of *the Qumran sect itself*. The commentary on Nahum interprets the biblical material of a different ethnic group from that of Qumran but *in the same contemporary setting*. The commentaries on Isaiah interpret the text of Isaiah *eschatalogically*.[6] The Habakkuk commentary illustrates all three procedures: interpreting the text in terms of (1) Qumran, (2) another contemporary group, and (3) eschatology.[7]

This approach to interpretation has plagued interpreters from the time of the Qumran community to the present day. One of the basic principles of sound interpretation is that a later interpreter must first find out what the author of an earlier writing was trying to convey to those who first read his words. Interpreters in Qumran forgot this in their haste to apply the Scriptures to themselves and their own times. If we first find the meaning of the author's words for his original readers, we can usually see what we have in common with these readers. At these points the application is not only obvious but has a convincing relevance. Such genuine relevance is missing, however, in interpretation that is arbitrary or ignores the context.

The Pairs. From Maccabean times to the end of the Herodian age (168 B.C.—ca. A.D. 10) interpretation was highlighted by a series of friendly debates between sets of two rabbis. The rabbis of each period had their respective followers. Hence "the pairs," as they were known, kept alive crucial differences in interpretation as well as preserving the main emphases of Judaism. The schools of Hillel and Shammai were probably the climax of this type of activity. In applying legal maxims, Hillel emphasized the qualifying factors of surrounding circumstances. Shammai interpreted with strict rigidity. Hillel was famous for (1) classifying the topical discussion of the biblical material into six orders and for (2) his seven exegetical rules.[8] Blackman summarizes his seven rules in this way:

> Rule 1 was called "light and heavy" and signified the inference . . . from the less to the greater. Rule 2, "equal decision," meant discernment of analogies and comparisons. Rules 3 and 4 were concerned with deducing the general implications from one passage, or from more than one passage; Rule 5 with a more precise statement of the general by reference to the particular, and vice versa; Rule 6 with the use of one passage to interpret an-

---

[6] Millar Burrows, *More Light on the Dead Sea Scrolls* (1958), pp. 166-67.
[7] *Ibid.*, p. 167.
[8] Farrar, *op. cit.*, pp. 65-66.

other; and Rule 7 with the use of the whole context to elucidate a verse or passage.[9]

These rules are helpful in that they stress logical procedures. Unfortunately, although the rabbis did apply these rules, they also utilized such practices as substituting one letter for another, forming new words, assigning a numerical value to words, etc. In Genesis 2:7 the Hebrew word "and he [the Lord] formed" has two yods (smallest Hebrew letter, equivalent to English "y") in the unpointed Hebrew text. In Rabbinic Hebrew the word impulse *(yētzer)* is a noun from the same root as "to form." Hence, the rabbis deduce that because of the two yods in Genesis 2:7—the first letter of the words "to form" and "impulse"—God created two impulses in man, a good impulse and a bad one![10] This makes us smile, but it at least shows that these interpreters carefully observed what was written. Unfortunately, instead of using their ingenuity to clarify the precise meaning conveyed by the language, they looked for "deeper hidden meanings."

Rabbinic Literature to the Completion of the Babylonian Talmud

This period extends from about A.D. 10 to A.D. 550. When we examine the sheer quantity of literature produced in this period, we are forced to admit that the Jewish people were zealous interpreters. When they were not interpreting the Scriptures themselves, they were interpreting the interpretations. Sometimes the interpretation of the interpretation of the interpretation had to be interpreted! This effort does indicate that the Jews were searching for the Scriptures because they believed that *in them* they had eternal life (cf. John 5:39). Only the briefest treatment of this period can be given.[11]

Two Literary Forms. For centuries the oral law had existed in Israel. When the materials finally were written down, two distinct forms emerged. The *midrash* or *midrashim* were running commentaries on the Old Testament. The three oldest Midrashim are on the Pentateuch: the Mekilta on Exodus, the Sifra on Leviticus, and the Sifre on Numbers and Deuteronomy. These dealt primarily with the legal material. The Bereshit Rabbah on Genesis is an example of a homiletic or devotional type of commentary. In addition to the commentaries

---

[9] A. C. Blackman, *Biblical Interpretation* (1957), p. 72.

[10] Berakhoth, 61ᵃ. See Herman L. Strack and Paul Billerbeck, *Kommentar zum Neuen Testament aus Talmud und Midrasch* (1928), IV, Part 1, Neunzehnter Exkurs: "Der gute und der böse Trieb," p. 467.

[11] An excellent summary of this literature can be found in Morton Scott Enslin, *Christian Beginnings* (1938), pp. 104-110.

was the *Mishna*. Here the biblical material was discussed and interpreted in a topical arrangement. Though Hillel started to classify the subject matter, the present categories are attributed to Akiba. The headings or topics are not theological. This becomes clear when we look at a listing of the topics: (1) Seeds *(Zeraim)*—Laws about agriculture, the seventh year, kinds of tithes. Prefixed to this section on seeds is a book of prayers, *Berakhoth,* that has the shema (Deut. 6:4-5), the eighteen benedictions, grace at meals and other prayers. (2) Festivals *(Moed)* —Feasts, Fasts, Sabbath Laws. (3) Women *(Nashim)*—Laws pertaining to all aspects of marriage, place of widows, vows, etc. (4) Injuries *(Nezikim)*—Civil and criminal laws, oaths. Appended to this category was the *Pirke Abot,* i.e., the sayings of the fathers. (5) Holy Things *(Kodashim)*—Sacrifices, meal offerings, the first-born, excommunication, measurements of the temple, etc. (6) Clean Things *(Toharot)*. The title of this classification is really an euphemistic expression for unclean things: Vessels, defilement from a corpse, leprosy, red heifer, ritual and purificatory baths for women because of menstruation, childbirth, sexual intercourse, contact with leprosy, a corpse, etc.

In the Mishna, biblical passages were rarely quoted as authority for the legislation. In the *Tosefta* (which is an amplification of the Mishna) the biblical passages serving as the bases for the legislation are frequently cited.

Several collections of Mishna, organized according to the six categories, circulated during the second century A.D. By the third century A.D. the collection of Judah the Patriarch had gained so much favor that it became known as the *Mishna*. Judah the Patriarch is really the editor of the work. In this "official" or "canonical" Mishna 150 authorities are cited. Individual sayings preserved from the other collections are called *Baraitas.*

Two Types of Content. Both the Midrashim and the Mishna have contents classified either as Halakah or Haggadah. Halakah was a discussion of the legal material in Scripture. Haggadah refers to the non-legal material—the history, the prophetic exhortations, the personal experiences of the psalmists. The Haggadah was devotional, sermonic, practical. Obviously a commentary could have both Halakah and Haggadah. Usually one emphasis stood out. Sometimes the Midrash was almost entirely one or the other. Likewise in the Mishna both elements can be found. The prayers and the sayings of the fathers are Haggadic in nature while the discussion of the law is decidedly Halakic in content. In all of this interpretive material the stress is on *what* God demands and *how* men should respond to him. The idea of *who* He is as something separate from his demands or the proper response of men to Him is scarcely if ever developed. There is a constant practical emphasis. Yet speculative imagination is present on almost every page. Rabbi Akiba held that every verse of Scripture has many explanations. Farrar points out how he extracted these:

> His principle was that a meaning was to be found in every monosyllable of Scripture. If there is a superfluous "and" or "also," or sign of case, these are always to be specially interpreted. If in 2 Kings 2:14 it said of Elisha that "he *also* had smitten the waters" it means that Elisha did more wonders at the Jordan than Elijah. If David says "Thy servant slew also the lion, also the bear," the meaning (by the rule of inclusion after inclusion), is that he slew three animals besides. If it is written that God visited Sarah (*eth* Sarah), it means that with her He visited other barren women. . . .
>
> But Aqiba went still farther. He not only explained every particle and copula, but said that there was a mystic meaning in every letter of Scripture, and in every horn and letter flourish of every letter, "just as in every fibre of an ant's foot or gnat's wing." The Rabbis delighted to tell how "many rules unknown to Moses were declared by Aqiba."[12]

We all agree today that any rule that permits an interpreter to get out of a text just what he wants is worthless. Further, any good principle which is wrongfully applied in order to extract an arbitrary meaning is likewise to be dismissed in its wrong application.

Two Talmuds. Interpretation did not stop with the "official" Mishna of Judah the Patriarch. The comments of the 150 authorities cited there were studied carefully. Soon it was felt necessary to explain their explanations. What did the scholars in the Mishna mean? Why should one writer say this and another writer say something else? In this way later scholars began interpreting the earlier scholars.

How could this growing body of literature be brought together? The biblical statements were explained by the Mishna and the Mishna was explained by later scholars. To bring this literature together the Talmuds were prepared. There was to be a complete Palestinian Talmud and a complete Babylonian Talmud. The rabbinical school in Tiberias was closed, however, before the Palestinian Talmud was finished. Hence it is not complete and is shorter than the Babylonian Talmud,

---

12 Farrar, *op. cit.*, pp. 73-75.

which has come down to us in complete form.[13] The Talmud really is a Mishna on the Mishna. Paragraph by paragraph, sentence by sentence the Mishna is cited. Then comes the opinions of scholars who seek to unfold the meaning of the earlier scholars. The Palestinian Talmud appeared in about A.D. 450 and the Babylonian Talmud between A.D. 500 and A.D. 550. The Babylonian Talmud is actually four times longer than the Palestinian Talmud. The Talmuds consist both of rabbinic Hebrew and Aramaic. They include Midrashim as well as Mishna. In all of this wide expanse of literature both Halakah and Haggadah are found in various proportions and relationships. Delitzsch describes the Talmud as "a vast debating club, in which there hum confusedly the myriad voices of at least five centuries."[14] Strack and Billerbeck have carefully sifted through this ocean of material to find parallels and other useful materials having a bearing on the interpretation of the New Testament. Acquaintance with this work of Strack and Billerbeck will help the student get a feeling for the procedures of interpretation followed in the Talmud.[15]

Two Groups of Interpreters. The scholars or interpreters who composed the Mishna were known as the *Tannaim* (teachers). Their period extends from about A.D. 10 to A.D. 220. Those who worked on the interpretation of their interpretation are called *Amoraim* (speakers, interpreters). The comments which they produced are designated as *Gemara.* Hence the *Amoraim* cover the period from A.D. 220 to A.D. 500.

Many lessons can be drawn from the study of Rabbinic literature. We see that quantity does not make for quality. We also find that confusion grows where there is no unifying principle or person to bring together the biblical material and to place it in a definite perspective. But most of all we see how far afield anyone can stray when the interpreter fails to start with the historical context of a passage.

Alexandrian Judaism

The Jews were scattered throughout the whole Mediterranean world and across the fertile crescent. Wherever they went, they maintained their ethnic culture. Although they appeared

---

[13] Epstein (ed.), *The Babylonian Talmud* (1948). Cf. Marcus Jastrow (ed.), *A Dictionary of the Targumim,* Talmud Babli and Yerushalmi, and the other Midrashic Literature (1950).

[14] Franz Delitzsch, *Jüdisches Handwerkleben zur Zeit Jesu,* p. 35, as quoted by Terry, *op. cit.,* p. 617.

[15] Herman L. Strack and Paul Billerbeck, *Kommentar zum Neuen Testament aus Talmud und Midrasch.* Vols. I-IV (1921-1928).

to be aloof and different from the people among whom they lived, yet the Jews did interact. For example, they not only spoke the Greek language but they actually made it their own. Consequently the Old Testament was needed in the Greek language. From this need grew the Septuagint, which was translated between 250 and 150 B.C. In Alexandria the Jews were able to grow numerically, religiously, and to some extent culturally. Nevertheless, Judaism in Alexandria and elsewhere in the dispersion held to the basic theological convictions of Palestinian Judaism. The differences lay only in peripheral matters.

Allegorical Method. In the allegorical method a text is interpreted apart from its grammatical historical meaning. What the original writer is trying to say is ignored. What the interpreter wants to say becomes the only important factor.

This method came into Alexandrian Judaism via Greek thought. Plato was acquainted with this method, and was so opposed to it that he did not want poets in his Republic! Homer was banned, with or without allegories! Theogenes of Rhegium (ca. 520 B.C.) is supposed to have been the first man to have allegorized Homer. In ancient times men allegorized for two reasons. First, they wanted to keep the poets from being ridiculed or ignored. Second, serious thinkers found that by means of allegory they could use past literature to promulgate their own ideas and outlook. By allegorizing they could maintain continuity with the past without getting too involved with undesirable elements in its literaure. The Homeric gods and the entire Greek pantheon could be allegorized in whole or in part. If one wanted to keep certain "values" of the gods, he could allegorize the accounts of their immoralities.

Among the Greeks the Stoics made use of allegorizing both to maintain their philosophy and to promulgate it. By allegorizing Stoicism could show that it was at home with the past while at the same time it could bring a fresh message into its contemporary world.

The Jews found that allegorizing could help them defend their faith. Aristobulus in the first half of the second century B.C. claimed that Moses really taught Greek philosophy and that the Greek philosophers had borrowed their ideas from Moses. The letter of Aristeas (written by an Alexandrian Jew about 100 B.C.) is famous for its account of how the Septuagint came into existence. But it also has good examples of allegorizing. It says, for example, that the dietary laws which made the Gentiles ridicule the Jews really taught various kinds of discrimination necessary to obtain virtue. Whether animals chew or do not chew the cud really points to the fact that "the act of chewing the cud is nothing else than the reminiscence of life and existence."[16] Traces of allegory may be found in the Book of Wisdom,[17] but there certainly is no widespread use of allegorizing in the Apocrypha. Yet by the first century A.D., Hellenistic Judaism was employing this method to communicate a variegated message.

Philo. Here was an Alexandrian who made allegory his principal method.[18] Philo was fully aware of the literal meaning of the Pentateuch. Moreover, he held a theory of inspiration which made it resemble dictation: the biblical writers, he said, wrote in a spirit of ecstasy, loosed from their natural powers.[19] Yet he believed that literal meanings were usually less important than those other ideas which he accepted from philosophical schools such as Stoicism and Neo-platonism, and hence he attempted to reveal the presence of these ideas in the Pentateuch by allegorical interpretation. Farrar describes the main emphases of Philo's rules of interpretation as follows:

> 1. The rules by which the literal sense is excluded are chiefly Stoic. It is excluded when the statement is unworthy of God; when there is any contradiction; when the allegory is obvious....
> 2. The rules which prove the *simultaneous* existence of the allegorical with the literal sense are mainly Rabbinic....
> 3. Again, words may be explained apart from their punctuation....
> 4. Again, if synonyms are used, something allegorical is intended....
> 5. Plays on words are admissible to educe a deeper sense....
> 6. Particles, adverbs, prepositions may be forced into the service of allegory.... [20]

As an exegete, then, Philo is an example of what not to do. As a thinker we see Philo interacting with ideas outside of Judaism while maintaining his allegiance to the main tenets of Judaism. He definitely enlarges upon certain aspects of Judaism, and he fails to see what his eclectic approach does to his ancestral faith. Unfortunately, the influence of his exegetical method far exceeded the influence of his philosophical and

[16] Letter of Aristeas, 154. See 150-156. R. H. Charles (ed.), *The Apocrypha and Pseudepigrapha of the Old Testament* (1913), II, 108-109.

[17] See Blackman, *op. cit.*, pp. 81-82.

[18] For an accurate picture of Philo as a thinker and theologian see Harry A. Wolfson, *Philo,* Foundations of Religious Philosophy in Judaism, Christianity and Islam, 2 vols. (1948).

[19] Farrar, *op. cit.*, pp. 147-48.

[20] *Ibid.*, pp. 149-151.

theological interactions. Allegorism became a permanent part of Alexandrian thought.

Patristic Period

General Characteristics

This period extends from Clement of Rome (who wrote *I Clement*, ca. A.D. 95) to Gregory I, called Gregory the Great, who became pope in A.D. 590. During this period the canon of the New Testament was established, the orthodox view of the deity and humanity of Christ was delineated, as well as the relationship of the Spirit to the Father and the Son. In all of these theological discussions the role of exegetical study cannot be minimized. Although the Greek and Latin fathers employed philosophical categories and used abstract nomenclature, they did make a careful and extensive interpretation of the New Testament the basis of key theological formulations.

Nevertheless, although there are examples of careful exegetical study on major questions, allegorizing itself continued to grow until it had a firm hold on biblical studies that could not be broken for one thousand years.

Second Century

Clement of Rome, who lived at the close of the first century, quotes at length from Scripture. He is not fanciful in his treatment. The Old Testament is treated as a preparation for Christ and is judged in the light of one who is dedicated to Jesus Christ. Although Clement does cite the legend of the phoenix,[21] he does not usually follow an extravagant interpretation. Rahab's scarlet cord in the window is an example of faith and also of prophecy—"foreshowing that all who believe and hope on God shall have redemption through the blood of the lamb."[22] Basically Clement uses Scripture to re-enforce his exhortation to faithfulness and service.

---

[21] *I Clement*, chaps. 25-26. The gist of the legend is this: A bird from Arabia called a phoenix lives for 500 years. When death is near the bird makes a sepulchre of frankincense and myrrh and other spices. Entering this sepulchre, the bird dies. As the flesh decays a worm emerges which feeds on the juices of the dead bird. As it grows the worm becomes a bird. Taking up the sepulchre and the bones of its predecessor the bird carries these things down to Egypt. In Heliopolis the bones are deposited at the altar of the Sun. The priests there observe their register of dates and find that this thing happens every 500 years.

[22] *I Clement*, chap. 12.

Ignatius' thinking is Christocentric. His letters, which have been preserved and which show his awareness of approaching martyrdom, contain many warnings against heresy and schism while emphasizing faithfulness to Jesus Christ. Ignatius alludes frequently to the Old and New Testaments, but seldom quotes them directly. When he does exegete Scripture, he usually avoids allegorizing and strained interpretations.

The Epistle of Barnabas uses extensive allegorizing. Barnabas taught that there was only one covenant and that the Jews misunderstood that covenant from the very beginning. This premise made it impossible for him to interpret literally the plain assertions of the Old Testament. Barnabas illustrates well the effect that wrong assumptions have on an interpreter.

Marcion's approach to the Old Testament was to throw it out. Of the Gospels, he accepted only Luke. Even there he eliminated from the Gospel what he regarded as Jewish interpolations or intrusions of alien Jewish ideas. Marcion was convinced that the God of the Old Testament was not the God and Father of Jesus Christ. As Barnabas illustrates an erroneous historical assumption, so Marcion illustrates an erroneous theological assumption.

Justin Martyr makes extensive use of the Old Testament. Unfortunately he provides us with many examples of arbitrary, artificial exegesis. He is so taken up with Old Testament teachings about Christ, that he rarely notes what the prophet was saying to his contemporaries.

Irenaeus lived both in the East and the West. In his battles against the heretics he insisted upon correct interpretation. His standard consisted of what was taught in the churches. Here are the beginnings of the concept of the church as the authoritative interpreter. Irenaeus had a sound historical perspective. He insisted that the Old Testament law had an important place in the history of the Jewish people. Although he pointed out the failures of the heretics in their treatment of Scripture, Irenaeus' own performance is not free of arbitrary procedures.[23]

School of Alexandria

The outstanding members of the school of Alexandria were Pantaenus, the first teacher of the school; Clement of Alexandria (ca. A.D. 155-215); and Origen (A.D. 185-254). This was not a school in a formal sense. Origen had to leave Alexandria because of persecution. He went to Caesarea in Palestine, where he established a school that flourished under his leader-

[23] Farrar, op. cit., pp. 174-177.

ship. But in Alexandria there was a group of scholars trying to make the Christian faith meaningful in the intellectual milieu of Alexandria, where the Scriptures were attacked as immoral, trivial, and absurd by such men as Celsus, Porphyry, and others. In the face of such Old Testament problems as Lot's incest, the drunkenness of Noah, Jacob's wives and concubines, Judah's seduction of Tamar, minute distinctions between what was clean and not clean in the animal kingdom, prohibitions against eating vultures, anthropomorphic descriptions of God, etc., the Alexandrians (particularly Origen) resorted to allegorizing.

Origen's allegorizing is often criticized, but many recent scholars, recognizing Origen's achievements in textual criticism, complete study of the whole of Scripture, apologetics, and human learning in general, have sympathetically examined his allegorical method in the light of his background.[24] This does not mean that the allegorizing of Origen or the school of Alexandria becomes a model for present day interpreters, but it does help remove our superficial disdain.

Using a word pattern from Paul (I Thess. 5:23), Origen spoke of a threefold sense of Scripture: body, soul, and spirit. The bodily sense supposedly involved the literal, the outward, the external events. The soul sense dealt with all of man's personal relationships and experiences with his fellow men. The spiritual sense concerned man's relationship to God and God's relationship to himself, his world, and especially to mankind. Origen found it useful to allegorize in the "soul" and "spirit" areas. And since the spiritual sense was regarded as the most important, Origen gave most of his thought (and his allegorizing) here. According to him Rebecca's drawing water for Abraham's servant and his cattle means that we must come to the wells of Scripture in order to meet Christ. In the story of the triumphal entry the ass represents the letter of the Old Testament; the colt or foal of an ass (which was gentle and submissive) speaks of the New Testament. The two apostles who obtained the animals and brought them to Jesus are the moral and spiritual senses.[25] Such examples illustrate how allegorizing

---

[24] See Blackman, *op. cit.*, pp. 95-103; Robert Grant, *The Bible in the Church*, pp. 65-72; James Wood, *op. cit.*, pp. 55-58; Bernard Ramm, *Protestant Biblical Interpretation* (1956), pp. 31-33. See especially the plea for a reevaluation of Origen in Jean Danielou, *Origène* (1948), English trans. by W. Mitchell (1955).

[25] Farrar gives some other examples on pp. 199-201. He makes this comment: "They do but weary and offend us with a sense of incongruous unreality. They change tender human narratives into dreary and ill-constructed riddles."

tells the observer clearly what the interpreter is thinking but it tells nothing about what the biblical writer was saying. His meaning is ignored. We are left with only the interpreter's arbitrary assertions. These in themselves may be good, but the interpreter should not pretend that his ideas are somehow found in, with, or under the biblical statements.

School of Antioch

Important representatives of this school were Theophilus of Antioch (ca. A.D. 115-188), Diodorus of Tarsus (died A.D. 393), Theodor of Mopsuestia (ca. A.D. 350-428), Chrysostom (A.D. 354-407), and Theodoret (A.D. 386-458).

These interpreters all emphasized historical interpretation. Yet this stress was no wooden literalism, for they made full use of typology. The school of Alexandria felt that the literal meaning of a text did not include its metaphorical meaning, but the school of Antioch insisted that the literal meaning cannot exclude metaphor.[26] "Literal" here means the customarily acknowledged meaning of an expression in its particular context. For example, when Christ declared that he was the door, the metaphorical meaning of "door" in that context would be obvious. Although metaphorical, this obvious meaning is included in the literal meaning.

Because of the theological controversies of the fourth and fifth centuries—the Nestorian controversy, for example (relationship of Christ's human and divine natures)—some of the school of Antioch were accused of departing from orthodoxy. The school began to lose influence. This loss was hastened when the church split into Eastern and Western segments. Without the opposition of Antioch, the Alexandrian school of allegorizing became more prevalent and so did the practice of allegorizing.

Jerome and Augustine

Jerome (ca. A.D. 347-419) is known primarily for his work as a translator, but he was also an interpreter of renown. In his early ministry he admired allegorizing, but later he grew discontented with its obvious weaknesses, and attacked it in his exegetical works. Yet he was apparently unable to throw off completely this earlier influence, for he continued to practice allegorizing. For example, to him all of the forty-four stations in the wilderness had a mystical meaning. Farrar, commenting

[26] Cf. R. Grant, *The Interpreter's Bible,* I, 111.

on Jerome, declares: "He flatters himself that he succeeded in steering safely between the Scylla of allegory and the Charybdis of literalism, whereas in reality his 'multiple senses' and 'whole forests of spiritual meanings' are not worth one verse of the original."[27] Jerome also suffered from haste. In writing his commentary on Galatians, he dictated as much as 1000 lines per day. This speed did not encourage originality. Despite these weaknesses Jerome was still a great scholar. His example shows us that clarity and directness in interpretation are difficult to achieve.

Augustine (A.D. 354-430) was a Manichaean before he became a Christian. The Manichaean religious movement (which began in the third century A.D.) pointed with scorn at the anthropomorphisms in the Old Testament. "Look how literal interpretation results in absurdity," the adherents to Manichaeanism exclaimed. All of this was meant to discredit the Old Testament and Christianity. Such objections kept Augustine, for a while, from embracing Christianity. Then came Ambrose who took Paul's statement that "the letter kills but the spirit makes alive" as a slogan for allegorical interpretation. In this approach Augustine found a way to overcome the objections of the Manichaeans to the Old Testament. Through allegorizing, traditional Christianity became tenable for Augustine. Augustine was an incisive theologian and a clear thinker. He knew that sound principles are important for interpretation.[28] Yet he himself allegorized extensively. For example, the psalmist talks about lying down, sleeping, and rising up again or awaking (Ps. 3:5). But what he really refers to is the death and resurrection of Christ! In the narrative of the fall, the fig leaves mean hypocrisy, the coats of skins are mortality, and the four rivers become the four cardinal virtues.[29] Augustine knew no Hebrew and his knowledge of Greek was meager. His main base for Bible study was the Old Latin. Jerome's Vulgate was a new translation which he did not trust. We see that with Augustine the tradition of the church is beginning to play a prominent role in controlling interpretation. Although Augustine's theological tractates have freshness and vigor, his biblical exegesis often fails to set forth with forcefulness and freshness what the original writer wanted to say. Allegorization soon was to take over the methodology of biblical scholars for a thousand years.

27 Farrar, *op. cit.*, p. 233.
28 Augustine, *Concerning Christian Doctrine*, chaps. 24-28, 42.
29 Farrar, *op. cit.*, p. 238.

THE MIDDLE AGES

THE MIDDLE AGES

General Characteristics

Throughout the Middle Ages interpretation is bound by a dull conformity. Church tradition stands supreme. The Scriptures and the fathers—or collections of sayings gathered from both—were offered as supports for tradition. Philosophical theology and theological philosophy controlled the thinkers. Inferences from basic ideas were more important than examining whether these basic ideas had any biblical validity. Except for an oasis here and there, the Middle Ages were a vast desert so far as biblical interpretation is concerned. As a result, no fresh, living message from the Lord sounded forth from churches and cathedrals. Amid the routine and drudgery of human existence the Church offered only another type of routine. The power, glory, and brightness of the biblical message seemed like past ideas rather than living realities confronting the worshipper when he stepped into the sanctuary.

Fourfold Interpretation

Interpreters during the Middle Ages saw a multiplicity of senses or meanings in Scripture. Revelation was not only expressed in Scripture, but it also was hidden in Scripture. Some Latin poetry of the sixteenth century expresses this well. A rough paraphrase keeping the metrical rhyme in English goes like this:

> The *letter* shows us what God and our fathers did;
> The *allegory* shows us where our faith is hid;
> The *moral* meaning gives us rules of daily life;
> The *anagogy* shows us where we end our strife.

Interpretation could be literal, allegorical, moral, or anagogical. "Jerusalem" for the medieval interpreters could refer to the literal city in Palestine. Allegorically it could mean the church. Morally (tropologically) it would refer to the human soul. Anagogically "Jerusalem" refers to the heavenly city. As Blackman points out, the literal is the plain, evident meaning; the moral sense tells men what to do; the allegorical sets forth what they are to believe; the anagogical centers in what Christians are to hope.[30]

This does not mean that interpreters always tried to find all

---

[30] Blackman, *op. cit.,* p. 111.

four senses. Sometimes two or three senses were sufficient to the task at hand. Unfortunately, however, this pursuit of multiple meanings is really a magical approach to language. It removes any certainty of meaning. It is true that a passage may have teaching that simultaneously applies to a man's conduct, to his belief, and to his hope. But not all these ideas are expressed by the original writer in the same word or phrase. Certain sections of a chapter may deal with conduct, or doctrine, or the consummation. But one particular expression like "Jerusalem" in any one passage has only one sense. Where it means the literal, earthly city, it does not refer to the heavenly city. One basic meaning may have a higher application of that meaning,[31] as the word "son" is used both of Solomon and of Christ (cf. "He will build a house for my name," II Sam. 7:14 together with Heb. 1:5). But in each context the train of thought determines the meaning it has in that particular place.

Prominence of Allegory

From A.D. 600 to 1200 allegory had a real hold upon the minds of medieval theologians. Collections of allegorical interpretations circulated. These showed how many meanings one word could have. For example, the word "sea" could mean a gathering of water, Scripture, the present age, the human heart, the active life, heathen, or baptism.[32] It is obvious that picking meanings out of a collection like this rather than on the basis of context can lead us far astray. Towards the end of the Middle Ages the use of allegory declined although it was still extensively used.

Glossa Ordinaria

Exegetical anthologies from the fathers were also in circulation. Such men as Augustine, Jerome, Ambrose, Bede, and Isidore of Seville were cited. The text of Scripture was printed by hand. Comments were written in the margin and between the lines of the text. When books were copied by hand, this method insured the most material for the available space! The citations were not chosen at random but to reach a conclusion based upon all the opinions cited. This was the extent of creativity in the Middle Ages. There was no fresh, creative thinking about the Scriptures themselves.

[31] Cf. Chapter 11.
[32] Alanus de Insulis, *Liber de distinctionibus dictionum theologiculium.* See Blackman, *op. cit.,* p. 112.

St. Thomas Aquinas (1225-1274)

Though famous as a theologian, St. Thomas also had a tremendous grasp of the content of Scripture. His extensive knowledge probably gave birth to the story that he had memorized the whole Latin Bible. In theory St. Thomas, as Augustine before him, believed that theological reasoning must be based only on the literal sense of Scripture. Yet in his *Summa Theologica* St. Thomas declares:

> God is the Author of Holy Scripture. He has given a meaning not only to the words but to the things they signify, so that the things signified in turn signify something else. *Primarily,* words signify things, which is the *historical* sense; secondarily, the things signify other things, and we get the spiritual sense. The latter is of three sorts. The Old Law is *allegorically* interpreted in the New Law, but the interpretation of matters affecting Christ and our obligation is *tropological,* and that which deals with the eternal glory is the *anagogical* or *celestial* sense. The literal sense is that which the author intends, but God being the Author, we may expect to find in Scripture a wealth of meaning.[33]

Consequently, although St. Thomas stresses the primary importance of the literal interpretation and represents a trend in the right direction, he is still deeply involved in the multiple sense practices. He compiled a catena (chain) of sayings of the fathers on the four Gospels. These came from twenty-two Greek and twenty Latin writers.[34] Farrar laments: "He accepts without hesitation their most tasteless and empty allegories."[35] The problem that St. Thomas faced—and that we still face—is the role and function of figurative language. How may it be recognized? What does it mean? St. Thomas' involvement in allegorizing made it almost impossible for him to handle objectively either literal or figurative language. Allegorizing is like a fog which at first renders objects indistinct and then finally blots them out altogether. In the presence of allegorizing both literal and figurative elements are obscured.

Nicholas of Lyra (1279-1340)

Nicholas of Lyra stands as a bridge between the Middle Ages and the Reformation. On the one hand, he accepted the practice of fourfold interpretation or "multiple sense." But on the other

[33] Part I, Question 1, Art. 10, cited by McNeil, *Interpreter's Bible,* I, 122.
[34] Farrar, *op. cit.,* p. 270.
[35] *Ibid.*

hand, being influenced by Rabbinic studies, he stressed the importance of the literal sense and criticized the Vulgate because it was not always true to the Hebrew text. He took explicit issue with some allegorical interpretations, and his general emphasis was sound. At the University of Erfurt, where Martin Luther studied, Nicholas' system of biblical interpretation prevailed. Luther respected Nicholas, and his thought was probably influenced by him.

It is significant that reformation began when men questioned the allegorical or mystical approach to Scripture. The Middle Ages reveal the tragic results of close alignment between allegorizing and ecclesiastical tradition. Buried but yet stirring beneath these forces was the potent reality of the message of God.

THE REFORMATION PERIOD: SIXTEENTH CENTURY

General Characteristics

In the Reformation the Bible came to be the supreme and sole authority. For Protestants, no assertion of Pope or Council was valid unless it was based upon the plain statements of Scripture. The battle cry of *sola scriptura* brought the Bible to the forefront. This emphasis advanced both the method of interpretation and the actual practice of interpretation.

Martin Luther (1483-1546)

No one factor can explain Luther's outburst of creative energy. His lectures on Romans and on the Psalms plus his own independent study of Scripture made him discontented with the traditionalism and allegorizing in the church of Rome. This dissatisfaction became a preparation for positive action.

Luther's own experience of justification by faith brought this teaching into focus as a major emphasis of both the Old and New Testaments.[36] He abandoned the fourfold interpretation of the medieval period and stressed the single fundamental meaning. The complexity of multiple meanings had brought only a confused babel to the simple believer. Luther's new emphasis led to a greater clarity of Scripture.

Luther not only cut away artificial complexity of meaning, but he also asserted the right of each believer to interpret the Bible for himself. But how could the believer do this if he

[36] See Blackman, *op. cit.*, p. 116. Blackman's whole summary of Luther is excellent. Note his evaluation on pp. 116-125.

did not have the Bible in his own language? Hence Luther's great work as a translator grew from his basic conviction about interpretation.

Luther also balanced the literal or grammatical sense with the spiritual depth of meaning. Depth of meaning is due to explicitly formulated ideas. Allegory for Luther had no depth. It consisted of "monkey tricks" to show the ingenuity of the exegete.[37] Luther knew that for genuine depth of spiritual meaning, we must experience the illumination of the Holy Spirit.

He also knew very well that training in linguistics, history, or even theological reasoning does not suffice. Many of his fellow monks possessed these skills. Apart from the quickening of the Spirit, the interpreter will have only words and phrases. Only through the Holy Spirit can he enter into the meaning of the biblical writers and express that meaning as a vital reality.

Luther's biblical interpretation is centered in Christ. To him, Scripture is a testimony to Christ. In those portions of Scripture where he did not find this testimony, he spent little time. Therefore, he selected out of the Scriptures what he wanted to stress. As a result Luther has been classified by some as "the most radical critic of the Church of the Reformation."[38] Such an evaluation is based on Luther's action rather than on his own enunciated beliefs. When both his actions and his beliefs are considered, Luther stands forth as an independent scholar and as a theologian of conviction. Luther never majored in minutiae. He underscored the main themes of the Gospel.

John Calvin (1509-1564)

Unfortunately, many people know Calvin only as the writer of his *Institutes*. They think of him only as a theologian who sought to bring all Scriptural teaching together in a rigid, logical system. If we like his system and its emphases, then to us Calvin occupies a pedestal of honor. If we think that his system is only a mixture of biblical truth and philosophical presuppositions, we dismiss Calvin as a vain articulator of the *decretum absolutum*. Either way, we tend to forget that Calvin was basically a biblical interpreter and only secondly a theologian. As McNeil points out, "His commentaries form the major portion of his writings. . . . He omitted from formal exposition only one book of the New Testament and eight of the Old."[39]

[37] *Ibid.*, pp. 120-21.
[38] See Farrar, *op. cit.*, p. 335.
[39] *Interpreter's Bible*, I, 124.

Furthermore, Calvin's commentaries are of such a calibre that they are still helpful to the modern interpreter.

Calvin interpreted grammatically and historically. Rarely did theological aprioris color his thinking. In the Psalms Calvin applied the writer's statements to the historical context of the particular psalm. Most interpreters today agree that messianic references in the Psalms are on the whole typological rather than alleged direct predictions which ignore the obvious context. Calvin himself shared this point of view. He maintained that Psalm 2 must be applied primarily to David. On the phrase "this day I have begotten thee" (Ps. 2:7), unlike theoretical thinkers of many epochs, Calvin removes himself from all speculation about eternal generation when he says:

> David, indeed, could with propriety be called the son of God on account of his royal dignity . . . David was begotten by God when the choice of him to be king was clearly manifested. The words *this day*, therefore, denote the time of this manifestation; for as soon as it became known that he was made king by divine appointment, he came forth as one who had been lately begotten of God . . . .[40]

To prevent hopeless subjectivity, Calvin brought together the Spirit's work in the inspiration of Scripture with the Spirit's illumination of the interpreter of Scripture. Calvin would never substitute human learning for divine instruction. Calvin's high view of inspiration did not, however, cause him to ignore the phenomena of the text. He noted the stylistic differences of the human authors. He recognized the lack of preciseness and even inaccuracies in trivia.[41] Calvin's standards for a commentary were clearness and brevity. It is because of his

---

[40] John Calvin, *Commentary on the Book of Psalms*, tr. Jas. Anderson (1845), I, 17-18.

[41] On the phrase "Zachariah, son of Barachiah" in Matt. 23:35 Calvin says: "But whether Jehoiada had two names, or whether (as Jerome thinks) there is a mistake in the word, there can be no doubt as to the fact that Christ refers to that impious stoning of Zechariah which is recorded in 2 Chron. 24:21, 22"—John Calvin, *Commentary on a Harmony of the Evangelists: Matthew, Mark, and Luke*, tr. William Pringle (1949), III, 104. On the phrase "through Jeremiah the prophet" in Matt. 27:9 Calvin remarks: "How the name of *Jeremiah* crept in, I confess that I do not know, nor do I give myself much trouble to inquire. The passage plainly shows that the name of *Jeremiah* has been put down by mistake, instead of Zechariah (11:13), for in *Jeremiah* we find nothing of this sort or anything that even approaches to it," *ibid.*, III, 272. On Acts 7:16: " . . . and they were carried over unto Shechem, and laid in the tomb that Abraham bought for a price in silver of the sons of Hemor in Shechem." Calvin comments: "And whereas he saith afterward, they were laid in the sepulchre which Abraham had bought of the sons of Hemor, it is manifest that there is a fault [mistake] in the word

own clear style, free from endless digressions, that Calvin's exegetical works are still used.

Beginnings of Creed and System Making

There were other significant interpreters and exegetes (Melanchthon, Bucer, Zwingli, Oecolampadius, Heinrich, Bullinger, etc.) which must be eliminated from this brief review. From the death of Calvin (1564) to the end of the sixteenth century, we see the beginning of creed and system making. The Council of Trent, which was in session off and on between 1545 and 1563, drew up a list of decrees setting forth the Roman Catholic dogmas and canons anathematizing the Protestants. With such an extensive production,[42] the Protestants began to reply in kind. New writings were geared to attract all who were dissatisfied with the church of Rome. The Council of Trent clarified the extent and nature of the reforms the Roman Catholic Church would accept. As a result Protestants in the last part of the sixteenth century prepared a great quantity of literature consolidating their biblical data. This literature continued into the seventeenth and eighteenth centuries. We must remember, however, that these theological statements forged in the heat of controversy often lacked the balance that comes from comprehensive exegetical study based on a dispassionate study of the Scriptures.

THE POST-REFORMATION PERIOD: SEVENTEENTH AND EIGHTEENTH CENTURIES

General Characteristics

A great variety of views appeared in these two centuries. Many chose reason as the final authority. Numerous philosophers competed for followers, such as Hobbes (1588-1679), Descartes (1596-1650), Spinoza (1632-1677), Locke (1632-1704), Berkeley (1685-1753), Hume (1711-1776), Leibnitz (1646-1716), and Kant (1724-1804). Empiricistic emphases came to the fore-

'Abraham.' For Abraham had bought a double cave of Ephron, the Hittite (Gen. 23:9) to bury his wife Sarah in; but Joseph was buried in another place, to wit, in the field which his father Jacob had bought of the sons of Hemor for an hundred lambs. Wherefore this place must be amended [hic locus corrigendus est = this passage must be corrected]," John Calvin, Commentary on the Acts of the Apostles, tr. Henry Beveridge (1844), I, 265.

[42] See Henry Denzinger, The Sources of Catholic Dogma, tr. Roy J. Deferrari (1957), pp. 243-304, pars. 782-1000.

front: Many were critical of any proposition that could not be proved by sense experience.

Reason, systems, and abstract formulations ruled in theology. Theology often controlled exegesis, in opposition to the correct order in which exegesis controls theology. Men looked for texts to prove their theology and explained away evidence that seemed to be contrary to their particular view.

Pascal (1623-1662)

Pascal never left the Roman Catholic Church although he was touched by the same forces that moved Luther, Calvin, and the other reformers. Living a century later than the pioneers of the Reformation, Pascal disliked the abstract categorizing of deity. He pointedly spoke of God as the God of Abraham, Isaac, and Jacob rather than the God (god) of philosophers. Revolting against the abstractness of a mere god of reason, Pascal put the emphasis on the heart which feels, senses, and experiences God. His view of Scripture shows careful, firsthand study. In the Bible, he asserted, "there is enough clarity to enlighten the elect and enough obscurity to humble them."[43] Pascal is evidence that the Bible was a living book for some who chose to remain within the Roman Church.

Anabaptists

Not only did the Anabaptists hold to a baptism of believers only, but they were even more insistent than the reformers that the Bible was their sole authority in faith and practice. They made strong use of the New Testament, stressed that the individual was illuminated by the Holy Spirit and could interpret the Scriptures for himself, and held that the individual had a right to live according to what he believed was the scriptural pattern. From our historical perspective, the Anabaptists and other Protestant groups of the post-Reformation period seem very similar since they all proclaimed the Scriptures as their authority. But while this common belief in the ultimate authority of the Scriptures did bring Protestants together, it is equally true that their different views as to what those Scriptures meant kept them apart. Despite so much to bind them together and with so urgent a task facing them, Christians began persecuting fellow Christians, such as the Anabaptists. This grim twist of misdirected zeal in the post-Reformation

[43] Pensées Frag. 578, Brunchwieg 497. See Grant, *The Bible in the Church,* p. 116.

times serves as a warning to each of us that Christian truth must be lived as well as analyzed, discussed, and classified.

Textual, Linguistic, and Historical Studies

During the seventeenth and eighteenth centuries great strides were made in determining the original text of the Bible. Scholars began to classify and evaluate the New Testament manuscript materials, and became increasingly aware of how much needed to be done in cataloguing all the variants in any particular passage and deciding which variant was the best. In the Old Testament, textual studies were hampered by a lack of textual materials. But even here progress was made, for scholars became aware of the lateness of the vowel points and that the Massoretic text in certain places was not always reliable.

Grammars and lexicons of Hebrew, Aramaic (Chaldean), and Greek began to circulate, aided by the discovery of printing in the fifteenth century. Although they were only beginnings, the advance over the Middle Ages was striking indeed.

Historical backgrounds of the biblical accounts came in for deeper study. Some interpreters began to see the inadequacy of looking at the Bible for proof texts while ignoring the historical situation into which the message first came. Johann Wettstein (1693-1754) and J. A. Bengel (1687-1751) were leaders in textual criticism and historical studies of Scripture. Others began literary analysis and the evaluation of the internal evidence of the books of the Bible in the framework of the traditional opinion of authorship. These were new dimensions in biblical studies.

Rationalism

Hobbes (1588-1679) and Spinoza (1632-1677), as representative rationalists, taught that the human intellect was capable of deciding what is true and false and what is right and wrong. It does this by reflection on all that the mind encounters in a time-space world, not by revelation from a transcendent God. According to the rationalists, the Bible is true where it corresponds to the conclusions of man's independent reason. The rest of the materials in the Bible may be ignored. Rationalism is closely interrelated with deism, humanism, and empiricism. Since interpreters are always influenced by thought movements of their times (whether they support them, oppose them or seek to modify them), biblical studies during this period show the impact of man's confidence in reason.

Hebrew Poetry

During the seventeenth and eighteenth centuries, scholars began to recognize that Hebrew poetry existed and that it was
extensively found in the Old Testament. In England Robert
Lowth (1710-1787) put out four editions (1753, 1763, 1775, 1787)
of *De sacra poesi Hebraeorum praelectiones academicae Oxonii
habitae.* The work was translated into English under the title:
Lectures on the Sacred Poetry of the Hebrews. In Germany
Johann Gottfried Herder (1744-1803) wrote *Vom Geist hebräi-
scher Poesie* (1782). From these works interpreters learned that
form influences content. The literary form by which a writer
conveys his ideas influences the meaning that they have upon a
reader. If we ignore the form, we cannot accurately understand
the meaning.

THE NINETEENTH CENTURY

Philosophical Assumptions

In the nineteenth century, a rigid historicism came to the
forefront and received a wide hearing. The roots for this approach were planted in the eighteenth century, but in the
nineteenth century historical criticism came into its own. Grant
points out that the extent and influence of historical criticism
was partially determined by the setting where it was promul-
gated.[44] Previously most study had been carried on in the surroundings of the church or a church-controlled school. Now
the scene shifted to the secularized German universities, where
distinct philosophical presuppositions guided the historical investigations. The rationalists' attitude toward miracles was
taken for granted: the universe is controlled by fixed laws
which allow for no suspension, alteration, or change. The
Bible is to be interpreted as any other book. This latter principle in itself is not dangerous unless it is dominated by naturalistic persuasions. We must take seriously the claims that any
book makes for itself. Evidence may demand a modification of
these claims. Yet many of the investigators of the nineteenth
century dismissed those claims of the Bible about itself without
even considering their bases. They insisted that the Bible was
like any other book, yet at the same time they described it as
being produced by a complicated array of sources, redactors,
and interpolators different from any other literary production.

[44] *The Bible in the Church*, p. 131.

We are referring here to the Bible's creative production, not to its transmission. Eventually it became apparent that their belief in its similarity to other books was limited to their assertion that it was a purely human product without any genuine interventions (acts) of God as its base or guidance of God in its production. They rejected the idea that God acted within history or that he communicated to chosen representatives (kings, prophets, priests, apostles, etc.) authentic messages which they relayed to others. The phrase "Thus saith the Lord" became a liturgical phrase or a psychological device to impress upon the hearer the solemnity of what was being said. In this atmosphere of immutable, impersonal law, many nineteenth century thinkers thought that they could find security. But their object of confidence was a "revelation" of self-sufficient reason.

Preoccupation with Historical Criticism

During the nineteenth century there was feverish activity to find out how the various books or groups of books of the Bible were written. In this period confidence in historical criticism grew. By the end of the century some were speaking of the assured results of such criticism on a whole host of things. Now historical criticism is an important study and should be supported and encouraged by all students of the Bible. But when historical criticism is controlled by a framework of naturalistic assumptions and philosophical aprioris, the results of painstaking historical investigation are vitiated. Looking back on such endeavors one may admire the work but reject many of the results because of the principles which controlled the investigators.

Living in an Hegelian world of development and dialectical contrast, Julius Wellhausen (1844-1918) worked out his J, E, D, and P hypothesis of the sources of the Pentateuch. Instead of the historical development being Law, Priests, and Prophets, Wellhausen changed the order to Prophets, Law, and Priests. Ferdinand C. Baur (1792-1860) was the New Testament counterpart to Wellhausen. Baur was a church historian and a fervent disciple of Hegel. Baur saw Peter and Paul as heads of two antagonistic groups and taught that the Petrine and Pauline parties were brought together in the second century church. He insisted that the book of Acts was a literary reminder of the compromise between these two contrasting elements. To carry out this scheme, Baur had to date most of the New Testament writings in the second century. He said only four of Paul's epistles (Romans, I & II Corinthians, Galatians) and the book of Revelation came from the apostolic age, i.e., the first century.

After Baur's death a strong reaction set in against his theoretical reconstructions. Nevertheless, many scholars did accept some of his particular ideas such as the elimination of the supernatural and miraculous elements, interest in Christian gnosis, objections to the pastoral epistles, etc. Baur was not as successful as Wellhausen in bringing scholars into his camp because the New Testament has many more external data available with which to compare it. Do New Testament writings exude the atmosphere of a Marcionite second century? Any careful study reveals that the differences far outweigh the alleged similarities. Further, the New Testament gives evidence of being composed over a relatively short span of time whereas the Old Testament, under any historical arrangement of the materials, demands a considerable period of time from the earliest to the latest writing.

As a result, Wellhausen's speculations can be refuted only by showing the presuppositions which controlled his investigations and by making a thorough study of all textual phenomena. Furthermore, since Wellhausen's time, a vast bulk of archaeological and linguistic evidence has accumulated. This must now be reckoned with. In contrast Baur could be refuted both externally and internally without any encyclopedic study of thousands of details ranging over a vast bulk of literature and a long period of time. Baur and Wellhausen both illustrate the procedures and conclusions of a rationalistic historicism.

Many others in the nineteenth century, whose work was colored only partly by rationalistic assumptions, worked in historical criticism. Still others renounced the arbitrariness of rationalism but accepted freely the demand for a careful weighing of historical evidence. Those with such an attitude produced exegetical commentaries of abiding value.

Theological attitudes have always colored historical research. There are many factors that tend to control an interpreter. Grant makes plain the impact of one dominant theological attitude:

> The nineteenth-century critical movement was not simply a movement in the history of interpretation, but (like every other exegetical school) had its own theological axes to grind. It stood for liberalism in theology. Any judgment on the work of the school must be made on the basis of this theological outlook as well as on the basis of the criticism itself. The two were closely

connected. Today, after two wars we are less optimistic over the possibility of a Christian world, and after nearly a half century of further criticism we begin to realize human potentialities for error and the limitations of the historical method. As pioneers, the old critics cut down forests with abandon. The axe of criticism will be only one of the tools we employ.[45]

Monumental Exegetical Commentaries

In spite of forces hostile to sound biblical interpretation, many exegetical commentaries were published in the nineteenth century that did not concentrate their efforts solely on historical, critical, and linguistic details. Most of these commentaries maintained a balance between secondary matters and the unfolding of the real message of each book. They dealt with such primary questions as: What are the main emphases of the book? What message were the first readers intended to appropriate and make their own? Why is theology, when it is properly drawn forth from the biblical writings, essential for Christian growth? These questions were dealt with by such men as E. W. Hengstenberg, Carl F. Keil, Franz Delitzsch, H. A. W. Meyer (and those associated with him), J. P. Lange (and those associated with him), F. Godet, Henry Alford, Charles J. Ellicott, J. B. Lightfoot, B. F. Westcott, F. J. A. Hort, Charles Hodge, John Albert Broadus, Theodor B. Zahn, and others. In the monumental commentaries of the nineteenth century the writers carefully blended together grammar, lexicography, and historical background with the message and particular truths of the book. They also made occasional allusion to literary criticism in the course of the commentary proper, with careful treatment of critical problems in the introduction to the book which was being interpreted. Most students will find points with which they do not agree in these works. But almost everyone who reads them will concede that these commentators, although far removed in time from the writings upon which they were commenting, wrote with genuine empathy for the basic convictions of the biblical writers who felt and declared the moving of God's Spirit in their lives. This is in marked contrast to the rationalistic interpreters of whom Ehrenberg comments: "If you wish to find the Holy Spirit in the Bible, you look for Him first in passages marked R [Redactor, i.e. later additions]."[46]

[45] *Ibid.,* p. 141.
[46] Cited by Blackman, *ibid.,* p. 146.

THE TWENTIETH CENTURY

General Characteristics

This is the century of far-reaching changes. When the century began, however, it was under the influences of the optimism of the nineteenth century. In the early years of the twentieth century interpretation was influenced more in the area of basic assumptions than in the area of methodological procedure. As the century moved on important changes in methodology also became clear.

One fact stands out: on the whole, interpretation in the United States has been more imitative than creative. By the end of World War I, German scholars were beginning to point out the weaknesses of many nineteenth century dogmas. But in the United States no such discontent was apparent until after World War II—i.e., until there had been time for the German writings to be digested and understood! Then, under the pressure of the newer trends of German scholars, Americans began to take a fresh look at Scripture, and even though these interpreters themselves were not fully aware of the great changes which were breaking into the interpretive horizon, the results were soon apparent in biblical and interpretative studies. A by-product of this trend was the fact that theology ceased being a bad word and became "interesting," "thought-provoking," or even "pertinent" to Christian living.

Evangelical or orthodox interpreters in the United States did not find stimulus for exegetical or theological thought from Germany. Rather, they tended to look backwards rather than outward and forward. The Anglican scholarship of J. B. Lightfoot, B. F. Westcott, F. J. A. Hort, Henry Alford and others together with the translated materials of C. F. Keil and Franz Delitzsch not only served as models but, with rare exceptions, comprised the basic exegetical authorities. American orthodox scholars in the first half of the twentieth century failed to produce works of the same caliber dealing with the concerns and questions of their own time. This made it appear that orthodoxy either had no vital interest in biblical interpretation or thought that the final word in exegesis had been said. In the latter half of the century there are signs of improvement as commentaries of depth, insight, and linguistic learning are appearing. Yet much remains to be done, especially regarding the Old Testament.

Commentaries Without Theology

From the beginning of the twentieth century to the close of World War II many commentaries appeared that were replete with studies of grammar, literary criticism, historical parallels, etc., but which assiduously avoided theology. Historical, antiquarian, linguistic, and cultural interests were satisfied. But the emphasis on a meeting with God, a definite involvement with particular truths of God, were conspicuously absent. God appears to have been an abstract idea to the interpreters. They limited themselves to factors associated with a preliminary preparation for full understanding. These preliminaries are essential if the commentary is to be more than a devotional treatise. But to give more attention to backgrounds than to the message about God or Christ that the original writer meant to convey indicates that the commentator is preoccupied with minutiae and that the real reason for all such studies—to make clear the essential message—has been relegated to last place.

The Old Quest for the Historical Jesus

During the nineteenth century many scholars were enamored with what they regarded as the theological wrappings that had come to surround the historical Jesus. They tried to reconstruct his biography in such a way as to free the man Jesus from all these later additions. When this "reconstructed," "historical" Jesus was unveiled, however, he turned out to be only an ethical teacher. He did no miracles. He had no interest in eschatology. He was a shadowy reflection of a nineteenth century liberal! Albert Schweitzer, who remained within the liberal tradition, protested. He insisted that to rely on that kind of Jesus took more than a super-colossal faith. It really demanded a naive dismissal of large sections of the Gospels. His famous volume *Von Reimarus zu Wrede,* published in Germany in 1906, was translated into English under the title: *The Quest of the Historical Jesus.*[47] Schweitzer emphasized the eschatological elements in Jesus' teaching, and his volume really ended the nineteenth century quest for the historical Jesus.

It was an unsuccessful quest, for a reason that Karl Barth was to point out in the Preface of his famous *Die Römerbrief* (1919; 2nd ed., 1922). According to Barth, historical-critical questions and methods provide only the preparation for understanding the Scriptures; genuine understanding requires a good deal

---

[47] Albert Schweitzer, *The Quest of the Historical Jesus,* tr. W. Montgomery (2nd ed., 1911).

more than these. In this emphasis on total understanding as
the goal of hermeneutics, Barth was unquestionably right.

The New Quest for the Historical Jesus

For about fifty years the old quest was merely a memory.
Some scholars were skeptical that we could ever know anything
about the historical Jesus; far removed from these were those
who were confident that the Christ of faith was the Jesus of
history and that it was not difficult to differentiate between
Jesus' words and deeds as separate from the interpretive meaning of these words and deeds. Yet it is apparent in the Gospels
that during Jesus' lifetime on earth the disciples understood
little of the significance of who Jesus was and why he did what
he did. They had occasional flashes of insight when God specifically revealed things to them, but many times they simply
stood in perplexity (cf. Luke 9:43b-45; Mark 9:32). It is a
complex but worthwhile study to see how Jesus appeared to the
disciples while Jesus walked with them for about three years,
and how the death, resurrection, and proclamation of good
news changed their initial impressions.

In 1959 James M. Robinson published a significant volume
entitled *A New Quest of the Historical Jesus.* [48] Robinson contrasts sharply the nineteenth century view of history with the
twentieth century view of history.[49] The objective, factual level
of the nineteenth century study is now regarded as only one
dimension of history. In the twentieth century, the distinctly
human, creative, purposeful aspects that distinguish man from
nature come into their own as the deeper dimension of history.
Robinson also points out that for primitive Christianity the
kerygma (message of good tidings *heralded forth* by the apostles,
prophets and followers of Jesus) was central. The early Church
was devoted to proclaiming the good tidings about Jesus to
everyone. This proclamation was not only about something
past but also about something *present.*

> Believing the witness about God's past action in Christ coincides
> with the occurrence of this divine action in my present life.
> Herein resides the unity of God's action in history, and ultimately

[48] James M. Robinson, *A New Quest of the Historical Jesus* (1959). The
chapter headings alone indicate a well thought out, overall plan of procedure: I, Introduction; II, The Impossibility and Illegitimacy of the Original Quest; III, The Possibility of a New Quest; IV, The Legitimacy of a
New Quest; V, The Procedure of a New Quest.
[49] *Ibid.,* pp. 28-29, 76, 85.

the meaningfulness of the Trinity. Thus both as witness to past event and as experience of present event, the *kerygma* is central in primitive Christianity and contemporary theology. It is for this reason that the *kerygma* has become a whole unified theological position which has just as nearly swept the field in twentieth-century theology as did the theology of the historical Jesus in the nineteenth century.[50]

The new quest appears to have a sounder outlook than the earlier quest. It recognizes quite forthrightly the limitations of older principles that supposedly distinguish the authentic material about Jesus from that which is kerygmatic and hence from the church.[51] Yet the procedures in the new quest, which distinguish kerygmatic interpretation and assertion (i.e., material which bears the stamp of the early Christian community) from the utterances and actions of Jesus (i.e., material which bears the stamp of Jesus' word and deed) still have an arbitrary ring to them. The individual interpreter is often too confident of his ability to judge whether one statement is a kerygmatic declaration while another tells what Jesus proclaimed or what Jesus did. Although it is true that current scholars are sifting the gospel material, not for the purpose of playing the kerygma over against the utterances and actions of Jesus, but for the purpose of having an encounter with both,[52] these same scholars confidently engaging in the new quest can easily fall into presumptions very similar to those of the nineteenth century positivistic historicism. The success of the new movement is dependent on how well they escape these kinds of presumptions.

Renewed Interest in Theology

Theology has come into its own through the influence of biblical interpretation. The study known as Biblical Theology is really an historical theology of the Old and the New Testaments. Theology is examined in the historical setting into which a particular teaching first came. The categories of such studies have a biblically orientated nomenclature rather than a philosophical one. Thus interpretation has brought into existence a highly developed linguistic, historical, and theological discipline. Likewise in reciprocal fashion biblical theology has provided the interpreter with more insights and depths of meaning than mere linguistic or historical study by itself could do.

50 *Ibid.*, pp. 42-43.
51 *Ibid.*, pp. 99-100.
52 *Ibid.*, pp. 104-05, 111.

Theological and Historical Studies

In 1928 Gerhard Kittel announced that he would produce a new theological dictionary which would bring up to date the old work of Cremer, *Biblico-Theological Lexicon of New Testament Greek*.[53] This new work was entitled: *Theologisches Wörterbuch zum Neuen Testament*. Volume I appeared in 1932-33. Volume II was published in 1935. Volume III appeared in 1938 while Volume IV came off the press in the midst of World War II in 1942. In 1948 Gerhard Kittel died. Gerhard Friedrich took his place. Volume V was published in 1954 and Volume VI was completed in 1959. Words which have theological significance are presented alphabetically. These six volumes cover the words beginning with *alpha* through those beginning with *rho*. Two volumes still in process will complete the Greek alphabet—from *sigma* to *omega*.[54]

This work is significant because it provides the interpreter with the Judaic and Hellenistic background of important words and the ideas which they convey. The use of a word in the various writings or groups of writings in the New Testament is carefully studied. This is not merely another lexicon with word equivalents but it involves the backgrounds for the total context-idea in which the word serves as one of the major contributing factors. This work alone is a monumental testimony to the revival of genuinely creative theological study.

Renewed Popular Interest in the Study of the Bible

Following World War II both Protestants and Roman Catholics produced commentaries for laymen. *The New Testament Reading Guide* consists of 14 volumes, produced in inexpensive paperback.[55] These will certainly be helpful to the Roman Catholic layman. Many Protestants also would benefit by a reading of them. Among college students in this country *The New Bible Commentary,* a one-volume commentary produced mainly by English scholars, has proved very useful. Another one-volume commentary produced by scholars from the United States has just appeared—*The Wycliffe Commentary.*

[53] Herman Cremer, *Biblico-Theological Lexicon of New Testament Greek,* tr. William Urwick (4th English ed., 1895).

[54] English-speaking students will long be indebted to the Wm. B. Eerdmans Publishing Company for publishing the English translation of this work. Volume I of the translation will appear in 1963.

[55] For complete data on this and other guides mentioned below, see Bibliography appended to this volume.

Likewise the *Interpreter's Bible* is being used by some laymen, although its bulk and cost—12 volumes—have prevented many from personally owning a set. *The Tyndale New Testament Commentaries* are adequate yet concise in their treatment of the writings of the New Testament. These are only a few of the numerous exegetical works to appear.[56] Such works indicate that many want to understand the message of the Bible rather than merely to know how it came to be written. An active, alert laity dedicated to the great truths of the Christian faith is essential if Christianity is to move forward in an ominous age.

BIBLIOGRAPHY

Blackman, A. C., *Biblical Interpretation* (1957).
Burrows, Millar, *The Dead Sea Scrolls* (1955).
————, *More Light on the Dead Sea Scrolls* (1958).
Denzinger, Henry, *The Sources of Catholic Dogma,* tr. Roy J. Deferrari (1957).
Enslin, Morton Scott, "The Genius of Judaism: Its Literature," Chapter VI, *Christian Beginnings* (1938).
Farrar, F. W., *History of Interpretation* (1886).
Grant, Robert M., *The Bible in the Church* (1948).
Wolfson, Harry A., *Philo* (1948).
Wood, James D., *The Interpretation of the Bible: An Historical Introduction,* 1st ed. (1958).

---

[56] One can only refer to a few. Students should consult current book catalogues and book stores carrying a wide variety of materials from which to make a selection.

III   Crucial Issues

During every age particular issues occupy the minds of those who interpret the Bible. These issues are never the same, although there are similarities with past issues. The answers, too, though similar, have a certain originality in every age. A fresh, creative answer is always essential because the combination of factors in any issue and their relative emphasis demand a response that comes from renewed and serious reflection.

No list of issues can ever be complete. Questions which disturb some do not bother others. Even major issues sometimes seem remote to the interpreter who is without technical training in languages, history, philosophy, and theology. This same interpreter may be more genuinely perplexed by minor matters. Many times we are aware of problem areas but are unable to isolate the particular point that needs clarifying. Following is a list of issues that are of major importance. They have been discussed at length in books and magazine articles. In this chapter we will merely show the main elements involved in these issues. In the course of the discussion the author's own attitude will be obvious. Men with similar training and ability often produce diverse interpretations because their approach to these crucial issues affects all of their exegetical work. Each interpreter carries his own attitudes and outlook into his task of unfolding the meaning of someone else's statements.

EXEGESIS AND EXPOSITION

Position of the Interpreter

Everyone who interprets a passage of the Bible stands in a *present* time while he examines a document that comes from a *past* time. He must discover what each statement meant to the original speaker or writer, and to the original hearers or readers, in *their* own present time. Then he must convey this message to his contemporaries. He must see what meaning these statements had in the past, but he must also show what is their meaning *for himself and for those to whom he conveys these ideas.*

Take Paul's opening statement in the Epistle to the Romans: "Paul, a slave of Jesus Christ" (1:1). Paul and his original readers understood well the status of a slave. They knew that a master owned his slave, directed his activities, and regulated his conduct. The slave had to obey. Yet Paul chose this expression to show his relationship and that of his fellow Christians to Christ (cf. Rom. 1:1; I Cor. 7:22; Phil. 1:1; Col. 1:7; 4:7,12). Christ had bought them. He owned them. To such a master—one who purchased believers at the cost of his own life—Paul could only give his complete allegiance. This became one of his favorite terms. But the average reader who picks up the King James Version reads: "Paul, a servant of Jesus Christ" (Rom. 1:1). He pictures a very wealthy man who is able to afford servants. To the average reader, servants are part of a bygone epoch. When wages were lower, servants did the things now done by an array of household gadgets. So when Paul speaks of himself as a servant of Jesus Christ he sounds like a domestic in Christ's household. What a distortion of Paul's metaphor![1] Exegesis of the word *doulos* ("slave") demands showing what this word meant for Paul and for his contemporaries. Exposition of the word *doulos* demands that the interpreter help the modern reader to get rid of his wrong ideas about "servant" and to overcome his emotional antipathy to the meaning "slave." Only then can he point out the true meaning that the expression should convey to the modern reader.[2] The interpreter must constantly involve himself both in the past and in the present.

[1] See Edgar J. Goodspeed, *Problems of New Testament Translation* (1945), pp. 139-41, 77-79.

[2] For the terms "exegesis" and "exposition" contrasted in a manner similar to this, the writer is indebted to James Smart, *The Interpretation of Scripture* (1961), pp. 40-44.

Independence of Exegesis and Exposition

There are two steps involved. First, we must discover the meaning of the expression or statement in the past. Then we must drive this meaning home to our present society with the same impact it had when it was originally written. It is easier to identify our errors in interpretation if these two steps are differentiated. In exegesis the interpreter sometimes ignores certain assertions of the Bible simply because what it says or claims is unacceptable to the interpreter, e.g. the claim of prediction. Or he may explain (away) the claim as an ancient form of writing history. In exposition, the interpreter may be so eager to convey an idea to modern man that the biblical idea becomes mixed with the interpreter's own ideas. For example, in discussing the New Testament concept of time we must show both the qualitative and quantitative aspects of time and how they are set forth. Which of these is in the ascendency in the New Testament? How are these aspects related to each other?[3] Should one build a case on biblical words apart from biblical propositions and assertions? How easy it is for us to attribute to the original speaker or writer ideas which never entered his mind when he uttered the expression which is being interpreted.

Inseparability of Exegesis and Exposition

Current attitudes on historical method have a real bearing on interpretation. Today's historian knows he must look not only at the "outside" of history—battles, length of wars, years of geographical discoveries—but also at the "inside" of history —why war came, what the war did and did not solve, the attitudes and outlook of colonists. James Smart has well said:

> All history is the history of thought, and there must be a re-enact-ment in the historian's mind of the thought whose history he is studying. Past and present cannot be cut apart without the past becoming a corpse and the exegete's task merely one of historical

[3] See for example Oscar Cullmann's *Christ and Time,* tr. Floyd V. Filson (1950). Prof. Cullmann stresses the New Testament quantitative emphasis upon time. He shows its abhorrence for a philosophical "timelessness" or "eternal now." Yet there is more to the qualitative aspects of time in the NT than Cullmann depicts. This may be due to the brevity of his treament and his desire to show the centrality of redemptive history. Though this latter proposition is qualitative, to be sure, Cullmann draws out its quantitative implications most fully. The need for careful terminological and lexical study on the words for time such as *kairos* and *aiōn* is brilliantly set forth by James Barr, *Biblical Words for Time* (1962), pp. 47-81.

dissection. Only the exegete who takes seriously the question, What does this text mean *for me now?* has any hope of getting inside the mind of the original author in order to understand what the words meant *for him then.*[4]

In this procedure the interpreter is simply starting where he is and is proceeding back to where the original author was. The interpreter is not a spectator who merely tries to report flawlessly what actually happened. He is a participant who enters into what happened or what was originally thought so that he can help his contemporary generation enter into the experience and thought of the original writer and readers or hearers. This puts a heavy demand upon the historian and the interpreter. As he enters into the meaning of the passage or event he will constantly modify and correct what he thought the text meant for him and what he thought it meant for the original readers or observers. The "correction" may be only a deepening of an original conviction. But this conviction about the meaning will be increasingly supported by objective factors—contextual, grammatical, historical, cultural, theological, etc.—that influence meaning. The honest and careful interpreter is always prepared to alter his ideas when he sees that extraneous or wrong assumptions have colored his original impressions. Interpretation must not consist of untested first impressions. Too often the interpreter never evaluates himself or his procedures. He simply uses biblical statements to enhance his own ideas or outlook. This is neither sound exegesis nor valid exposition. Correct interpretation demands both sound exegesis and valid exposition. To bring out the true meaning of a biblical statement, the interpreter must be involved in the earlier epoch as well as being vitally related to his contemporaries—those to whom he must communicate the meaning of a statement that comes out of the past.

Purpose of Exegesis and Exposition

The purpose of exegesis and exposition is to communicate the meaning of an earlier statement to those living at the same time as the interpreter. The interpreter is talking neither to himself nor for himself. He is conveying biblical ideas about God and man, not his own opinions. This is easier to say than to do. But it is the aim of every faithful interpreter to be involved in what he communicates without expanding or contracting the biblical ideas which he is communicating.

4 Smart, *op. cit.,* p. 43.

EVENT AND INTERPRETATION

In our day there has been a heightened interest in the activity of God in historical events and in the meaning of these events. This interest has made theology a more concrete study as compared to the abstract study of carefully worked-out propositions. The previous emphasis on propositions as final entities with little or no relation to the historical activity of God made theology seem like an abstract philosophy under a different name. The discussion of events and their interpretation benefits all participants.

Importance of the Acts of God

Throughout the Old Testament, but especially in the Psalms, the mighty acts, deeds, and works of God are celebrated.[5] Sometimes God's acts or works of creation are spoken of, but most of the emphasis falls on God's acts of deliverance and judgment. Israel is to have nothing to do with idolatry. Israel's allegiance is to be to "Jehovah, who brought you up out of the land of Egypt with great power and with an outstretched arm, him shall ye fear, and unto him shall ye bow yourselves, and to him shall ye sacrifice" (II Kings 17:36).[6] In communicating with his covenant people, God identifies himself as the one who brought them up out of the land of Egypt. Orthodoxy has always stressed that in these acts God took the initiative with Israel (and through Israel with mankind) to bring men into a living relationship with himself. God acted against the Egyptians to make them eager to get rid of a foreign minority group. God acted on behalf of the Israelites to deliver them from slavery ("a house of bondage") but also to make them aware of the covenant relationship that existed between themselves (Abraham's descendants through Isaac) and God. From Egypt to

[5] The Hebrew word *gᵉvurah* (*strength, might*), in the plural *gᵉvurōth*, means *mighty deeds*. It is used of God in the following passages (references are to Eng. txt.): Deut. 3:24; Ps. 20:6; 71:16; 106:2; 145:4,12; 150:2; Isa. 63:15. The noun *maⁿᵃseh* refers to the *deed(s)* or *work(s)* of Jehovah especially in deliverance and in judgment in these passages: Deut. 3:24; 11:3,7; Josh. 24:31; Judges 2:7,10; Ps. 28:5; 33:4; 66:3; 86:8; 92:4,5; 104:24; 106:13; 107:22,24; 111:2,6,7; 118:17; 139:14; 143:5; 145:4,9,10,17. The noun *pōⁿal* is used of the *deed* or *thing done* by God in deliverance, Ps. 44:1; 77:12; 90:16; 92:4; 95:9; 111:3; 143:5. In one passage the noun *pᵉⁿullah* (*work, recompense*) in the plural refers to the *deeds* of Jehovah: Ps. 28:5.

[6] God's bringing Israel out of Egypt is a constant theme: Exod. 17:3; 32:7, 23; 33:1; Deut. 20:1; Josh. 24:17; Judges 2:1; 6:8,13; I Sam. 10:18; II Kings 17:7,36; I Chron. 17:5; Neh. 9:18; Ps. 81:10; Jer. 16:14-15; 23:7-8; Amos 2:10; 3:1; 9:7; Mic. 6:4.

Canaan, Israel met God both in mercy and in judgment. Some responded by trust and obedience. Others responded by distrust and disobedience. In both instances, those who responded responded inwardly to outward situations. In the miracles, God showed his power to his people—"with great power and with an outstretched arm"—to produce an immediate effect upon the people and also a later effect. The meaning and significance of God's action *into* and *in* and *through* history become the basis for man's inner response. In rejecting God, the individual Israelite was not simply rejecting an idea. In accepting God, he was not simply accepting an idea. He was responding to the living God. God confronted man in both the inward and outward spheres. In both of these spheres, man accepted or rejected him.

Emphasis on the acts of God is found in the titles of some works.[7] Gilkey points out that this language about the acts of God, as it occurs in much of modern theology, really is ambiguous.[8] If Calvin were asked what God actually did at the Exodus, he would tell the questioner to read the book of Exodus and see the account of the plagues, the pillar of cloud, and the different places where God spoke.[9] But when he asks this question of Wright or Anderson[10] the answer is extremely elusive. Many modern scholars, unlike Calvin, deny a univocal (one meaning) understanding of theological language:

> To us, theological verbs such as "to act," "to work," "to do," "to speak," "to reveal," etc. have no longer the literal meaning of observable actions in space and time or of voices in the air. The denial of wonders and voices has thus shifted our theological language from the univocal to the analogical.[11]

Those who hold that this language is completely analogical (proportional meaning: related to one meaning yet different from it) cannot explain why God's action in the Exodus made this the major event in Israel's national-religious history. To be sure, the absence of an answer is not immediately recognized because religious language of some kind is brought in to fill the gap.

[7] Cf. George Ernest Wright, *God Who Acts* (1952). George Ernest Wright and Reginald H. Fuller, *The Book of the Acts of God,* Contemporary Scholarship Interprets the Bible (1960).

[8] Langdon B. Gilkey, "Cosmology, Ontology, and the Travail of Biblical Language," *The Journal of Religion,* XL (1961), 200.

[9] *Ibid.,* p. 198.

[10] B. Anderson, *Understanding the Old Testament* (1957).

[11] Gilkey, *op. cit.,* p. 196.

In sum, therefore, we may say that for modern biblical theology the Bible is no longer so much a book containing a description of God's actual acts and words as it is a book containing Hebrew interpretations, "creative interpretations" as we call them which, like the parable of Jonah, tell stories of God's deeds and man's response to express the theological beliefs of Hebrew religion. Thus the Bible is a book descriptive not of the acts of God but of Hebrew religion. And though God is the subject of all verbs of the Bible, Hebrew religious faith and Hebrew minds provide the subjects of all the verbs in modern books on the meaning of the Bible.[12]

Gilkey goes on to point out that those who use biblical language analogically rather than univocally are often not very clear about what they are doing. If they do not know what one term of the analogy means, what God *really* did or said, then the analogy is unintelligible. It is not analogical language but rather equivocal language (different unrelated meanings)![13]

Gilkey puts forth a fervent plea for clear thinking. Ambiguous theological language is a credit to no one. On the other hand, many representatives of modern biblical theology would object to the substitution of "the Hebrew mind" or "Hebrew religious faith" for God as the subject of all verbs of the Bible. However, if they really object to such substitution, then perhaps they should accept the fact that God did act! Of course, if they hold to a closed continuum where law is supreme, where cause and effect are never interfered with by either God or man, they can hardly believe that God really acted. Hence such an apriori in any form should be renounced as contrary to all that the Bible says about God's freedom. Not only do the Scriptures assert that God has freedom, but that he has exercised his freedom in the past and will do so in the future. The world is a controlled continuum, and it is God who is exercising the control.

Inseparability of Event from Interpretation

Every mature person knows that life is full of events whose meanings are inscrutable. Even events that can be interpreted or explained are frequently of such a nature that they require much time and effort to make the explanation. An airplane crashes. After many months of painful investigation the Civil Aeronautics Board may explain why it crashed. This explanation is an "interpretation" of a tragic event. In 1939 Germany

12 *Ibid.*, p. 197.
13 *Ibid.*

invaded Poland and in 1941 she invaded Russia. The meaning of these events was not clear at that time. Those who had read Adolf Hitler's *Mein Kampf* understood more. The meaning of every historical event demands the perspective of time. Yet mere time is no guarantee of a fair evaluation. In the world today we have many different evaluations of the meaning of the Russian revolution. The meaning of the spread of Communism after World War II is interpreted one way by a professor of history in Russia and in quite a different way by a professor of history in England, France, West Germany, or the United States. Serious thought can never be content with a simple listing of events. Germany did invade Russia in June of 1941, but the thinking person wants to understand the reasons. We can seldom give final and complete answers to the "why" questions, but we do want some meaning. The biblical writers believed that God acted in decisive events for the redemption of his people. They were decisive not only for Israel (and, in the New Testament, for the Church), but they were decisive for mankind. Therefore, when such events are recorded, interpretation or meaning is also recorded. How much significance is seen in the event and the amount of interpretation provided is influenced by the nature of the event. The events of Christ's death and resurrection are regarded as climactic. God acted once and for all for men and for their salvation. Therefore the message of good news includes events *plus* meaning.

Meaning in History. Meaning in history is a personal matter. Many people may see the same meaning in certain historical events. But it is, nonetheless, *their* meaning. An individual may accept uncritically a meaning offered by someone else. Nevertheless, until he arrives at a different meaning for himself, the first is *his* meaning. In the German language two words are used in theology in reference to history. *Historie* focusses the attention upon "the causal nexus in the affairs of men."[14] Here the emphasis is upon facts. The historian is supposed to divorce himself of all presuppositions and prejudices (an obvious impossibility). Objective facts are the only goal when one is pursuing historical research along the lines of *Historie*. *Geschichte* focusses the attention upon "the mutual encounter of persons."[15] Here impartiality is not even attempted. The historian experiences an encounter in *Geschichte* that affects his personal existence. In this encounter certain demands and responses become evident. The person thus affected makes resolves and decisions.

---

[14] Julius Schniewind, "A Reply to Bultmann," *Kerygma and Myth*, A Theological Debate, ed. Hans Werner Bartsch (1961), p. 82.
[15] *Ibid.*

He shows love or hate. He is involved. In translating the volume *Kerygma and Myth*, Reginald Fuller translated the adjective *historisch* by the English words "historical" or "past-historical." The adjective *geschichtlich* is translated by the English word "historic."[16] Schniewind suggests that in *Historie* one finds a "neutral" approach to historical data, while in *Geschichte* one encounters a "personal" approach.

Such distinctions are elusive. Events do not occur with identification tags stipulating their meaning. The commendable effort to avoid bias, prejudice, and partiality must not be vitiated by an endeavor to avoid becoming involved in an historical event. The interpreter merely seeks to become involved in the right way. The individual who originally acted in the actual historical event should have no grounds to say to the historian: "You have completely misunderstood my experience or message," or "You have introduced elements into my message or my experience that distort the basic facts." He should be able to say instead: "You have entered into my message or my experience and reported it to your contemporaries in the way that I would do if I understood your times as well as I do my own." No historian can fully reach this goal. But the extent to which he does is the criterion of his faithfulness as an historian. Thus history consists of facts (events, persons, institutions, tools, weapons, etc.) and personal encounter with facts. There was a personal encounter when an event first took place or when a message was first given, another personal encounter when the event or message was later recorded, and there must be a third when the record is interpreted. History involves event, encounter, and interpretation. One may separate these analytically, but not at the expense of their basic inseparability.

For Bultmann the cross is both an historical fact and an historical event.

> In its redemptive aspect the cross of Christ is no mythical event, but a historic *[geschichtlich]* fact originating in the historical *[historisch]* event which is the crucifixion of Jesus. The abiding significance of the cross is that it is the judgment of the world, the judgment and the deliverance of man. So far as this is so, Christ is crucified "for us," not in the sense of any theory of sacrifice or satisfaction. This interpretation of the cross as a permanent fact rather than a mythological event does far more justice to the redemptive significance of the event of the past than any of the traditional interpretations. In the last resort mythological language is only a medium for conveying the significance of the historical *[historisch]* event. The historical *[his-*

16 R. Fuller, *ibid.*, pp. xi-xii.

torisch] event of the cross has, in the significance peculiar to it, created a new historic *[geschichtlich]* situation. The preaching of the cross as the event of redemption challenges all who hear it to appropriate this significance for themselves, to be willing to be crucified with Christ.[17]

But the cross for Bultmann is not followed by another event, namely the resurrection, although it is so stated in all four Gospels. For Bultmann the cross and resurrection "form a single, indivisible cosmic event."[18] For Bultmann "resurrection" is only interpretation. It is an article of faith but not a separate fact of history. "An historical *[historisch]* fact which involves a resurrection from the dead is utterly inconceivable!"[19] That the resurrection is *first* an event, and second, an interpreted event or an article of faith is impossible for Bultmann. He cannot conceive of this because he has already predicated that the universe is a closed continuum, and resurrections do not occur in that kind of a universe. In contrast the Scriptures simply assert the event—"He is risen" (Matt. 28:6; Mark 16:6). But usually the notice of the event is either directly interpreted or occurs in a context of such interpretation—". . . to those trusting in the One who raised up Jesus our Lord from the dead, who was handed over for the sake of our trespasses, and he was raised for the sake of our acquittal [or justification]" (Rom. 4:24-25). But why should such interpretation militate against the historicity *[Historie]* of the event? All important events are expounded as well as asserted. To expound them, the historian becomes involved (or has an encounter) with them. If this is true of other important events, how much more of the resurrection.

Although the cross for Bultmann is *Geschichte* and *Historie,* he has no interest in Christ as *Historie* or even *Geschichte* separated from the kerygma.

> So far, then, from running away from *Historie* and taking refuge in *Geschichte,* I am deliberately renouncing any form of encounter with a phenomenon of past history, including an encounter with the Christ after the flesh, in order to encounter the Christ proclaimed in the kerygma, which confronts me in my historic situation.[20]

Bultmann's anchor point is not the historical Christ, nor the historic Christ, but the kerygmatic Christ. It is true, of course, that the Christ of the proclamation (kerygma) is historic

---

[17] "New Testament and Mythology," *ibid.,* p. 37.
[18] *Ibid.*
[19] *Ibid.,* p. 39.
[20] "Reply to Theses of Julius Schniewind," *ibid.,* p. 117.

(geschichtlich) because I encounter him in my own situation. But this is no encounter with a phenomenon of past history but an encounter with one who meets me in my history. This existential emphasis ignores the fact that the one who meets me now has had a specific past history which determines all that he is and can do for me now. The interpreted Christ of the kerygma has a meaning that God has revealed. God's disclosure of the meaning of Christ, i.e. of who he is, began during Christ's earthly (i.e. *historisch*) life. " Flesh and blood did not reveal this to you but my Father who is in Heaven" (Matt. 16:17). But Bultmann has reconstructed the materials in the Gospels according to his pattern of a closed continuum and according to the premise that one can be sure that materials from the tradition are genuine (i.e. from Jesus) only if they could not possibly come from rabbinical sources or church sources. The only statements that can be certain not to have come from rabbinical or church sources are those that are contrary to what was taught by the rabbis or by the early Church. To Bultmann and many of his followers only a small portion of the materials in the Gospels are actually from Jesus; the larger portion is from the early Church. Unless you share the premises of this school, this procedure seems highly arbitrary. In actual results we find that certain sayings or events from Jesus' life that lie side by side are assigned to one category or the other. The reasons for the choices are based on rationalistic assumptions derived from a contemporary philosophic world view. The basic convictions of the New Testament writers themselves are ignored even while such interpreters are trying to show the meaning of what the New Testament writers are saying. Such a procedure can bring only distortion.

Revelation in Event. In contrast to Bultmann, who minimizes the event in favor of the kerygmatic declaration, there are others who apparently equate revelation with the events in history. James Smart cites Wright[21] and Dodd[22] as providing examples of this type of procedure. He points out the error in such a procedure:

> However, in this emphasis upon event, the fact is lost from sight that in both Testaments the event is always an interpreted event. Event in history and interpretation are inseparable, so that the event without the interpretation would not be a revelation to anyone.... This tendency to equate revelation with the historical events fails to take account of the fact that, everywhere in Scripture, the revelation, which is the inmost meaning of the

21 Wright, *op. cit.*
22 C. H. Dodd, *The Apostolic Preaching and Its Developments* (1936).

event, is hidden until it is revealed by the Spirit of God to the faith of man. The event itself is capable of receiving other interpretations.[23]

Revelation in Interpreted Event. From all that has been said it is clear that revelation involves the meaning of the redemptive actions of God. Take, for example, the death and resurrection of Christ. His death could be construed as the death of a martyr. His resurrection could be understood as a proof of his innocence. But the New Testament does not interpret the death and resurrection in this way. His death involved a complex transaction among the members of the Godhead and between the triune God and man. Such a transaction involves many facets and elements. His resurrection stands primarily for his victory over man's foes: the law (in one sense), sin, death, hostile forces—human and superhuman, etc. From whence comes the meaning of the event? The New Testament answers this question clearly. Interpretation is not by human inference but rather by God's disclosure to particular servants concerning what he has done, is doing, and in some cases of what he will do. Of the cross, Smart declares: "The revelation of its meaning is nowhere described as a human inference from a divine event but as a direct revelation of God to man of what he is doing."[24] God grants to his selected men an understanding of what he did at the cross and in the resurrection. This kind of interpreted event is revelation. The goal of interpreters (i.e., those who set forth by exegesis and exposition *an* interpretation of *the* interpretation), is to say neither more nor less than the Spirit of God conveyed to those to whom he first disclosed the meaning. Later disclosures of God may shed light on earlier disclosures. But the interpreter must not read back into earlier statements truths which he knows only from later disclosures.

SUBJECTIVITY IN INTERPRETATION

The interpreter, like the historian, must become involved. Hence, he cannot be a neutral spectator. It is true that this involvement may bring a wrong kind of subjectivity—that is, the interpreter may pretend to be clarifying the idea of Paul or John when in reality he is setting forth his own idea. No procedure could be more erroneous. Yet we cannot escape subjectivity in our interpretation of the Bible. An interpreter brings to bear upon the text all that he is, all that he knows, and even

23 Smart, *op. cit.,* pp. 172, 173.
24 *Ibid.,* p. 173.

all that he wants to become. It will help us just to be aware that this is so. Knowing this, we must try to be so molded by God that the distortion brought about by our subjectivity will be at a minimum. In this molding, the believer is not passive but very active. If intellectual development is part of our salvation, then the believer works out his intellectual growth "with fear and trembling" because God is the one who is working in him both the willing and the working on behalf of God's good will (cf. Phil. 2:12-13). Interpretation is more than intellectual procedures, attitudes, and assumptions, but these do enter into a man's subjectivity and consequently must always be open to correction. Failing to be open to self-correction is like a man's having 20/200 vision and steadfastly refusing to wear glasses.

Earlier liberalism was under the illusion that it was objective. Bultmann saw clearly that the interpreter must surrender any pretense of neutrality and come to the text fully recognizing his own attitude and the framework of thought in which he operates.[25] The earlier Bultmann had as his own framework the tradition of the Church and the Church's faith.[26] But the Bultmann of twenty-five or thirty years later talks about a "pre-understanding."[27] The current framework for his "pre-understanding" is existentialist philosophy. For all of us this "pre-understanding" comes out of certain interests. These interests control the interpreter whether he be an historical scholar, a psychologist, a student of aesthetics, or an existentialist philosopher.

> Hence it is evident that each interpretation is guided by a certain interest, by a certain putting of the question: What is my interest in interpreting the documents? Which question directs me to approach the text? It is evident that the questioning arises from a particular interest in the matter referred to, and therefore that a particular understanding of the matter is pre-supposed. I like to call this a pre-understanding.[28]

This pre-understanding controls what a man sees in a passage and what part of it he stresses. Bultmann operates from an existentialist perspective because he thinks that from this perspective he sees what is relevant to the needs of modern man.

[25] This was in 1925 when he wrote an essay on "The Problem of a Theological Exegesis of the New Testament" (*Zwischen den Zeiten*). See Smart, *op. cit.*, p. 47.

[26] Smart, *op. cit.*, p. 47.

[27] Rudolf Bultmann, *The Presence of Eternity*, History and Eschatology (1957), p. 113.

[28] *Ibid.*

Yet Bultmann and many modern scholars bring other subjective perspectives to bear upon the text besides existentialism. How much does their pre-understanding influence their interpretations? Because our universe is one of cause and effect, many conclude that God did not intervene in this world in any way that would alter the constancy of inexorable natural law.

> The causal nexus in space and time which Enlightenment science and philosophy introduced into the Western mind and which was assumed by liberalism is also assumed by modern theologians and scholars; since they participate in the modern world of science both intellectually and existentially, they can scarcely do anything else.[29]

It would have been more accurate to say "is also assumed by *some* or by *many* modern theologians and scholars." The statement rather implies that one who does not assume this is neither a theologian nor a scholar! Yet this assumption is only a presupposition that his experience is the only possible experience and represents the only experience of any other person or group of persons who have lived on this planet. The scholar who assumes this has made his empirical experience and that of his contemporaries the sole criterion of what is possible. Any other evidence is ruled out as unconvincing, irrelevant, or unsatisfactory to "scientific" minds. For scholars with such assumptions their "pre-understanding" has shut out material or evidence that questions the soundness of such a premise. Without openness of mind, there is no way for self-correction to root out distortions.

> Therefore, when we read what the Old Testament seems to say God did, or what precritical commentators said God did (see Calvin), and then look at a modern interpretation of what God did in biblical times, we find a tremendous difference; the wonder events and the verbal divine commentaries, commands, and promises are gone. Whatever the Hebrews believed, *we* believe that the biblical people lived in the same causal continuum of space and time in which we live, and so one in which no divine wonders transpired and no divine voices were heard.[30]

One can find similar utterances in Bultmann.[31] But here is subjectivity being impinged upon by the arbitrary assumption that man lives in a closed continuum instead of a controlled continuum. To believe in a miracle one must believe in an or-

---

[29] Gilkey, *op. cit.*, p. 195.

[30] *Ibid.*, p. 196.

[31] See for example: "Is Exegesis Without Presuppositions Possible?" *Existence and Faith*, pp. 291-292.

derly universe. Only two classes of people *cannot* believe in miracles: those who see nothing but chaos in the universe, and those who see an order so unalterable that God is virtually a prisoner of his own laws. But those who believe in a controlled continuum, where God is free in the orderly universe that he has established, have no difficulty with the idea that he may act in his universe as he pleases. Such an approach is also a "pre-understanding" which affects the interpreter in his work.

If the subjectivity of the interpreter includes concepts hostile to God and the revelation found in Scripture, or in a milder way which can prevent the interpreter from grasping this or that truth, how can this situation be remedied? Smart summarizes Barth's answer to this question by saying:

> It is true that what each man hears [in Scripture] will be profoundly affected by whatever may be the character of his existence and by where he happens to be in his understanding of the world and himself. But his ability to understand Scripture will increase not through any conscious attempt on his part to secure in himself a standpoint in harmony with Scripture but through the reshaping of his mind and spirit and his total understanding of life by what he hears in Scripture itself. It is God himself who, through his Word and Spirit, creates in man the necessary presuppositions and the perspective for the understanding of Scripture.[32]

Barth says that mental resolve without an inward change is ineffective. Yet acquiring sound presuppositions does demand that the interpreter have an openness of mind which permits him to observe and correct his own aprioris and presuppositions. Many who have been Christians for a long time have made few if any corrections for years. This could indicate that their subjectivity has been molded by God. But it could also indicate that their "pre-understandings" have prevented them from being open to a needed revision and correction.

MYTHOLOGY AND DEMYTHOLOGIZING

Current theological literature dealing with certain parts of the Bible discloses a frequent use of the terms "myth," "mythology," and "demythologizing." The present interest in these themes goes back to an essay by Rudolf Bultmann in 1941 which has been translated into English under the title: "New Testament and Mythology."[33] In 1951-1952 while on a lecture

---

[32] Smart, *op. cit.*, p. 50.
[33] See *Kerygma and Myth,* pp. 1-44.

tour of the United States Bultmann further popularized his views on mythology.[34] In its broadest sense "mythology" for Bultmann is anything in the Bible which is contrary to a modern scientific world-view.[35] He cites as examples: a three story universe—heaven, earth, hell; intervention of supernatural powers in the course of events—angels, demons, Satan; and all miracles. Bultmann admits that this modern scientific world-view does not comprehend the whole reality of the world, yet he insists that faith offers no corrective to this world view but merely adopts it.

> Faith does not offer another general world-view which corrects science in its statements on its own level. Rather faith acknowledges that the world-view given by science is a necessary means for doing our work within the world. Indeed, I need to see the worldly events as linked by cause and effect not only as a scientific observer, but also in my daily living. In doing so there remains no room for God's working. This is the paradox of faith, that faith "nevertheless" understands as God's action here and now an event which is completely intelligible in the natural or historical connection of events.[36]

Since many things in the Bible are contrary to the modern scientific world-view, Bultmann feels that much of the Bible conveys little or nothing to modern man. "For modern man the mythological conception of the world, the conceptions of eschatology, of redeemer and of redemption, are over and done with."[37] For Bultmann, "to de-mythologize is to reject not Scripture or the Christian message as a whole, but the world-view of Scripture. . . . To de-mythologize is to deny that the message of Scripture and of the Church is bound to an ancient world-view which is obsolete."[38] This means that demythologizing is a hermeneutic method[39] which employs an existentialist philosophy to clarify for personal existence those truths found in mythological language.[40] For example, the cross and the resurrection bring judgment to the world and open for men "the possibility of authentic life."[41] Mythological thinking in the Bible, according to Bultmann, conceives of the action of God as intervening between natural, historical, or psychological events. "It [the

---

[34] Rudolf Bultmann, *Jesus Christ and Mythology* (1958).
[35] *Ibid.*, p. 15.
[36] *Ibid.*, p. 65.
[37] *Ibid.*, p. 17.
[38] *Ibid.*, pp. 35-36.
[39] *Ibid.*, p. 45.
[40] See "New Testament and Mythology," *Kerygma and Myth*, pp. 17-44.
[41] *Ibid.*, p. 39.

action of God] breaks and links them at the same time. The divine causality is inserted as a link in the chain of the events which follow one another according to the causal nexus."[42] But non-mythological thinking, accepting the modern scientific world-view, rejects God's action as occurring *between* the worldly actions or events and posits God's action as happening *within* them.[43]

In contrast to Bultmann, those who take seriously the basic emphases of Scripture must insist that faith offers a much-needed corrective to the modern scientific world-view. God's action involves his intervention *into* history as well as his working *in* and *through* history. This conviction rises from historical data that became intelligible to one or more observers only on the grounds that God came *into* their history for the purpose of revealing himself. It is true that these interventions can be explained in other ways. But there is always a variety of possibilities which may be put forth to explain any historical event. The one which is most valid is the one which does justice to *all* of the evidence. The Gospel of John related Jesus' agony of soul as he drew near to the experience of his death (John 12:27-33). Should Jesus pray to be saved from this hour? He quickly dismisses this possibility by saying that he came for this very hour. Instead he prays that his father will glorify his own name. A voice from heaven brings assurance to Jesus: "I glorified it [i.e. the Father's name] and I will glorify it again." Those in the crowd differed as to what happened, and they knew nothing of a modern world-view. Some said that there was no voice at all, but only thunder. Others maintained that an angel spoke to Jesus. Jesus' own comment, according to John, was that the voice was not for his benefit but rather for those who were around him. He does not say whether the voice came for an immediate effect or whether its coming was for its later results. Either way, Jesus heard again that he would bring glory through suffering. God's free action can be explained away or taken seriously. The biblical writers take his actions seriously, not because they were superstitious, dull, or naive, but rather: "We cannot but speak the things which we saw and heard" (Acts 4:20). They were convinced by what for them was irrefutable, empirical evidence. For moderns to disregard such evidence only shows that they select the empirical evidence that suits them, and on the basis of this selection they choose the interpretation which suits them. Hence the outcome of research

---

[42] *Jesus Christ and Mythology*, p. 61.
[43] *Ibid.*

is controlled by the "pre-understanding" rather than by all of the evidence.

In adopting any technical language we must ask: what does this expression mean today? Yet before one uses the terms "myth," "mythology," and "demythologizing" he should at least find out the status of myth in the Bible.[44] Wright points out that "the Bible definitely and consciously repudiates the gods of the nations together with their mythology and their magic."[45] We need only read the tales about the gods in Greek thought and in the thought of the nations surrounding Israel to see why they were rejected. Yet some say it is not fair to tie together the past and present usages of the word "myth." Though moderns differ in their use of the term, it is clear that they do not mean by myth what the pagans meant in ancient times. Wright certainly realizes how terms are given an extended or even a different meaning. Yet if the older meaning is still needed and still must be employed, then to use this term with new and different meanings leads to confusion. This is especially true of the word "mythology."

> It has its own proper meaning in the history of religions; it refers to the religious literature of the polytheist religions which concentrated attention upon the life of nature and saw in it the life of the gods. Nature is alive for the polytheist; it is filled with powers to which man must integrate his own existence. When he spoke about the gods, he too told stories; but they are not set in history, nor primarily concerned with history. Actually, they combine a faith with imagination and pre-logical, empirical observation in order to depict the working, the life of nature. The polytheist has the "deep conviction of a fundamental and indelible *solidarity of life* that bridges over the multiplicity and variety of its single forms.... To mythical and religious feeling, nature becomes one great society, the *society of life*. Man is not endowed with outstanding rank in this society. He is a part of it, but he is in no respect higher than any other member. Life possesses the same religious dignity in its humblest and in its highest forms. Man and animals, animals and plants are all on the same level."

> In this context the word "mythology" makes definite sense. Yet modern theologians, with scarcely more than the most cursory regard for the word's proper meaning and with the most scanty attention to the theology of polytheism, now cheerfully "steal" the word and say to the modern world: "Christianity is mythology

[44] For an excellent treatment of "myth" etymologically, its meaning in Greece and Hellenism, in the Old Testament and Judaism, and in the New Testament see Gustav Stählin, *"muthos," TWNT*, IV, 769-803. For a brief treatment, yet one which is very incisive, see George Ernest Wright, *God Who Acts*, pp. 116-128.

[45] Wright, *op cit.*, p. 119.

and to understand it we must demythologize it for you." Or, they
say: "Christianity is mythology, but it is a true mythology, for
you can only comprehend ultimate meaning in the world in terms
of mythology."[46]

Certainly it is clear that myth in a polytheistic society has a
central place. With no particular perspective on history and
with no concept that history is going anywhere (except the
rhythmic pattern of nature or the more extended cyclical pattern of longer epochs) such a society found myths a good way
to give meaning to existence. But with the biblical conviction
that history is the sphere in which God acts, that history is moving toward a goal or destiny appointed by God, the meaning
of life is set in history and is primarily concerned with history.
Interpreters in the history of the Church have often tried to escape this fact. But there is no way to avoid the history-centered
emphasis of the Bible.[47]

Further, myth and truth are contrasted even in Greek
thought. Stählin remarks:

> The contrast between myth and truth already existing before the
> New Testament obtains in the New Testament a completely dif-
> ferent depth through the new filling of the concept "truth" with
> the whole reality of salvation which occurred historically and
> with Christ, the fullness of God having become flesh. In contrast
> to myth there stands here [in the N.T.] no longer an abstract
> concept of truth or only a prosaic, factual, earthly event, but on
> the contrary a divine fact with the whole emphasis of historical
> reality. The New Testament is not able to say that it contains a
> word or an historical "truth," if the truth has nothing in common
> with the reality. One stands either on the side of myth or upon
> the side of New Testament truth.[48]

After dealing with the New Testament passages where *muthoi*
(myths) or *muthos* (tale, story, legend, myth, fable) are mentioned, Stählin concludes:

> The decisive renunciation of myth belongs to those distinctions
> which are peculiar to the New Testament. Myth is a pagan cate-
> gory. It may still be visible in rudiments in many parts of the
> Old Testament and in the New Testament in "metamorphoses."
> Myth as such has no place upon biblical grounds either (1) as di-
> rect communication of religious "truths," or (2) as parable, or
> (3) as symbol.[49]

---

[46] *Ibid.*, pp. 125-26. The quotation in Wright about man and nature in a
polytheistic society comes from Ernst Cassirer, *An Essay on Man* (1944),
pp. 82-83.

[47] See Gustav Stählin, *"muthos," TWNT*, IV, 791-793.

[48] *Ibid.*, p. 793.

[49] *Ibid.*, p. 800.

In place then of the term "mythical language" this writer would prefer such expressions as "metaphorical phraseology," "designed metaphor," and "undesigned metaphor." Designed metaphor is intentional metaphorical language; undesigned metaphor is metaphorical language without a full consciousness of all of its figurative characteristics. Metaphorical language is abundant. God has neither hands, nor feet, nor eyes, nor lungs. Consequently, God's "seeing" involves metaphorical language. His "breathing" likewise is metaphorical language.[50] Because breath for man indicates life, this metaphor describes the living God imparting life to his creature, man. Since all of God's actions are historically centered, the term "mythological" does not fit. God is far greater than the sum total of all that man encounters in his experience. Therefore, man has no alternative than to use metaphorical language to describe vividly the reality of God.

LANGUAGE

Another issue now receiving much attention[51] is that of language. A whole chapter will be devoted to the interpreter's use

[50] Gen. 2:7. For a further discussion of biblical metaphors, see below, Chapter 14.

[51] Bibliographical materials are endless. Here are a few recent works showing how extensive are the issues and how divergent are the opinions regarding language. Jules Moreau, *Language and Religious Language*, A Study in the Dynamics of Translation (1961). I have received much help from Chapter III of Professor Moreau's book: "Language and Meaning: Linguistics and Semantics," pp. 74-105. James Barr's volume is exceedingly helpful in the area of the use of language: *The Semantics of Biblical Language* (1961). Gordon H. Clark in his volume *Religion, Reason, and Revelation* (1961) criticizes the behavioristic view of language as well as the contention that "strictly there are no literal sentences." See Chapter III of this work: "Inspiration and Language," pp. 124-134. In Willem F. Zuurdeeg's *An Analytical Philosophy of Religion* (1958), pp. 173-308 the author considers the background of modern man's language structures and the language structures which assist modern man in establishing his existence. For an incisive critique of Professor Zuurdeeg's position see Arthur F. Holmes, "Three Ways of Doing Philosophy," *The Journal of Religion*, XLI (1961), pp. 206-212. In place of the idealism which Zuurdeeg rejects and the language analysis with its anti-metaphysical perspective which Zuurdeeg espouses, Professor Holmes argues cogently for a realism that analyzes concepts, not language, *per se*. Such a realism, unlike language analysis, shifts the focus of attention "from the nature of religious *language* to the nature of religious concepts, beliefs, and experience. Religious language, expressive of religious beliefs and experience, is certainly convictional and emotive, but it is also indicative and predicational. The Apostles' Creed is as clear an example as any. As soon as we reintroduce predication, we are compelled to reintroduce two further aspects of traditional religious philosophy: the study of analogical predication

of language to determine meaning. Here we will merely consider why language is assuming a key role in current discussions on interpretation.

All types of scholars have been working on language: linguists, philosophers, educators, psychologists, and social scientists. Naturally each one's discussion stresses the peculiar interest of his own field. Ironically, those investigating particular aspects of language tend to communicate mainly to others interested in the same aspect with the result that the separate threads are not being brought together. Since the areas overlap, a standardized terminology would be helpful. But even here there are too few signs of teamwork and consolidation. Technical jargon is essential for linguists, but a good glossary of terms is equally essential for the novice. In spite of these difficulties, real progress has been made toward a sound methodology for achieving understanding in language.

Modern linguistic studies are all inductive. In the past many errors have resulted from incomplete induction or from applying inductively arrived at conclusions in one language to another language without seeing whether the second language supports such conclusions. Out of inductive research we have learned that descriptive studies (present characteristics of a language) should precede historical studies (past characteristics of a written language). Both of these approaches precede comparative studies (noting similar and dissimilar characteristics among languages).

Study of language normally consists of the analysis of sounds, of words looked at independently, and of words considered in their relation to other words. The linguist analyzes these ele-

and the truth value of religious language. These are aspects of religious philosophy which Dr. Zuurdeeg's situational analysis altogether overlooks" (p. 211). For a concise statement of the contributions of analytic philosophy to a methodology of Christian philosophy, see another article by Professor Holmes, "The Methodology of Christian Philosophy," *The Journal of Religion*, XLII (1962), pp. 220-222. The stress in analytic philosophy on meaning receives praise from realist Holmes when he says: "Most of all, the analyst has given us a sensitivity and a set of tools—a sensitivity to meaning which should be ingrained into every philosopher's conscience and a variety of tools for getting at meaning—tools of assorted value, it is true, but largely precision tools which our forebears lacked. Clarity, meaning, understanding, precision of thought and expression—these ideals of philosophy à la Dilthey now promise to be actualized by analytic and critical methods" (p. 220). For the student interested in bibliography on language see the books listed in Chapter III of Moreau's work, Chapter III of Clark's book, and the references found throughout Barr's book as well as the select bibliography at the end, pp. 299-303.

ments in terms of present time and past time, in terms of form and meaning.

Here are the ingredients of linguistic analysis stated for the most part in non-technical terms.[52]

DISTINCTIVE SOUNDS (PHONOLOGY)
    Of a language as spoken today
    Of a language as spoken in the past
WORDS IN THEIR FORM (MORPHOLOGY) AND
MEANING (LEXICOLOGY)
    Form of words today
    Form of words in the past
    Meaning of words today
    Meaning of words in the past
RELATION OF WORDS IN THEIR FORM AND
MEANING (SYNTAX)
    Form of relationships today
    Form of relationships in the past
    Meaning of relationships today
    Meaning of relationships in the past

The completeness of this approach to language will prove helpful to students in every stage of language study and in whatever aspect they are working. In ancient languages form and meaning in different periods of history receive careful consideration. Since the nineteenth century language study has become increasingly thorough, so that the interpreter has access to every linguistic factor which may influence meaning.

Semantics (or meaning) is also a growing field of study. Education, psychology, and epistemology stress the relation of thinker and thought to event or object of thought. Philosophical semantics, especially logic, stresses the kind of judgments made, criteria of truth and error, and the relation between symbol (written or oral expression) and what it refers to. Linguistic semantics explores the possible variations in understanding between thought and symbol (written or oral expression).

Ogden and Richards have clarified these dimensions by a "triangle of meaning." In the following diagram the basic idea is that of Ogden and Richards with other clarifying aspects inserted.[53]

The solid line indicates that meaning can be traced only by going from referent (object) to thought to symbol. Yet in logic one is concerned with the truth or falsehood of a person's expressions about an object. We ask: is his reasoning sound?

---

[52] For a more technical discussion, see Moreau, *op. cit.*, pp. 83-87.
[53] *Ibid.*, pp. 90f.

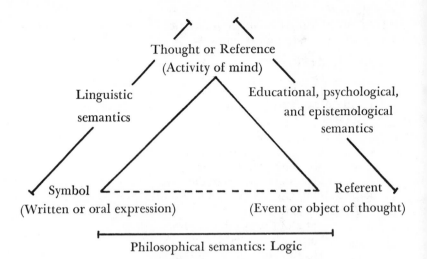

Here the person is judged by the product—i.e., how accurately the symbol (written or oral expression) reflects the reality for which it stands. Hence philosophical semantics, although it does proceed from referent (object) to thought to symbol, also covers the coherence of a person's expressions. The dotted line indicates this dimension.

Formal logic is concerned to eliminate the ambiguities of ordinary language, and hence it uses an abstract mathematical language. Distinguishing between form and content, formal logic devotes itself only to form. With its own abstract language, formal logic considers criteria of meaningfulness and validity of inference. To see how complex this becomes, we need only consult a dictionary of philosophy under the headings: "Logic, formal"; "Logic, symbolic"; "Logistic system"; and "Semiotic, Theory of Signs."[54]

Great importance has also been placed upon definitions. Alfred Korzybski in his book *Science and Sanity: An Introduction to Non-Aristotelian Systems and General Semantics* urges people to observe their own processes of evaluation.[55] His rules for how to convey meaning emphasize use and life situations. Korzybski uses the term *intensional* valuation for the definition of

[54] See, for example, Dagobert D. Runes (ed.), *Dictionary of Philosophy* (1961), pp. 170-183; 288-298.
[55] Moreau, *op. cit.*, pp. 93-94, 197.

a word in terms of other words. An *extensional* or *operational* valuation, however, means that a word is defined in terms of something to be performed or experienced. Words or concepts are viewed as being a part of a "systematic organization of observed life facts."[56] It is obvious that Korzybski's discussion is empirical in its outlook. Although we believe that the empirical is only one method of obtaining meaning, even from this approach we can see that for words to have meaning the reader or hearer must himself become involved. What is defined must be related to his experience. Hence an adequate definition demands more than a correct formulation of words. It means that the formulation must enter the experience of the reader or hearer.

Repentance in the New Testament is defined experientially in terms of the believer's total transformation in an extensional manner.[57] Approaching repentance from the standpoint of an *intensional* valuation while keeping in mind only some of the experiential data, the theologian Strong confines repentance to an inward, mental response.[58] Correct definitions are hard to make because of all that they ought to contain. Carefulness here will at least bring improvement.

There are also languages within languages. In the physical sciences, the biological sciences, the social sciences, and the humanities, almost every area has its own technical vocabulary. We easily recognize this in the sciences but tend to forget that the humanities also have a technical jargon. All such languages within a language have one purpose: to describe clearly and accurately various kinds of phenomena. When a student of Hebrew sees a verb in the Qal stem preceded by a Qal infinitive absolute (Gen. 2:17) he knows exactly what this "language" means. A Greek student who declares: "A substantival infinitive of apposition illustrates well the fact that an infinitive is a *verbal noun* with the stress on *noun*" is depicting accurately one of the functions of a Greek infinitive. We need technical language to describe linguistic data. A man must be thoroughly acquainted with a particular field (in the examples above, Hebrew and Greek) to see how essential such technical vocabulary is. In all disciplines technical vocabulary is undergoing constant refinement. For example, in the old Hebrew lexicons, Aramaic was called Chaldean. But since Aramaic was spoken in Palestine and across the Fertile Crescent, the use of such a local place name was unfortunate. Change in technical language

56 *Ibid.*, p. 94.
57 See Bauer, pp. 513-514. Behm, *TWNT*, IV, 997-998.
58 Augustus Hopkins Strong, *Systematic Theology* (1907-09), III, 832-836.

simply indicates how important such language really is. It must constantly be improved.

Moreau rightly points out that the languages of physical, biological, and social sciences are largely denotative,[59] that is, the words have precisely defined meanings acknowledged by all the members as conveying certain basic ideas. The literature of a people—i.e., the literary masterpieces that have met the test of time—is full of connotations and words with suggestive significance. Religious language, too, is connotative, often carrying a freight of emotional and experiential meaning. For example, the language of Christianity (and of Judaism for that matter) is the language of commitment. Take the man who says: "Christ is my Savior." In telling us what this means to him he may explain the Saviorhood of Christ both negatively and positively: "Here are the things *from* which I am saved or delivered. Here are the things *for* which I am saved and *to* which I am committed." Such explanation has a connotative dimension as well as a denotative one. All things become new because the "I" looks at life with a heart attitude that is concerned for God and for fellow man. Its old concern for self has been removed by "the expulsive power of a new affection." Love for God has flooded the inner man. With this love has come an abounding love for fellow believers and for all men as well. In such a situation the connotative dimension of language is highly significant. Then there are times in which for many reasons spiritual vision grows dim. We grasp only a small part of what is connoted. We miss many nuances of meaning. Yet on other occasions with certain needs, with a deep sense of urgency, and with the illumination of God's Spirit these nuances will break through. Because of this access to the connotative dimension of language, the basic denotative freight of meaning is made vital to us in many different ways.

SIGNIFICANCE OF THESE ISSUES

The new aspects of exegesis and exposition place the interpreter in two spheres—the past as well as the present. The acts of God occurred in history. They are historical and historic (*historisch* and *geschichtlich*) events. Because event and interpretation are inseparable it is crucial that the student have a passion for right interpretation. Subjectivity on the part of the interpreter is as inescapable as a man's leaving his fingerprints on all that he touches. The important question is: what colors my subjectivity as an interpreter? Figurative language must be

59 Moreau, *op. cit.,* p. 101.

meaningful to modern man. But to call such language "myth-ology" and to "demythologize" its content only adds more am-biguity while claiming to explain the particular figurative expression or section. The terms "designed metaphor" and "un-designed metaphor" allow the interpreter to describe what he observes both from the standpoint of the original author and from his own standpoint as an interpreter.

Issues such as are discussed in this chapter remind us of the intense complexity of sound interpretation. Though the proc-ess of interpretation may be complex, the result is profound only when it is clearly and simply stated.

BIBLIOGRAPHY

Barr, James, *The Semantics of Biblical Language* (1961).

Bultmann, Rudolf; Lohmeyer, Ernst; Schniewind, Julius; Thielicke, Helmut; and Farrer, Austin: *Kerygma and Myth,* ed. Hans Werner Bartsch (1961).

Bultmann, Rudolf, *Jesus Christ and Mythology* (1958).

Gilkey, Langdon B., "Cosmology, Ontology, and The Travail of Biblical Lan-guage," *The Journal of Religion,* XLI (1961), 194-204.

Holmes, Arthur F., "Three Ways of Doing Philosophy," *The Journal of Re-ligion,* XLI (1961), 206-212.

———, "The Methodology of Christian Philosophy," *The Journal of Reli-gion,* XLII (1962), 220-222.

McKenzie, John L., "Problems of Hermeneutics in Roman Catholic Exe-gesis," *Journal of Biblical Literature,* LXXVII (1958), 197-204.

Moreau, Jules Laurence, *Language and Religious Literature* (1961).

Richardson, Alan and Schweitzer, Wolfgang, eds. *Biblical Authority for To-day* (1951).

Ristow, Helmut und Matthiae, Karl, *Der historische Jesu und der keryg-matische Christus* (1961).

Robinson, James M., *A New Quest of the Historical Jesus* (1959).

Smart, James D., *The Interpretation of Scripture* (1961).

Stählin, Gustav, *"muthos," Theologisches Wörterbuch zum Neuen Testament,* IV (1942), 769-803.

Westermann, Claus, ed. *Probleme alttestamentlicher Hermeneutik* (1960).

Wright, George Ernest, *God Who Acts* (1952).

Zuurdeeg, Willem F., *An Analytical Philosophy of Religion* (1958).

IV   The Bible as a Unique Book

The unique characteristics of the Bible are sometimes forgotten. For some it is merely an ancient book. There are others who insist that the Bible is unique because of a specific list of differences. These characteristics and these alone supposedly stamp the Bible as unique. But when we give serious thought to the question, we find that the true uniqueness of the Bible is derived from the character of its message to meet the basic need of man. No list of its special characteristics can be complete. Some of these qualities will, however, be briefly treated in this chapter. This list is by no means exhaustive, but it will help to show that the uniqueness of the Bible lies in the combination of such characteristics.

CLAIMS OF AUTHORITY

There are claims made throughout the Old Testament that Jehovah or Yahweh is speaking to the prophet, to the king, to the priest, and to the people. There are four basic words or phrases in Hebrew that frequently declare that God has something *to say* in the pages of the Old Testament. He is not only the God *who acts,* but he is also the God *who speaks.* This point is often lost sight of by many interpreters.

The first of these expressions is *ne'um yhwh,* literally *the utterance* or *declaration* of Jehovah.[1] There are several variations

---

[1] Francis Brown, Samuel R. Driver, and Charles Augustus Briggs, *A Hebrew and English Lexicon of the Old Testament with an Appendix Containing the Biblical Aramaic* (1907), p. 610. Hereafter in citations from this lexicon, the letters BDB will be employed.

The four letter Hebrew word *yhwh* has the vowels of the word "Lord" of the basic formula, "the utterance of Jehovah." These are: "the utterance of Jehovah of Hosts"; "the utterance of the Lord Jehovah"; "the utterance of the Lord, Jehovah of Hosts"; and "the utterance of the King whose name is Jehovah of Hosts." In every case the context stresses that the declaration is made by the covenant God of Israel.[2] He is the Lord, Jehovah of Hosts. The solemnity and importance of what he declares is clear. There is a ring of authority. Men are called to hear what God has to say to them.

The second expression asserting God's authority is the verb 'amar, "to speak."[3] In combination with the adverb kōh[4] and the Hebrew consonants for the covenant name of God (yhwh)

because out of respect the Hebrews did not want to pronounce out loud the covenant name "Yahweh." Although the word "Jehovah" did not exist among those who spoke and wrote Hebrew, more clearly than any other alternative it expresses the difference between Lord ('adonay) when applied to God and YHWH as a covenant name for God.

2 The following passages are taken from the concordance of Gerhard Lisowsky, Konkordanz zum hebräischen Alten Testament (1958), pp. 886-888. This concordance also gives a basic meaning of the Hebrew word in German, English, and Latin. The versification follows that of the Hebrew Bible. This is usually the same as in English except for the book of Psalms. The arrangement of the books in the Hebrew Bible differs from English, Genesis being the first book and 2 Chronicles being the last. However, the Old Testament for Protestants has the same books as the Hebrew Old Testament. Note how this first expression comes predominantly from the prophets: GEN. 22:16. NUM. 14:28. I SAM. 2:30(twice). 2 KINGS 9:26(twice); 19:33; 22:19. ISA. 3:15; 14:22-23; 14:22; 17:3,6; 19:4; 22:25; 30:1; 31:9; 37:34; 41:14; 43:10, 12; 49:18; 52:5(twice); 54:17; 55:8; 56:8; 59:20; 66:2,17,22. JER. 1:8,15,19; 2:3,9,12,29; 2:19; 2:22; 3:1,10,12(twice), 13,14,16,20; 4:1,9,17; 5:9,11,15,18,22,29; 6:12; 7:11,13,19,30,32; 8:1,13,17; 8:3; 9:2,5,8,23,24; 9:21; 12:17; 13:11,14,25; 15:3,6,9,20; 16:5,11,14,16; 17:24; 18:6; 19:6,12; 21:7,10,13,14; 22:5,16,24; 23:1, 2,4,5,7,11,12,23,24(twice), 28,29,30,31,32(twice), 33; 25:7,9,12,31; 25:29; 27:8,11, 15,22; 28:4; 29:9,11,14(twice), 19(twice), 23,32; 30:3,10,11,17,21; 30:8; 31:1,14, 16,17,20,27,28,31,32,33,34,36,37,38; 32:5,30,44; 33:14; 34:5,17,22; 35:13; 39:17,18; 42:11; 44:29; 45:5; 46:5,23,26,28; 46:18; 48:12,30,38,39,43,44,47; 48:15; 48:25; 49:2,6,13,16,30,31; 49:5; 49:26; 49:32,37,38,39; 50:4,10,20,21,30,39,40; 50:31; 51:24,39; 51:25,26,48,52,53; 51:57 EZEK. 5:11; 11:8,21; 12:25,28; 13:6,7; 13:8,16; 14:11,14,16,18,20,23; 15:8; 16:8,14,19,23,30,43,48; 16:58; 16:63; 17:16; 18:3,9,23, 30,32; 20:3,31,33,36,40,44; 21:12,18; 22:12,31; 23:34; 24:14; 25:14; 26:5,14,21; 28:10; 29:20; 30:6; 31:18; 32:8,14,16,32,37; 33:11; 34:8,15,30,31; 35:6,11; 36:14, 15,23,32; 37:14; 38:18,21; 39:5,8,10,13,20,29; 43:19,27; 44:12,15,27; 45:9,15; 47:23; 48:29; HOSEA 2:15,18,23; 11:11; JOEL 2:12. AMOS 2:11,16; 3:10,15; 3:13; 4:3, 6,8,9,10,11; 4:5; 6:8,14; 8:3,9,11; 9:7,8,12,13. OBADIAH 4;8; MICAH 4:6; 5:9; NAHUM 2:14; 3:5. ZEPH. 1:2,3,10; 2:9; 3:8. HAGGAI 1:9; 1:13; 2:4(twice), 14,17,23; 2:4,8,9,23; 2:23. ZECH. 1:3,16; 1:4; 2:9,10(twice),14; 3:9,10; 5:4; 8:6,11; 8:17; 10:12; 11:6; 12:1,4; 13:2,7; 13:8. MAL. 1:2. II CHRON. 34:27. As subject: ISA. 1:24. PSALMS 110:1.

3 BDB, pp. 55-56.

4 BDB, p. 462.

one finds the basic formula *kōh 'amar yhwh*—"thus says or speaks Jehovah." This basic formula, too, has many variations. These are: "thus says Jehovah, the God of Israel;" "thus says Jehovah, the God of the Hebrews;" "thus says Jehovah of Hosts;" "because thus said the Lord unto me;" "thus saith the Lord, Jehovah;" "thus saith the Holy One of Israel;" "thus saith Jehovah, the God of David thy Father;" "thus saith God, Jehovah;" "thus saith Jehovah, the King of Israel, and his Redeemer, Jehovah of Hosts;" "thus saith Jehovah, the Redeemer of Israel and His Holy One;" "thus saith thy Lord Jehovah and thy God;" "thus saith the high and lofty One, the One who inhabits eternity and holy is his name;" "thus saith Jehovah, the God of hosts;" "thus saith Jehovah of Hosts, the God of Israel;" "thus saith Jehovah, the God of hosts, the Lord;" "thus saith Jehovah, my God." In context these formulae introduce solemn utterances on the part of God to his people. The formulae occur over and over. This constant repetition apparently has one main purpose which is to impress upon the hearers of the prophet's message the fact that they are being confronted with the declaration of God.[5] Whether the statement or com-

---

[5] The formula "Thus speaks Jehovah" or variations thereof is found in the following passages. These references are taken from the concordance of Solomon Mandelkern, *Veteris Testamenti Concordantiae: Hebraicae Atque Chaldaicae* (1955), I, 532-533. The citations are from the Hebrew text. One will notice as he goes through this list of verses, that a series will go through the whole book. Then another variation will go back to the beginning and start again. This is because all of the expressions listed in the text are found as one goes through the various books of the Old Testament. Furthermore, a phrase which can be translated in only one way may be listed twice or even three times because in one instance a dash (technically known in Hebrew as a *Maqqēph*) may be present or absent. Or some accent mark may be found on one occasion and not on the other. Mandelkern has enough of the Hebrew text (unpointed to be sure) before the citation of each particular expression to show what form of the formula is being employed. To save space contextual elements will not be included. The basic element "Thus speaks Jehovah" is found in all of the citations. EXOD. 4:22; 7:17,26 [Eng. 8:1]; 8:16; 11:4. 5:1; 32:27; 7:16. JOSH. 7:13; 24:2. JUDGES 6:8. I SAM. 2:27; 10:18; 15:2; II SAM. 7:5; 12:11; 24:12; 7:8; 12:7. I KINGS 5:25; 12:24; 13:2,21; 20:13,14,28,42; 21:19(twice); 22:11; 14:7. II KINGS 1:4,6, 16; 2:21; 3:16; 7:1; 9:3,12; 19:6; 20:1; 22:16; 3:17; 4:43; 9:6; 19:20; 22:15,18; 19:32; 20:5; 21:12; 22:18. ISA. 7:7; 49:22; 8:11; 18:4; 31:4; 10:24; 22:15; 21:6; 21:16; 28:16; 65:13; 29:22; 37:33; 30:12; 30:15; 52:4; 37:6; 38:1; 43:16; 45:14; 49:8; 50:1; 56:1; 65:8; 66:1; 37:21; 38:5; 42:5; 43:1; 43:14; 44:2; 44:6; 44:24; 45:1; 45:11; 45:18; 48:17; 49:7; 49:25; 52:3; 56:4; 66:12; 51:22; 57:15. JER. 2:2,5; 6:16,22; 8:4; 9:22; 10:2; 12:14; 13:9,13; 15:2; 17:5,21; 18:11; 19:1; 21:8; 22:1,3, 30; 26:2,4; 27:16; 28:11,13; 29:31; 30:18; 31:1 (2), 14 (15), 15 (16), 34 (35), 36 (37); 32:3; 33:10,20,25; 34:2; 36:29; 37:9; 38:2,3; 44:30; 45:4; 47:2; 49:1,28; 51:1; 4:3,27; 10:18; 16:3,5; 20:4; 22:6,11; 24:8; 29:10,16; 30:5,12; 31:6 (7); 32:42; 33:17; 48:40; 49:12; 5:14; 6:6; 27:19; 29:17; 6:9; 9:6; 11:22; 23:15; 25:8; 33:12; 6:21; 11:11,21; 14:15; 15:19; 18:13; 22:18; 23:38; 28:16; 29:32; 32:28;

mand involves judgment or blessing, it has behind it the covenant God of Israel, a God of holiness, righteousness, power,
and love. Often Israel disregarded these communications, but
the preservation in writing of the message of the prophets reminded future generations of God's claim upon his people and
their position under the authority of God.

The common verb *davar* is the third term in Hebrew indicating that God speaks and testifies to the authority of his own
assertions (as these are now recorded in the Scriptures). This
verb has the meaning "to speak" both in the simple stem (Qal)
and in the intensive stem (Piel).[6] The subjects of this verb are
"Jehovah," "God," "Lord," "Spirit of Jehovah," and "the
mouth of Jehovah." However, the most common of these subjects is "Jehovah" (*yhwh*). There are no repetitive formulae here
as in the other two expressions. Jehovah speaks unto Moses, to
one of his prophets, or to his people. The first person singular
is often employed. The variety found in the use of this word[7]

34:17; 36:30; 51:36; 7:3,21; 9:14; 19:3,15; 25:27; 27:4; 28:2; 29:4,21,25;
31:22 (23); 32:14; 35:13,18,19; 39:16; 42:15; 43:10; 44:2,7,11,25; 48:1; 50:18;
7:20; 9:16; 23:16; 19:11; 25:28,32; 26:18; 29:17; 49:7,35; 50:33; 51:58; 9:21;
11:3; 13:12; 21:4; 24:5; 30:2; 34:2,13; 37:7; 42:9; 45:2; 13:1; 17:19; 27:2;
14:10; 16:9; 27:21; 28:14; 29:8; 32:15; 42:18; 51:33; 21:12; 23:2; 32:36;
25:15; 32:4; 29:16; 33:2; 34:4; 35:17; 38:17; 44:2. EZEK. 2:4; 3:11,27; 5:5;
6:3,11; 7:2,5; 11:16,17; 12:10,19,23,28; 13:3,18; 14:4,6; 16:3,36; 17:3,9,22;
20:3,5,27,30,39; 21:3,31,33; 22:3; 23:22,32; 24:3,21; 25:3,8,12,15; 26:15; 27:3;
28:2,12,22,25; 29:3; 30:2,10,13; 31:15; 32:3; 33:25,27; 34:2,10,17; 35:3,14;
36:2,3,4,6,13,22,23,37; 37:5,9,12,19,21; 38:3,10,14,17; 39:1,17; 43:18; 44:6,9;
45:9,18; 46:1,16; 47:13; 5:7,8; 11:7; 13:8,13,20; 15:6; 17:19; 21:29; 22:19;
23:35; 24:6,9; 25:13,16; 26:3; 28:6; 29:8,19; 30:22; 31:10; 34:20; 36:5,7;
39:25; 11:5; 21:8; 30:6. 14:21; 16:59; 23:28,46; 26:7,19; 29:13; 32:11; 34:11;
21:14; 22:28. AMOS 1:3,6,9,11,13; 2:1,4,6; 3:12; 3:11; 5:3; 5:4; 5:16; 7:17.
OBAD. 1. MICAH 2:3; 3:5. NAHUM 1:12. HAGGAI 1:2; 1:5; 1:7; 2:11;
2:6. ZECH. 1:3,4,14,17; 3:7,8,21; 4:6,7,9,19,23; 1:16; 2:12; 8:14; 6:12; 7:9; 8:3;
11:4. MAL. 1:4. I CHRON. 17:4; 21:10,11; 17:7. II CHRON. 11:4; 12:5;
18:10; 21:12; 34:24; 20:15; 24:20; 32:10; 34:23,26.

6 BDB., pp. 180-82.

7 The passages where Jehovah speaks (or where one of the other designations is employed) are all listed in Lisowsky's concordance, pp. 337-345.
He has an unusual feature in his treatment of verbs. By a clever system
of footnotes (using Hebrew letters rather than Arabic numbers) he makes
clear who or what is the subject of the verb in most of the textual (book
by book) listings of the verb's occurrence. The references here with God
as subject of the verb are selected from the total listings of the verb *davar*:
Qal, GEN. 16:13. EXOD. 6:29. ISA. 45:19. JER. 32:42. JONAH 3:2. Piel,
GEN. 8:15; 12:4; 17:3,22,23; 18:19; 21:1,2; 24:7,51; 28:15; 35:13,14; 35:15;
44:7. EXOD. 4:30; 6:2,10,13,29; 7:13,22; 8:11,15; 12:25; 13:1; 14:1; 16:11;
16:23; 19:8; 20:1,19; 20:22; 23:22; 24:3,7; 25:1,22; 30:11,17,22; 31:1; 32:7,13,
14,34; 33:1,9,11; 34:32; 40:1. LEV. 1:1; 4:1; 5:14,20; 6:1,12,17; 7:22,28;
8:1; 10:3,8,11; 11:1; 12:1; 13:1; 14:1,33; 15:1; 16:1; 17:1; 18:1; 19:4; 20:1;
21:16; 22:1,17,26; 23:1,9,23,26,33; 24:1,13; 25:1; 27:1. NUM. 1:1,48; 2:1;

indicates that the other two expressions cannot be dismissed as mechanical stereotypes of a prophetic style. The verb *davar*, like "the utterance of Jehovah" and "thus speaks Jehovah" implies God's presence among his people. He is present with them in judgment and blessing. They are not left to guess; he interprets to them the meaning of judgment and blessing. We see the combination of Jehovah's speaking and acting, his proclamation and performance in the life of the prophet Ezekiel (cf. 17:24; 22:14; 36:36; 37:14). A study of these passages reveals that throughout the Old Testament God communicated to his people through his chosen messengers in such a way that those who really listened were aware that it was God speaking rather than the prophet.

The last of the four expressions showing the Old Testament claim of authority is the noun *davar*, whose basic meaning is "speech" or "word."[8] This noun is employed extensively throughout the Old Testament.[9] But of special importance is its meaning "word of God," as a divine communication in the form of commandments, prophecy, and words of help to his people, used 394 times.[10] It is also a part of a number of formulas: "then the word of Yahweh [use of vowels "a" and "e"

3:1,5,11,14,44; 4:1,17,21; 5:1,5,11; 5:4; 7:89; 8:1,5,23; 9:1,9; 10:1,29; 11:17,25; 12:2(twice), 6,8; 13:1; 14:17,26,35; 15:1,17,22; 16:20,23; 17:1,9,16; 17:5; 18:8, 25; 19:1; 20:7; 22:8; 23:17,19,26; 24:13; 25:10,16; 26:52; 27:23; 28:1; 31:1; 32:31; 33:50; 34:1,16; 35:1,9. DEUT. 1:6,11,21; 2:1,17; 4:12,15; 5:4,22 (19), 24 (21),26 (23),27 (24),31 (28); 6:3,19; 9:3,10,28; 10:4,9; 11:25; 12:20; 15:6; 18:2, 21,22; 19:8; 26:18,19; 27:3; 29:12; 31:3; 32:48. JOSH. 1:3; 4:8; 5:14; 11:23; 13:14,33; 14:6,10(twice), 12(twice); 20:1,2; 21:45; 22:4; 23:5,10,14,15; 24:17. JUDGES 2:15; 6:17,22,36,37. I SAM. 3:9,10,12,17(twice); 15:16; 16:4; 25:30; 28:17. II SAM. 7:7,19,25(twice), 28,29; 23:2. I KINGS 2:4,24,27; 5:19,26; 6:12; 8:15,20(twice), 24(twice), 25,26,53,56(twice); 9:5; 12:15; 13:3,22,26; 14:11,18; 15:29; 16:12,34; 17:16; 21:23; 22:23; 22:24,28,38. II KINGS 9:36; 10:10(twice), 17; 14:25,27; 15:12; 17:23; 19:21; 20:9; 21:10; 22:19; 24:2,13. ISA. 1:2,20; 16:13; 20:2; 21:17; 22:25; 24:3; 25:8; 28:11; 37:22; 38:7; 40:5; 45:19; 46:11; 48:15,16; 52:6; 58:14; 63:1; 65:12; 66:4. JER. 1:16; 4:12,28; 7:13,22; 9:11; 10:1; 13:17; 13:15; 14:14; 16:10; 18:7,8,9; 19:2,5,15; 22:21; 23:17,21,35,37; 25:13; 26:13,19; 27:13; 30:2,4; 32:24; 33:14; 34:5; 35:14; 35:17(twice); 36:2 (twice), 4,7,31; 37:2; 40:2,3; 42:19; 46:13; 50:1; 51:12,62. EZEK. 2:1,2,8; 3:10, 22,24; 5:13,15,17; 6:10; 12:25(twice), 28; 13:7; 17:21,24; 21:22,37; 22:14,28; 23:34; 24:14; 26:5,14; 28:10; 30:12; 34:24; 36:5; 36:6,36; 37:14; 38:17,19; 39:5,8; 44:5. HOSEA 1:2; 2:16; 12:11. JOEL 4:8. AMOS 3:1,8. OBAD. 18. JONAH 3:10. HAB. 2:1. PSALMS 2:5; 50:4,7; 60:8; 62:12; 85:9(twice); 89:20; 99:7; 108:8. JOB 33:14; 42:7,9. DAN. 9:12. I CHRON. 17:6,12,23 (twice), 26; 21:9; 22:11. II CHRON. 6:4,10(twice), 15(twice), 16,17; 10:15; 18:22,27; 23:3; 33:10. Hithpael, EZEK. 43:6.

8 BDB, pp. 182-184.

9 For all the places where the noun *davar* is found see Lisowsky, pp. 345-355; Mandelkern, pp. 282-288.

10 BDB, p. 182.

with the Hebrew letters *Yhwh,* covenant name of God] came
unto," "the word of Jehovah came unto," "behold, the word of
Jehovah came unto," "the word of Jehovah came by the
agency of," "then the word of Jehovah came by the agency of,"
"the word of the Lord which came unto," and "the word which
came unto."[11] Jehovah "sends" his word. He makes it an object
of vision. He commands it. This word is active, not static. The
authority of the word is not abstract; neither is the activity of
the word artificial. "Yahweh confirms his word of promise, Dt.
9:5; I S. 1:23 . . . I K. 2:4; 6:12; 8:20; Je. 29:10; 33:14, and his
word of warning, I K. 12:15; Dan. 9:12; his word stands forever,
Isa. 40:8; it is settled forever in heaven, Ps. 119:89; he remembers his *holy word,* . . . Ps. 105:42 (. . . cf. Jer. 23:9); he himself
—Joel 2:11; the angels—Ps. 103:20, and forces of nature—Ps.
148:8 . . . do his word of command; by his word the heavens
were made, Ps. 33:6; it is near his people, in their mouth and
heart, Dt. 30:14; a lamp to their feet, Ps. 119:105."[12] Procksch
shows how the noun *davar* becomes detached more and more
from representative imagery and in usage becomes a term for
the purest expression of revelation.[13] But in all such uses it is no
mere statement, but an explosive word of power that calls men
to decision.

How tragic that the Church has not heard this word of authority in the Old Testament! The New Testament has the
same ring of authority. The imperative mood is used so frequently that it is a grammatical phenomenon familiar to all
careful students. Jesus proclaimed good news. Jesus also acted.
The events of his life, though without parallel ("We never
saw it in this manner," Mark 2:12), were overshadowed by the
events of his death and resurrection. The Church proclaimed
the meaning of what Jesus said and did. Both in Jesus' life
and in the proclamation about his life, death, and resurrection,
action and speech are united. Regarding the Gospel of John,
Kittel says: "The entire composition of the gospel rests in its
essential parts upon the complete unity of action and discourse;
the action is the theme for the discourse and the discourse is
the interpretation of the action."[14] The authority of the New
Testament lies in the person of Jesus Christ—his acts, his words,
and his disciples' proclamation of what God would do for men
who by faith enter into a living relationship with the risen
Lord.

11 *Ibid.*
12 *Ibid.*
13 Otto Procksch, " 'Wort Gottes' im AT," *TWNT,* IV, 94. Procksch's
whole treatment deserves careful attention; see pp. 89-100.
14 Gerhard Kittel, " 'Wort' und 'Rede' im NT," *TWNT,* IV, 131-132.

UNITY OF THE BIBLE

As one considers the factors which make for unity of the Bible, he also becomes aware of elements showing the Bible's diversity. Unfortunately, many become so involved in the elements of diversity that they either cannot or do not list the factors of unity. Is the question of unity theological in nature? That is, is the unity provided by the theologian's system of thought rather than by the data of the Scriptures themselves? Actually, the question is theological, historical, and literary. Each thinker, by virtue of the activity of his own mind, does create a framework of unity. But the crucial questions remain: are the factors in this framework basic and essential elements in the Bible? Do they act as unifying elements for a vast quantity of other materials or are they merely independent particulars? Unifying elements in a framework of thought would correspond to the weight-supporting beams of a house. Independent particulars are similar to partitions in a house (such as closet walls) which separate one part from another but do not carry any weight. The answer to the question of unifying factors is a value judgment, and hence there will not be agreement on every detail. Nevertheless, it would seem evident that the Bible does contain at least the following elements of unity.

Action of God as Creator

The Scriptures emphasize the action of God as Creator. There are many facets to the subject of creation.[15] But one thing is clear: God has brought into existence all that is. He creates, forms, makes what he wants for the purposes he has in mind. Creation involves not only matter and persons but also the transformation of a rebel into a disciple and a sinner into a consecrated Christian (II Cor. 5:17). Creation is past and present. But there is also a future dimension of creation. This future aspect gives meaning and unity to Scripture and history (Isa. 65:17; II Pet. 3:13; Rev. 21-22). The narrative of human history begins with creation. The final removal of sin and rebellion will be climaxed by creation. Here a factor of unity shows itself to be also a factor of harmony.

Action of God with His People, Israel

Another element of unity is the action of God with his people, Israel. God's actions in the present are related to his action

---

[15] Werner Foerster, "Ktizō, ktisis, ktisma, and ktistēs," TWNT, III, 999-1034.

in the past: "I am Jehovah thy God who brought thee up out of the land of Egypt" (Ps. 81:10, cf. further Haggai 2:5). From the time that God laid hold of Abraham until the birth of Jesus, Israel's Messiah, the theme of promise and fulfillment runs through Israel's history. The reason is that God renewed his promises, gave new promises as well as elucidated earlier promises, and fulfilled some promises. As centuries rolled by for Israel and as the centuries have rolled by since the Incarnation, the evidence of this theme—promise and fulfillment—has grown. God has done great things not only for Israel but for all mankind as well. This involves not only history prior to the banishment of sin but also history with sin totally removed. The choice of the nation Israel, the covenant with Israel, and the role of Israel among the nations are part of the unfolding of promise and fulfillment. Therefore, the action of God with his people draws together all the details of their life. There is obviously much diversity in the total life of a people. The unity lies in the unfolding of God's plan for his people.

Action of God in Christ

A decisive factor affecting the unity of the Bible is found in the action of God in Christ. Here is ultimate fulfillment. Yet this is not complete fulfillment. Christ's action for his people had more meaning than was unfolded during the days of his flesh. Further, the concept "his people" is far broader than Israel had conceived.[16] The concept of the solidarity of the people of God in Christ emerges in the New Testament, but all that this means will be unfolded in history. "There is no Jew or Greek, there is no slave or free, there is no male or female because you are all one in Christ Jesus" (Gal. 3:28). But sexual distinctions and particular responsibilities of husbands and wives are still here. Israel, God's elect but at present rejected people, is still the object of anti-Semitism. Gentile nations still seek to control and dominate others. Slavery raises its head in various forms. Diversity is present, sometimes painfully so. Yet this diversity is still under the unifying factor of God's action in Christ. The Christian church is (or ought to be) a present sample of what will be when God's kingdom comes, when his will is done on earth as it is in heaven (cf. Matt. 6:10). The unifying factor in history or in the Scriptures is Jesus Christ himself. The interpreted Christ of the New Testament is not a full picture of all that he is, but it is an adequate picture, and as

---

[16] For an excellent treatment of the concept "people of God," see Hermann Strathmann and Rudolf Meyer, "*laos*," *TWNT*, IV, 29-57.

such it holds together and unifies elements which at first seem quite diverse. Jesus Christ is the fulfillment of the Old Testament promise. In him the promise was fulfilled as a present reality, but its total content was not fully actualized. He gave meaning to all of God's action in the past so that Paul could write: "But when the fulness of time came, God sent forth his son, born of a woman, born under the law in order that he might redeem those under the law, in order that we might receive the adoption" (Gal. 4:4-5). He gives meaning to all that God will do in the future. Paul asserted further that Christ redeemed from the curse of the law, so that the blessing of Abraham might be to the Gentiles in Christ (Gal. 3:13-14). Unity is not uniformity. He who was the fulfillment of the Old Testament promise came to make disciples of all nations. Matthew, citing the LXX of Isaiah 42:4, speaks of the Gentiles "hoping in his name" (Matt. 12:21). Although the Old Testament centers in the Jewish nation, it often speaks of God's interest in the Gentiles, and this interest comes to a fulfillment in Christ who is the link between Jew and Gentile.

Action of God with Those in Christ

The last unifying factor is the action of God with those who are in Christ. These belong to Christ's body, his Church. Mankind had been divided into two categories: Jew and Gentile. Paul makes it clear that a third order has come into existence —the Church of God (I Cor. 10:32). Both Jews and Gentiles who are joined to Christ by faith are created "into one new man" (Eph. 2:15). This third order of "man" is God's way of making peace between Jew and Gentile because both are transformed in Christ into something new and distinct. The characteristics of the Christian order of man, the power and purpose of the members of this order, all these things point to the creative activity of God. Much of the New Testament consists of letters written to individual churches, to groups of Christians over a wide geographical area, or to individuals. The New Testament concept of unity in Christ and in the Church, which is his body, binds these groups together. In his discussion of the Church, Schmidt points out that every group of believers is a local manifestation of the Church or the body of Christ. "Strong support is found in I Cor. 1:2 and II Cor. 1:1 for the contention that the Church is not a great community made up of an accumulation of small communities, but is truly present in its wholeness in every company of believers, however small. The proper translation in those verses is not 'the Corinthian Congregation'—taking its place beside the Roman, etc.—but 'the Congregation, Church, Gathering, as it is in Corinth.' "[17] Since the participle *ousēi* is in the restrictive attributive position to the noun *ekklēsiai* one could heighten the emphasis of Schmidt by translating the phrase: "the church of God which lives (or resides) in Corinth." Schmidt's rendering is certainly the mildest way that the expression can be paraphrased. The mildest translation would be: "the church of God which is in Corinth." If Paul had wanted to write "the Corinthian congregation" in Greek, his literal order would have been: "the in Corinth church of God." The New Testament is a unity not only because of the centrality of Christ's words and deeds but also because the local groups of believers who proclaimed the good news to mankind are bound together in a living connection with the risen Lord. The message of the New Testament reflects this relationship.

DIVERSITY OF THE BIBLE

If the unity of the Bible lies in the area of relationship—between the creator and what he has created, between God and his people (O.T., Israel; N.T., those in Christ)—and in the basic convictions or agreements of those within this relationship, then all elements of diversity are also within this relationship. God not only controls the diversity but he uses it to clarify the meaning of life and his relationship to man. Man is pictured realistically rather than poetically. Men who fail to face this realism may minimize the diversity in the Bible because they do not see its purpose.

One of the roots of diversity is found in the differing situations of the people of God. Little is said of this group before Abraham. But from Abraham to the Apocalypse (Revelation) the people of God were located geographically in Palestine, Egypt, Assyria, Babylonia, and around the whole of the Mediterranean. Sometimes the nation Israel governed itself, but most of the time it was oppressed by foreigners. In these varying situations there was no uniform response to either adversity or prosperity. Similar judgments or similar blessings did not bring similar responses. Not only did the response of the people vary, but God's action varied. He takes into account all factors as he works out his own counsel in history. Paul's sundry experiences in prison illustrate this well—Jerusalem, Caesarea, Rome. Paul accomplished as much for the advance of the gospel in prison

[17] Karl Ludwig Schmidt, "The Church," *Bible Key Words* from Gerhard Kittel's *Theologisches Wörterbuch zum Neuen Testament* (1951), I, 10.

as outside of prison. Yet each of his experiences in prison, as they are described in the New Testament, was different and God's action toward Paul in these situations likewise varied.

Diversity also comes from the different kinds of messengers through whom God spoke. The Old Testament prophets, the apostles, and the New Testament prophets were all distinct personalities. Their actions and words reveal their own personal traits and thought patterns. During the last one hundred years, biblical scholars have painstakingly analyzed stylistic traits and characteristics of biblical writings. The inferences drawn from these studies regarding authorship and sources may or may not be valid. But the characteristics and traits of style in the Hebrew, Aramaic, or Greek text are made clear for all to study. Some of these traits or emphases in the narration are apparent even in the English translation. Consider the story of the woman who was healed from a flow of blood after hemorrhaging for twelve years (Matt. 9:20, Mark 5:25, Luke 8:43). Mark concisely but forcefully sets forth her trying experiences at the hands of many physicians for many years. Not only was she not benefited but she grew worse (Mark 5:26). In contrast Luke does not mention these adverse experiences. He merely informs the reader that she was a difficult case "who was not able to be healed by anyone" (Luke 8:43). These differences show the background of the writers and their different interests. Mark wanted to show why she was so insistent—she was progressively deteriorating. Luke simply told what was wrong with her and that no one could heal her. It is not certain whether he sought to keep the physicians from being put in a bad light. But the diversity is clear. Yet all three Gospels agree on the central elements: a woman with a long-standing illness, her touching of Christ's garment, and the reason for her cure being her faith. Because of such diversity, the Bible conveys rich, warm, human experiences.

Diversity also is caused by the different purposes the writers had for their writing and for their preserving of the historical records. This is seen, e.g., in the contrasts between Kings and Chronicles: the former devotes attention to the Northern and Southern kingdoms, the latter is concerned just with the Southern kingdom. The different emphases in the accounts of Paul's conversion reflect the different reasons for retelling the event; e.g., in Acts 9 and 22 Paul receives his commission from Christ through Ananias (9:10-19; 22:12-16) while in Acts 26 Ananias is not mentioned at all (26:16-18).

Finally, the varying needs of those to whom the message comes produce differences in the way the message is presented.

The message is not changed but the manner of presentation adapts to the need. Observe the various ways a holy life and consecrated living is presented to the seven churches of the Apocalypse (see Rev. 2-3).

Diversity is most obvious when one examines the biblical evidence concerning a particular doctrine—e.g. election, second coming of Christ, holiness or sanctification. Such an examination only confirms the judgment of the history of doctrine. Christians over the centuries have differed as to how certain passages should be integrated and which should receive the most emphasis. Yet each biblical writer or speaker has a perspective intentionally limited by God. Paul makes this clear when he wrote: "Now we know in part and we prophesy in part, but whenever the perfect comes, that which is in part will pass away. . . . Now I know in part, but then I will know completely just as I have been completely known (I Cor. 13:9-10, 12b). This means that not one of God's inspired servants received *all* the truth. Each was given certain fragments. Hence, if we could integrate perfectly all of that which has been revealed (a task of no mean proportions), the result would still be fragmentary. Lietzmann is right when he says: "At the Parousia [return of the Lord] everything will be allotted to the believers in completeness: then, of course, the present imperfect endeavors will become worthless."[18] Paul says: "That which is in part will pass away." The limited perspective will be replaced by the comprehensive viewpoint. Since God is the unifying force in the midst of diversity, we know that the diversity plays just as great a role in God's purpose as unity. Herein is the uniqueness of the Bible.

INSPIRATION OF THE SCRIPTURES

Everyone who has ever tried to formulate his own statement on the inspiration of the Bible discovers that it is easier to memorize someone else's! Yet the man who makes himself put into words a fresh, personal statement—however inadequate— soon sees the need constantly to improve it. As he weighs and evaluates what he finds in Scripture, he is both humbled and challenged by the task.

How should we as interpreters proceed to formulate a view of inspiration? First, we must consider every statement which refers to God's action with a writer (speaker) or the writers

---

18 D. Hans Lietzmann, *An die Korinther, I, II* ("Handbuch zum Neuen Testament;" Herausgegeben von Günther Bornkamm; Tübingen: Verlag J. C. B. Mohr [Paul Siebeck], 1949), p. 66.

(speakers) of Scripture. We should study what the Scriptures have to say, directly or indirectly, about their own inspiration. What do the biblical writers actually claim? Second, in the light of these claims we must examine the performance of the biblical writers. Does the record which came from their pens support the kind of inspiration they claim or is the record incongruous with the kind of inspiration claimed? Do their writings help us to understand *the nature* of inspiration as well as the assertion of *the fact* of inspiration? This writer believes that the actual claims of the biblical writers for the inspiration of Scripture find support in their performance. Finally, taking into account the testimony of the writers and the performance of the writers, the one seeking to define inspiration should state simply what it seems to him is involved in the inspiration of the Bible.

The biblical writers make some basic assertions about God's action in bringing the Scriptures into being. Throughout the Old Testament one finds the claims to authority (see beginning of this chapter). In the New Testament we have statements such as: "Every scripture passage is inspired of God" (II Tim. 3:16). This is given as a statement of fact. The writer means that the Old Testament, viewed as Scripture passage after Scripture passage, is inspired of God. Inspiration involves the product. Inspiration also involves the persons who produced the product. "Having come to know this above all, that not any prophecy of Scripture is a matter of one's own private interpretation. Because prophecy was never produced by an act of human will, but *men spoke from God being put in motion by the Holy Spirit*" (II Pet. 1:20-21). Here is a picture of inspired men. When they spoke (and, by inference, when they wrote) with a God-directed sense of urgency, they were speaking and writing as divinely energized persons. Further, inspiration involves the words which were spoken or written: "which things also we speak, not in words taught of human wisdom but in words taught of the Spirit, interpreting spiritual truths to those who possess the Spirit" (I Cor. 2:13). Note that words are vehicles that convey spiritual truths to those who possess the Spirit. Hence such words are not to be taken apart artificially and examined atomistically without regard for context. Verbal inspiration simply means language inspiration. It refers to the inspiration of a statement or of a series of statements that convey truth. The Bible indicates that inspired messages were sometimes regarded as merely human utterances. Paul gave thanks to God because the Thessalonians did not take his message to be merely that of a traveling Jewish teacher: "Because when you received the message of divine preaching that goes out from us you did not receive it as the message of men but just as it truly is the message of God, who is at work in you who are believing" (I Thess. 2:13). What the message "truly is" and how it is sometimes regarded shows that there is a clear division between the message itself and the response or condition of those who hear it.

Interpreters sometimes do not stop to listen to the biblical claims for inspiration. Some brush these claims aside. Others mingle their own ideas or those from a venerated antiquity with the biblical claims. Yet the biblical assertions of inspired persons, inspired writings, and inspired language are beautiful in their simplicity and profound in their meaning.

The scholar faces a tremendous task when he sets out to examine the phenomena of the Bible. The phenomena must be examined first hand. This demands a careful study of the Hebrew, Aramaic, and Greek texts of the Scriptures. He should also know archaeological and historical data (taken from Scripture and from parallels outside). He must compare biblical materials with biblical materials and study whatever other relevant information is available to understand the habits, customs, and procedures of the biblical writers. Any good handbook in archaeology will provide many examples of the accuracy and historical preciseness of biblical narratives. On the other hand, the individual who is interested in formulating a correct view of inspiration also finds instances where the biblical writers were not as accurate and precise as historians would be today. They give approximations, general identifications, and popular descriptions that those who examine details may not always appreciate. However, when we discover the writer's main purpose and see how carefully he handles this, the failure to be preoccupied with minor details may then appear as an asset and not a liability. For example, Mark observes the chronological order when he records the cursing of the fig tree as occurring on one day while the drawing of the lesson from the cursed fig tree took place on the next day (Mark 11:11-25). In contrast, Matthew condenses. According to his account the cursing of the fig tree and the drawing of the lesson occur on the same day (Matt. 21:11-22). Both writers are interested in the main purpose of the narrative: the making of the fig tree into an object lesson. To insist that two gospel writers must give identical accounts of an incident is to ignore these very differences that give freshness and vitality to each Gospel. There is no routine sameness about the Gospels. In the passion week accounts, where all four Gospels provide similar information, the in-

dividual approaches enhance their value as historical witnesses.
The differences as well as the similarities support their claim of
being eyewitness reports. Had the Church later polished off and
created the narratives in the way that some imagine, the reader
would find traces of a studied, intentional collusion. Instead, he
finds basic agreement without artificiality, unity without uniformity, and commonness of conviction without a monotonous
pattern of details.

Revelation encounters modern man in the text of Scripture.
Smart well says:

> The revelation is *in the text itself,* in the words that confront us
> there in all their strangeness, and not in a history or a personal
> biography or an event that we reconstruct by means of the text.
> The event of revelation is available to us only through the text
> of Scripture interpreted in the context of the church. It is through
> these words and no others that God intends to speak to us, and,
> when he does, we know that there is no other kind of inspiration
> than verbal inspiration. Far from implying any divinizing of the
> words of Scripture, verbal inspiration understood in its Biblical
> sense takes the words of the text with full seriousness as the words
> of real men, spoken or written in a concrete human situation,
> and yet at the same time words in which God ever afresh reveals
> himself to me.[19]

The biblical writers were real men who spoke freely in a concrete human situation. They were involved in the message with
their whole being. Kantzer deals with the charge that inspiration and freedom are mutually exclusive:

> To argue that a divine inspiration must necessarily negate the
> freedom and humanity of the Biblical writers is scarcely possible
> for one who pretends to be a Christian. Whatever may be said
> for or against a rational solution of this problem, it ought to be
> abundantly clear that no theist who believes in God's providential
> control of the universe can possibly use this objection against the
> inspiration of the Bible. The God of Romans 8:28, who works
> all things together for good, including the sinful acts of wicked
> men, could certainly have worked through the will and person-
> ality of His prophets to secure the divine Word which He wished
> to convey through them.[20]

Inspiration means the action of God in the lives and utterances
of his chosen servants so that what they declare conveys to men
what God wants men to know. The Scriptures are the inspired
word of God because they represent all that God deemed it

[19] James Smart, *The Interpretation of Scripture,* pp. 195-196.
[20] Kenneth S. Kantzer, "The Authority of the Bible," *The Word for
This Century,* ed. Merrill C. Tenney (1960), p. 46.

necessary to preserve from the past so that succeeding generations could know the truths he conveyed to men of earlier generations.

Because the Bible is an inspired book, it is a unique book. The reason for its inspiration is to bring men into a living encounter with the living God. Hence the Bible came into existence for interaction and reflection—for good hard use. All valid principles of interpretation are to insure that we use the Bible correctly.

BIBLIOGRAPHY

Kantzer, Kenneth S., "The Authority of the Bible," *The Word for This Century,* ed. Merrill C. Tenney (1960), p. 46.

General Hermeneutics

V Context

This chapter on context as well as the next two chapters—
one on language and the other on history and culture—are all
a part of general hermeneutics. They are classified thus because
these subjects must be of constant concern to all biblical interpreters and apply to all portions of the Bible. There are
some portions of Scripture—as will be shown—where the context
provides no help for the interpreter in arriving at the meaning.
But on the whole, context must be seriously considered. Therefore the tools, techniques, and principles of general hermeneutics
can be applied almost every time one interprets the Scriptures.

PRIMACY OF CONTEXT

Neglect of context is a common cause of erroneous interpretation and irelevant application. For example, Arthur W. Pink
interprets John 1:35-43 as presenting a typical picture of the
Christian dispensation. He asserts that the phrases "the next
day after, John *stood*" (vs. 35) and "the tenth hour" (vs. 39)
mean "the end of John's *activities* were now reached."[1] Such
an application is entirely out of context, for in John 3:23 John
the Baptist is portrayed as a very active man: "And John also
was baptizing in Aenon near to Salim, because there was much
water there; and they came and were baptized."
We will discuss principles of application more fully in the
chapter on Devotion and Conduct.[2] When interpretive applica-

[1] Arthur W. Pink, *Exposition of the Gospel of John* (1945), I, 75.
[2] Chapter 17.

tions are contrary to the context, many thinking readers lose confidence in all applications of that interpreter. Context is basic because it forces the interpreter to examine the entire line of thought of the writer. When the interpreter projects his own ideas into the thought he is interpreting, he ceases being an honest interpreter and becomes a personal propagandist under the guise of explaining the work of another.

Context is important because thought is usually expressed in a series of related ideas. Occasionally a person does make a swift and radical departure from the train of thought he is pursuing. Sometimes thoughts are tied together loosely by a general theme. But whether ideas are thus bound by close logical union or whether the main propositions are developed by repetition, the meaning of any particular element is nearly always controlled by what precedes and what follows.

TOOLS FOR MASTERING CONTENT

Sometimes the obvious is forgotten simply because it is so self-evident. One cannot properly handle context until he has a good grasp of biblical content. The interpreter must know the content of the book from which the particular passage he is interpreting comes. He needs to know the content of books in which there are passages devoted to the same theme which he is interpreting. Sometimes the passages only appear to be parallel but in reality are not. In other parallels the first glance discloses little in common but careful examination reveals decisive points of similarity. Biblical content is essential for the much-needed grasp of context.

Where can one find actual or real parallels? Marginal references in various Bibles are famous (or infamous) for providing other materials which have a real or supposed bearing on the passage being studied. While these should be used, they should also be critically evaluated to see whether the citation is an actual parallel, merely a chance resemblance, or an apparent resemblance but without true similarity of thought pattern. To the writer's knowledge, there is no better collection or grouping of marginal references than that in Nestle's *Greek New Testament*. The verses listed from the Old Testament are from the Hebrew text unless a Greek version is indicated. The marginal notes of the *American Standard Version* (1901)[3] also have

---

[3] This is a very useful translation in its original form. Being a very literal translation, the ASV can be used in conjunction with modern versions to check whether a free paraphrase has added anything to the original. The Lockman Foundation of La Habra, California is publishing the Ameri-

higher accuracy than the marginal notes found in many editions
of the King James version. Good commentaries also list parallel
passages.

But even the best sources of parallels are not enough. The
interpreter should know well the content of the whole Bible.
How can he achieve this? And if he does achieve such a knowledge, how does he retain it? Mastery of biblical materials is
something like the mastery of a musical instrument. Without
consistent practice the musician loses his touch with his instrument. The same is true regarding the biblical material. There is
no substitute for constant study and review. The writer has
found that one aid to mastering the content of the Bible and
retaining that content is to use a wide margin Bible. Such a
Bible, with margins at least an inch wide on top, bottom, and
sides, provides space for the interpreter's own summaries and
outlines. Or he can use the space to jot down a good outline by
another. (In my own wide-margin Bible, I have a harmony of
the Gospels in the top and bottom margins of each Gospel.)
Concise summaries, paragraph by paragraph, in the margins
enable the interpreter to grasp quickly the content of one
chapter, several chapters, or of a whole book. Since these are
personal summaries, the individual who writes them has a
fresh statement in his own phraseology of the content of each
book. By persistence he can soon have the whole Bible summarized. By frequently scanning a well-marked Bible and by
reviewing the personal summaries, the interpreter will keep the
contents fresh in his mind.

There are one column New Testaments which have as much
space for writing notes as is devoted to the printed text. These
are helpful for detailed Bible study and exegesis. But for the
mastery of content, this much space is not needed for paragraph
summaries. The summaries should be as brief as possible, so
long as the phrase or sentence captures the emphasis of the
paragraph. Since the one column Testaments with extremely
wide margins are not a part of a whole Bible, they are profita-

can Standard Version in a revised format. Paragraphs are indicated by
bold face verse numbers. One column of text per page is employed. Textual variants and marginal notes are found in outside margins. Second
person plural pronouns are noted ("you^{pl}"). Unfortunately nothing is done
about 2nd person verb forms. But the marginal notes are both copious
and readable. To go from the small upraised letter in the text to the marginal note is easy and inviting. The arrangement has been made so clear
that the first cross reference in each verse begins with "a." Succeeding references in the same verse are "b," "c," etc. Some editing of the original
ASV(1901) is evident, but this is only in small details. Basically, the original version is presented.

bly employed for the detailed study, while any one-inch margin
Bible may be used for mastering the content of Scripture.

VARIETIES IN CONTEXT SITUATIONS

Immediate Context

The first responsibility of every interpreter is to note carefully
what precedes and what follows any verse or passage which he
is interpreting. This often involves going back two or three
paragraphs and ahead two or three paragraphs. Chapter divisions do not necessarily serve as boundary lines. One may need
to go back to the preceding chapter or ahead to the next chapter to get the true context. It is surprising how much light a
careful study of context sheds on any one verse or group of
verses. As an example, consider Ephesians 3:4-6:

> When you read this you can perceive my insight into the mystery
> of Christ, which was not made known to the sons of men in
> other generations as it has now been revealed to his holy apostles
> and prophets by the Spirit; that is, how the Gentiles are fellow
> heirs, members of the same body, and partakers of the promise in
> Christ Jesus through the gospel (RSV).

In these verses Paul declares that he has understanding in the
mystery which is Christ (genitive of apposition) or about, re-
lating to Christ (objective genitive). Either of these syntactical
usages comes to about the same meaning. The relative pronoun
"which" (vs. 5) has for its antecedent "mystery." Christ and all
that is involved in him was not made known in past generations
"as it is now revealed to his holy apostles and prophets by the
Spirit." The last verse of the three (vs. 6), beginning "that is,
how the Gentiles . . ." has an infinitive (in Greek) as the main
verbal element. The verse can be regarded either (1) as an
appositive to the relative pronoun "which" (vs. 5), or (2) as the
subject of the verb "revealed" (vs. 5), or (3) as indirect discourse
after the verb "revealed" (vs. 5). If the third possibility is
chosen, the connection then would be: "It was revealed that
the Gentiles are. . . ." If one selects the second construction, he
would translate the verses (vss. 5b-6): "As the fact of the Gentiles being heirs together *with* Israel [or the Jews], and belonging to the same body *with* Israel, and sharers together *with*
Israel of the same promise in Christ Jesus through the Gospel
has now been revealed to his holy apostles and prophets by the
Spirit." If it is the first alternative, the verse would read: "As
it [the mystery] is now revealed to his holy apostles and proph-

ets by the Spirit, that is that the Gentiles should be heirs together *with* Israel (or the Jews), and belonging to the same body *with* Israel, and sharers together *with* Israel of the promise in Christ Jesus through the gospel."

The writer prefers the first alternative because it makes the smoothest flow of thought. The mystery, Christ (or about Christ) involves the Gentiles as heirs together, members of the same body, and sharers together in the promise *with* the believing Jews who accepted the Messiah. "And if you are Christ's, then are you Abraham's seed, heirs according to promise" (Gal. 3:29). The stress on "with" in the passage points forcefully to the existence of a new relationship.

These three verses (Eph. 3:4-6) are part of a section in Ephesians where Paul treats the relation of Jew and Gentile to God. In 2:11-22 he develops the idea of the union of the Jew and Gentile in the Church. God creates the two—Jew and Gentile—into one new man. This is the Christian man (see Eph. 2:15). Christ reconciles both Jew and Gentile to God through his cross. On the cross he slew the enmity between Jew and Gentile as well as the enmity between man and God. These reconciled ones who belong to the new order of man—the Christian man—also are placed by this reconciliation in one body (Eph. 2:16). This body is the Church (cf. I Cor. 10:17; Eph. 4:4,12; 1:22-23; Col. 3:15). Christ preaches peace to both Jew and Gentile—those who historically were near and those who historically were far off from the covenants. Through Christ both Jew and Gentile may approach God in one Spirit (Eph. 2:18). Gentiles instead of being strangers and foreigners are now fellow citizens with the saints (Eph. 2:19). This means that the Gentiles are fellow citizens with the Jewish saints, both past and present. The Gentiles are members of the household of God.[4] They are a part of God's household or family. This sheds great light on Ephesians 3:6. Who are the fellow heirs, fellow members of the same body, fellow sharers in the promise? They are Gentiles who, we are told in the previous chapter, are fellow citizens with the saints and fellow members of God's household.

In 3:1-13 we see Paul's role in cementing the union of Jew and Gentile. Paul's stewardship on behalf of the Gentiles put his life in jeopardy. He was a prisoner, Christ Jesus' prisoner, on behalf of the Gentiles. By revelation Paul knew the secret or

---

4 Otto Michel, *"oikeios," TWNT*, V, 136-37: "The members of the household are the Christians in the family of God." See also *"oikos,"* "6. 'House of God' as an early Christian figurative expression for the Church," V, 128-131. See Chap. XIII, pp. 301-2, f.n. 18.

mystery of what God would do for the Jews and Gentiles in Christ. Therefore, he wanted to tell his Gentile readers how he obtained this understanding. God had revealed to his Jewish people truth about the Messiah and the people of the Messiah. But this revelation was only a beginning. The revelation of past times was not full. It was not to the same degree *"as it is now* revealed to his holy apostles and prophets in the Spirit" (Eph. 3:5). The mystery or secret was revealed to Christ's apostles and prophets (for their importance see I Cor. 12:28; Eph. 4:11). The apostles and prophets of the New Testament came to know by revelation what God was doing for mankind in Christ. This was the mystery or secret which once had been hidden but was now revealed. Paul's main activity (he who also had been called to be an apostle) was to bring this good news to the Gentiles. To them he proclaimed what before had been a secret (3:9)—i.e., the how or the manner in which God would bring mankind, Jews and Gentiles, into a living relationship with himself. The Church is to manifest this manifold wisdom of God not only to mankind but also to the rulers and authorities in heavenly places (the cosmic powers, Eph. 3:10). God purposed all these things in Christ Jesus. Because of their faith in him, the Gentiles have the access and approach to God. Since Paul is carrying out this magnificent purpose of God, his Gentile readers must not faint (lose heart) at his afflictions on behalf of them (Eph. 3:13).

Thus we can see that by observing what precedes and follows a passage, the interpreter has greater opportunity to see what the writer was seeking to convey to his original readers. These readers did not plunge into the middle of the letter and seize out a few consecutive sentences. They read carefully the whole document. To treat material fairly the modern interpreter must enter into the total train of thought. Originally there were no verses or chapter divisions, so we must note carefully the breaks or shifts in thought. Many times chapter divisions do indicate breaks in thought, but there are other places where chapter divisions artificially obscure the continuance of thought. The interpreter must decide for himself where there are genuine breaks in thought.

Context in a Particular Writing

What are parallels? Parallel material means identical or similar language, or identical or similar ideas found in a different context from the one being studied. When the parallel is found in other material in the same writing, one should be alert to see whether the fuller presentation of the subject in different contexts helps to clarify the meaning in any one context.

In considering parallels, the interpreter should understand the purpose and outline of each particular book. However, it is not enough simply to appropriate someone's outline or statement of purpose unless this outline and purpose is first tested by a firsthand knowledge of the book. The more intense our study of the Bible, the more eager we are to revise or improve either our own outlines or those of others. Alliteration does not improve accuracy. To insist on having the same letter begin each point may lead to inferior headings. But usually an outline is of real help in seeing how the thought is developed. Where an idea or an expression occurs frequently in the same book, the reason can often be seen from the outline. In some books the purpose of the writer is explicitly stated (Prov. 1:1-6; Luke 1:1-4; John 20:31 etc.). In many others it is not. But a study of the content of the book usually shows why the author wrote as he did to his readers. As we understand the purpose of the original writer, we are deterred from attaching ideas to his writings that are completely foreign to his purpose or development of thought.

Context has particular significance with regard to parallel sayings in different parts of the same Gospel. Interpreters of the sayings of Jesus are sometimes so unduly influenced by their own theoretical reconstructions of how the Gospels were written or how the sayings were collected and finally put down that the sayings themselves are treated as secondary. Some commentators seem to think that the origin and transmission of the sayings is more important than the message they convey. This is unfortunate. To be honest we must admit that every theory as to just how the Gospels were written is no more than a working hypothesis. For example, the tests by which some determine whether a saying or incident is genuine (i.e., comes from Jesus) or is a reconstruction of the Church are often worthless. A pre-understanding or a concisely worded definition of what can and cannot be genuine may make genuineness impossible by definition. Any good test of historicity should be just as applicable to extra-biblical material as to biblical. If a given principle is to measure whether a saying of Jesus is genuine, the same principle should be able to determine whether a saying of Socrates is genuine. A frequent pattern of thought among some current scholars is the assumption that if the Church is seen to be in agreement with any of Jesus' sayings, then the Church created the saying! Now apply this principle to

Socrates and Plato. We would have to assume that Plato's recorded sayings of Socrates could only be the utterance of Socrates if they are contrary to what Plato thought. If Plato should be in agreement with Socrates, then he must have created the saying and it could not come from Socrates. This is clearly ridiculous. Instead we assume that Plato has recorded Socrates' sayings and that these represent what Socrates taught unless strong evidence is presented to the contrary. This is obviously a sounder procedure.

The sayings of Jesus may be found in different parts of a Gospel for a number of reasons. Jesus repeated himself in his travels throughout Galilee and Perea. The Gospel writers often grouped sayings together to acquaint their readers with all they knew he taught on particular subjects. The slightly different forms of the sayings are often helpful in interpreting the meaning. The differences as well as the similarities help to clarify the meaning. The brief statement of Jesus on divorce in Matthew 5:31-32 has a parallel in Matthew 19:3-12 where the interpreter has more context. The sayings which deal with physical members which cause an individual to sin are found in two different contexts in Matthew. A study of both contexts shows the forcefulness of these sayings—cf. Matthew 5:29-30 with 18:8-9. Parallels in one Gospel as well as parallels found in two or more Gospels demand careful study. The results of such study become a larger context in which to unfold the meaning of the saying.

We have already considered the importance of the immediate context on Ephesians 3:4-6. The larger context of the whole book sheds light on particular aspects of Ephesians 3:4-6. The word "mystery" or "secret" is found in 1:9; 3:3; 3:9; 5:32; 6:19. These passages all help the interpreter enter into the meaning that Paul associated with this word.

On the phrase "holy apostles and prophets" in Ephesians 3:5, there is an excellent parallel in Ephesians 4:11. In this passage the exalted Christ gives gifts to his Church in terms of specific officeholders. Heading the list are apostles and prophets.

For the phrase "members of the same body" (ASV) in 3:6 the interpreter should consider the teachings of Ephesians on "the body" and on the "Church." In the following passages the word "body" gives a greater depth of meaning to the phrase "belonging to the same body" (1:23; 2:16; 4:4,12,16; 5:23,30). One finds the word "Church" in the following passages in Ephesians: 1:22; 3:10,21; 5:23,24,25,27,29,32. All of these passages are parallels in that they show what is involved in belonging to the same body. The metaphor of the body is remarkable.

No one who seriously studies the above references can regard the Church as an abstract institution.

Finally, this short section of Ephesians has two different words for revelation: "to make known" *(egnōristhē)* and "to reveal" *(apekaluphthē),* Ephesians 3:5. Elsewhere in Ephesians the word "mystery" is associated with expressions of revelation —the noun "revelation" (3:3), and the verb "to make known" (1:9; 3:3).[5] The noun "revelation" is also used in 1:17. These parallels show the nature of the truths being discussed. God discloses truths which for a long time had been hidden (either completely or in part). This is what a "mystery" or a "secret" is—not something "mysterious" but rather a truth previously withheld but now revealed and proclaimed.

Context in Other Writings

Parallels in other writings are the same as parallels in one particular writing. They consist in identical or similar language, identical or similar ideas in other writings.

Since no two people think exactly alike, the claim is often made that apparent similarity or identity found in different authors is partly the creation of the reader. Of course there are differences among the various writers of the Bible. And it is even true that such a simple concept as "rest" has many meanings. Take its usage today for example. If a man says he wants to get some rest, it may mean that he wants a nap. If a medical doctor (general practitioner) says he needs a rest, it means that he ought to take a trip to relieve the tension of his 24-hour-a-day job. There is a far different meaning in the figurative statement: "He was laid to rest in a quiet garden overlooking the Hudson." This asserts that he was buried. Consider the meaning of "rest" in this sentence: "The union and the company could not get together on the time allotted for rest periods." Here "rest" refers to a break in the routine of assembly line workers. In each instance the context makes clear the difference.

Where there are similar contexts—even though the writers or speakers are different—one expects some similarity of meaning. This is especially true in the Scriptures. Although there are many authors, all are members of the same community—the community of Israel, or the community of the Church. The word "election" (casting of a ballot) means one thing to a citizen of Russia and something else to a citizen of the United

---

[5] See Gunther Bornkamm, *"mustērion," TWNT,* IV, 827.

States. Each group associates a certain meaning with the term "election." Similar agreement is also true for the members of the commonwealth of Israel in the Old Testament and the members of the Church in the New Testament. Terms have a relatively common meaning for members of the same group. This common frame of reference eases communication and thereby opens the door to a greater understanding of truth via the commonly understood language. Growth and enlargement of meaning are found side by side with a basic continuity of meaning.

When we study a parallel from another book of the Bible which may or may not involve the same author, the interpreter must understand the purpose of the other book and the way the author unfolds his thoughts (outline). Only then can the student of Scripture assess the contribution of the parallel to the meaning of the context he is studying.

Parallel material in other Gospels is a big subject in itself. Already some dangers confronting the interpreter of the Gospels have been pointed out (see pp. 105-106). We must beware that theories of how the Gospels were written do not take precedence over what has been written. A student of the Gospels should surely make use of a harmony.[6] Burton and Goodspeed, for example, print parallel materials in parallel sections in regular type. "Parallel sections are sections which by position and content or by content only are shown to be as sections basically identical—narratives of the same event, or discourses dealing with the same subject in closely parallel language. They may differ greatly in extent by reason of one evangelist including material which another omits."[7] Parallel material in non-parallel sections is put in small type. "Parallel passages in non-parallel sections are passages which, though standing in sections not basically identical, closely resemble each other in thought or language."[8] Examples of parallel materials in parallel sec-

---

[6] One of the best harmonies of all four Gospels in English is Albert C. Wieand, *A New Harmony of the Gospels*. In Greek there are two fine harmonies on the Synoptic Gospels: Albert Huck, *Synopsis of the First Three Gospels* (1949), and Ernest De Witt Burton and Edgar J. Goodspeed, *A Harmony of the Synoptic Gospels in Greek* (1947). The procedure in Burton and Goodspeed of putting parallel material in parallel sections in regular type with the parallel material in non-parallel sections in a smaller type is very useful in studying the variety of parallels. Even though parallels between John and the Synoptics are found mostly in the Passion Week, a harmony of all four Gospels in Greek would be a help to the student of the Gospels. Absence of parallels is as significant as is the fact that there are parallels in two, three, or even four Gospels.

[7] Burton and Goodspeed, *op. cit.*, p. vi.

[8] *Ibid.*

tions are: The Centurion's Servant, Matthew 8:5-13, Luke 7:1-10; The Transfiguration, Matthew 17:1-13, Mark 9:2-13, Luke 9:28-36; The Feeding of the Five Thousand, Matthew 14:13-21, Mark 6:31-44, Luke 9:11-17, John 6:1-14. An example of parallel material in non-parallel sections is seen in the discourse on counting the cost, Luke 14:25-35. Parallels to parts of this discourse are found in Matthew 10:37,38; Matthew 16:24b, Mark 8:34b, Luke 9:23b; Matthew 5:13b; Mark 9:50a. In the Gospel of Luke (Luke 17:20-18:8) Christ talks about the kingdom of God, the revelation of the Son of Man, and the importance of prayer for believers under pressure. Parallels to parts of this discourse are found in Matthew 24:23,26,27; Mark 13:21; Matthew 16:21, Mark 8:31; Luke 9:22; Matthew 24:37-39; Matthew 24:17-18; Mark 13:15-16; Matthew 10:39; Matthew 24:40-41; Matthew 16:24, Mark 8:35, Luke 9:24; Matthew 24:28.

There are also significant parallels in the epistles. Consider again Ephesians 3:4-6. The Gentiles are not only fellow heirs with the believing Jews, members with them in the same body, but also sharers together with them in "the promise" in Christ Jesus. How can one find out who are the receivers of the promise, what is the content of the promise, and the present and future blessings of the promise? We must examine the word "promise" and the other expressions which are related to it in a variety of contexts. Note how Friedrich does this:

> The receivers of the promise are Abraham and his seed (Rom. 4:13); "that the promise might be certain to all the seed not only that which is from the Law but also to the seed which is from the faith of Abraham" (Rom. 4:16). Thus the Jews in the New Testament salvation history received the various promises of the Messianic Salvation (Rom. 9:4), while the Gentiles are "strangers from the covenants of the promise" (Eph. 2:12). Because the Messiah should come out of Israel, Jesus had to become a Jew "on behalf of the truth of God for the purpose of confirming the promises of the fathers" (Rom. 15:8). The promises, first of all, have value for the Jews. Out of them salvation must come to the peoples. However, now not only are the natural descendants sons of Abraham, but also those who believe just as he did. Therefore, the Gentiles "are sharers together [with the Jews] of the promise in Christ Jesus through the Gospel" (Eph. 3:6). What first was promised to Israel, now is made accessible to all the Gentiles. The Gospel mediates to them the blessings of salvation. Paul understands Gal. 3:16ff, "to thy seed" different from Romans 4. The seed is not the natural descendants, nor either is it those from faith. On account of the singular he confines it to the one from the seed of Abraham: Christ. He is the true heir of the promise, the universal heir, and he determines the fellow heirs. Whoever has put on Christ (Gal. 3:27), whoever is in Christ

Jesus (Gal. 3:28), whoever belongs to Christ are the seed of Abraham, "heirs according to promise" (Gal. 3:29).

The content of the promises, the blessing of the promise, whether it is called on the one hand "inheritance" (Rom. 4:13; Gal. 3:18,29) or "life" (Gal. 3:21; Rom. 4:17) or "righteousness" (Gal. 3:21) or "Spirit" (Gal. 3:14; Eph. 1:13) or "sonship by adoption" (cf. Gal. 4:22ff and Rom. 9:8f), is always the Messianic Salvation. Therefore, one may speak of the "promises" in the plural number or also of the "promise." They have become a reality in Christ (Rom. 15:8). He is the "yes" to the promises of God. He is the fulfillment of salvation in his person. Thereby it has happened that he has come to earth. God has acknowledged his promises; for in Christ they have all been fulfilled (2 Cor. 1:20). He has done away with the curse of the law, "in order that we might receive the promise of the Spirit through faith" (Gal. 3:14). In the gift of the "Spirit" each Christian has the fulfillment of the promise. The Spirit is the "first-fruit" (Rom. 8:23) or the "first installment" (2 Cor. 1:22; 5:5) of the final realization ". . . when you believed, you were sealed with the Holy Spirit, the promise, who is the first installment of our inheritance" (Eph. 1:13f). The Spirit promised in the Old Testament and then again through Christ is the token of the complete realization. He is the "seal" of the fulfillment which has commenced and is the "security" of the consummation still to be expected.[9]

This kind of comparative context study demands hard, careful work. But the results give the worker the feeling of unfolding a theme which has far more grandeur than he ever realized when he set himself to the task.

Likewise "the secret" or "mystery" of Ephesians 3:4 which involves what God will do for the Jew and Gentile in Christ is developed by Paul in other parts of Ephesians and in other of his epistles. The following passages in Colossians are excellent parallels to the ones in Ephesians and help to give greater clarity to this expression: Colossians 1:26,27; 2:2; 4:3. Taking Colossians 1:27, Ephesians 3:4-6, and Ephesians 1:9-10 Bornkamm paints the following picture of what "the secret" or "mystery" involves:

In Col. 1:27 the content of the "mystery" or "secret" is declared with the formula "Christ in you" i.e. it is in the indwelling of the exalted Christ "in you," the Gentiles. Eph. 3:4ff designates the participation of the Gentiles in the inheritance, in the body —the church, and in the promise in Christ as the mystery. This union of Gentiles and Jews in one body under the Head Christ is an eschatological-cosmical event; there occurs in it already the

9 Gerhard Friedrich, "epaggelia in the NT," TWNT, II, 579-80.

"mystery" of the bringing together of the whole created world in Christ, in which experience the totality also receives Christ as its head and sum (Eph. 1:9-10).[10]

The phrase "holy apostles and prophets" in Ephesians 3:5 indicates that God appointed certain offices in the Church. Christ is looked upon as "giving" these officers to the Church in Ephesians 4:11. In I Corinthians 12:28 it is God who "appoints in the church, first apostles, second prophets . . . ." In the context of I Corinthians 12:28-31 Paul shows why God revealed to his holy apostles and prophets what had formerly been a secret—how God would bring Jew and Gentile together in Christ. Certain gifts and tasks are assigned to particular officers. Only those who are appointed by God can play the role which each office demands.

The phrase "members of the same body" (RSV) can also be rendered "belonging to the same body" (Eph. 3:6). By studying the use of the metaphor "body" in the other Pauline letters we find that the expression designates Christians who are bound to Christ in a living relationship. The word "church," when it indicates all believers in Christ, also sheds light on the phrase "members of the same body." In Colossians 1:18 and 1:24 the words "body" and "church" are found together. In Colossians 2:19 and 3:15 more information is provided on the metaphorical use of the word "body." These contextual parallels help us see the significance in the statement that Gentiles belong to the same body with the believing Jews. In the doxology in Ephesians 3:20-21 Paul ascribes glory to God "in the Church and in Christ Jesus unto all generations, forevermore" (vs. 21). This means that the Church will endure as long as earthly generations continue and then forevermore. The Church and Christ are placed side by side. In both Hebrew and Greek eternity is expressed through time-centered formulas. When these are intensified, the writers merely build upon their temporal base. Sasse does a good job in showing how these intensified or strengthened forms arise:

> Also the doubling of *aiōn* in the formula *eis ton aiōna tou aionos,* Heb. 1:8 (Ps. 44:7) serves for the intensification of the concept of eternity. In 21 passages the doubling is connected with the plural form so that the formula so characteristic for the Pauline writings and Revelation (not to mention Heb. 13:21; I Pet. 4:11; 5:11) *eis tous aionas tōn aiōnōn* arises. Finally, there are cases in which the *aiōn*-formula is blended with similar turns of expression. Thus we recognize in the expression *eis pasas tas geneas tou*

10 Gunther Bornkamm, *"mustērion," TWNT,* IV, 827.

aiōnos tōn aiōnōn, Eph. 3:21 (cf. Col. 1:26) the constituent parts *eis pasas tas geneas* and *eis ton aiona tōn aiōnōn;* and *eis hēmeran aiōnos* 2 Pet. 3:18 allows itself to be analyzed into *eis hēmeran* (supply *kuriou*) and *eis ton aiōna.*[11]

Thus by context and parallel the phrase "members of the same body" (RSV) takes on greater depths of meaning.

Elsewhere in Paul one finds the word "mystery" or "secret" connected with expressions of revelation: the noun "revelation" in Romans 16:25; the verb "to reveal" in I Corinthians 2:10; the verb "to make known" (Rom. 16:26; Col. 1:27); and the verb "to be manifested, become visible or known" (Rom. 16:26; Col. 1:26).[12] What is revealed is no longer hidden or secret. Such truths were not and are not mysterious. They were simply unknown by God's people until he made them known. They can now be clearly grasped and can become a basic part of the believer's understanding of God's plan of redemption.

Absence of Context

In the Wisdom Literature (e.g. Job, Proverbs, and Ecclesiastes) where there are sayings, proverbs, and various kinds of epigrammatic statements, the interpreter gets very little help from the immediate context. However, the editor or collector of the proverbs often groups them topically. On the whole, much of Proverbs and Ecclesiastes consists of individual units which are complete in themselves. Indeed, these units circulated by themselves. But parallels elsewhere may shed some light on meaning and should be studied carefully to see what help they can provide.

In the Gospels there are groupings of Jesus' sayings in which the immediate context provides little. The interpreter can make use of parallels elsewhere, but the specific context does not provide the information which would give him an understanding in depth. Take for example Luke 12:49-59. Just before this section Jesus contrasts the faithful and unfaithful steward (Luke 12:41-48). Just after this section are Jesus' comments on the tragic news report about the Galileans slain by Pilate (Luke 13:1-9). The verses between these two sections (Luke 12:49-59)

---

[11] Hermann Sasse, *"aiōn," TWNT,* I, 199. For the phrase "unto all generations" see Exod. 12:14. For a less developed blending of formulas involving the combination of "generation" and "age," see LXX of Tobit 1:4; 13:12 [Goodspeed translation of Apocrypha 13:10]; see also Enoch 103:4; 104:5.

[12] For further material see Gunther Bornkamm, *"mustērion," TWNT,* IV, 827.

touch upon the following themes: one purpose for Christ's coming—to bring fire upon the earth (vs. 49); Christ's impending baptism (vs. 50); the kind of division which Christ brought (vss. 51-53); those who interpret the weather but do not discern the character of their time (vss. 54-57); the coming to a settlement with one's adversary (vss. 58-59).

In Luke 16:14-18 five topics are discussed. The first two have a connection with the preceding context, but after that the immediate context contributes little. Just before this section is the account of the unjust steward (Luke 16:1-13). Just after this section is the story of the rich man and Lazarus (Luke 16:19-31). Note how the material in the intervening section moves away from the contextual topics of thought: (1) the Pharisees ridicule Jesus for his teaching on wealth (vs. 14); (2) Jesus declares God's knowledge of men's hearts (vs. 15); (3) the law and the prophets were until John; followed by the proclamation and response to the kingdom of God (vs. 16); (4) disappearance of heaven and earth easier than the invalidity of the smallest part of the law (vs. 17); (5) a saying on divorce (vs. 18).

It appears that the fact that the sayings circulated orally has affected both their independence and certain groupings as well. Examples as difficult as these should make the interpreter thankful for the amount of context he does have in the materials which have come from Jesus.

PRINCIPLES FOR INTERPRETING FROM CONTEXT

1. Observe carefully the immediate context—that which precedes and follows the passage.

2. Observe carefully any parallels in the same book to the materials in the passage being interpreted. Be aware of the purposes and development of thought in the book.

3. Observe carefully any parallel in another book by the same author or in other books by different authors. Take into account the purpose and development of thought in these books.

4. Where the immediate context is of little or no value, try to find genuine parallels which come from the same period or time.

5. Bear in mind that the smaller the quantity of material to be interpreted, the greater the danger of ignoring context. No axiom is better known and more frequently disobeyed than the oft quoted: "A text without a context is only a pretext." Somehow, to discern this kind of error in someone else is easy but to recognize this same fault in ourselves is most difficult.

Faithful adherence to context will create in the interpreter a genuine appreciation for the authority of Scripture.

VI Language

The purpose of this chapter is to acquaint the interpreter with the basic elements in language. If he does not understand these elements and take them into account as he interprets, he may miss the real meaning of the biblical passage. This chapter is not a study of linguistics, linguistical theory, or the fine details of grammar. We will look rather at the main role of language. Although there must be some technical classifications, the discussion will seek to be meaningful to the person who has had no formal study in Hebrew, Aramaic, and Greek. If he understands how these biblical languages are put together, the English equivalents in the more literal English translations will take on new significance. For the reader with some formal study in the biblical languages, this survey may remind him of his need to be constantly aware of these building blocks of thought. True language consciousness on the part of the interpreter is essential. To develop this in the original languages (Hebrew, Aramaic, Greek) is very rewarding. Constant use of them will bring a steady growth and greater results. Putting time and effort into language study is like putting money in the bank. As one's capital increases, so does the interest. But if one cannot study the original languages, then a language awareness in English will help the interpreter to escape many pitfalls and to lay hold of many truths which he might otherwise pass by.

SOUND OF WORDS (PHONOLOGY)

People sometimes forget that the biblical languages were used far more in oral form than in written form. The Hebrew,

114

Aramaic, and Greek languages were used by peoples in a variety of circumstances. Whether they lived in small settlements, or in fairly large cities, the spoken word was even more important in their lives than in our own. With no newspapers, few books, and with much illiteracy, communication was often confined to speech.

The sounds and pronunciations of Hebrew, Aramaic, and Greek words are surrounded by some mystery. The original biblical texts were written in the Hebrew and Aramaic manner of omitting all vowels. Only the consonant sounds were written down. In the A.D. 500's the Massoretic scholars inserted the vowel points into the Hebrew and Aramaic texts. In so doing, they preserved for us the sounds of the Semitic words. On the other hand, there are many uncertainties associated with Massoretic vowel points. The common pronunciation of Greek words goes back to the times of the Renaissance. Erasmus furthered a revival of learning among biblical scholars by working out a pronunciation of the Greek words. This "Erasmian" pronunciation has an artificial ring to it. Even though the Greek language has changed much since Paul's day, it is likely that Paul would better understand the pronunciation of modern Greek than the academic sounds of Erasmian Greek. Yet the Erasmian pronunciation has been useful and has helped many students develop a first hand sense or feeling for the Greek language.

Vocalizing of the language is being increasingly employed in the study of Hebrew and Aramaic, and to a lesser degree in Greek. Speaking a language helps the student to absorb the vocabulary and learn more quickly to think in the language. It also helps him to experience the Hebrew, Aramaic, or Greek idioms from the standpoint of the people who spoke in this idiomatic way. Germany has produced some of our greatest linguists and has always had many scholars who were strongly in favor of vocalization. In their classes students are not permitted to translate a line of Greek until they each read it aloud. Language sounds, therefore, have an important role in the communication of meaning. Sounds are the gateway to ideas.

FORMS OF WORDS (MORPHOLOGY)

Students of a foreign language soon are aware of the forms of the words. Languages such as Hebrew, Aramaic, Greek, Latin, German, etc. are highly inflected languages. Tense, mood, voice, person, and number all influence the form used. "I say," "you (sg.) say," "he says," "we say," "you (pl.) say," "they say" may all be different forms even though they are found in the same tense. Changes in the tense, a shift from an active to a passive voice, change from statement to command—all such changes influence the form. Very little of this appears in English. We do have the shift from "you (sg.) say" to "he says." But English-speaking students are not usually prepared for the vast number of changes in the declension of nouns and in the conjugation of verbs that they find in Greek and Latin. The Hebrew noun does not change as frequently as the Greek noun, but the changes that do occur influence the meaning decidedly. The Hebrew verb system is complicated, and there is no easy way to master it. Aramaic, though a cognate language to Hebrew, has its own peculiarities in forms. A student who knows Hebrew well will not be able to read on sight a passage of Aramaic. He will find difficulty even though the Aramaic words are parallel to the Hebrew words. The changes in form will confuse him. After he masters the changes in form, he soon learns to assess both similarities and differences. Only at this point will he be able to state how much alike the two languages are and what are the more important differences.

One cannot overemphasize the importance of knowing and recognizing forms. In first year study of any inflected language this receives high emphasis. The student may feel that this is only a mechanical process and that when he really knows the language, he can forget such things just as he usually does in English. But there is a difference. In speaking a modern language, if a man does not understand what his neighbor means, he merely asks the neighbor to clarify himself. In ancient languages one cannot ask the writer for a further explanation. The interpreter must be able to recognize the form and all the possibilities of meaning which the form may carry. Error in the first of these procedures makes any valid thinking on the second procedure impossible. Therefore, the recognition of forms is highly important in determining the meaning of thought. Some students lean on analytical lexicons (dictionaries which tell the student the main root from which the form comes). Occasionally such a lexicon does provide help on a difficult form. But the need to refer constantly to such a device is a danger signal. Short range gains are not worth the long range liabilities. It is somewhat like learning to type. To type correctly takes more effort at first than the "hunt and peck" system. But no one who has mastered the correct technique would go back to the two-finger typing that seemed easier at first. Likewise, the student who has learned to recognize forms for himself will never go back to depending on an analytical lexicon to read each verse.

Standard lexicons that give the meanings of words also include among the entries clues to help the student find the more difficult forms. It is far better for a student to use these helps than to use an analytical lexicon.

MEANING OF WORDS (LEXICOLOGY, LEXICOGRAPHY)

Tools

Never before has the interpreter had such fine tools as are now available to him. In some ways this makes his task easier —others have done work that he should otherwise have to do. On the other hand, these good tools demand more of the interpreter. He must weigh several possible meanings and must have good reasons for the one which he chooses. But without the tools such rigorous and incisive thought would be impossible.

One appreciates lexicons more and more as he gains experience in interpretation. The basic lexicons in Hebrew and Aramaic are: Francis Brown, Samuel R. Driver, and Charles A. Briggs, *A Hebrew and English Lexicon of the Old Testament with an Appendix Containing the Biblical Aramaic;*[1] Ludwig Koehler and Walter Baumgartner, *Lexicon in Veteris Testamenti Libros.*

The basic lexicons in Greek are: George Henry Liddell and Robert Scott, *A Greek-English Lexicon;* Walter Bauer, *A Greek-English Lexicon of the New Testament,* ed. and trans. William F. Arndt and F. Wilbur Gingrich; Gerhard Kittel and Gerhard Friedrich (eds.), *Theologisches Wörterbuch zum Neuen Testament;*[2] James Hope Moulton and George Milligan, *The Vocabulary of the Greek Testament,* Illustrated from the Papyri and Other Non-Literary Sources. All of these works have their own particular emphasis. Liddell and Scott is the most comprehensive Greek lexicon. It covers the Greek language from 1000 B.C. (traditional date of Homer) to and partly into the Byzantine period (A.D. 529 to A.D. 1453). Bauer

---

[1] See the appended bibliography for further information on this and other books mentioned below.

[2] Harper and Row have translated and published *Bible Key Words,* a four-volume work, four words per volume (Vols. I and II). These volumes contain some important words that have been extensively treated in the *TWNT*. At the present time Geoffrey Bromiley is supervising the translation of the entire *TWNT* from German into English for the Wm. B. Eerdmans Publishing Company. This herculean task will be a monumental work of translation. It is greatly needed in the English-speaking world to acquaint interpreters with the amount of careful lexical and theological work done on words to give us a better perspective on their meaning.

(Arndt and Gingrich) covers the New Testament and the early Christian literature. Kittel and Friedrich's *Theologisches Wörterbuch* covers all aspects of a word to bring out its theological significance. Take the Greek word *orgē* (wrath).[3] Here is how it is discussed: Outline of article (one page); Wrath in the Classical Age (9½ pages); The Wrath of Men and the Wrath of God in the Old Testament (18 pages); The Wrath of God in the Septuagint (3½ pages); Late Judaism—The Apocrypha and Pseudepigrapha, The Rabbis, Philo, and Josephus (5½ pages); The Wrath of Men and the Wrath of God in the New Testament (28½ pages). The whole article consists of sixty-six pages. Approximately twenty-three pages are in smaller type while forty-three pages are in larger type. All footnotes (some of which are extensive) are in smaller type. This means that the maximum amount of material is crowded into the smallest amount of space. Reading an article like this gives one an increased understanding of the word in a broad perspective. Yet there is still work to be done. Monographs, theses, various kinds of devotional and theological studies should be written on particular aspects that are merely touched upon in this broad survey. But the survey gives the right kind of perspective in which to do more detailed studies. It also provides some excellent statements on meaning in particular passages. Moulton and Milligan's *The Vocabulary of the Greek Testament* shows the use of the words in the papyri. This means that the interpreter can find out what the word meant in ordinary life among people who lived from approximately the third century B.C. to the sixth century A.D. The beginning student will find Moulton and Milligan difficult because the Greek examples often are not translated. This proves to be a barrier to those with a limited vocabulary. Yet all the meanings are listed in English. Terse comments are also given in English.

Many students of the Bible first became aware of concordances through the use of *Cruden's Complete Concordance*. The author of this concordance was born in 1701 and died in 1770. The first edition appeared in 1737, the second in 1761, and the third in 1769. Concordances, like lexicons and grammars, are invaluable. Improvements are made by building upon the work of those who have gone before. The concordances now available to the student of the original languages are of a high calibre.

---

[3] Hermann Kleinknecht, Oskar Grether, Otto Procksch, Johannes Fichtner, Erik Sjöberg, and Gustav Stählin, "*orgē, orgizomai, orgilos, parorgizō, parorgismos*," *TWNT*, V, 382-448.

The following concordances to the Old Testament are very helpful: Solomon Mandelkern, *Veteris Testamenti Concordantiae: Hebraicae Atque Chaldaicae;* Gerhard Lisowsky, *Konkordanz zum hebräischen Alten Testament* [Aramaic section follows Hebrew]; Edwin Hatch and Henry A. Redpath, *A Concordance to the Septuagint* and the Other Greek Versions of the Old Testament (Including the Apocryphal Books); *The Englishman's Hebrew and Chaldee Concordance of the Old Testament,* Being an Attempt at A Verbal Connexion between the Original and the English Translation with Indexes, A List of the proper Names and Their Occurrences etc. Mandelkern is the most complete concordance. Although the Hebrew text is unpointed (a disturbing factor to beginning Hebrew students) the concordance has excellent material. Lisowsky, the most recent concordance, is a fine intermediate concordance. The original manuscript (done by hand) was photographed rather than printed. Yet the concordance is easy to read and the Hebrew text has vowel points. Further, the subject of all verbs is indicated by a clever system of footnotes. Brief meanings of the words are given in German, English, and Latin. The concordance of Hatch and Redpath to the Septuagint is one of the finest. Not only is it remarkably complete, but it indicates every Hebrew word or expression which the Greek word translates. A common word like "the earth" *(gē)* or "land" covers fifteen pages with three columns per page. There are twenty-five Hebrew words or expressions that have *gē* as the Greek translation. There are really more, since one finds 2.a, 2.b, and 2.c with the inclusion of synonymous expressions (including Aramaic words as well). Wherever one finds a (2.c) after a passage the word *gē* is translating the Hebrew noun *e'retz. The Englishman's Hebrew Concordance* takes up all of the Hebrew and Aramaic words alphabetically. The Hebrew verbs are analyzed in terms of their stems, infinitives, participles. The text of the passage is in English, but the word itself is given in Hebrew. After the Hebrew word the editor has put the equivalent for the Hebrew in English letters as a help to the beginner in Hebrew.

The following concordances to the New Testament are most useful: W. F. Moulton and A. S. Geden, *A Concordance to the Greek New Testament;* Alfred Schmöller, *Handkonkordanz zum griechischen Neuen Testament;* Kurt Aland and H. Riesenfeld, *Vollständige Konkordanz des griechischen Neuen Testament* unter Zugrundlegung aller modernen kritischen Textausgaben und des textus receptus; *Englishman's Greek Concordance of the New Testament.* Moulton and Geden is the most complete of the older concordances. The Greek words are listed alphabetically. The context for the word is given in Greek. Hence a student can learn much about the word simply by reading through all the entries under the word. Where a formal quotation is made from the Old Testament, Moulton and Geden print the Hebrew text of the passage below the Greek. Schmöller has less context in the entries than Moulton and Geden. He does not have the degree of completeness of Moulton and Geden, but this is still an excellent intermediate concordance. Brief meanings of the words are given in Latin. While Moulton and Geden, and Schmöller follow a specifically selected textual base, Aland and Riesenfeld have created a concordance based on the widest possible text base. *The Englishman's Greek Concordance* has the textual entries in English with the Greek word serving as the heading to the list of passages where the word occurs.

The most complete concordances for those who are not acquainted with the original languages are: James Strong, *The Exhaustive Concordance of the Bible,* and Robert Young, *Analytical Concordance to the Bible.* There are no lexicons or dictionaries in English that are comparable to those available in the original languages. To find the meanings of words, the English student must consult dictionaries of theology, Bible encyclopedias, and up-to-date commentaries on Scripture. One of the outstanding rewards of the study of the biblical languages consists in the tools that such a study makes available to the interpreter. The student who cannot work in the biblical languages should consult those works which show evidence of having consulted the basic sources.

Factors Influencing Meaning

Etymology. Etymology is the study of the roots or primitive forms from which words are derived. This may be a highly theoretical reconstruction. Rightly done it becomes an introduction to the history of known usage, but it must not be confused with historical studies of usage. Ultimate etymological origin is usually wrapped in vague shadows. From similarities among words of one language and from similarities of words in cognate languages, the trained linguist can construct some plausible hypotheses of development, growth, or relationship. But even for these hypotheses, he is dependent on historical usage. Hence the interpreter must never consider etymology apart from usage. Since usage is so important, a safe rule for the interpreter is to leave etymology in the hands of the experts and to apply himself diligently to context and usage.

Etymological studies throughout the years have intrigued all classes of people. Laymen and scholars alike try to "discover an original meaning." On the basis of this alleged or actual meaning they then propound inferences. We must be aware of the pitfalls of this practice. James Barr devotes fifty-four pages to "Etymologies and Related Arguments."[4] He points out that the etymology of a word may be no help to understanding its current meaning. For example, the English word "nice" comes from the Latin *nescius,* "ignorant." Obviously, there is no connection between the current meaning of "nice" and its etymology. Barr shows the fallacy of trying to connect the English word "holy" with the words "healthy" or "sound." How often great weight has been placed upon the etymology for the Greek word *ekklēsia* ("assembly," "congregation," "church"). The two Greek words *"ek"* and *"kaleō"* seem to point to a derivation meaning "to call out." Hence members of the church are "called out ones." Such an argument may be tied to election or to the proclamation of the Gospel and those who respond to it. Barr takes up the connection of the Greek word *ekklēsia* with the Hebrew word *qahal.*[5] He discusses at length the supposed connection of *qahal* ("assembly") with the Hebrew word *qōl* ("voice"). He shows all the complexities of the various etymological arguments. If there is a connection between *qahal* and *ekklēsia* it is because of the meaning in usage which they share in common of "assembly." Barr shows other possible connections between *ekklēsia* and the Aramaic word *kᵉneset.* He lists theological inferences drawn from etymological connections. He shows how the interpreter can choose what he wants. "The interpreter enjoys a great power of selection not only over the etymological 'connection' which he cares to notice for the words but also over the strand or aspect of biblical thought which he makes them fit."[6] Correct biblical ideas are often falsely ascribed to erroneous etymological connections. Because the idea may be true, people fail to notice how erroneous was the procedure used to arrive at it. Karl Ludwig Schmidt in his article on *ekklēsia* in *TWNT* puts etymology as point VII.[7] "We have left the etymology of the word *"ekklēsia* to the end, because its history is more important.... The truth in matters of verbal usage is not to be reached by adventurous ingenuity,

---

4 James Barr, *Semantics of Biblical Language,* pp. 107-160.
5 *Ibid.,* pp. 119-29; 138-40.
6 *Ibid.,* p. 139.
7 *Bible Key Words,* "The Church," 57-61.

but by a careful study of the actual use and abuse of words."[8]
This means that meaning must be based on usage and context.
Without these, brilliant conjectures of etymology should be
simply dismissed as "adventurous ingenuity."

Usage. Lexicons or dictionaries that give the meanings for
Hebrew, Aramaic, and Greek words are very helpful. The
newer and more recent Old Testament lexicons show parallel
words in such cognate languages as Ethiopian, Egyptian, Egyptian Aramaic, Akkadian, Amorite, Old Babylonian, Old South
Arabic, Babylonian, Hurrian, Hittite, Canaanite, Moabite, Na-
bataean, Modern Arabic, Persian, Syriac, Samaritan, Ugaritic,
etc. These are of value for the scholar, but the significance of
parallels in cognate languages for particular scriptural passages
is difficult for even the scholar to judge. Hence the average interpreter may note these parallels but had best stay with the
use and context in either Hebrew or Aramaic of the Old Testament unless no sense can be made of the wording of the text
as it stands.

The lexicon of Liddell and Scott gives extensive examples of
various meanings of Greek words during the whole classical
period as well as the Koine period (including the LXX). Bauer,
edited and translated by Arndt and Gingrich, lists examples of
Greek words in the Septuagint, in the papyri of the Koine period, in the writers of literary Koine, and in the early Christian
literature. Such listings in these lexicons indicate when a word
had certain meanings, when other meanings began to appear,
which meanings were more frequent, and which ones were rather
rare.

Yet the most important thing in a Hebrew-Aramaic lexicon
of the Old Testament or a Greek lexicon of the New Testament is the separation and classification of meanings. All uses
or meanings of the word are immediately brought to the attention of the interpreter. In Bauer at the close of the information on a word one asterisk (*) indicates that all passages in
which the word occurs in the NT, the Apostolic Fathers, and
the other early Christian literature are listed in this entry. The
double asterisk (**) means that only the NT passages are
given.[9] In this way the lexicon serves as a classified or topical
concordance. In Brown, Driver, and Briggs a dagger (†) is
usually prefixed to a word to indicate that all passages in the
Old Testament are cited. Lexicographers or editors of a lexicon
are not infallible. Their classifying of a passage under one par-

---

[8] *Ibid.*, pp. 57-58.
[9] Bauer, p. xxvii.

ticular meaning does not automatically exclude all other possibilities. The listing of passages after any one particular meaning obviously represents the opinion of the editor. His opinion
should be respected. Bauer devoted forty years of his life to revising and developing a Greek lexicon. Such study naturally
develops a feel for words and their meaning in particular contexts that only constant experience can create. But Bauer and
all other good lexicographers often note that a particular passage could be classified under meanings 1 or 2. As the subpoints under a word become finer, the possibilities increase of
other categories of meaning for a particular passage. This
means that when the interpreter finds a meaning of a word
that he thinks is well suited for that context, he may adopt
that meaning. But his choice of that particular meaning must
be supported by specific contextual reasons for one meaning as
being more probable than another. Sometimes the lexicographer
and interpreter differ because they see the context differently.
Sometimes the lexicographer and the interpreter differ because
of frameworks of thought (with foreign assumptions) that take
precedence over anything in the context. How important is
context? Context influences meaning in proportion to its proximity. The immediate context should receive prime consideration. The context of the book itself is next. Then the context
of Scripture itself is third.

Let us consider a word such as the noun "truth" *(alētheia)*.
Bauer lists three main meanings. Note also the subpoints under
meaning number two. "1. *truthfulness, dependability, upright-
ness* in thought and deed. 2. *truth* (opposed to falsehood). a.
generally. b. especially of the content of Christianity as the absolute truth. 3. *reality* as opposed to mere appearance (opposite
to pretext)."[10] Here the classification of all uses of the word
alētheia is not too difficult. Category 2.b. has the largest number of references. Within this category there is wide variety.
One finds "the message" *(logos)* of truth (Eph. 1:13; Col. 1:5;
II Tim. 2:15; James 1:18), the Spirit of truth (John 14:17; 15:26;
16:13; I John 4:6), Christ himself as the truth (John 14:6), the
knowing or knowledge of the truth (John 8:32; I Tim. 2:4;
4:3; II Tim. 2:25; 3:7; Tit. 1:1; Heb. 10:26), etc. Yet in all of
them "truth" is opposed to falsehood. The various aspects of
truth in the Christian faith are listed concisely. When categories are broad and well defined, there is rarely difference of
opinion over classification of meaning.

In the Old Testament counterpart for *alētheia,* the inter-

10 Bauer, pp. 35-36.

preter finds more categories. The word *'emeth* means *firmness, faithfulness, truth.*[11] Here are the categories of meaning: "1. *reliability, sureness.* 2. *stability, continuance.* 3. *faithfulness, reliableness,* (a) *of men,* (b) *an attribute of God.* 4. *truth,* (a) *as spoken,* (b) *of testimony and judgment,* (c) *of divine instruction,* (d) *truth* as a body of ethical or religious knowledge. 5. adv. *in truth, truly."* This plurality of categories shows the interpreter alternatives in classification. When he consults another lexicon he finds other ways of setting forth the meanings. Take Koehler and Baumgartner on the same word, *'emeth:* "1. *firmness, trustworthiness,* 2. *stability, constancy,* 3. *faithfulness (not always to be safely discerned from* 2. *constancy* and 4, *truth),* a) *faithfulness of God,* b) *of men.* 4. *truth, reality*... adv. *truly, really."*[12] Various classifications and meanings make it possible for the interpreter to find the one that fits the context. Through the lexicon he becomes a part of a living stream of communication. And through these words in context God communicates to men what they need to know about him, about their world, and especially about themselves.

Periods or Epochs in the history of language. Hebrew and Aramaic stretch from the middle of the second millennium B.C. to the Persian period (539-331 B.C.). From the Persian period to the time of Christ Hebrew ceased being the language of the people and Aramaic became the spoken and written language of the common man of Palestinian Judaism. During these centuries Hebrew and Aramaic grew and developed as do all languages. Unless we recognize growth and change in language we can never understand what language is. God's revelation throughout history has always used the language as it was at the time when the revelation was given. For example there are two words in Hebrew for "congregation"—*"edah* and *qahal.* In Numbers *"edah* is very frequent (81 times); *qahal* is infrequent (11 times). In Ezekiel there is no instance of *"edah* while *qahal* occurs 15 times; I Chronicles has no examples of *"edah,* yet there are six examples of *qahal.* II Chronicles has one example of *"edah* while there are 24 examples of *qahal.* On the other hand *"edah* is found 11 times in Joshua while *qahal* is found only once. Since Ezekiel and Chronicles are post-exilic in date *qahal* seems to be the more popular word at this period. In Joshua and Exodus, *"edah* is the common word. Yet in Deuteronomy *"edah* does not appear at all while *qahal* occurs 11 times. Frequency of words is controlled by the au-

[11] BDB, p. 54.
[12] Koehler-Baumgartner", pp. 66-67.

thor's preference, the subject matter, and usage at the time of the original writing (or later editing). However, all of these factors are controlled by God. He uses the language of any period to unfold truth about himself. One of the important features of the Dead Sea Scrolls is the light they shed on late Hebrew and Aramaic.

Greek is also an old language, with a continuous history from before 1000 B.C. to the present. The Koine period from 322 B.C. to A.D. 529 (closing of the Academy of Plato at Athens by Justinian) provides the setting for New Testament Greek. The discovery of great quantities of papyrus letters, commercial contracts, etc., at the close of the nineteenth century made it clear that the Greek of the New Testament was the Greek of ordinary life. In carefully examining the papyri, scholars had proof that the Greek of the New Testament was the Greek of everyday life. The writers of the New Testament were God's chosen servants to speak his message in language which their hearers could clearly understand. True, there is in the New Testament a greater depth of meaning than any of the hearers first realized. But they could still understand the message sufficiently to come into living fellowship with Christ or otherwise to reject the message and cling more tightly to Judaism or paganism.

Septuagint. For most of the early Christians, the Septuagint was their Bible. This Greek version of the Old Testament came into existence in Alexandria (or found wide acceptance and use there) between 250 and 150 B.C. It was the first large-scale translation of the Hebrew Old Testament into another language. It was prepared for Jews who were scattered abroad from Palestine. These Jews in the Diaspora wanted to read their Old Testament in the language which they now spoke. Thus the Septuagint met a real need.

The first Christians (cf. the 120 of Acts 1:15) spoke Aramaic. Soon a number of Greek-speaking Jews came into the fellowship. The problems that developed caused the church to appoint seven Greek-speaking deacons to solve these difficulties (see Acts 6). Jews who spoke Greek were called Hellenists. The most prominent of these was Stephen. The Bible for the Hellenists was the Septuagint. During Paul's missionary journeys when the Gentiles came into the Church in large numbers, the Septuagint became even more important. Hence the New Testament writings were originally written to a people who for the most part knew of the Old Testament through the reading of the Septuagint.

Paul, although he knew Greek, Hebrew, and Aramaic, made most of his quotations either from the Septuagint or from a

Greek version not too far removed from it. Earl Ellis points out that fifty-one of Paul's ninety-three Old Testament texts "are in absolute or virtual agreement with the LXX."[13] Paul's style and vocabulary show definite affinities with the LXX.[14] This means that the LXX played a role in moulding the technical or theological language of the New Testament. The New Covenant was the fulfillment of the Old Covenant. The God who revealed himself at Mt. Sinai revealed himself with greater depth and detail at Calvary and in the resurrection. As Christians came to understand the meaning of God's actions in Christ, they found the language of God's earlier revelation to be most helpful. Thus the two covenants are bound together by the vocabulary and ideas of revelation. This vocabulary, consisting of Hebrew and Aramaic in the Old Testament and Aramaic and Greek in the New Testament (the words of Jesus were originally in Aramaic) belongs not only to the life situation of the epoch from which the writing comes but also from the life situation of previous periods. Hence revelation did not become creative by bringing into existence a core of new words. The creativity of revelation lay in the deeper meaning and insight given to words already in use. The word "righteousness" is a good example. The noun, the adjective, and the verb (often translated "to justify") have certain meanings in the LXX.[15] The New Testament writers brought to these same words an even greater significance. This significance can be seen by examining these words in their New Testament context.

Synonyms. The older works devoted many pages to synonyms, i.e., words with similar meanings.[16] In today's lexicons, e.g. Bauer's and Kittel's, the material on the synonyms is found under the individual words. This is preferable because the man who becomes too involved with words that have the same meaning or similar meaning is tempted to see different shades of meaning in the words themselves. A careful study of all usages may show occasions where two words are actually interchangeable. In other contexts, different emphases make this impossible. The Greek words *logos* and *rēma* are often translated

[13] *Paul's Use of the Old Testament* (1957), p. 12. See Appendix II, pp. 155-185.

[14] *Ibid.*, p. 13.

[15] Gottfried Quell and Gottlob Schrenk, "Righteousness," *Bible Key Words*, 1-4, 16-17, 29-31, 57-59.

[16] See Milton S. Terry, "Synonyms," *Biblical Hermeneutics*, pp. 191-202. R. C. Trench, *Synonyms of the New Testament* (1890). G. Heine, *Synonyme des neutestamentlichen Griechisch* (1898). Herman Cremer, *Biblico-Theological Lexicon of New Testament Greek*, tr. William Urwick (1895), pp. 924-928.

"word." Both words have many separate meanings, especially *logos*.[17] Again, in different contexts the same word (e.g. *logos*) has different meanings. For example, the use of *logos* in John 1:1-18, where Jesus is called the living Word or *logos*, in no way controls the meaning of *logos* in Ephesians 6:19, where it means "speaking." Hence where *logos* and *rēma* have the same shade of meaning, it is because the context makes it so. In I Peter 1:23 the word *logos* is used; in I Peter 1:25 *rēma* is employed. Both words in this context have the meaning "message," i.e., the Christian message or gospel. Through this message believers were born again (vs. 23). The message of the Lord which abides forever is expressly said to be the gospel in verse 25: "And this is the message which was proclaimed as good tidings ('gospelized') to you." Synonyms are determined by context.

Modern lexicons have canvassed synonyms and particular examples far more thoroughly than the earlier lexicons did. For example, the Greek words *boulomai* and *thelō* both have the meanings of "wish, will, be willing." After noting the basic meaning of *boulomai*, Bauer adds "no longer different in meaning from *thelō*."[18] Or take the Greek words *agapaō* with the basic meaning of "love, cherish," over against *phileō* with the meanings of "love, have affection for, like." Whatever the reason, the New Testament writers prefer the *agapaō* family to the *phileō* family. The verb *agapaō* is found approximately 139 times, the noun *agapē* ("love") is found approximately 117 times, while the adjective *agapētos* ("beloved, only beloved, dear friends," etc.) is found approximately 51 times. In contrast the verb *phileō* occurs only 23 times (8 times in the Synoptics, 11 times in John, 4 times in the rest of the New Testament). The noun *philēma* ("kiss") occurs 7 times. The noun *philia* ("friendship") occurs once. In general one may conclude that the *agapaō* family is more comprehensive in meaning. The elements of choice, compassion and decision found in the context of the *agapaō* family show that this term came to stand for one of the essential characteristics of God and of Christianity. Yet *phileō* is used of the Father's love for the Son (John 5:20) and for the disciples (John 16:27), and for the disciples' love for Jesus (John 16:27). Hence *agapaō* and *phileō* can be equivalents. In John 21:15-17, where very likely there will always be a difference of opinion because of the nature of the context, Bauer takes *agapaō* and *phileō* to be synonymous. "*Agapaō and phileō* seem to be used interchangeably here; cf.

---

17 Bauer, *logos*, pp. 478-480; *rēma*, pp. 742-743.
18 *Ibid.*, p. 145.

the frequent interchange of synonyms elsewhere in the same chapter (*boskein-poimainein* [feed, tend / herd, tend], *arnia-probata* [sheep, lamb / lamb, sheep], *helkuein-surein* [drag, draw, haul / drag, pull, draw, drag away])."[19] In a passage such as this where the interpreter finds a multiplicity of synonyms, it seems that these synonymous expressions are placed in close proximity to each other to re-enforce the basic idea. Sheep or lambs are to be cared for. Metaphorically, Peter is to care for believers, God's sheep or lambs. The shift in words is only to drive home the truth. This is also true of the two words for love. Interpreters who, unlike Bauer, believe that there are shades of meaning should not deny the major purpose of the synonyms—to probe into the kind of affection which Peter had for Jesus. Whether the term *agapaō* or *phileō* is used, the test of affection is the same. *Affection is seen by what a man does.* As Peter feeds God's sheep, he will be demonstrating his love or affection.

Principles for the Interpreter in Lexicography

Words are building blocks of thought. But words are not like stone blocks or bricks, for one block may be cemented to another block without itself being changed. This is not true of words. Words are changed by the words which surround them. Hence the interpreter must proceed with certain principles in mind.

1. Know all possible meanings of the word in the period of its occurrence.

2. Decide which meaning fits best into the context of the writer. Give reasons rather than saying: "Oh, it sounds best to me this way." The familiar will often sound best although it may be inferior to another rendering.

3. Consider carefully the context (or life situation) of your listeners or readers so that they will not unconsciously read their own ideas into a biblical passage where they do not belong. God did not necessarily anticipate and answer all of modern man's questions on various details. God has not told us whether there is life on Mars or what kind of life it is. He does not tell us the age of the earth. He does not tell us whether saints who "are absent from the body and present with the Lord" are aware of the course of human history after they leave this earthly scene.

4. Beware of all etymological pronouncements that are not

19 *Ibid.*, p. 4. The other synonyms in John 21 mentioned by Bauer are in verses 6, 8, 16, 17.

well supported by contemporary usage. Etymology used as a preface to a discussion on usage is helpful. But etymology is of no value when used to "prove" a particular meaning of a word in a particular context apart from usage. If usage is mentioned but the main stress is on etymology, the interpreter should still be wary. Etymology may sound erudite but when wrongly handled it leads to mistakes.

5. Beware of fine distinctions of meaning in synonyms that are not supported by the context in which they are found. When synonyms are used, we should see how these synonyms give added force to the idea being conveyed. If the context supports fine distinctions of meaning, additional light is shed upon the idea that is being unfolded. But in practice many "ingenious insights" are devoid of textual foundation. The fine distinctions then become only human cleverness and are actually rationalism in a spiritual guise. Such practices deceive many into accepting interpretations that have no basis except in some interpreter's imagination. Here as in many other aspects of hermeneutics, the law of *parsimony* has a definite place: all other factors being equal, the simplest explanation of meaning is to be preferred as the true one. Complicated "explanations" often are a form of *eisegesis*—the reading in of a meaning which the author did not intend.

If we are aware of the context in the writing we are interpreting, and if we are aware of the backgrounds of those to whom we minister, we can both unfold the true meaning and make this meaning relevant to the listener. Never be so intent upon application that there is no serious attention to what the biblical writer has actually asserted. Careful interpreters are not content with any application; they want a valid application.

RELATIONSHIP OF WORDS (SYNTAX)

How words, phrases, and clauses are related to each other is a fascinating study. Even in inflected languages that make greater precision possible, usually there are two or more ways that a construction can be understood. Syntax is a study of thought relations. These elements in thought cannot be analyzed as the various chemicals in hard water are analyzed. But syntactical categories (if they are not treated mechanically) enable us to penetrate thought to a degree impossible to one unacquainted with syntactical procedures. Unquestionably, every alert reader does grasp some of the thought even though he has no understanding of syntactical categories. But he misses many connections of just what is related to what. Often such connec-

tions or relations are essential to an understanding of what
the writer is saying. Our comprehension of the relationship
of words, phrases, and clauses affects our understanding of
thought.

Tools

Grammars analyze sounds (phonology), forms (morphology),
and relationships (syntax). It is to the latter that we now give
attention. The grammars here listed are not beginning grammars (except in Aramaic). In a first year text book of a highly
inflected language the main emphasis falls on the forms of the
noun, verb, and clause, with a secondary emphasis on vocabulary and basic syntax. Intermediate and advanced grammars
give major emphasis to a more comprehensive treatment of
syntax.

In Hebrew, two grammars have long been used: E. Kautzsch
and A. E. Cowley, *Gesenius' Hebrew Grammar,* and H.
Bauer and F. Leander, *Historische Grammatik der hebräischen Sprache des Alten Testaments.* Recently a newer Hebrew grammar has appeared: Benedict Hartmann, *Hebräische
Grammatik.*

In Aramaic the standard grammar has been H. Bauer and
P. Leander, *Grammatik des Biblisch-Aramäischen.* Two older
briefer grammars are: H. Bauer and P. Leander, *Kurzgefasste
biblisch-aramäische Grammatik,* and D. Karl Marti, *Kurzgefasste Grammatik des biblisch-aramäischen Sprache.* Recently, a beginning grammar in Aramaic has appeared in
English: Franz Rosenthal, *A Grammar of Biblical Aramaic.*

In Greek the figure of A. T. Robertson has dominated the
American scene for 60 years, although he died in 1934. His
most famous work was *A Grammar of the Greek New Testament in the Light of Historical Research.* He also wrote a
shorter grammar in which W. Hershey Davis contributed the
section on accidence (forms): A. T. Robertson and W. Hershey
Davis, *A New Short Grammar of the Greek Testament* for
Students Familiar with the Elements of Greek. In the Robert-
sonian tradition but with many fresh ideas of their own is the
grammar of H. E. Dana and Julius R. Mantey, *A Manual
Grammar of the Greek New Testament.* All of these grammars,
for many different reasons, have either remained unchanged or
(as in the case of Dana and Mantey) only slightly altered during the past forty-odd years.

Revision, however, is the life-blood of a grammar. Friedrich
Blass was a contemporary of A. T. Robertson. He himself put

out three editions (1896, 1902, 1911) of his *Grammatik des
neutestamentlichen Griechisch.* Then after his death Albert
Debrunner kept revising the work. He put out a 4th edition in
1913, a 5th edition in 1921, a 6th edition in 1931, a 7th edition
in 1943, an 8th edition in 1949, a 9th edition in 1954, and a
posthumous (Dr. Debrunner died in 1958) 10th edition in 1959.
Some of these editions had only minor changes; others included
more involved alterations. Throughout all of these changes
the hand of Blass is still to be seen, although a greater grasp
of the Koine is clearly evident in the later editions. Because
Robert Funk was preparing to translate this grammar into
English, Debrunner put into his hands an extensive set of notes
which he had prepared for another German edition. His death
prevented these notes from being utilized in the latest German
edition. Funk took these notes and with them revised the 9th-
10th German editions before translating the work into English.
The book appeared in 1961: F. Blass, Albert Debrunner, and
Robert W. Funk, *A Greek Grammar of the New Testament and
Other Early Christian Literature,* A Translation and Revision
of the ninth-tenth German edition incorporating supplementary notes of A. Debrunner.

Here are the tools for handling syntax. If the interpreter
knows none of the biblical languages, he should use a literal
translation such as the American Standard Version (1901). By
applying his knowledge of English grammar to such a translation, he can observe many thought connections and thought
sequences that will greatly increase his understanding of the
passage.

Basic Syntactical Elements—Verb, Noun, and Clause

Verbs and their relationships, nouns and their relationships,
and clauses or grouping of words functioning as a unit constitute the basic elements of syntax.

Older grammarians worked out syntactical categories for
Latin and Greek. Then they tended to impose these categories
on other languages, thus squeezing them into a foreign mould.
But categories of syntax should, of course, provide ample room
for the distinctive elements of each language. In modern linguistics all labels are functional. No grammatical or syntactical
category is sacred, since our understanding of language functions is always capable of improvement. If a student forgets the
particular syntactical label which describes a certain relation,
then his "home-made" label is better than nothing. He will
find, however, that the syntactical labels in the grammars are

not only convenient but usually they are more concise and accurate than his own terminology.

Although syntactical categories of one language should not be imposed on another, there are many similarities in the syntactical structures of related languages and also between languages in different families. It is these similarities that the beginning student finds helpful. What he observed in Latin, e.g., gives him understanding of something in Greek. But the student must be careful not to confuse similarity with identity. Careful examination is sometimes necessary to reveal the difference.

In this brief survey of syntactical categories in Greek and Hebrew the writer proposes to show the basic elements and why these must be observed to penetrate thought. Since there is so little biblical Aramaic in the Old Testament, Hebrew will receive most of the attention in the Old Testament. A few examples will show that syntactical labels are not dry categories of embalmed thought. Rather, they describe vital possibilities of living thought. Not only was the language of the Bible spoken, but it still speaks. God is conveying his thoughts to us through this language. He does not use some ethereal language, but Greek, Hebrew, and Aramaic. He uses the thought patterns of his chosen servants. Hence syntax is indispensable for our understanding of ideas.

Verb

Greek. The following elements may be classified under the category of verb: *tense, mood, voice, person, number, infinitive, participle, adverb, conjunction,* and *particle.* To state briefly what each of these involves demands oversimplification. There are exceptions in every language. Yet organization is based upon regularity, major and minor emphases, and frequency of clearcut examples. Simplicity and clarity must characterize all of these basic elements, or the student will spend his time trying to understand the grammar rather than using it.

Tense in Greek refers primarily to *kind of action* rather than *time of action.* (1) Action may be regarded as continuous or linear. He *was writing* a letter. This kind of action is expressed by the imperfect tense, by most occurrences of the present tense, and by some occurrences of the future tense. (2) Action may be regarded as complete, i.e., a state or condition which resulted from past action and remains. He *has written* a poem. The perfect tenses are nearly always in the indicative mood (only in the indicative mood of Greek does tense have time implications). Here in the perfect tenses time and kind of action work together. The present perfect signifies a state existing in the present time. Darkness *has come.* The past (plu)perfect signifies a state existing in past time. Darkness *had come.* The future perfect signifies a state existing in future time. Darkness *will have come.* (3) Action may be regarded as a totality, i.e., wholeness of action. He *wrote* a letter. The totality indicated by the action may be a split second or a thousand years. But the action focuses attention upon wholeness. Sometimes this kind of action is referred to as point action or punctiliar action. Such action is conveyed by the aorist tense, by many examples of the future tense, and by a very few examples of the present. Where a tense may be linear or punctiliar (as in the present or future) the student must observe the context. But he should always take into account the known frequency of kind of action of each tense. The present tense is ninety-five per cent or more linear. The future is probably sixty per cent punctiliar and forty per cent linear, yet some might want to raise the punctiliar and reduce the linear percentages. Time in Greek is confined to the indicative mood. Past time is conveyed by the aorist, imperfect, pluperfect, and present (rare) tenses. Present time is conveyed by the present and the present perfect tenses. Future time is conveyed by the future, future perfect, and present (rare) tenses.

Mood in Greek deals with the relation of a verbal idea to reality, i.e., it deals with the way a man affirms a thing to be. In the indicative mood he affirms a thing to be an *actuality.* The subjunctive, optative, and imperative moods are moods of *contingency* or *possibility.* This first example illustrates *actuality:* "Because the law *was given* through Moses, but grace and truth *came about* through Jesus Christ" (John 1:17). The second example exemplifies *contingency:* " . . . if one *would proceed* to them from the dead, they will repent" (Luke 16:30). The subjunctive and optative moods are found both in main clauses and subordinate clauses. The imperative mood, expressing mostly commands and prohibitions, is confined largely to short sentences. Although there are some exceptions, the statement of Dana and Mantey is still valid that the affirmation in the subjunctive mood is *objectively possible,* in the optative mood it is *subjectively possible,* and in the imperative mood it is *volitionally possible.*[20] The last three moods are moods of potentiality, yet the indicative in some constructions involves itself in potentiality. This shows that thought patterns are not worked out in neat, logical sequences. Grammatical classifica-

[20] Dana and Mantey, *op. cit.,* p. 166.

tions must make room for deviations while at the same time they show customary or usual practices.

Greek has three voices. The active voice is similar to that in English where the subject does the acting. In the passive voice, the subject is acted upon. In the middle voice the subject is intimately involved in the action. He both produces it and participates in its results. The active voice states *the fact* of doing. The middle voice states both *the fact* of doing and *the attitude* of doing: "But clothe yourself (direct middle) with the Lord Jesus Christ, and stop making provision for yourself (indirect middle) for the flesh to arouse desires" (Rom. 13:14).

Person and number in Greek are important because of their preciseness. Second person singulars and second person plurals are never confused since the endings are different. This is true both in verb forms and in pronouns. In Romans 11:11-32 if one observes carefully the second person singular and plural pronouns and verb forms, he will find his observations very instructive. The Gentiles as a group are in the apostle's mind (cf. 11:12,25). But also he thinks of the individual Gentile and the importance of his individual response (11:16-24). Only by observing person and number will the truths tied to the grammatical facts of number break in upon the reader. "Behold, therefore, the goodness and severity of God. On the one hand, to those who fell, severity; but to *you* [sg.], the goodness of God, if *you* [sg.] continue in the sphere of [God's] goodness; for otherwise if *you* [sg.] do not continue in the sphere of God's goodness, *you* [sg.] also will be cut out" (Rom. 11:22).

The infinitive in Greek is a verbal noun. In all of its uses both qualities will be present. In some instances the verbal aspects will predominate and in others the noun aspects will be in the ascendancy. It has such verbal uses as purpose, result, time, cause, command. The noun or substantival uses find the infinitive acting as subject, object, possibly as indirect object, instrumental (dative), apposition, and as modifier—complementary infinitive with nouns and complementary infinitive with adjectives. In indirect discourse (e.g. after a verb of saying) the noun and verbal aspects are well-balanced. The infinitive is the object of a verb, yet it is functioning as a main verb. Because of its verbal aspects the infinitive has voice and tense. It may take an object and be modified by an adverb. In addition to the noun uses listed above, the infinitive behaves as a substantive by being accompanied by a preposition, by an article, and by being qualified by adjectives. With this picture of the Greek infinitive it is easy to see why even the most literal of the English translations cannot render exactly some infinitive constructions.

One can also see why English paraphrase is the only way to convey all the aspects of one Greek infinitive construction.

The participle in Greek is a verbal adjective. As such it has functions associated with the verb in its broadest aspects and also with the adjective in its wide scope. The *adjectival* use of the participle involves all the functions of an adjective in Greek. Like the adjective, the participle may also function as a substantive. In the *circumstantial* use of the participle, though the participle is in agreement with the word it modifies, it presents an additional thought that affects the verbal action. The sentence would be complete without the presence of the participle, but the additional thought would be lacking. Because of the context, this additional thought may involve such ideas as purpose, time, cause, condition, concession, means, manner. The participle itself says, for example, "having seen" (Matt. 2:10). The context provides the basis for the translation "When they saw [having seen] the star, they rejoiced very much with intense joy." The *supplementary* use of the participle is found where the participle supplements another verb. Without the participle the other verb would be powerless to convey any meaning. The periphrastic construction (usually the verb "to be" in finite form plus participle) is one type of supplementary participle. The participle following such verbs as "begin," "continue," "cease," etc. is also supplementary. "... on behalf of you we did not cease *praying* and *asking* that . . ." (Col. 1:9). The participle in indirect discourse can be classified as a supplementary participle as well: "Know that Timothy, our brother, has departed[21] (and is absent) [from me]" (Heb. 13:23). The phrase "has departed (and is absent)" is a participle in Greek. In the *independent participle* the participle is used as the main verb in a sentence. Or it may be used in a clause where it is the main verbal element, the clause itself being grammatically independent from the sentence in which it is found. As a main verb in a sentence the participle is used as an imperative and as the indicative. In clauses one finds the nominative absolute (rare), the accusative absolute (very rare), and the genitive absolute (common). Thus the versatility of the Greek participle and its frequency means that the interpreter must watch these grammatical units carefully. The participle often can be construed syntactically in two ways. Sometimes there is no difference in meaning. Other times there is. Commentaries may not help. The commentator himself may not have seen the two possibilities, or because he was limited in

---

21 See Bauer, *op. cit.*, p. 96: 2.b. and 3.

space he may have given only the possibility which seemed best to him or which most other commentators have supported.

Adverbs in Greek, like adverbs in English, modify verbs, adjectives, adverbs, and occasionally also they modify substantives. Often an adverb may be translated in more than one way. For example, when Jesus healed the deaf man with a speech impediment in Decapolis, he asked those who brought the man not to spread the news abroad. But the more Jesus tried to stop the news from spreading, the more they proclaimed these tidings. In their amazement Christ's admirers said: "He has done everything very well indeed [or 'splendidly,' 'in the right way']; he even makes the deaf to hear and the dumb to speak" (Mark 7:37). The adverb "very well indeed" brings into focus their evaluation of Jesus. This last miracle seemed to build the evidence to towering heights. The adverb captures their feeling.

Conjunctions connect sentences, clauses, phrases, and words. In Greek there are two main kinds. Coordinate conjunctions join together elements which are grammatically equal. Subordinating conjunctions join together unequal grammatical elements, usually a dependent clause to an independent clause. Hence subordinate conjunctions and dependent clauses belong together. The coordinating conjunctions may be adversative ("but," "except"), emphatic ("yea," "certainly," "in fact," etc.), inferential ("therefore," "then," "wherefore," "so"), explanatory ("now," "for instance"), transitional or continuative ("and," "moreover," "then," etc.), causal (i.e., ground or reason: "because," "for"), adjunctive ("also"), ascensive ("even"), and responsive (in dialogue: "in reply," "in response," "in return"). For the variety of meanings possessed by both coordinate and subordinate conjunctions the interpreter should consult Bauer's lexicon. To observe conjunctions will help the interpreter: "Christ freed us for the freedom [see Gal. 4:21-31]. *Therefore,* keep standing firm and cease being loaded down again with a yoke of bondage" (Gal. 5:1). This "therefore, stand" has a real basis in Paul's context. Understanding his reason for inserting this inferential conjunction gives us a new concept of Christian freedom. In such a freedom the Christian is to stand firm.

One finds these kinds of particles in Greek: negatives, emphatic or intensive particles, interrogative particles, and particles of affirmation and confirmation. The negative *ou* in Greek is a clearcut negation while the negative *mē* involves a qualified negation. In questions, *ou* expects an affirmative answer while *mē* anticipates a negative answer. Often the emphatic or intensive particles are not translated although the original author used them to intensify the idea (see *men* and *ge* in Phil. 3:8). The interrogative particles are important because questions play a large role in the teachings of the New Testament. To the *ei* in Acts 1:6 ("Are you at this time restoring the kingdom to Israel?") Jesus gave a clearcut answer in Acts 1:7-8: "The knowing of the times or seasons which the Father placed under his own authority is not yours [to know]." The affirmatory particles often re-enforce a statement which immediately precedes: "Blessed are the dead who from now on are dying in the Lord. *Certainly* [*or indeed*] the Spirit declares that they will rest from their toils [labors] because their deeds go along with them" (Rev. 14:13).

Hebrew. Under the verb in Hebrew one may discuss *tense, stem, mood, voice, person, number, infinitive, participle, adverb, conjunction,* and *particle.* Although the categories are the same as in Greek, the function of these elements is different in Hebrew. Yet all these functions observed by grammarians are most pertinent for the interpreter. The meaning carried through these elements can be grasped in part even though one cannot accurately describe the syntax. But to know what each particular mechanism of language involves, what possibilities it offers in meaning and translation, and how this syntactical construction is related to the other constructions brings the interpreter to a higher level of understanding.

The Hebrew tenses of perfect and imperfect involve two kinds of action. The perfect tense presents action as *complete* whether this action is in the past, the present, or the future. The imperfect tense presents action as *incomplete* whether it is in the past, the present, or future. Snaith argues for a third tense which is both complete and incomplete because it involves action in the future (immediate or more distant) which in the mind of the prophet is certain to be fulfilled. He maintains that the perfect tense in Hebrew with the strong *waw* is the Akkadian "permansive" and he describes it as "definitely a present-future tense."[22] Snaith has the form clearly identified but his description of the function is not clear. Tense in Hebrew denotes basically kind of action. Whether it occurs in the past, present, or future, whether the action is continuous, momentary, attempted, or initiated—these are all determined by context. The forms and structure of tense in Hebrew cannot convey these differences.[23] Under tense in Hebrew one does

---

[22] Snaith, *op. cit.*, p. 222.
[23] See Barr, *op. cit.*, pp. 80-81: "The main point is that systematic morphological distinctions such as tense are abstractions from the totality of an action referred to...."

have conjugations or stems. The simple stem is called the Qal: "He *kills*." the passive and reflexive of the Qal is the Niphal: "He *kills himself*," "he *is killed*." The intensive active stem is the Piel: "The slaves *massacred* their masters." The intensive passive stem is the pual: "The masters *were massacred*." The causative active stem is the Hiphil: "Jealousy *caused him to kill* his brother." The causative passive stem is the Hophal: "Jealousy *caused his brother to be killed*." The intensive reflexive is called the Hithpael: "In order to carry out orders, the faithful soldiers *massacred themselves* when they entered into battle horribly outnumbered." Very few verbs appear in all tense stems. But the great variety of meaning here gives to Hebrew a richness in its verbs that compensates for lack of distinctions in time and kind of action.

Mood in Hebrew is different from Greek. Positive commands are expressed in the imperative mood, second person singular or plural. The cohortative imperfect is an imperfect first person singular or first person plural with an *âh* or *ĕh* attached to the form. The cohortative stresses the resolve, determination, and interest of the one who is carrying out the action. Just as the cohortative is a lengthened form of the imperfect so the jussive is sometimes a shortened form of the imperfect although it may be the same form as a regular imperfect. It is found in the second and third persons, singular and plural. It expresses a conviction, persuasion, or desire that something should or should not happen: "Let there be light" (Gen. 1:3). "May Jehovah lift up his face unto thee and may he establish peace for thee" (Num. 6:26). In these uses of mood one sees clearly the attitude of the speaker. Whether he speaks in the first, second, or third person, there is a sense of urgency about action which should or should not happen. As in similar constructions in other languages, here the interpreter comes close to the speaker or writer himself. He can often catch a glimpse of the man's inner responses and aspirations.

In the area of voice Hebrew has two voices: active and passive. The following stems are active: Qal, Niphal (when reflexive), Piel, Hiphil, and Hithpael. The following stems are passive or may be occasionally used as passives: Qal (participle), Niphal, Pual, Hophal, and Hithpael (rare). Thus in either the simple stem of ordinary statements and affirmations, or the intensive, causative, or reflexive stems, the subject may act or be acted upon.

Like other inflected languages, person and number in Hebrew indicates clearly who is the speaker. In the perfect tense there are two forms for the third person singular (masc. and fem.), two forms for the second person singular (masc. and fem.), and one form for the first person singular. In the plural, only the second person has two forms (masc. and fem.). The third and the first persons have only one form for both masculine and feminine. In the imperfect tense in both the singular and plural there are two forms (masc. and fem.) for the third and second persons. In the first person there is one common form in the singular and one common form in the plural for both masculine and feminine. Hebrew has grammatical gender as well as physical gender. The nouns "stone" *('ĕvĕn)*, "wind," "spirit" *(ruach)*, "light" *('or)*, etc., are all feminine (with rare exceptions). The nouns "vision" *(chazōn)*, "flesh" *(basar)*, "rock, cliff" *(tzur)*, and "crag, cliff" *(sela")*, etc., are all masculine. So the gender, number, and person in the verb form help to clarify what is the exact subject of the verb. In Daniel 9:27 the last clause is translated in various ways in English translations. Yet the subject of this part of a difficult verse is very clear: "But strict decision [or that which is strictly determined] will pour forth on the horror causer." "Strict decision" is a feminine Niphal participle of *charatz*. It functions as a noun and is subject of the verb "to pour forth" *(nathak)*. This verb is in the Qal imperfect, third feminine singular, in order to agree with its subject. The form of the verb is the same as a second person masculine singular. But there is no "you" (masc. sing.) in the context to function as subject. In contrast the feminine noun precedes this verb.

The infinitive in Hebrew as in Greek is a verbal noun. In most stems there are two forms of the infinitive. The shorter form is called the infinitive construct and the longer form is the infinitive absolute. The infinitive construct is flexible and versatile. The infinitive absolute by comparison is rather rigid and inflexible. The infinitive absolute emphasizes the idea of the verb in the abstract.[24] The agent of the action in the verb, and the time and mood under which it takes place, are of no concern to the infinitive absolute. Being a verbal noun, the infinitive absolute may function as subject, predicate, object, or as a noun governed by another noun (genitive). It can take an object. It is used as an adverbial accusative: "And I will feed you knowledgewise and insightwise" (Jer. 3:15). It is commonly used to strengthen and intensify the idea of the main verb: "Thou shalt surely die" (Gen. 2:17). The infinitive absolute is sometimes used as a substitute for the finite verb. In this way it is used for an imperative in Deuteronomy 5:12: "Keep [Qal

24 See Gesenius-Kautzsch-Cowley, pp. 122-23; 339-40.

infin. absolute] the day of the Sabbath to observe it as holy [Piel infin. construct] just as Jehovah thy God commanded thee." The infinitive construct is far more frequent than the infinitive absolute. As a verbal noun it is used as subject, object, and genitive. It is used frequently with prepositions (this is not true of the infinitive absolute) which constructions, because of the verbal element, are often translated in English as clauses (temporal, causal, purpose, or aim). The construct itself takes an object. In a construction characteristic of Hebrew the subject of the action described by the construct is often in the noun which follows the construct: "... as the loving of Jehovah the sons of Israel" (Hos. 3:1). The frequency and importance of the Hebrew infinitive should not be overlooked.

The Hebrew participle is a verbal adjective. Only the Qal stem has two participles—an active and a passive participle. In the rest of the stems the participles follow the pattern of the stem. Hence the Piel participle will be an intensive active participle while the Pual will be an intensive passive participle, etc. The active participles depict the person or thing as being engaged without interruption in the exercise of the activity indicated by the verb. The passive participle pictures the person or thing in a state brought about by the external actions of someone else or something else. The time of such activity is determined by the context. Participles take objects which are either in the accusative case or are nouns and pronouns preceded by a preposition. Passive participles may be in a shortened form (construct) followed by a noun which is under the government or rule of the participle: "Blessed is he who is *forgiven in respect of* transgression, *covered in respect of* sin" (Ps. 32:1). Very frequently the participle is used as a predicate. This means that it functions as a finite verb (or at least as a main verb in a "subordinate" clause: "And Lot *sat* in the gate of Sodom" Gen. 19:1). The Hebrew participle, though it does not have the versatility of the Greek participle, is vibrant with action, alive with meaning, and descriptive of all aspects of human existence.

Hebrew, like all other languages, has its own ways of forming adverbs, but the adverb in Hebrew functions much as it does in other languages. The intensity of action in Hebrew verbs and nouns makes the adverb all the more forceful. Note the action in this proverb and the forcefulness of the adverb: "A man of reproofs who stiffens his neck will *suddenly* be broken in pieces and there is no cure [healing]" (Prov. 29:1).

The study of Hebrew conjunctions shows that Hebrew is a paratactic language, i.e., the emphasis of the language is on coordinate construction. The Hebrew language uses subordination, but coordinate construction plays the dominant role. In Hebrew, coordinate construction is expressed without conjunctions. However, the Hebrew *waw* *(w^e)* is used in coordinate construction, e.g. in a continuative sense and in an adversative sense. The use of this same word in subordinate clauses seems strange to the Greek student because he knows that he must depend solely on context to determine which it is—a fact which makes Hebrew clauses puzzling to nearly all Hebrew students. The *waw* for example may introduce circumstantial clauses, causal clauses, comparative clauses, purpose clauses, result clauses, etc.[25] The subordinate conjunctions in Hebrew are not confined to object clauses, causal clauses, temporal clauses, etc. For example, the conjunction *kiy* in Hebrew is used in object clauses, clauses introducing direct narrative, causal clauses, conditional clauses, asseverative or confirmatory clauses, adversative and exceptive clauses, temporal clauses, and result clauses.[26] Hebrew does not have as many conjunctions and phrases as Greek, but it uses extensively the ones it has.

Hebrew, likewise, has only a limited number of particles. But particles are found in interjections, exclamations, oaths, and negatives. Their function is similar to those found in other languages. The Hebrew interjection *hinneh* (behold!) takes up four pages and eighteen columns in Mandelkern's concordance.[27] A shorter form, *hēn,* extends to almost two columns in this concordance. Note how majestically Isaiah 42 begins with the interjection: *"Behold* my servant, whom I uphold, my elect [or chosen] one, in whom my soul delighteth." What Hebrew lacks in variety it makes up in quantity of usage so far as interjections are concerned. The negative *lō',* like *ou* in Greek, is used for objective and unconditional negation. On the other hand *'al,* like the Greek *mē,* expresses a subjective and conditional negative.

English equivalents. The student should use a fairly literal English translation to become aware of syntactical equivalents for these Greek and Hebrew verb constructions. For some of these constructions only the person who is trained in Greek and Hebrew can recognize the English rendering which is conveying, say, a Greek middle voice or a Hebrew cohortative. Yet others of these the English student can note. For example, these English renderings, "I speak," "I was speaking," and "I spoke"

---

[25] *Ibid.,* paragraph 154.
[26] *Ibid.,* p. 555.
[27] Mandelkern, *op. cit.,* pp. 335-39.

would be the equivalent to the Greek present *(laleō)*, the Greek imperfect *(elaloun)*, and the Greek aorist *(elalēsa)*. "I have spoken" equals the Greek perfect *(lelalēka)*, active voice. "I have been addressed (or spoken to)" corresponds to the Greek perfect passive *(lelalēmai)*. The simple "he that believeth on the Son" expresses the linear or durative action in the verb. Faith or committal of oneself to Christ involves a constant trust. Though other tenses are used in Greek, the frequency of the present tense when it comes to faith or trust should not escape the interpreter's attention. Because the verb is such a basic part of both Greek and Hebrew, the interpreter should be aware of the main elements and how they function.

Noun

Greek. The following elements may be classified under the category of noun: *case, preposition, adjective, pronoun,* and *article.* An inflected language differs from English, but the over-all function of these syntactical elements should be familiar to the English student.

In studying cases in Greek, one must decide between two schools of thought. One says that the number of cases is controlled by case forms and functions within that case form. The other holds that historical grammar and case functions should determine the number of cases. Those who have taken the former point of view have been five-case grammarians (with many variations) while those who have taken the latter point of view have been eight-case grammarians (also with some variety). This writer is a modified five-case grammarian because he holds to the importance of form (descriptive syntactic morphology) while also noting the main functions associated with each form. The following chart presents a summary of cases in Greek.

Case	Basic Idea or Ideas	Particular Uses
1. Nominative	Specific designation	Of subject, predicate, to introduce names, parenthetical assertions.
2. Vocative	Address	Vocative case form with ō [voc. case form is really stem of word]. Nominative form used as vocative.
3. Genitive		
a. Genitive Proper	Specifies by definition, description, or qualitative differentiation	Of possession, of relationship, partitive, of quality (description), of time or place, with

Case	Basic Idea or Ideas	Particular Uses
		adjectives and adverbs, with nouns of action—subjective and objective genitives, of apposition, of price or value, of material or content, of direction and purpose, of agency, in absolute construction, with verbs whose meaning causes their object to be in the genitive rather than in the accusative (verbs of sensation; of emotion or personal response; of sharing, partaking, filling; of ruling; of buying, selling, being worthy of; of accusing and condemning).
b. Ablatival Genitive	Separates by noting point of departure, by distinguishing persons or things so as to set them apart as distinct in their context	Of separation, of source, of means or agency, of comparison, with verbs (of departure and removal; of ceasing and abstaining; of missing, lacking, and despairing; of differing and excelling).
4. Dative		
a. Dative Proper	Personal interest	Of indirect object, advantage or disadvantage, possession, respect, with verbs (serve; show, reveal; tell to; censure, command; trust, obey; be angry, envy, thank, owe), with adjectives (having meanings similar to above verbs).
b. Instrumental-associative dative	Means or association	Of means, of cause of personal relations, of accompanying circumstances and manner, with adjectives and adverbs, with verbs (follow; draw near; join, have fellowship with; have intercourse with, either friendly or hostile; make use of; be like).
c. Locative dative	Location or position	Of place, time, and sphere.
5. Accusative	Limitation or extension	Of direct object, with verbs of fearing and of swearing, cognate accusative, double accusative, of respect or reference, adverbial accusative, of extent (space or time).

This chart is not exhaustive. But it conveys the main ideas and the subordinate uses associated with the cases in Greek. Since nouns, pronouns, adjectives, infinitives, and participles all function in case relations, the interpreter never fails to get a good workout when he asks: "What is the particular case usage here and how can I express in English the thought which the writer intends to convey?"

Prepositions are used often in Greek. Adverbial prepositions (sometimes called "improper" prepositions) are words which sometimes function as adverbs and at other times function as prepositions. An adverb qualifies a verb by modifying its action, motion, or state. This may be in terms of manner, place, time, or extent. A preposition, although it may have some of these functions, is primarily concerned with the *direction* and *relative position* of the verb's action, motion, or state. Prepositions are helping words (i.e., they help to make clear the relationships that cases are also employed to convey). They help to make more precise what the verbal idea is asserting. Prepositions may be either separate, preceding the noun and standing as independent words, or they may be compounded with verbs or nouns. If no preposition were used, the case alone would eventually be enough to give the reader the right idea. But he would have to ponder hard and long over the context. With the preposition the precise idea is often much easier to discover. Paul tells about Epaphroditus, who "drew near until death [or came close to dying] *because of* the work of Christ" (Phil. 2:30). The Greek preposition *dia* shows that the work of Christ was the reason for Epaphroditus' illness. But if the *dia* were not there, we could not easily tell whether "the work" was in the accusative or nominative case since the form of neuter nouns is the same. We would very likely assume that "the work" was nominative and supply a "him" for the object. This would result in the wrong translation: "The work of Christ brought him close to death." Eventually we might come upon the idea and translation: "He came close to dying for the work of Christ." But the presence of the preposition and the accusative case enables us to settle upon this translation as the right one quickly and with little effort. The five-case grammarian finds it easy to classify prepositions in the New Testament in terms of the case that follows them. Some prepositions are followed by only one case. Others may have one case in one context but a different case in another. Still others may be followed by one of three cases depending upon what the author wanted to convey in a given context. Basic meanings of a preposition, case that follows it, and context that surrounds it all help to unfold the meaning of a preposition in a particular passage. When a preposition is compounded with another verb, the resulting compound may intensify the meaning of the simple verb or noun, it may alter that meaning, or because of frequency of use, the compound may have the same meaning as the simple verb or noun. Prepositions are important and the student should consult frequently Bauer's lexicon on these words.

Adjectives in Greek are descriptive. When adjectives function as adjectives they may be attributive or predicate. There are two forms of the attributive adjective: (1) "the *faithful* brother" (I Pet. 5:12); (2) "the witness, the *faithful* [one]" (Rev. 1:5). The predicate adjective is like English: "But the Lord is *faithful . . .* " (II Thess. 3:3). The adjective "faithful" can also have the meaning "cherishing faith or trust." Thus it can be used as a substantive meaning "the believers, i.e., the Christians." Paul speaks of foods "which things God created for a receiving by *the faithful* [or by the believers, i.e., the Christians]" (I Tim. 4:3). Adjectives have three degrees as in English: positive, comparative, and superlative. Many superlative forms of the adjective do not mean the highest degree possible but are rather emphatic—*very* or *exceedingly* great, tall, wide, etc. Since the participle may function in Greek like the adjective, the adjectival construction is common in Greek. In English we have article, adjective, and noun. Greek may do likewise. But in Greek one may also have a much more involved construction. Between the article and the noun with which it agrees there may be an adverb, a participle, and another noun. Jude urges Christians "to contend for *the* once for all having been handed over to the saints *faith*" (Jude 3). No English translation would follow this order. But the order does show how the original writer wanted a particular noun to be modified. Adjectives as modifiers may greatly enrich ideas.

The New Testament is rich in pronouns. There are personal pronouns ("I," "we," "you," etc.), reflexive pronouns ("himself," "themselves," etc.), possessive pronouns used as pronouns ("mine," "yours," etc.) and adjectives, reciprocal pronouns ("one another," etc.), intensive pronouns ("the Spirit himself"), demonstrative pronouns ("this," "that," etc.), relative pronouns ("who," "which," "what," etc.), interrogative pronouns ("who," "which," "what," etc.), indefinite pronouns ("anyone," "anything," etc.), correlative pronouns ("as much as" . . . "so much as," etc.), and pronominal adjectives ("each," "other," etc.). When one understands the nouns for which they stand, the antecedents to which the relatives (definite relatives) refer, the case and particular function of each relative in its context, he is amazed at how much the thought is clarified.

The article in Greek serves as a pointer to individual identity and emphasizes the particularity of that which it modifies. In this connection Greek differs from English in that the article may particularize other parts of speech besides the simple noun or substantive. Articles in Greek are found with infinitives, adverbs, phrases, clauses, and even sentences. Whatever the size of the unit, the whole unit is particularized by the article. The absence of the article indicates quality. The article may be classified by noting its functions and the parts of speech with which it works. (1) The article may function as a pronoun. (2) The article is commonly used with substantives. It denotes the individuality of persons, places, and things. It indicates previous reference to this person, place, or thing. With certain kinds of nouns and with prepositional phrases the article may or may not be present. One needs to consult a grammar as to what the presence or absence of the article in these particular cases means.[28] The article is present and absent with abstract nouns, and with nouns governing a genitive. The presence of the article with proper names, geographical names, and names for people[29] shows great variation. All of these cases involving the presence or absence of the article have their own peculiarities. Yet apart from such instances where it is difficult to explain the presence or absence of the article the basic rule of the particularizing force of the article can be relied upon. (3) The article is found with adjectives used as substantives. In those rare cases where it is absent, the stress is on quality. (4) The article is used with numerals and adverbs. (5) It is used with appositives —an explanatory phrase ("Philip, the evangelist," Acts. 21:8). (6) The article is used with substantives where there are two or more words (adjective, adverb, participle, numeral, etc.) modifying a noun. (7) The article plays a key role in determining whether any modifier (especially an adjective or participle) is in the attributive or predicate position. (8) Occasionally, the article is found with predicate nouns. (9) The article is found frequently with pronouns and pronominal adjectives. (10) The article with two or more substantives connected by *kai* (and) helps to make clear whether the writer is thinking of these substantives as designating the same person or thing or different persons or things. On the whole, where one article is found with two nouns joined by *kai* both nouns refer to the same person

[28] Blass, Debrunner, and Funk, *op. cit.*, paragraphs 253, 254, 255, 256, 257.

[29] *Ibid.*, paragraphs 258, 259.

or thing. Where there are two articles, one with each noun, the identity of each is maintained.[30] In Titus 2:13 the phrase "the great God and our Saviour Jesus Christ" has one article. By this grammatical procedure the writer indicates that the nouns "God" and "Saviour" refer to the same person. One must never be pedantic about the use of the article. Over-refinements are to be avoided. Yet by the presence or absence of the article the Greeks achieved a precision and forcefulness in the use of cases, prepositions, adjectives, pronouns, infinitives, and participles which not only gave beauty to their language but also increased its capacity for expression.

Hebrew. The following elements, in Hebrew, may likewise be classified under the category of noun: *contextual relations of the noun, prepositions, adjectives, pronouns,* and *articles.* As in the verb, so in the noun, Hebrew has its distinctive elements.

Unlike Greek, Hebrew employs no noun case endings or inflected articles. Direct objects in Hebrew are recognized either by the context (as in English), or some form of the particle *'eth* may be placed before the object. The object may have the same root as the verb (cognate accusative)—to sin a sin, to fear a fear etc. Hebrew has double accusatives and adverbial accusatives of place, time, measure, cause, and manner. Prepositions are also used to subordinate nouns to verbs. One of the most common ways for one noun to be related to another noun is by a unique method in Hebrew called the construct state. A noun can have two forms: a regular form and a shortened form. The Hebrew word for "word" is *dâvâr.* Its shortened or construct form is *devăr.* In the phrase "the word of the Lord" the word "word" is in the construct state (ruling noun) and the word "Lord" is in the genitive (ruled noun). As a genitive it would be subjective in the sense that the Lord produces his own word. There are other constructions where the Hebrew genitive has some things in common with the Greek objective and partitive genitive. Yet often the noun which follows the construct is a nearer definition, a further expansion of the ruling noun. Thus Hebrew nouns stand in distinct relationships to each other. The same relationship may be shown in more than one way. Yet each way brings with it certain emphases.

Hebrew has fewer prepositions than Greek (*'el, be, le, min, "al,* etc.), but their variety and range of meaning are very impressive. Not only are they alternatives for the accusative, but *be,* for example, may mean "among," "at," "on," "to trust *in*,"

[30] See A. T. Robertson, *A Grammar of the Greek New Testament,* pp. 785-789.

"to share *in*," "by, with," and "at the cost of." To study Hebrew prepositions, a student should consult a Hebrew lexicon such as Brown, Driver and Briggs which treats prepositions extensively. In this lexicon b^e receives almost three and one half pages.[31] Careful exegetical work demands a painstaking scrutiny of prepositions.

The adjective in Hebrew usually stands after the substantive and agrees with it in gender and number. Comparative and superlative degrees in Hebrew have nothing of the inflectional preciseness of Greek. For the comparative the preposition *min* is with the word following the adjective. In the superlative degree the adjective is made definite either by the article or by a following genitive. By these devices the reader knows that the quality set forth in the adjective is in a class by itself. By the context it becomes clear that this quality belongs to the highest class. Jonah tells about the men of Nineveh who put on sackcloth "from the greatest of them even to the least of them" (Jonah 3:5).

In pronouns, Hebrew has greater simplicity than Greek. Personal pronouns are used for emphasis. They can be used as demonstratives or reflexives. Possessive pronouns are attached to nouns or to substantival elements ("I will restore the ones judging thee, i.e. thy judges," Isa. 1:26). They are not separate words. The demonstrative pronoun *zĕh* usually points out a new person or thing present while *hu'* points out a person or thing already referred to or known. Several interrogative pronouns are available. Dependent relative clauses in Hebrew are adjectival while independent relative clauses are substantival.

The article in Hebrew makes a noun definite or determinate. A genitive following a noun or a pronoun attached to a noun also makes it definite or determinate. In Hebrew the letter *h* (*hē*) usually with a short "a" under it (*hă*) is placed before the noun and the first consonant of the word is strengthened. In contrast to this Hebrew procedure, Aramaic adds an *aleph* (first letter of the alphabet) at the end of the word. The word "king" for example has the same vowels in Aramaic as in Hebrew. So it is spelled exactly the same (*mĕlĕk*, with short e's). To say "the king" in Hebrew the article is placed before the noun and the initial consonant is strengthened by being doubled,—*hammelek*. In Aramaic a short vowel and an aleph are added to the end of the word. Because the end of the word is stressed, the vowel is lengthened. Hence to say "the king" in Aramaic results in the word *mălkâ'* (the ' = aleph). Aramaic and Hebrew here

---

[31] BDB, pp. 88-91.

differ only in the method by which they make a noun definite or determinate. The article in Hebrew is used with individual persons, places, and things. It is used with adjectives which modify substantives. It is used with titles, with classes—"the lion," "the enemy," "the Canaanite," etc., and even with the vocative. The article is used with the noun in the genitive case following the construct (shorter form of governing noun)—"the word of the prophet" (Jer. 28:9). As in Greek, the article in Hebrew is also fascinating. Because of its demonstrative background it retains the force of a pointer. Since the genitive alone makes the preceding Hebrew noun definite, English translations must put the article with the governing noun although in Hebrew it occurs only with the second noun (or not at all). Abraham's servant is to swear by "Jehovah, the God (no article in Hebrew) of the Heavens (article in Hebrew) and the God (no article in Hebrew) of the Earth (article in Hebrew)" (Gen. 24:3). The article, then, does give the interpeter a good clue to the proper placing of emphasis.

English Equivalents. The student who observes Greek and Hebrew nouns, prepositions, and the like in a fairly literal English translation will find connections and relationships which open new horizons of thought. When he studies Hebrew and Greek he will begin to see still more, until at last he can look at the connections of ideas for himself. Over and over again he will find that the firsthand look brings a fresh awareness of truth.

Clauses

Clauses can perform all the main functions previously attributed to verbs and nouns, although they are, of course, larger units of language.

Greek. We first consider the *structural relation* of Greek clauses, and then the various kinds: *relative, causal, comparative, local, temporal, purpose, result, conditional, concessive,* and *substantival. Indirect discourse* together with *commands* and *prohibitions* round out the picture.

Clauses are either coordinate (both independent) or subordinate (at least one independent clause and one or more dependent clauses). The dependent clauses function as substantives, adjectives, or adverbs.

Relative clauses function either as adjectives or substantives. Adverbial flavors (e.g. causal, concessive, conditional) which are sometimes associated with relative clauses are due entirely to context. The clause itself is strictly adjectival or substantival. The relatives are often translated "who," "which," "whoever," etc. The most common conjunctions introducing relative clauses are the relative pronouns *hos, hostis.*

Causal clauses may be either coordinate or subordinate. The Greek word *gar* often introduces coordinate causal clauses. Numerous particles and phrases introduce the subordinate causal clauses. These clauses are adverbial and state the ground or reason for action: "And the hope [the one just mentioned] does not disappoint *because* the love which God bestows has been poured forth in our hearts" (Rom. 5:5).

Comparative clauses are also adverbial and often answer the question "how." The comparison has greater meaning if the interpreter understands exactly what is being compared. In Ephesians, husbands are told: "Love your wives just as Christ loved the Church" (5:25). If the reader does not know how Christ loved the Church, then the comparison is of little value. But if he does, then the command followed by this adverbial clause of "how" makes him aware of how poorly he loves his wife and how great his love ought to be.

Local clauses are adverbial and answer the question "where." "Where I am going, you are not able to come" (John 8:21-22). In examining such clauses the interpreter should ask: "Why is the place important?" In the Johannine passage the very next verse (vs. 23) clarifies why the same local clause in two succeeding verses is so important.

Temporal clauses are obviously adverbial. In Greek the temporal limitation may be either stated as definite or assumed to be real. In such cases the indicative mood (stress on actuality of verbal idea) is used in the temporal clause. However, where the temporal clause refers to the future, is an indefinite possibility, or if its temporal aspect is in any way contingent, then the subjunctive mood (mood of possibility) is employed in the temporal clause. The indicative mood is employed in the following example: "But when the fulness of the time came, God sent forth his son born from a woman, born under the law . . ." (Gal. 4:4). Notice how the temporal clause refers to a definite past action. At the exact time that God wanted, Jesus Christ was born, lived among men, died, and rose again. To meditate upon this temporal clause in its relationship to the main verb brings the interpreter face to face with God's control of history. In another kind of temporal setting the subjunctive mood is found: "Count it all joy, my brothers, whenever you fall into a situation where you are surrounded by various trials" (James 1:3). The action in this temporal clause is future. The believer should count it all joy on those occasions when the trials of life put pressure upon him. The uncertainty here lies in the exact time when these trials will come, but not in the fact that they *will* come. This is the reason for the subjunctive mood in temporal clauses in Greek.

Clauses or expressions of purpose in Greek are introduced by such conjunctions as *hina* and *hopōs*, by the infinitive by itself and with *tou*, by the articular infinitive and article with the prepositions *eis* and *pros*, etc. Negative purpose is expressed by *hina mē* and by *mē*. One needs only to meditate upon purpose clauses to see their significance. In Ephesians 5:25 Paul tells how Christ handed himself over on behalf of the Church. In the next two verses there are three *hina* clauses of purpose stating why Christ handed himself over to suffering and death: (1) to consecrate or sanctify the Church, (2) to present the Church to himself as glorious (splendid, i.e., brilliant in purity), and (3) to make the Church to be holy and without blame. Christ's action becomes more significant in the light of these purposes.

Result in the New Testament is expressed by *hōste* with the infinitive, rarely with the indicative, and occasionally in still other ways. Take the example in II Corinthians 3:7-8 of *hōste* and the infinitive: "If the ministry of death having been engraved in stone letters originated in splendor [glory, radiance], as a result [so that] the sons of Israel were not able to gaze at the face of Moses . . . . how much more . . . ." The divine origin of the Mosaic law had certain results. One of these left its imprint upon the face of Moses. Moses' use of a veil to conceal the departure of the radiance is developed later in the chapter (vss. 12-18). This result clause earlier in the chapter contains an idea which dominates the thought of the apostle in this section of II Corinthians.

Conditional sentences in the New Testament are common. In technical language the conditional part ("if . . .") is called the *protasis*. The conclusion is called the *apodosis*. The key to conditions in Greek is the mood (indicative, subjunctive, or optative) found in the conditional part of the sentence. The condition may be assumed as real, as unreal, as possible, and as remotely possible. There are places where what is assumed as unreal, for example, is not unreal at all (cf. Luke 7:39). But on the whole, the assumptions of the writers or speakers correspond to the facts of the case. In Matthew 12:27, for the sake of argument, Christ assumes the position of the Pharisees that he casts out demons by Beelzebub. He frames his conclusion as a question to show the serious implications for the Pharisees of such an assumption. In the next verse, however, he assumes what is in fact true: "Since I by the Spirit of God cast out demons, then the reign of God has come to you." The assumption is valid, and consequently the conclusion is of great importance as well. Christ's miracles and his power over the demons were only samples of what the reign of God will be in its fulness. But in these samples, the reign of God was actually present. The age to come had broken through in mighty power. Modern scholars may continue to speculate as to whether Jesus proclaimed a present or future reign of God, or whether he proclaimed both. But in this condition (Matt. 12:28) assumed as real and in the conclusion which follows, there can be no doubt as to what the New Testament record says. The reign of God had come. It was and is a live option for men.

Concessive clauses differ from conditional clauses in Greek in the way that the conclusion is related to the concession proper. In the conditional sentence just discussed, the conclusion is the logical outcome of the condition. In a concessive clause, the conclusion is asserted in spite of the content of the concessive clause. "Though our outward man is being destroyed, certainly our inward man is being renewed day after day" (II Cor. 4:16). In spite of the existential fact that the Christian's physical condition is deteriorating, Paul proclaims the increasing soundness of the inner, spiritual man.

Substantival clauses in Greek are used as subject, as object, or in apposition. The following constructions are found in all of these functions: the infinitive, the conjunction *hoti*, and the conjunction *hina*. Note how a *hina* clause is used in John 15:8: "My Father is glorified in this, that [*hina*] you bear much fruit." The clause is in apposition to the "this" *(en toutōi)*. The present tense in this apposition clause shows that a Christian is to be constantly producing fruit. This kind of action glorifies or extols the father.

Indirect discourse in Greek is really a distinct form of an object clause. There are indirect statements, indirect questions, and indirect commands. This is part of the rhetorical style of the writer. All of these could be expressed in direct statements, in direct questions, or in direct commands. In Luke 11:18, for example, the words of the Pharisees are recorded in an indirect statement: "Because you say that I cast out demons by Beelzebub." With indirect discourse, it is well to state what the form of the direct discourse would have been. In this way the vividness of direct discourse is kept before the mind of the interpreter.

Commands and prohibitions in Greek are independent

clauses. Their frequency brings to the New Testement a note of authority. The present tense of the imperative stresses continuous or repeated action. The aorist tense of the imperative emphasizes wholeness of action. In prohibitions, the present imperative urges the ceasing of that which is already in progress: "Stop being deceived, my beloved brothers" (James 1:16). The aorist subjunctive carries the idea of "do not begin to do this or that." "If, therefore, they say to you, 'Behold, he is in the desert,' do not begin to go out; 'Behold, he is in one of the inner [secret] rooms,' do not begin to believe it" (Matt. 24:26).

Hebrew. The Hebrew language also has distinctive features in *the structural relation* of clauses. Then Hebrew, like Greek, has *relative clauses, causal clauses, comparative clauses, local clauses, temporal clauses, purpose clauses, result clauses, conditional clauses, concessive clauses, substantival object clauses, disjunctive, adversative,* and *exceptive clauses,* and finally *prohibitions.*

Sentences or clauses in Hebrew are broken up into two classes: noun clauses and verbal clauses. In noun clauses the subject consists of nouns or their equivalents (such as participles): "Now the men of Sodom [were] wicked and sinners" (Genesis 13:13). Usually there is no verb expressed. For a predicate the verb "to be" is simply assumed as in the above example. In verb clauses the subject is a noun (or pronoun with verb) and the predicate is a finite verb: "And many nations will come . . . " (Micah 4:2). The noun clauses tend to emphasize a state or being. The verbal clauses tend to emphasize movement and action. With this basic structure in mind, the interpreter can see why the Semitic languages are coordinate in structure. The coordinate elements may function like subordinate clauses in other languages. Nevertheless, structurally, the language is made up primarily of grammatically independent units.

Relative clauses in Hebrew are adjectival units that are dependent either on a noun or a substantive, thereby standing as independent nominal expressions. The most common conjunction for relative clauses in Hebrew is *'asher,* but one also finds *zeh, zo, zu,* and sometimes the article. Unlike Greek both noun and verbal clauses in Hebrew may function as relative clauses without any relative pronouns as indicators. Because of context simple coordination in structure may involve subordination in thought: "Happy [is] the man [who] seeks refuge in Him" (Ps. 34:9 [34:8, Eng. txt.]). The above sentence reads literally: "Happy, the man; he seeks refuge in Him." The absence of an actual relative pronoun does not obscure the fact that the verse is really a unit consisting of two parts: a command for action ("taste and see that Jehovah is good") and a promise of blessing ("happy is the man who seeks refuge in Him"). Purely contextual connections allow for differences of opinion as to whether the clause is relative, causal, temporal, etc. Usually the context gives adequate grounds for preferring one possibility.

The causal clause in Hebrew may be a coordinate clause introduced by *waw*, or the causal clause may be introduced by a whole variety of conjunctions, *kiy* being one of the most common. In Isaiah 6:5 there are three *kiy* clauses. The first tells the cause or reason for Isaiah's declaration: "Woe is me." In these three clauses we see: (1) the effect of the vision upon the prophet himself, (2) his awareness of his own condition and that of his people, (3) his own vivid meeting with God—"My eyes have seen the king, Jehovah of hosts." The last two clauses are dependent on the first one and tell why the prophet is so shaken. "I am undone [ruined] *because* I am a man of unclean lips and I dwell in the midst of a people of unclean lips *because* my eyes have seen the king, Jehovah of hosts." If the interpreter will only reflect upon clauses like this, he will be able to enter more fully into the experience of the prophet. The sharing of an experience is essential for the interpretation of the meaning of the experience.

Comparative clauses in Hebrew are found in two coordinate clauses joined by a *waw*, the second of which provides the comparison. Sometimes even the *waw* is missing. Comparative clauses are also found with conjunctions *(ka'ᵃsher, 'ᵃsher, kēn)*. "And Jehovah spoke unto Moses face to face *just as* a man speaks unto his friend" (Exod. 33:11). How apt are such clauses to convey the nature of Moses' encounter with God!

Local clauses in Hebrew are actually a species of circumstantial clauses. These clauses may be either noun or verbal clauses. They tell the how or the where of the action. "And Abraham pitched his tent, Bethel on the west and Ai on the east" (Gen. 12:8). Local clauses are also introduced by conjunctions—e.g. *'ᵃsher* or compounds of *'ᵃsher*.[32] Note Elisha's words to the Shunammite woman: "Arise and go, thou and thy household and sojourn *in the place where (ba'ᵃsher)* you may sojourn because Jehovah has called for a famine, and it will surely come unto the land for seven years" (II Kings 8:1). The local clause is followed by a causal clause. Thus in this one verse the interpreter is confronted with the importance of the

---

[32] See BDB., 4.b.beta, gamma, p. 82.

Hebrew clause as a key element to get at the meaning. Elisha is rather indefinite as to where the woman should go and very definite as to why she must go. Thus uncertainty and certainty have a place in the prophet's command.

Temporal clauses in Hebrew occur with two clauses joined by *waw* or *hinnēh*, with two clauses placed side by side without any connective or exclamatory adverb, and with numerous conjunctions that introduce clauses of time. For example, take the temporal phrase *"adth 'asher*: "I will go and I will return unto my place, *until* they bear their punishment, and they will seek my face, in their distress they will seek me earnestly" (Hosea 5:15). Hebrew is rich in temporal constructions. The quantity or extent of time is not always specified. This is left in the hands of God. But the kind or quality of time (the existential now) is often stated. This is clear in the passage from Hosea. God returns to his place until the Israelites bear their punishment. The temporal period is one of experiencing divine punishment. Inherently, quality of time is more important than quantity of time. Temporal elements usually include both, but some moderns tend to be too preoccupied with quantitative considerations of time. Biblical writers stress the qualitative or content aspects of time. Note Psalm 110:1: " . . . sit at my right hand *until* I make thy enemies as a footstool for thy feet." Quantity of time is not important here. But the quality or content of what takes place during the period of sitting is all important.

Purpose clauses may be introduced by a *waw* at the beginning of a second coordinate clause. There are a number of conjunctions that introduce subordinate purpose clauses. The content of the purpose clause often discloses the character of the speaker. Note David's words: " . . . Thou art lifting me up from the gates of death *in order that (lᵉma"an)* I may recount all thy praise (Ps. 9:14-15 [13-14 Eng. txt.]).

Result clauses can also be introduced by a *waw* at the beginning of a second coordinate clause: "God is not a man that [as a result] he should lie or the son of man, that [as a result] he should repent" (Numbers 23:19). The common conjunctions *kiy* and *'asher* which introduce many other kinds of clauses also introduce result clauses. Israel is to hear and to observe all of Jehovah's commandments *"that as a result* [so that] it may be well for thee and *as a result* [so that] you may become exceedingly many, as Jehovah the God of thy fathers spoke to thee" (Deut. 6:3).

Conditions in Hebrew reflect the attitude of the speaker or writer. The writer declares whether the condition is capable of fulfillment (conditions dealing with the past disclose this) or is incapable of fulfillment. Conditions may be formulated without the use of conditional conjunctions. Where conditional particles are employed, the use of *'im* or *lu'* (and the tenses utilized with them) indicate whether the condition is already fulfilled, whether the condition may possibly occur in the present or future, whether the condition is represented as not fulfilled in the past, and whether the condition is not capable of being fulfilled in the present or future. The tense employed in both the conditional part of the sentence and in the conclusion illustrate well that in inflected languages conditions are highly complex. Hebrew is no exception. Yet the basic principles are not too difficult to grasp.[33]

Concessive clauses are expressed by coordinate constructions such as the imperative mood and circumstantial clauses. They are also introduced by such expressions as *'im, gam kiy, gam, kiy gam,* and by the preposition *''al.* Isaiah 1:18-20 illustrates both the concessive and conditional use of the same conjunction. In vs. 18 *'im* is concessive because the context (Isa. 1:2-17) shows how rebellious and sinful the people were. In vss. 19-20 the *'im* is conditional. These verses deal with action which is possible in the present and future. If they take one course, God will prosper them. If they take another course, they will suffer adversity. "*Though* your sins be like scarlet [in guilt], they will grow white as snow, *though* they show redness like scarlet stuff, they will be as wool. *If* you [plural] be willing and obedient, you will eat the good of the land. But *if* you refuse and be disobedient, you will be consumed by the sword, because the mouth of Jehovah hath declared it."

Substantival clauses in Hebrew are object clauses used in indirect discourse. After verbs of mental action the reader notes the content of that action. Hence one should look for this kind of object clause after verbs of seeing, hearing, knowing, perceiving, believing, remembering, forgetting, saying, and thinking. The clause may follow such verbs without any conjunction. Sometimes the clause is coordinated with the preceding clause by a *waw*. Usually the object clause is introduced by the conjunctions *kiy* or *'asher*. In object clauses these conjunctions are translated "that." Observe the object clause after the verb of remembering: "And they remembered that God was their rock and the Most High their redeemer" (Ps. 78:35).

---

[33] Gesenius-Kautzsch-Cowley (paragraph 159) do a masterful job of presenting main principles as well as the multitude of small details found in Hebrew conditional sentences. Hebrew, being the kind of language it is, makes such a balance difficult to achieve.

The Hebrew language in clauses can show various alternatives (cf. Ezek. 14:17,19, *'ow*), great contrast (cf. I Sam. 8:19, *kiy 'im*), and make qualifications or exceptions ("Thus is my word which proceeds from my mouth; it will not return to me without effect, *except [kiy 'im]* it do what I delight in and experience prosperity in that to which I sent it," Isa. 55:11). These kinds of constructions give beauty and balance and also profound ideas that are set off in sharp distinction from others.

Prohibitions in Hebrew are expressed by *'al* and the jussive (sometimes a shortened form of the imperfect) or *lo'* with the imperfect. The second of these constructions is the stronger prohibition. An example of the first construction is Proverbs 3:7: *"Do not be wise* in your own eyes." An example of the second construction is Exodus 20:4-5: *Thou shalt not make* for thyself an idol or any representation . . . . *Thou shalt not prostrate thyself* before them and *thou shalt not serve* them . . . ."

English Equivalents. In a literal translation (such as the American Standard Version) the interpreter can observe the presence of one or several clauses in a verse, and in many instances he can observe the kind or kinds of clauses that the translator endeavored to set forth in an English equivalent. However, the English word "that" is very ambiguous. It can designate an object clause, a purpose clause, a result clause, a clause in apposition, etc. In Hebrew the conjunctions can introduce several kinds of clauses. The coordinate *waw* is also employed to introduce several subordinate relations. In fact a clause may follow another clause simply by proximity without any introductory word. Good commentaries list the various possibilities and also tell the reader which one the commentator prefers and why he prefers it. Greek clauses are more precise, but in themselves they are not confined to one possibility. It is the context which brings about the limitation. The conjunction *hina* may introduce purpose clauses, substantival clauses (subject, object, apposition), result clauses, and indirect commands, etc. For this reason the interpreter must closely examine the context. Only rarely does the interpreter find it difficult to determine clause usage after he has thoroughly considered the context.

Principles for the Interpreter of Syntax

1. Have well-marked-up grammars available for consultation. No one can keep all of the details of grammar in his head. With the major points in his mind, the interpreter can use the

particular grammar he needs to find the small detail that may explain the construction and shed light on meaning.

2. Understand the basic elements under verb, whether the passage be in Greek, in Hebrew, or in Aramaic. Look to see whether any of these are carrying important ideas and how the particular function sheds light on the meaning.

3. Understand the basic elements under noun, whether the passage be in Greek, in Hebrew, or in Aramaic.

4. Understand the basic elements under clause, whether the passage be in Greek, in Hebrew, or in Aramaic.

5. Keep in mind that lexicons also give help on syntax—e.g., Bauer lists over a half dozen syntactical uses of *hoti,* see pp. 592-594.

6. Note all the syntactical factors in any one verse or group of verses but pay special attention to the ones which carry the greatest freight of meaning.

7. Consult good commentaries that treat syntax in an adequate manner. Beware of commentaries that habitually give only one syntactical possibility. Sometimes the context overwhelmingly supports one use. Unfortunately, where different doctrinal emphases are made, the context may be the main reason for these possibilities! In using commentaries every interpreter must evaluate the evidence for himself. Do not assume that any particular commentary must be right. Infallibility eludes the grasp of all present-day commentators!

8. Respect the syntactical links as connections forged by another. Do not try to separate what the author joined together. All such separations (for even the most noble of purposes) will only lead to eisegesis (reading in of one's own ideas). Eisegesis is the substitution of the authority of the interpreter for the authority of the original writer.

BIBLIOGRAPHY

Barr, James, *The Semantics of Biblical Language* (1961).
Danker, Frederick W., *Multipurpose Tools for Bible Study* (1960).

VII History and Culture

Since the middle of the nineteenth century grammatical-historical interpretation has been a basic premise of all serious interpreters. Yet with this basic premise there is the constant danger that the study of history and culture may make the background appear more important than the actual content being examined. It is certainly true that without knowledge of history and culture the interpreter may easily fall into many errors. But if he is preoccupied with history and culture, the interpreter can treat the content as secondary to the reconstruction of the original setting. History and culture, then, as secondary elements, are essential for the understanding of content. Out of a complex maze of events and into the agonizing pressures of daily existence, God's message came and confronted men with God himself.

MEANING AND SIGNIFICANCE

History involves the selection of *various factors* which make up the life of an individual, of groups of individuals within a nation, of nations themselves or of groups of nations. On the basis of the factors selected, the historian gives meaning (i.e., his meaning) to the acts or purposes of an individual, a group, or a nation. A record of past events may seem to deal with such impersonal factors as "the history of the automobile." But any given history of the motor car would involve a selection of facts to show how the automobile was developed from a horseless carriage to the latest model. Yet this "thing," i.e. the automobile, turns out to be a composite production of many minds. Consequently, history as it is carried out by historians,

159

or would-be historians, is man-centered. Both the events and the record of the events are called history. Whether the record be written or oral, interpretation is unavoidable. The selection of details is itself a matter of interpretation. The Christian believes that history is the unfolding of God's plan or purpose (Eph. 1:7-11). The Christian cannot center history in man and ignore God. Such a course would be indicative of humanism, idolatry, or both. In Scripture, the actions of men and the actions of God take place in the same historical continuum or course of events. Intellect and emotions as well as the body are a part of the historical process. Each man moves in *one* history. It is there that he meets God, and spiritual life and meaning come to him. History is a God-ordained sequence of experiences in which man discloses his estrangement and hostility to God or his reconciliation to God in Christ. All of the details of life indicate that a man is responding either by further revolt from God or by an ever-deepening commitment to him. Such a view makes meaningless any division of history into the secular and sacred. Secular history appears to be the story of man trying to get along by and with himself. The idea that such independence from God is possible is one of man's sinful delusions (Acts 17:28ff).

Culture

Culture is part of history because it concerns the creative result of man's actions. Culture involves the ways, methods, manners, tools, institutions, and literary productions of any people.[1] These reveal how a people lived, what values they stressed, and why they did or did not prosper. Culture involves the totality which emerges out of the elements that make up everyday life. The terms "Egyptian Culture," "Palestinian Culture," "Greek Culture," etc., are not abstractions. These terms denote the way of life of these people. Idolatry and sorcery as well as the forms of worship of the living God are all a part of a people and their culture.

Divergent Historical Backgrounds

Whatever historical period and background the interpreter attaches to a book, he should make use of all external evidence (historical materials outside the book) and internal evidence (historical materials within the book) which has any bearing

[1] Cf. Ramm, *Protestant Biblical Interpretation*, p. 96.

upon the meaning. Sometimes the internal evidence is such that it could be fitted into several periods. Take the book of Obadiah. Trinquet points out that the book has been dated anywhere between the ninth century B.C. and the Greek epoch. He himself dates the book between 587 and 312.[2] Young puts it before Jeremiah and says that Davis may be right in putting it in the time of Ahaz.[3] This would place the historical setting of the book in the last quarter of the eighth century B.C. Pfeiffer dates one part of the book from 460 B.C. and another part from about 400 B.C.[4] Schultz notes four times when Jerusalem was subjected to invasion.[5] These were by Shishak in the days of Rehoboam (931-913 B.C.), by the Philistines and Arabians in the time of Jehoram (848-841 B.C.), by Joash of Israel in the time of Amaziah (796-781 B.C.), and by Nebuchadnezzar in the period from 605-586. Robinson holds that Obadiah was written after the fall of Jerusalem (587-86) and then proceeds to show what relationship the book may have to Jeremiah 49:7-22 which, he holds, comes *before* the fall of Jerusalem.[6]

All of this may puzzle the reader. If the historical background is uncertain for trained experts, what can the average interpreter do? First, he should recognize that the reconstruction of historical backgrounds is more difficult than first appears. In many instances, after one has looked at all the internal and external evidence he can give good, compelling reasons for putting the writing at some particular time. For some books there is a general consensus. For others, reasons are given for different dates of the book as a whole or of parts of the book. Where there is a difference of opinion, the interpreter should recognize the various viewpoints and have his own reasons for favoring one of these viewpoints.

Second, the interpreter should recognize that the historical situation is more important than the precise historical date. Let us consider Obadiah again. The book deals with: (1) Edom's security (vss. 1-9), (2) Edom's indifference and hostility toward Judah (vss. 10-14), (3) Edom's judgment by the nations in the day of the Lord (vss. 15-16), (4) Edom's judgment by the house of Jacob (vss. 17-18), and (5) Edom's successors (vss. 19-21). The historical situation obviously was one of conflict between two peoples who, be-

2 J. Trinquet, "Abdias," *La Sainte Bible* (1956), p. 987.

3 Edward J. Young, *An Introduction to the Old Testament* (1949), p. 253.

4 Robert H. Pfeiffer, *Introduction to the Old Testament* (1941), pp. 584-586.

5 Samuel Schultz, *The Old Testament Speaks,* p. 404, n. 2.

6 D. W. B. Robinson, "Obadiah," *The New Bible Commentary,* ed. F. Davidson, A. M. Stibbs, and E. F. Kevan (1956), p. 710.

cause of their early ties of blood, should have been friendly toward each other. Instead, the prophet laments of Esau: "You also were as one from them [i.e. the foreign invaders]" (vs. 11). Judah in a dark hour found a brother showing violence rather than help (vs. 10). This is the historical situation. The prophet's words about judgment for Edom, about the day of the Lord being near to all the nations, and about the kingdom being Jehovah's, are the outcome of this situation. But whether the situation occurred in the ninth century, the sixth century, or some other century makes little difference to the understanding of the vision of Obadiah.

On the other hand, some interpreters have placed certain books in a late period so that what the author claims to be a foretelling of future action (both of God and man) had already occurred. The interpreter then insists that the author was really using only another way of writing history. In such cases the interpreter shows that he is controlled by a rationalistic apriori such as this: "If God makes disclosures to man, these must deal only with the past or present." But interpreters who are not controlled by such presuppositions foreign to the main emphases of Scripture will often differ as to the historical settings of some biblical materials. If the basic historical situation is understood, as in the case of Obadiah outlined above, the different historical settings are of no serious consequence.

Finally, complex historical reconstructions and also those that involve some inferential conjecture should be regarded only as working hypotheses rather than as final solutions to historical questions. Some questions tantalize interpreters because they are sure that certain clues will give the answer. Who was the Chronicler (i.e., who put the books of Chronicles into their present form)? When did the Exodus take place? Who wrote Hebrews? Why are there four accounts of the feeding of the five thousand and is there any interdependence involved? Answers to such questions should be viewed as working hypotheses. Questions of this kind are secondary. When we put too much mental energy into secondary tasks and ignore the primary task—for example, the basic emphases of the book of Hebrews—we have lost our vision of what a faithful biblical interpreter is to be doing.

Position in Life and Perspective in Faith

A German phrase, *Sitz im Leben,* has almost become a part of the English language among those who investigate historical backgrounds. This phrase means "life situation." No matter how hard one studies the life situation of the biblical writers, such study by itself will not bring him to the biblical perspective of life in faith. Minear points out that the *Sitz im Leben* is only one part of the picture. There is also the *Sitz im Glauben*,[7] i.e., the "faith situation"—that which brings about a position and perspective in faith. The position of the biblical writers is that of men in a relationship with God. The problems with which they wrestle are not merely problems of *thought* but also problems of *destiny*.[8] How important it is for the interpreter to enter into the biblical perspective! Minear assumes "that there is a recoverable unity in the outer and inner dimension of biblical experience."[9] The biblical perspective and its unity (see Chapter 4) escape the notice of many modern interpreters as they struggle with details. Because the biblical framework is assumed by the original writers rather than being explicitly formulated, Minear tells what this means to him as he considers the contemporary interpreters in their approach to the Bible.

(1) The strangeness of the biblical perspective; (2) the unity of this perspective throughout the biblical period; (3) the futility of trying to understand any segment of thought detached from its hidden context; (4) the germinal power and universal reluctance that emerges whenever that context is uncovered and appropriated; (5) the unsuspected value of the more objectionable patterns of thought in locating distinctive dimensions.[10]

One may begin his study of the Bible as if it were merely a literature of past peoples—the Judaic-Christian heritage. For

7 Paul S. Minear, *Eyes of Faith* (1948), p. 181.
8 *Ibid.*, p. 118.
9 *Ibid.*, p. 1.
10 *Ibid.*, p. 2. Paul Minear's *Eyes of Faith* is a challenging book. He points out in the Introduction the causes of listener resistance to the prophetic point of view (pp. 5-6): (1) the unconscious worship of modernity; (2) the assumption that any ancient point of view is invalidated by defects of the primitive mind; (3) the nest of emotional and intellectual antipathies where minds snuggle down in comfort, and (4) the uneasiness of men in the presence of scathing condemnation of sin, assertion of final authority, and demand for total obedience. The freshness of thought found in this volume is most stimulating. PART I. THE ANGLE OF VISION. 1. God Visits Man. 2. God Chooses Man. 3. God Says, "Choose." 4. Men Seek Other Lovers. 5. God Creates a People. 6. God Appoints Times. 7. Man Builds a House. PART II. THE FOCUS OF VISION. 8. God Conceals His Word. 9. God Reveals His Will to the Prophets. 10. The Prophet Speaks Parables. 11. Signs Witness to the Word. PART III. THE HORIZONS OF VISION. 12. Israel Forgets and Remembers. 13. Israel Despairs and Hopes. 14. Prophets Look Beyond History. PART IV. REVISION OF VISION. 15. The Messiah Comes. 16. The Christian Sees New Horizons. EPILOGUE: TO SEE OR NOT TO SEE.

such an interpreter the *Sitz im Leben* seems to be quite sufficient. But when the interpreter grows aware of the biblical
perspective—God confronting men with himself and men called
upon to choose whom they will serve (Joshua 24:14-15)—then
the *Sitz im Glauben* becomes essential to understanding. The
interpreter must examine both of these dimensions—the hori-
zontal: man and his environment; the vertical: man and his
relationship to God. Only then can he adequately expound the
biblical message.

TOOLS FOR THE INTERPRETER

To study history and culture, the student needs Bible atlases,
histories, and anthropological treatments of peoples and cultures.

Bible atlases are not merely collections of maps. They usually
include a commentary about peoples and nations that came
into contact with Israel and the early Christians. They point
out important literary and archaeological discoveries. Chronological outlines of ancient history are helpful because they show
the history of the patriarchs, Israel, and the early Christians as
it really was—one of interaction with world empires, peoples,
and nations who moved across the horizons of Near Eastern
civilizations. A careful study of maps and of textual explanations will give to the student an indispensable picture of the
setting for the biblical narrative.[11]

Works on historical backgrounds are often long and complex.
Hence we tend to ignore these. However, indices often prove
helpful.[12] One of the tests of a good commentary is whether

[11] Many good atlases have appeared recently. See for example George
Ernest Wright and Floyd V. Filson, *The Westminster Historical Atlas to
the Bible* (1956). Charles F. Pfeiffer *et al* (eds.), *Baker's Bible Atlas* (1961).
Emil G. Kraeling, *Rand McNally Bible Atlas* (1956).

[12] An old work (end of the 19th century—German 4th edition, 1910)
which is extremely helpful and has excellent indices is Emil Schürer, *A
History of the Jewish People in the Time of Jesus Christ*, trans. John Mac-
pherson, Sophia Taylor, and Peter Christie (1890-93). The index to the entire work is in Div. II, Vol. III, at the end of the volume (99 pages in
this index). The index contains the following divisions: Index of Scripture
Passages, of Hebrew Words, of Greek Words, and of Names and Subjects.
For the backgrounds on the Dead Sea Scrolls see Millar Burrows, *The
Dead Sea Scrolls* (1955) ; and Burrows' second book, *More Light on the
Dead Sea Scrolls* (1958). *The Dead Sea Scrolls* has a bibliography on pp.
419-435. *More Light on the Dead Sea Scrolls* has a bibliography on
pp. 411-424. This second volume has an index to both volumes on pp.
425-434. The following volumes are a select list of works covering basic
areas of historical background. William F. Albright, "The Old Testament

the reader is supplied with good notes on historical background in the commentary portion itself. An introductory section on historical background is not enough. For example, a commentary on Paul's Corinthian letters should show in nearly every passage the situation of Paul's original readers. The questions they wanted Paul to answer came straight from their own "life and faith situation." Christianity came to Corinth, a city with a great history and with distinct cultural patterns. Only when these are understood will the reader grasp the significance of some of Paul's statements on marriage (I Cor. 7), on conduct in public meetings (I Cor. 14), on separation from idolatry (II Cor. 6:14-7:1), etc.

Anthropology is valuable because it helps us see how the way of life of the group profoundly influences the actions and responses of the individual. Today in some societies the emphasis is on the group; in others, on the individual. In the biblical materials we also find both emphases.[13]

BASIC ELEMENTS

Geographical Factors

Palestine was in truth the crossroads of the Near East. Through this land marched the great leaders of the world empires. But whether the setting is Palestine, Egypt, Syria, Assyria, Babylonia, Asia Minor, Greece, Italy, or any of the islands of the Mediterranean, the interpreter should know such factors as climate; relation of the setting to the sea, desert, mountains, etc.; roads and the kind of terrain; and how the

World," *The Interpreter's Bible*, I, 233-271. George Ernest Wright, *The Old Testament Against Its Environment* (1950). William Fairweather, *The Background of the Gospels* (1926). Floyd V. Filson, *The New Testament Against Its Environment* (1950). Merrill C. Tenney, *New Testament Survey* (1961), pp. 1-120: "Part I: The World of the New Testament." Morton Scott Enslin, *Christian Beginnings* (1938), pp. 1-143: "Part I, The Background." Robert H. Pfeiffer, *History of New Testament Times* (1949), pp. 1-230: "Part I, Judaism From 200 B.C. to A.D. 200." The best brief survey in terms of maps and pictures as well as text of the Dead Sea scrolls is J. T. Milik, *Ten Years of Discovery in the Wilderness of Judea*, trans. J. Strugnell (1959).

13 For further material on ways of life and culture patterns see Ruth Benedict, *Patterns of Culture* (1934). Alfred Lewis Kroeber, *Anthropology* (1948): VII, The Nature of Culture; VIII, Patterns; IX, Culture Processes; X, Culture Change. Herbert C. Jackson, "The Forthcoming Role of the Non-Christian Religious Systems as Contributory to Christian Theology," *Occasional Bulletin, Missionary Research Library*, XII, No. 3 (March 15, 1961). A cross-cultural perspective should be gained by all interpreters.

people were distributed in the particular geographical situation. When the interpreter is aware of such things, the message he is interpreting or the history which he is reviewing becomes real. Such an interpreter knows that the land of Palestine meant much to the people of Israel. This was the land that God had promised to them (cf. Gen. 35:12; Heb. 11:9). The plains, the deserts, the Great Sea, i.e. the Mediterranean, the rivers, the Sea of Galilee, the Dead Sea, the hills, and the mountains—all of these made up *the land*. The modern Jew, whose heart is often far from God and upon whose heart a veil still remains (cf. II Cor. 3:15-16), has at least one thing in common with his ancient Jewish brother—he is passionately devoted to *the land*. In fact the land has become almost an idol taking the place of God. But when God and *the land* are rightly conceived, the land becomes the place where God wrought many of his mighty acts. The land is important because of what God did and said there.

Political Factors

In both the Old and New Testaments political rulers and leaders often played an important role in the life of the Jewish people and the early Christians. Where a ruler or leader is mentioned by name, we should get all information possible about him. The historian Josephus gives excellent accounts of Roman procurators who governed Palestine.[14] If the Jews had grounds for not liking the Romans, the Romans also had grounds for not liking the Jews! Both sides tried—sporadically at least—to irritate the other. The war that brought the destruction of Jerusalem in A.D. 70 had long preparation. Conditions steadily deteriorated, and soon war became inevitable. It became only a question of when it would begin. It was in such a setting that Jesus was put to death and arose again on the third day. In this same setting the good news of Christianity spread throughout Palestine, north to Syria, and then westward across Asia Minor, Greece, and to Italy. Early Christianity did not have ideal political connections. But the exact nature of the political surroundings at the time of any writing—especially those of early Christianity—is of great help in interpreting the meaning of the writing.

Not only should the interpreter know the historical situation behind any narrative or passage, but he should know the past history behind any particular incident. The woman with whom

---

[14] *Antiquities of the Jews*, Books XVIII-XX. *Wars of the Jews*, Book II.

Christ talked at the well in Sychar had behind her five hundred years of conflict that colored her feelings and attitudes. Some of her remarks and the brief editorial insertion ("now Jews do not associate on friendly terms with Samaritans" John 4:9) point to an animosity which was accepted as a way of life—just as between the modern Jew and Arab. Hence past history as well as contemporary history often work together to give important insights.

The international situation—activities of surrounding nations—also may have a bearing on interpretation. If one is interpreting Isaiah 7-10, he should know the situation in Judah under Ahaz, in the Northern Kingdom under Pekah, the situation in Syria under Rezin, and the larger shadow of Assyria which ominously spread over all three kingdoms. The prophet Isaiah spoke to a people under pressures from many sources. He spoke of deliverance for Judah from both Syria and Israel (see Isa. 7:16; 8:4). A knowledge of these political factors will help clarify the particular assertions of Isaiah in chapters 7-10. Some of the sayings transcend this background but they cannot be separated from this background.

Environmental Factors of Everyday Living

Material Culture. This involves the things people use in their daily existence. It includes the homes people live in, the objects in their homes, the tools for their work, the kind of clothing they wear, their weapons for war, the implements for getting food, the means of transportation, etc. The importance of the material culture in any narrative may not be immediately apparent. Take Jesus' healing of the paralytic who was carried by four men (Matt. 9:1-8, Mark 2:1-12, Luke 5:17-26). Because of the crowd, his friends who served as stretcher carriers went up on the roof. From this elevation they lowered the man into the presence of Jesus. Edersheim discusses the various kinds of Palestinian homes.[15] From the data, he assumes that this house was one of the better dwellings of the middle class. It probably had a central courtyard with rooms going out from this courtyard on three sides. The courtyard would be open. An overhang extending outward from the U-shaped living quarters would make it possible for those living in the house to go from one room to the others around the courtyard without getting out in the sun or rain. Edersheim thinks that the Pharisees and

[15] Alfred Edersheim, *The Life and Times of Jesus the Messiah* (1927), I, 501-503.

teachers of the law may have been sitting in the guest chamber where Jesus was staying. The people thronged into the courtyard to listen to Jesus. So Jesus eventually would have to stand in the doorway to his guest chamber and speak to the people in the courtyard because there was no longer any room even at the place near the door (Mark 2:2). The men then took the sick man up on the roof, took off some of the roofing from the overhang, and lowered the man down before Jesus who for the reasons suggested may have been standing in the doorway. Whether this reconstruction is correct in all details matters little. What is important is the interpreter's awareness of Palestinian homes, the possibility of people coming off the streets into private living quarters, and the general situation which caused those bringing the paralytic to take such extreme measures to get him near Jesus. It is no wonder that Jesus saw *their* faith—that of the man and the four who carried him (Matt. 9:2, Mark 2:5, Luke 5:20). Material culture in this case is important in revealing one of the main elements of the study —how faith influences action.

Social-Religious Situation. Another large segment of everyday living has to do with our social relationships from birth to death. After the birth of a child there were customs to be observed. In Israel these involved the place of worship, the priest, the parents and the child. Among all peoples there are specific customs that surround marriage. Legal transactions in ancient times often took place at the gate of the city. Here the courts held session. The religious life found its expression in the tabernacle, in the temple, in the synagogues, and in the local congregations of Christians. The latter was a tightly knit group. Christians were accused by the pagans of immorality, of eating their children, and of other vicious practices. These slanders grew because the outsiders were conscious of the group solidarity of the Christians.

The role of the city in the life of ancient peoples is in itself an interesting phenomenon. People lived in the cities and went outside of the city by day to work in the fields. For safety they returned at night to a fortified place. The Roman roads made possible trade and travel between cities. This brought increased social interaction and awareness of the activities of other cities. Travel to the various oracles and shrines was simplified. Asia Minor and Greece were overrun with temples and religious sites to which people came from miles around. The Jews of the diaspora looked with disdain on all such pagan centers, but they themselves came to the temple at Jerusalem for one of the major feasts at least once in their lifetime if at all possible.

Thus Hellenistic Judaism and Palestinian Judaism were bound together by the temple and by the reading of the Old Testament Scriptures in the synagogues. The social structure of the slave and freedman, of the poor and the rich (with a middle class minority) makes ancient society quite different from the kind of society we know in the West.

Stability of Economy. When we look at the historical scene into which the message of God was proclaimed, we see that matters of trade, agriculture, craftsmen and their products, travel by sea and by land all help determine whether the economy was stable or unstable. Absence of rainfall meant famine. Earthquakes blotted out whole cities. The ravages of war remained for generations. Whole populations were removed and deported to other locations. For example, many Jews were not interested in going back to Palestine even though Cyrus, the Persian, made this possible. They found a stable economy where they were and they were prospering. They looked at the unstable economy of Palestine—their former home—and found it uninviting. These environmental factors are rarely referred to in Scripture. The message supersedes all such detail. Nevertheless, the stark realities of life and death, of the struggle to obtain the bare essentials of life—these things daily confronted ancient man. His span of life was short; the threats to his existence were many. Stability of the economy or of his way of life was the exception rather than the rule. Those who live in our modern urban centers (even with the threat which automation poses) are hardly aware of the relative stability of our economy compared with that of the original hearers or readers of the biblical message. Without an understanding of this difference, the interpreter cannot enter into a message which came to a particular people in a particular situation.

DIVERSITY IN HISTORICAL CULTURAL SITUATIONS

If the culture of a people is narrowed, as Redfield defines it, to the people's "total equipment of ideas and institutions and conventionalized activities,"[16] or as Nida says, to "the whole behavior patterns of a particular people,"[17] then the wide variety among cultures becomes apparent. Language plays a leading role in revealing ideas, institutions, and the whole gamut of conventional activities. Therefore, language opens up to us most vividly the diversity in historical cultural situations.

[16] Robert Redfield, *The Primitive World and Its Transformations*, p. 85, quoted in Eugene A. Nida, *Message and Mission* (1960), p. 35.

[17] Nida, *op. cit.*, p. 35.

Influence of Cultural Diversity on Communication

What we say is thoroughly colored by our behavior patterns. Hence communication apart from cultural influence is impossible. When God spoke to men, he used their cultural situation to help convey to them what he wanted them to know. How we handle cultural factors will determine how clearly we communicate, whether we are speaking to people in the same culture as ours or to those in a dissimilar culture. In any cultural situation certain elements are basic to communication.

Source-Message-Receptor. Eugene Nida has made very clear that these three factors are the basic components in communication in any total cultural context.[18] God reveals his truth through his "messengers"; he is the *final source,* and the human messenger is the *immediate source.* The human messenger stands within a people and within a culture, proclaiming a *message.* The "receptor(s)" are those who hear the message. The manner of life of a people regulates the form and function of language and controls how they will understand the message. If we list the letters S—M→R, we will have the ingredients of communication, each of which is in a vital relationship with culture.

Total Cultural Framework. Nida has depicted with charts the diverse cultures which influence the communication of the biblical message.[19] In the diagram (p. 171), the triangle represents the particular biblical culture which influenced the first source, message, and receptors. The square represents the culture of the modern Western world. The circle represents modern cultures differing from that of the Western world. The hyperbolic curve at the top represents the fact that God is the ultimate source of revealed truth.

The individual triangles, squares, and circles describe the involvement of the source, message, and receptors in the particular biblical culture, the culture of the modern Western world, and other contemporary cultures of our world. The interpreter has to be aware of this involvement. He himself stands in a modern culture, whether this be Western or another. He must understand the particular biblical culture which influenced the original source, message, and receptors. He must note both how it differs and how it resembles his own. Only then can he effectively communicate the message from one culture pattern to another. The complexity of this process stands out when an interpre-

18 *Ibid.,* pp. 36-39.
19 *Ibid.,* pp. 47, 222.

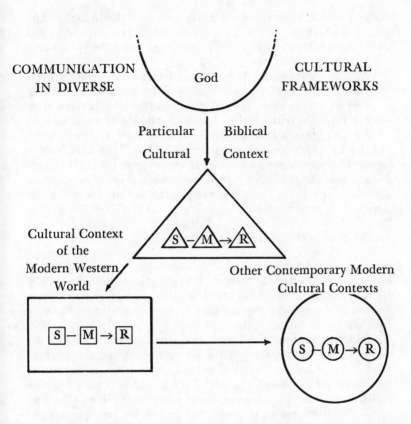

COMMUNICATION IN DIVERSE CULTURAL FRAMEWORKS

God

Particular Cultural | Biblical Context

Cultural Context of the Modern Western World

Other Contemporary Modern Cultural Contexts

ter must grapple first with the biblical cultural pattern, then with his own modern cultural pattern, and then with still another modern cultural pattern. Yet this is what most missionaries must do day by day.

To go from the triangle to the square to the circle demands a breadth of understanding possessed by too few people. A thorough knowledge of history and culture is not merely intellectually desirable but a practical necessity. Where differences prevent understanding, functional equivalents must be employed. For example, in many modern cultures the "heart" is not the center of a man's inward being. In these cases we must use the expression that has this meaning. Nida points out that in the Sudanic languages of northern Congo, the liver describes the center of man's inward being: "These people honor me with their mouths, but their livers are far from me" (Matt. 12:34).[19] We

19 *Ibid.*, pp. 190-91.

make a similar shift when we move from the psychological language employed in particular periods of Hebrew culture to our own modern Western culture. In place of the kidneys or reins, we substitute "heart" or "inward part."

When it comes to a total cultural framework, an interpreter must never think of himself merely as a spectator. He is an active part of his own cultural pattern. He must become thoroughly involved both in the particular biblical cultural context of the passage with which he is dealing and in any modern culture to which he is communicating. Only frustration results when we try to communicate what we understand only vaguely because we are prisoners within our own culture. Ignorance of the cultural context is often a main factor in our failure to understand or communicate.

Indigenization Contrasted with Syncretism

In communicating any message from one culture to another, we seek not to alter the message but to make it understandable. This is particularly true of the Gospel of Jesus Christ. Indigenization is the use of various forms of communication and transmission found in the culture to which a speaker or writer is bringing his message. Paul does this when he makes use of the term "secret" or "mystery" to describe the unique thing which God did in Christ. Syncretism, on the other hand, is an invalid procedure by which the content of the gospel is changed or partially assimilated by a hostile world view found in another culture. The interpreting of a message in one culture by someone who lives in another culture has its risks. The interpreter can unwittingly change the message while communicating it. Unless he uses cultural equivalents, the message will probably be altered. If he does not get the right equivalent, he may be guilty of syncretism. Careful interpretation in handling the biblical materials will prevent syncretism. But such interpretation demands a rigorous study of the particular biblical cultural context, the modern cultural context of the interpreter, and the modern cultural context of his hearers. To be aware of these differences in historical cultural situations is basic to sound interpretation and sound communication.

CURRENT EMPHASIS ON HISTORY AND CULTURE IN INTERPRETATION

Existentialist Hermeneutics

The movement known as existentialist hermeneutics represents a break with all earlier approaches to hermeneutics.

Wilder[20] summarizes its *raison d' être* very well when he says that this movement has turned the spotlight upon the historical character of the understanding which belongs to the interpreter. The forces, factors, attitudes, etc., within his personal history deeply influence how he understands. This emphasis is existentialist because it stresses all that faith or commitment does for the individual in his life situation. Faith is an historical response conditioned by historical factors. With this response there comes a new understanding, so that the historical character of understanding is as important as the historical character of faith.

The older historical interpretation gave the appearance of being detached. Existentialist interpretation insists that it is involved. In contrast to the older historical interpretation, existential hermeneutics systematically catalogues all life situation factors having to do with an ancient text.[21] The interpreter is existentially identified with the ancient writer and event. This identification of today's interpreter with past events is part of the general picture of the totality of things (phenomena) and how man is related to this totality (phenomenology).[22]

In the older historical approach the interpreter came to a document as an expert who scrutinized what it had to say. He was the subject, and the document was the object. But existentialist hermeneutics has reversed this approach. The interpreter comes to be scrutinized. The subject-object relation is reversed. The text scrutinizes the interpreter. Furthermore, the interpreter must submit to the text, not only intellectually but morally. But it is very difficult for interpreters to allow the contents of a document to search their moral point of view. A change may be demanded that he is unwilling to make. Hence exegesis becomes a case of a changing, growing person rather than a person merely examining data.

Fuchs speaks of the various "worlds" in which men live. These worlds consist of what men choose, agree upon, take for granted, seek after. The life experience and life meaning espoused in such worlds, Fuchs calls "speech" *(Sprache)*. The speech-event of the gospel is that which liberates men from other "worlds." By involving ourselves in the speech-event *(Sprachereignis)* of the gospel we can be freed from our "own self-understanding and world-understanding and history-under-

---

20 Amos Niven Wilder, "New Testament Hermeneutics Today," *Current Issues in New Testament Interpretation,* ed. William Klassen and Graydon F. Snyder (1962), pp. 38-52.

21 Ernst Fuchs, cited by Wilder, *op. cit.,* p. 43.

22 *Ibid.*

standing."[23] Openness to the message brings us into another world.

Thus hermeneutics for the existentialist is involved in two historical realities. The historical reality of the proclaimer (Jesus in the days of his flesh) or of the apostles of the early Church is one of these, while the other consists in the one who is confronted with this message—each man today as he encounters the kerygma. How are these two historical realities related? Among those adhering to an existentialist hermeneutics there is the growing conviction that there is no radical discontinuity between the kerygma of the church and the person and message of Jesus.[24] This growing agreement on basic unity between the historical Jesus and the resurrected Christ naturally gives rise to greater unity between the history of Jesus and the history of the believer.

There is only one area where existentialist hermeneutics binds itself to the older liberal perspective. It fully concedes the role of empiricism (the use of observation and experiment to establish cause and effect relationships) in interpreting Scripture.[25] When empiricism moves into a sphere where its method is not adequate to handle all the data the claimed objectivity in empiricism is illusory. Empiricism has no way to judge the unique. It is concerned with the regularly occurring, the oft-repeated. Objectivity, in the old liberal sense of neutrality, is impossible. But objectivity in terms of divinely interpreted events, persons, and power brings both a dedication to God and a detachment in the treatment of history. This kind of "objectivity" has a right to the name because there were the exodus, the exile, the cross, and the resurrection. Most certainly the divinely given meaning to these events is not exhaustive but normative. It came in a multiplicity of ways and through many channels. The results are found in the Old and New Testament Scriptures. The focus is on redemption, judgment, vindication, and total transformation. These events or experiences were unique not only in their historical occurrence, but because, in God's purpose, they make an effect upon succeeding generations. Each generation can become contemporaneous with these events. This brings us to another emphasis on history and culture in interpretation.

Actualization of Past Realities by Later Generations

The character of past realities for Israel did not consist of

23 *Ibid.*, p. 47.
24 *Ibid.*, p. 49.
25 *Ibid.*, p. 51.

mythical-poetical fancies. The structure of reality for Israel was historical. To actualize the past does not mean to re-enact a series of myths. Actualization has to do with historical realities.

Brevard S. Childs describes the redemptive events of the Old Testament as follows:

> These redemptive events of the Old Testament shared a genuine chronology. They appeared in history at a given moment, which entry can be dated. There is a once-for-all character to these events in the sense that they never repeated themselves in the same fashion.[26]

Yet these events lived on. Succeeding generations responded to them. The nature of this response is seen in the definition of actualization: "Actualization is the process by which a past event is contemporized for a generation removed in time and space from the original event."[27] This means that neither Judaism nor Christianity was tied to a mere historical record of past exploits. Both in Judaism and in Christianity response brings a contemporary encounter with the event and its meaning.

In contrast to German positivistic historians, Childs asserts that the event must not be separated from its interpretation. "The interpretation is not something added to the event, but constitutes the real event."[28] Neither should the interpretation be separated from the event by applying some *a priori* imagination by which the historian can rearrange all data and tell exactly what happened. Childs feels that R. G. Collingwood falls into this error. No historian is given such ability to recapitulate the past and re-create ancient situations that this ability becomes a private source of historical data withheld from others. "There are no avenues to the history of which the Bible speaks except through Scripture's own testimony to these events."[29]

When successive generations re-interpret the same events in terms of their own encounters, one may be tempted to think that these successive layers or accretions will overshadow the original determinative events. Childs maintains that the role of memory in Israel brings about no such result. Rather the whole of Old Testament redemptive history is one of God's action and Israel's response. The response shows great variety, yet there is continuity with the original redemptive event. "The remembered event is equally a valid witness to Israel's encounter with God as the first witness. Israel testified to the continuing na-

---

26 Brevard S. Childs, "Memory and History," *Memory and Tradition in Israel* (1962), p. 83.

27 *Ibid.*, p. 85.

28 *Ibid.*,   p. 86.

29 *Ibid.*, p. 88.

ture of her redemptive history by the events of the past in the light of her ongoing experience with the covenant God."[30]

Principles and Procedures

1. Know the people or peoples who are involved in the section being interpreted.

2. Determine what period is the most likely temporal setting for the materials to be interpreted. Remember that it is more important to know the historical situation than the precise historical date.

3. Check the place or places which provide the geographical setting.

4. Note the customs, objects of material culture, or social-religious relationships that are evident in the narrative or that lie behind the narrative.

5. Recognize how the history which took place before the times of the original hearers or readers influenced their responses and attitudes.

6. Examine the forces that brought about stability or instability of the economy.

7. See how the narrative transcends its surroundings. Some scholars who are well trained in history and culture spend most of their time showing similarities between the biblical narrative and the surrounding history and culture. The differences are important too.

8. Be aware of the similarities and differences between the historical-cultural elements surrounding the original writer and his readers and the historical-cultural elements surrounding the interpreter. We must recognize these similarities and differences if we are to convey the message to our contemporaries.

BIBLIOGRAPHY

Albright, William F., "The Old Testament World," *The Interpreter's Bible,* I (1951).

Bultmann, Rudolf, *Primitive Christianity in Its Contemporary Setting,* tr. R. H. Fuller (1956).

Burrows, Millar, *The Dead Sea Scrolls* (1955).

———, *More Light on the Dead Sea Scrolls* (1958).

Edersheim, Alfred, *The Life and Times of Jesus the Messiah* (1927).

Filson, Floyd V., *The New Testament Against Its Environment* (1950).

Milik, J. T., *Ten Years of Discovery in the Wilderness of Judea,* tr. J. Strugnell (1959).

Minear, Paul Sevier, *Eyes of Faith* (1948).

Nida, Eugene A., *Message and Mission* (1960).

Schürer, Emil, *A History of the Jewish People in the Time of Jesus Christ,* tr. John Macpherson, Sophia Taylor, and Peter Christie (1890).

Wright, George Ernest, *The Old Testament Against Its Environment* (1950).

[30] *Ibid.,* p. 89.

Special Hermeneutics

Material Involved in Special Hermeneutics

Special hermeneutics deals with definitions and principles which make it easier to interpret special literary forms or to convey the meaning found in specific topical areas treated in the biblical materials. The principles of special hermeneutics are to be applied only to these special forms or themes. However, these forms and themes appear frequently in the Bible, so that the interpreter often has need to refer to these definitions and principles.

Special hermeneutics involves the following aspects: First, figurative language—its variety and kinds (Chapters 8-12). Second, the language and content of prophecy (Chapter 13). What do the biblical writers consider to be prophetic materials and how should we interpret these materials? Third, creation and climax—a consideration of the language depicting the beginning and consummation of history (Chapter 14). Fourth, poetry—its characteristics and the proper procedures for interpreting it (Chapter 15). Fifth, doctrinal teachings—sound methods for formulating particular doctrines (Chapter 16). Sixth, devotion and conduct—sound methods of Bible study for Christian growth in grace that will transform daily living (Chapter 17).

The biblical materials which pertain to these areas are constantly encountered by the careful Bible student. Because of the importance of these materials, the student cannot afford to use a haphazard procedure. Neither can he use one that appears to be good, but which in reality either leaves out important elements or introduces that which is foreign to the biblical emphases. Special hermeneutics needs particular attention and must be mastered in order to insure sound biblical interpretation.

VIII Short Figures of Speech

In studying figurative language we are confronted with many semantical-philosophical questions as to whether all language is figurative and whether particular "figures" are only more figurative than the socially acknowledged meaning that may be designated as "literal." We shall not try to answer the questions that are wrapped up in the nature of language. They necessitate a careful distinction between "symbol" and "figure," and they require a careful weighing of the different meanings conveyed by "symbol" as against "symbolical." These chapters on figurative language will deal rather with the various kinds of figurative language. *By literal meaning the writer refers to the usual or customary sense conveyed by words or expressions.* This view of literal meaning is not to be confused with the idea that language, like the multiplication table, is made up of units that always have the same value. This is far from the truth. *By figurative meaning the writer has in mind the representation of one concept in terms of another because the nature of the two things compared allows such an analogy to be drawn.* When Jesus says: "I am the bread of life" (John 6:35), he uses this metaphor because he is to man spiritually what bread is to man physically—the source and sustenance of life.

SOURCES OF IMAGERY

Nearly all figures of speech come out of the life of the speaker or writer who uses them. This means that the student who understands the background of the writer (discussed under "History and Culture") will better understand his figurative

179

language. Most writers, for example, use comparison to explain the unfamiliar by that which is already familiar to the reader.

Jesus often employed figurative language. He used many figures of speech, but he is best known for his parables. It is remarkable that when Jesus used figurative language his listeners were often unaware of the figure. They apprehended meanings almost immediately; the figures reached their mark. His opponents as well as his disciples grasped enough of his message to know that Jesus' good news involved a radical change of perspective. Jesus used figurative language to convey how radical was his call to repentance, how decisive was the commitment demanded by his proclamation about the reign of God, and how far-reaching were the implications of a man's decision.

Where did Jesus obtain his imagery or figurative language?[1] The sources for the imagery in the Gospel of Luke alone are amazing.

Jesus showed his interest in the sphere of nature by the number of figures he utilized from this source. From the animal world he refers to wild animals (foxes, 13:32) and domestic animals (sheep, 10:3; 12:32; 15:4-7; camel, 18:25) and farming animals such as the ass and the ox (13:15,16; 14:5). Birds, such as sparrows or ravens, serve as a source of figures (12:6,7; 12:24). Animal habits enter into the imagery: maternal instinct (13:34, 35), scavenging birds (17:37), and ravenous beasts (20:46,47). The way men capture animals and catch fish serves as a basis for imagery (5:10; 7:23; 21:34,35). Wild plants and trees contribute to the imagery: lilies (12:27,28), the reed (7:24), and the leafing of trees (21:29-31; 23:31). Agriculture and cultivated plants are used: plowing (9:62), sowing (8:5-8), harvesting (10:2), sifting (22:31), and growth (13:18,19; 17:6). Fruit growing is also useful (6:43,44; 13:6-9). From the domain of weather, allusion is made to the signs of the weather (12:54,55) and to the suddenness or brilliance of lightning (10:18; 17:24). Material elements are not overlooked: dust (10:11; 9:5), and stones (19:40).

Jesus draws upon the sphere of domestic and family life to provide imagery. He speaks of wedding customs such as the joy of the bridegroom and his friends (5:34,35). He notes the significance of the father-son relationship (15:11-31; 11:11-13). Fam-

[1] Mary Ruth Howes, "Jesus' Use of Comparative Imagery in the Gospel of Luke" (Unpublished Master's thesis, The Graduate School, Wheaton College, 1957), pp. 30-58. Miss Howes in this thesis has exhaustively examined Jesus' use of imagery in the Gospel of Luke. After showing the various areas of life from which these images come, she points out how the character of Jesus is illuminated by the great variety of figures which he employed.

ily ties are given a larger meaning (8:21). The qualities of children are compared (18:16,17; 10:21; 9:48; 7:31,32). Jesus speaks of parts of houses and those who seek to enter into them: a door (13:24-30), a key (11:52), and a thief (12:39). He uses household items and activities: clothing (24:29), mending and sewing (5:36), cleaning (11:39,40; 15:8-10; 11:25), and sleeping (8:52). Jesus knew well the need of illumination for any family unit to function. In figurative language he draws the spiritual lesson (8:16,17; 11:33,36). Jesus speaks of fire in a figurative way (12:49). The ingredients of cooking provide figures: bread (22:19), drink (5:37-39; 22:20; 22:42), salt (14:34,35), leaven (12:1; 13:20,21). Eating and feasting play their role in Jesus' imagery (14:8-11, 12-14, 16-24). The physical body—parts, health, and function—is utilized: hair (21:18), action of a physician (4:23; 5:31), vision or eyesight (6:39; 6:41,42; 11:33-36). Life and death provide images (9:60; 11:44,47,48; 15:24,32; 20:37, 38). The language of the afterlife has a metaphorical base: Hades (16:19-31) and Gehenna (12:5).

To the sphere of daily life and business life Jesus makes many allusions. Work in general is used (10:7; 11:46), building construction (6:47-49; 14:28-30), various aspects of business: weights (6:38), debts (7:41-43; 11:4), trading (9:24-25; 21:19), economic gain and loss: treasure (6:45; 12:21; 12:33,34; 18:22), wealth (6:24,25; 12:16-20), and poverty (6:20,21). Legal matters enter into daily life. The language has significance for higher dimensions (6:37; 18:2-8). Punishment or disaster provides language for instruction: drowning (17:2), crucifixion (9:23; 14:27), stripes (12:42-48). Travel serves as a base for the parable of the Good Samaritan (10:30-36). War served as a vehicle for figurative language because it came from the daily life of the people (14:31,32; 11:21,22). Government as well as the whole idea of a reign or kingdom played a key role in Jesus' teaching: enrollment (10:20), rulers (22:25-27), kingdoms in conflict (11:17). The servant-master relationship is also employed: lordship (6:5, 46), stewards and servants (12:35-38; 12:42-48; 16:1-13; 17:7-10; 19:12-27), husbandmen (20:9-16).

Jesus alluded only a few times to religious imagery: passover (22:15,16), baptism (12:50), prayer (18:10-14), secrets or mysteries (8:10). However, Jesus called God "Father" in his personal prayers (10:21,22; 22:42; 23:34,46), in his instruction (6:36; 11:13; 12:30,36; 22:29; 24:49), and in his teaching on prayer (11:2) he speaks of the finger of God (11:20).

Imagery for Jesus is the language of life. So it was for the Old Testament prophets. Because it comes from so many sources, such imagery can be applied and used in a large variety of ways.

FIGURES EMPHASIZING COMPARISON

Simile

A simile is an explicitly stated comparison employing words such as "like" and "as." In approaching similes the interpreter should seek to understand fully the two things compared. The understanding of the simile can usually be gained *by reflection* without any historical research because that which follows the "as" or "like" is a commonly known item of experience. "Is not my word or message... *like a hammer that breaks the rock in pieces?"* (Jer. 23:29). Because similes are easy to grasp is no reason for hurrying by them. Reflection always deepens one's understanding.

When Jesus sent forth the seventy to prepare the way before his coming (Luke 10:1-2), he told them explicitly what their situation would be (Luke 10:3): "Go, behold, I am sending you as lambs in the midst of wolves." This figure brings out the undercurrent of antipathy to Jesus, the fact that the seventy had no experience or personal qualifications for such conflict, and the increasingly sharp division between those who followed Jesus and those who opposed him.

Jesus, in his lament over Jerusalem, contrasts his own desire for the city with the obdurate response of the city toward him. Only a simile could capture his pathos and concern: "How frequently I willed [wished] to gather together your children as a hen gathers together her brood under wings, but you would not" (Matt. 23:37; Luke 13:34). In his comparison, Jesus shows the protection and care he wanted to give to his own people. The attitude of Jerusalem reflected the cross-currents of thought that were spreading out through the whole country. This simile shows Jesus' love and concern for a people who were following the familiar road of departure from the God of Jacob.

With great vividness Jesus employs similes to describe his second coming: "Therefore, if they should say to you [i.e., the disciples who were the apostles of the Christian church]: 'Behold he is in a desert place,' do not begin to go out; 'behold, he is in the inner or secret chambers,' do not begin to believe it. Because, just as the lightning comes out of the east and shines unto the west, in this fashion will be the coming of the son of man" (Matt. 24:27, cf. Luke 17:24). The coming of the Son of man for his disciples will be like the lightning that flashes across the sky. The simile is employed to correct any erroneous reports of a secret coming with Christ in some desert place or inner storehouse.

The Old Testament is full of similes: see, for example, Isaiah 1:8; 29:8; 55:10-11; Jer. 23:29; Malachi 3:2, etc.

Similes are also found throughout the epistles of the New Testament (cf. I Cor. 3:15; 13:11; I Thess. 5:2, etc.), but most of all in the book of Revelation.[2] There are so many, in fact, that the reader may forget to think about each one. One should ask himself: (1) Why did John feel the need to employ simile in this particular place? (2) How does the simile enable the reader to grasp better the idea that is being presented? (3) In the book of Revelation it is always good to ask one further question: Even with simile, what is there in this assertion that still is either unknown to the reader or is understood only in a very general way? Similes do bring an increased understanding, but they do not guarantee a complete picture or understanding. While the interpreter should be thankful for what they illuminate, he should never be overzealous to make them say more than they obviously intend to convey. Similes are like wild flowers: if you cultivate them too strenuously, they lose their beauty.

Metaphor

Metaphor is comparison by direct assertion, in which the speaker or writer describes one thing in terms of something else. Most metaphors are *designed;* i.e., the author intends to make a direct comparison. These can usually be identified from the context, though not always with certainty. *Undesigned* metaphors are metaphors presumed to be unintentional.

The word "lord" (*kurios* in Greek) provides a good example of designed and undesigned metaphor. The literal meaning of *kurios,* as found in Greek literature, is *head* (e.g. of a family) or *master* (of some group).[3] This is no doubt the meaning which the disciples frequently had in mind when they called Jesus "Lord"; he was the master of their group. The metaphorical meaning of *kurios,* however, is *ruler,* even *sovereign ruler.* Thus there is a conscious metaphorical use of *kurios* in Revelation 19:16, where Christ is called "King of Kings and Lord of Lords." Moreover, a conscious use of metaphor is evident in the fact that the vowels added to the Hebrew "Yahweh" (Je-

---

2 After *homoios* the following similes or comparative expressions occur: Rev. 1:15; 2:18; 4:3(twice); 4:6,7(twice); 9:7,10,19; 11:1; 13:2,4,11; 14:14; 18:18; 21:11,18. Numerous examples are found after *hōs:* Rev. 1:10,14,15, 16,17; 2:18,27; 3:3,21; 4:1,6,7; 5:6,11; 6:1,6,11,12,13,14; 8:8,10; 9:2,3,5,7,8,9,17; 10:1,9,10; 12:15; 13:2,3,11; 14:2,3; 15:2; 16:3,13,15,21; 17:12; 18:6,21; 19:1,6,12; 20:8; 21:2,11,21; 22:1.

3 Liddell and Scott, p. 1013.

hovah in the ASV) have the meaning of "ruler." In the AV and the RSV this word is therefore translated "LORD."

Thus it may very well be pointed out that when Jesus' disciples called their leader "Lord," intending no metaphor, they nevertheless were using an unconscious metaphor. They were suggesting a link between Jesus and the covenant God of Israel; they were recognizing implicitly the legitimacy of Jesus' claim to be establishing the kingdom of God. Later, as they came to absorb Jesus' teaching, and particularly after Jesus' death and resurrection, the disciples became aware of the metaphorical meaning of "lord" and used it deliberately to refer to the deity of Christ (cf. Hebrews 1:10-12 with Psalm 102:25-27). As Paul was later to say, to pronounce Jesus "Lord" is to be moved by the Holy Spirit (I Cor. 12:3). Eventually, the use of *kurios* to mean "sovereign ruler" became no longer metaphorical but literal; this transition from unintentional to intentional metaphor, and thence to literal meaning, is thus indirectly an account of a growing appreciation of Jesus' divine prerogatives.

Jesus frequently used metaphors. "Fear not or cease being afraid, *little flock*, because your father has resolved [considered it good] to give you the kingdom" (Luke 12:32). Jesus' concept of the Church is made clear by the same metaphor: "And I have other sheep which are not of this fold; I must also lead these other sheep, and they will hear my voice, and they will become *one flock*, one shepherd" (John 10:16). Jesus taught that his kindred were not those with physical ties but those who responded to the message of God, thus showing a spiritual relationship to God. "These are my *mother* and *brothers*: those hearing and doing [keeping] the message of God" (Luke 8:21). Sometimes metaphor and simile are found side by side. "Simon, Simon, lo Satan has asked for you [plural] for the purpose of *sifting* [you, pl.] *as wheat*" (Luke 22:31). This comparative imagery depicts the severe testing which all the disciples would go through. Simon Peter, however, is singled out as the spokesman and verses 32-34 are concerned solely with Peter. Jesus says that he especially will be tossed around like wheat. He will experience the sifting process that will bring out the depth of his devotion. The metaphor speaks vividly of Peter's existential situation. Nevertheless, the language of Peter's situation describes sharply the condition of many contemporary Christians. They too are "being sifted." Hence Jesus' language may properly be applied to their present condition as well.

Metaphors also are common in the Old Testament (one of the most powerful of all is found in Jer. 2:13). They are found in descriptions of the activities of God. One such kind of metaphor is anthropomorphism—the ascribing to God of bodily members and physical movements. "Behold, Jehovah's hand is not shortened that it cannot save; neither is his ear heavy, that it cannot hear" (Isa. 59:1). The phrase "the arm of God" is often used to describe God's power and victory. Numerous examples can be found: Deuteronomy 4:34; 5:15; 7:19; 9:29; 11:2; 26:8; 33:27; Psalms 44:3(twice); 77:15; 89:10,13,21; 98:1; 136:12; and Isaiah 40:10,11; 44:12; 48:14; 52:10; 53:1; 59:16; 62:8; 63:5,12. Another variety of metaphor is anthropopathism—the ascribing to God of human emotions, feelings, and responses. God's grief is stressed in Psalm 95:10; Hebrews 3:10, 17. God's anger *(thumos)* is seen in Revelation 14:8,10,19; 15:1,7; 16:1,19; 18:3; 19:15. His wrath *(orgē)* also plays a prominent role: cf. Matthew 3:7; Luke 3:7; John 3:36; Romans 1:18; 5:9; Ephesians 5:6; Colossians 3:6; I Thessalonians 1:10; 5:9; Hebrews 3:11; 4:3; Revelation 6:16,17; 11:18; 14:10; 16:19; 19:15. Grief, anger, wrath, etc., are all genuine responses of God. The metaphorical element arises from the fact that human grief, anger, and wrath are a complex array of elements. Grief can involve self-pity; anger can be filled with an irrational obsession for revenge; wrath can be overlaid with a passion to return in kind. Yet these elements must be excluded from an accurate picture of God's grief, anger, and wrath. God's response is genuine; it is the human counterpart that is tainted by corrupt elements. Hence, when the interpreter recognizes these anthropopathisms, he can make an effort to remove all human self-centeredness from such emotions as grief, anger, or wrath. In doing so he gains a clearer picture of God's responses.

We may be unable to exclude all foreign elements from the metaphorical language about the being of God. Notwithstanding, such language is indispensable. The fact that God feels grief, anger, and wrath shows that the Holy Being of the Bible is not an abstract idea with an abstract set of attributes. The metaphor, therefore, is an extremely important vehicle for conveying truth and must not be dismissed.

FIGURES INVOLVING ASSOCIATION

Metonymy

Metonymy means using the name of one thing for another thing because the two are frequently associated together or because one may suggest the other. A common example of metonymy is the use of "the White House" to refer to the President, e.g. "The White House decided to release the speech earlier

than usual." Of course it was the President or a member of his
staff who made this decision. Substitutions of this kind are natural to our thinking, so it is not surprising that they occur in
Scripture. In the account of the rich man and Lazarus, Abraham
will not allow any particular representative to go back to earth
to warn the rich man's brothers. There is no need for this type
of warning because "they have Moses and the prophets. Let
them listen to them" (Luke 16:29, cf. also Luke 24:27). Here
"Moses and the prophets" stands for the writings of Moses and
the writings of the prophets. In this kind of metonymy the
author is put in place of his writing, or to put it abstractly,
the cause is put in place of the effect.

Metonymy is also found in the Old Testament. Jacob does
not want to permit Benjamin to go back to Egypt with his sons
to purchase more food. He knows how much he grieved over
the loss of his son Joseph. If harm should befall Benjamin in
the way, Jacob declares: "You will bring down my grey hair
[hoary head] in sorrow to Sheol" (Gen. 42:38). Here the grey
hair or hoary head stands vividly for an old man who, if he
should lose his youngest son, would come to his grave in great
sorrow.

Paul gives a good example of metonymy in Romans 3:27-30.
"Where, therefore, is boasting? It is eliminated. By what kind
of a law? By a law or system of works? No, but by a law of
faith [or a faith kind of system]. Now we hold [reckon] that a
man is justified by faith apart from the works of the law. Is
God only God of the Jews? He is also God of the Gentiles, is he
not? Of course he is also God of the Gentiles, since God is one
and the same who will justify [acquit] the circumcision because
of faith and the uncircumcision through faith." The context
indicates that "circumcision" stands for the Jew and "uncircumcision" stands for the Gentile. The participation or lack or participation in a ceremonial rite is used as a designation for a
whole people, and for all other peoples. Mankind, including
both Jew and Gentile, can be justified only by faith. This example of metonymy reflects Paul's Jewish point of view that
divides mankind into these two categories.

Synecdoche

A synecdoche is a figure of speech in which a part is used for
a whole or a whole for a part. An individual may be used for a
class or a class for an individual. A singular may be used for
a plural and a plural for a singular. In metonymy the associations are established by the situation or living context of the

writer or speaker, i.e., the relationship is *in the mind* of the one making the association. In synecdoche the association is rooted in physical or categorical dimensions, i.e., the relationship is due *to the nature* of the things associated.

Here are some examples of synecdoche. "And Jephthah judged Israel for six years. Then Jephthah, the Gileadite, died, and he was buried in the cities of Gilead" (Judges 12:7). After the death of this judge, he was buried among his own people. Although he served the interests of all the tribes, his own tribal loyalty becomes clear at his death. Of course he was buried in only one of the cities of Gilead, but the plural shows the loyalty which his own people felt for Jephthah. Synecdoche underlines the strength of tribal ties.

Both Micah and Isaiah depict the house of Jehovah as occupying a central place at the end of the days. All nations stream to it. Their purpose is to learn from the God of Jacob, so that they may walk in his paths. From Zion goes forth the law, and from Jerusalem the word of the Lord. Not only will there be instruction but there will also be judicial decisions affecting peoples near and far. In this context we read: "And they will beat their swords into ploughshares, and their spears into pruning knives" (Micah 4:3; Isa. 2:4). Here is synecdoche where the abandonment of two weapons—swords and spears—stands picturesquely for total disarmament. In Joel 3:10 the picture is reversed. There the stress falls on armament: "Beat your plowshares into swords and your pruning knives into spears." Again the use of part for whole is more effective than to say: "Arm yourselves for war; organize the people for military conflict."

FIGURES STRESSING A PERSONAL DIMENSION

Personification

In personification a thing, quality, or idea is represented as a person. "Do not begin to worry about tomorrow, because the morrow will worry about itself. Sufficient [or adequate] for the day is the evil which belongs to that day" (Matt. 6:34). In the Old Testament, Psalm 114 celebrates God's great deliverance of Israel from Egypt. The psalmist personifies the various environmental factors that were barriers or obstacles to be conquered. He singles out the Red Sea, the Jordan river, the mountains and the hills, and finally the earth itself. The Red Sea is described as fleeing. The Jordan is driven back or turns back. The mountains skip like rams and the little hills like lambs. The earth is commanded to tremble at the presence of the Lord. Here personification and simile lie side by side. God's victory at the Exodus is made very clear by this figure of the Red Sea fleeing. The words of Jesus, "the worrying for the morrow" followed by "the morrow worrying about itself" point to the tendency of Christians to be deeply anxious over things they must face day by day. They torture themselves by a prolonged anticipation of what may or may not come. But Jesus stresses the actual as against the possible. How forceful is his conclusion: "The evil which belongs to that day is sufficient for the day" (Matt. 6:34).

Apostrophe

This figure is akin to personification. In apostrophe words are addressed in an exclamatory tone to a thing regarded as a person (personification), or to an actual person. Whether the person or thing is present or absent is not important. Most frequently apostrophe is found where the person using it is thinking out loud, as it were, and the object of his thoughts is not physically in his presence. Such words of address often appear somewhat parenthetical, like a digression in speech or literary writing.

In Psalm 114 apostrophe and personification are both used: "What aileth thee, O thou sea, that thou fleest? Thou Jordan that thou turnest back? Ye mountains, that ye skip like rams; Ye little hills, like lambs" (ASV, Ps. 114:5-6). David's lament over Absalom is a dramatic example of apostrophe: "O my son Absalom, my son, my son Absalom! Would I had died for thee, O Absalom, my son, my son!" (II Sam. 18:33). Again, the Song of Deborah is vivid Hebrew poetry (Judges 5)[4] which contains apostrophe in vss. 3-4 and vs. 31. In verses 3 and 4 there is also personification: "Jehovah, when thou wentest forth out of Seir, When thou marchest out of the field of Edom, the earth trembled, the heaven also dropped, Yea the clouds dropped water. The mountains quaked at the presence of Jehovah, Even yon Sinai at the presence of Jehovah, the God of Israel." Here Jehovah is addressed and the effects of his action are carefully listed. Finally, at the close of the poem, Jehovah is addressed again: "So let all thine enemies perish, O Jehovah; but let them that love him be as the sun when he goeth forth in his might." Here is a mixture of apostrophe, simile, and personification. There is power in this imagery. Those who love Je-

---

[4] Richard G. Moulton, *The Literary Study of the Bible* (1899), pp. 133-142.

hovah are compared with the sun in its majestic movement. It appears each day to move across the heavens. Nothing blocks its path, and its power is felt by all. Since Jehovah is addressed, it is he who controls both the destiny of his enemies and the situation of those loving him. How fitting a conclusion for a poem of great freshness and beauty!

FIGURES DEMANDING ADDITIONS TO COMPLETE THOUGHT

Ellipsis (Brachylogy)

Ellipsis refers to an idea not fully expressed grammatically so that the interpreter must either supply words or expand and alter the construction to make it complete.

In repetitional ellipsis that which is to be supplied is expressed earlier in the context or is clearly related to that which has been explicitly expressed. In Galatians 3:5 Paul declares: "Now the one giving to you the Spirit and producing miracles among you [namely God], (*did he give* the Spirit and *produce* miracles) because of the works of the Law or because of the preaching which demanded only faith?" The main verbs in this sentence must be supplied from the two participles with which the sentence opens. The next verse (vs. 6) shows that Paul is thinking of God, who reckoned Abraham's faith for righteousness. Another example of repetitional ellipsis is found in Romans 11:22. Here a whole clause needs to be repeated: "Behold, therefore, the goodness and severity of God. On the one hand, to those who fell, severity; but to you [sg.; i.e., the individual Gentile reader] the goodness of God, if you [sg.] continue in the sphere of God's goodness; for otherwise [*if you do not continue in the sphere of God's goodness*], you [sg.] also will be cut out." The italicized material must be supplied to make the sentence complete. That which is to be supplied is explicitly stated in the context which immediately precedes.

Non-repetitional ellipsis means that that which is to be expressed is not explicit in the context. To the Jews at Corinth Paul said: "Your blood upon your head" (Acts 18:6). Many translations supply only the verb "to be." Your blood *be* upon your head." But it would seem better to supply the verb "come" (*elthatō*): "Let your blood *come* upon your head" (cf. Matt. 23:35).[5] In Romans 8:3 Paul says literally: "Now the impossibility of the law, because it was weak through the flesh." The phrase "the impossibility of the law" exemplifies the type of

---

[5] Blass-Debrunner-Funk, paragraph 480(5).

ellipsis which can be remedied only by recasting or adding to the wording. When such an ellipsis is filled out, we usually have greater clarity: e.g., "what was impossible for the law, because it was weak through the flesh...."[6] Just how the ellipsis is to be filled out is, however, often a matter of interpretation. Although translations represent the judgment of one or several mature linguists, they are not the final word. The basic question always is: exactly what did the biblical writer mean? The interpreter must judge whether any particular expansion of the statement is what the original biblical writer would have written if he had done his own "filling out," or whether he would be puzzled by the additions made. Ellipses are not an invitation to the interpreter to put his own ideas into the biblical text.

The so-called *constructio praegnans* is really a form of ellipsis or brachylogy involving prepositions. In II Timothy 4:18 the ASV reads: "The Lord... will save me unto his heavenly kingdom." The Greek word *sōzō* in this passage may have the meanings: "bring safely into,"[7] "bring Messianic salvation," "bring to salvation."[8] If the first meaning is selected, then the ellipsis disappears. But if one adopts the meaning "bring to salvation" then he must fill out an ellipsis: "The Lord... will bring me to salvation by leading me [*agagōn*] into his heavenly kingdom."

Zeugma

Zeugma is a specialized form of ellipsis. In certain contexts words are placed together which properly do not belong together. In I Timothy 4:3 false teachers are called liars "who forbid marriage *ordering* [*keleuontōn*] *Christians* to abstain from foods." The italicized words make clear that the infinitive "abstain" is not to be tied to the participle "forbid" but in reality is dependent upon a participle which is not expressed. Zeugma demands the supplying of some form of the verb to clarify the meaning.

Paul's concise language in I Corinthians 3:2 also illustrates zeugma: "I gave you milk to drink, not solid food." By the addition of a verb like *epsōmisa* the statement is rounded out to its full form: "I gave you milk to drink; *I did not feed* you with solid food."[9] The full form of the statement enforces Paul's

6 *Ibid.*
7 *eis*, 7. *Bauer*, p. 229.
8 *sōzō*, 2., *ibid.*, p. 806.
9 Blass-Debrunner-Funk, paragraph 479(2).

argument. Infants must have milk to drink. Older persons can get along on solid food. When Paul was teaching the Corinthians, he could not give them the spiritual truths he wanted them to have because they were not ready for such "solid food." He could give them only milk to drink. Note how metaphor and zeugma are combined.

Aposiopesis

In aposiopesis a part of a sentence is consciously suppressed either because the writer is strongly moved emotionally or because he wants to achieve a rhetorical effect—perhaps the awareness that an alternative with serious consequences is being presented. In the parable of the man who for three years came seeking fruit from his fig tree, Jesus refers to the owner's desire to cut the tree down. The gardener or vinedresser pleaded for the tree. He would dig around the tree and fertilize it for one more year. Here is his conclusion: "If, indeed, it bears fruit for the future, [the tree should be allowed to grow]. Otherwise, [if it does not bear fruit for the future] you shall cut it down" (Luke 13:9). But the bracketed material is not there. The emphasis falls upon removing the tree. Yet the possibility of its being spared is also a vital part of the narrative, although it is not explicitly stated. This delicate shift in alternatives shows Jesus' skill as a teacher.

Near the end of Jesus' life, the high priests, scribes, and elders asked him by what authority he carried out his ministry. Jesus answered with a counter question. Was the baptism of John from heaven (i.e., from God) or from men? Jesus said he would answer their question when they had answered his. The religious leaders did not like the dilemma inherent in Jesus' question. If they replied that the baptism of John was from heaven, then they would have to explain why they did not believe John. "On the other hand, should we say from men? . . . " At this point the narrative is broken off. Some such conclusion as this must be supplied: "There will be a riot, and we will be stoned." Mark concludes by saying: "They feared the crowd because all had regard for John that he was really a prophet" (Mark 11:32). The way Mark broke off at this point makes his narrative very effective (cf. Mark 11:32 with Matt. 21:26 and Luke 20:6). In a dramatic way, the reader is impressed with how the religious leaders always wanted to do what was politically wise. It was politically foolish to say anything inopportune. Loss of control would mean loss of power. A riot would indicate loss of control. Therefore, Jesus' questioners were very silent!

When one completes these figures, he truly enters into the thought. Thus such figures are a mental stimulant. The interpreter must identify himself with the writer or speaker.

FIGURES INVOLVING UNDERSTATEMENT

Euphemism

In euphemism a word or phrase that is less direct is substituted because the writer believes that the direct form would be distasteful, offensive, or unnecessarily harsh. In Acts 1:24-25 the small band of early disciples prayed about the one who was to take the place of Judas. They wanted God to make clear to them which of two men was best suited to take this position. They regarded Judas as having turned aside from the ministry and office of an apostle: "From which Judas turned aside to proceed *to his own place*" (vs. 25). This is certainly a euphemism for the place of Judas' final destiny.[10] Judas had been a member of the group. The early disciples could not avoid alluding to the fate of this man who had walked up and down Palestine with Jesus only to turn aside at the end. Yet when they speak about this matter they do so euphemistically.

Discussions in the Old Testament about sex are phrased in euphemistic language: "Every man of you shall not come near unto flesh of his flesh to uncover nakedness; I am Jehovah" (Lev. 18:6). The phrase "flesh of his flesh" means blood relatives. The verb "come near" means "to approach sexually."[11] The infinitive phrase "to uncover nakedness" involves the idea of having sexual intercourse with[12] plus the idea of contracting marriage.[13] In this section laws against incest are delicately phrased. An excellent standard is set here. The language is direct enough so that the first readers—i.e., the Hebrew people —knew exactly what was being discussed. Yet there is no morbid preoccupation with details. The Old Testament is neither prudish or prurient in dealing with sex. Euphemism plays a part in this achievement. The interpreter in such instances must be sufficiently direct so that the reader has no doubt about God's standard. This means that he must clarify some things that were clear to the first readers but are no longer so. At the same time,

---

[10] Bauer, l.g., p. 830: "Of the place of torment or evil...Acts 1:25b... W. gen. . . . Luke 16:28."

[11] BDB, p. 897.

[12] *Ibid., "erwah*, p. 789: "chiefly euphemism for cohabitation."

[13] *Ibid., galah*, p. 163: "Piel, 1. *uncover*, a. *nakedness* (oft = *contract marriage* . . .)* Lev. 18:6-19; 20:11-21 (Holiness Code 23 times) ; Ezek. 22:10."

because the holiness of marriage is the basis for all such detailed laws, there is no need to dwell on that which violates the holiness of the marriage relationship. It must be shown for what it is and then left to stand under God's condemnation.

Litotes or Meiosis

In this figure a negative statement is used to declare an affirmative truth. A milder form is found where simple understatement heightens the action which is being described.

Jesus' words in Acts 1:5 are reported in the form of litotes: "But you [pl.] will be baptized with the Holy Spirit *not long after these days* [= within a few days]." This same kind of understatement describes the storm in Acts 27:13-14: ". . . when they weighed anchor, they were sailing along Crete. *Not long afterward* [after not much time = soon afterward], a hurricane wind, called a North-Easter, rushed down against Crete."

A negative with simple understatement is very forceful in Paul's description of the Jews: "Who killed both the Lord Jesus and the prophets, and who persecuted us, and *who are not pleasing God,* but are hostile to all men who are hindering us from speaking to the Gentiles that they might be saved. . ." (I Thess. 2:15-16a). In describing the Jews as "not pleasing God" Paul really meant that they displeased, vexed, and angered God. Of this particular generation of Jews Paul utters a solemn verdict: "But wrath has come upon them through all eternity."[14] Not to please God is most serious indeed. On the other hand, to please God ought to be the Christian's constant ambition (cf. II Cor. 5:9).

FIGURES INVOLVING AN INTENSIFICATION OR REVERSAL OF MEANING

Hyperbole

Hyperbole is conscious exaggeration by the writer to gain effect. The last verse in the Gospel of John contains a classical example: "But indeed, there are many other things which Jesus did, which if they were written one by one, I do not suppose *that the world itself could contain the books being written*" (John 21:25). John states here that his Gospel, like the others, is a selection of incidents and sayings from the life of Jesus. Hyperbole drives home this point.

In Deuteronomy we find most of the people of Israel using

---

[14] Bauer, p. 819: *telos,* l.d. gamma, *eis telos . . . forever, through all eternity.*

hyperbole when they refused to enter the land of Canaan. Note how the hyperbolic statements of those sent to spy out the land —except Caleb and Joshua—stuck in the minds of the people. Moses quotes the people who, in turn, quote the spies: "Whither are we going up? Our brethren have made our heart to melt, saying, 'The people are greater and taller than we; the cities are great and *fortified up to heaven;* and moreover we have seen the sons of the Anakim there!" (Deut. 1:28). Bigger people, greater cities, and fiercest of all enemies—it was a realistic appraisal. And the hyperbole was part of the realism. However, a response of faith on their part would have had the same realism (cf. Rom. 4:19-22) with the opposite conclusion (see Num. 14:6-9).

Irony

In irony the writer or speaker uses words to denote the exact opposite of what the language declares. To the query: "How was the exam?" a student may answer: "Simple! Simple!" Yet the tone of his voice indicates that his reply is ironic. He means that the exam was very difficult. Context is essential in recognizing irony. We must know the surroundings of the speaker and his relationship to the person to whom he speaks. Irony is vivid. When it is grasped and recognized, it often carries a significant freight of meaning.

In Matthew 23 Jesus pronounces woes against the scribes and Pharisees. He speaks of them as building the tombs of the prophets and decorating the memorials of righteous persons. These leaders had stated confidently that if they had been living in the days of their fathers, they would not have murdered the prophets. Jesus, however, pointed out that by their own ad- mission they were sons of men who did murder the prophets (Matt. 23:31). Then Jesus remarks further: "And you [pl.] make full [or fill up] the measure of your fathers" (Matt. 23:32). The best textual reading here is that of the aorist imperative. It is also the more difficult reading since some scribes substituted an easier reading because they did not grasp the fact that Jesus was using irony. In place of the aorist imperative they put the aorist indicative (see manuscript D) or the future (see manuscript B). But Jesus is using irony here. He says: "All right, go ahead, make full the measure of sins which your fathers did not com- plete." Here is a people bent upon a certain course. No miracles on his part, no amount of teaching will change their attitude. Therefore Jesus simply gave them up to their self-chosen destiny. In these ironic words, the destiny of the religious leaders is sealed.

Paul also employed irony. In I Corinthians 3 and 4 Paul deals
with the party spirit in Corinth. He comments about their
loyalty to Apollos and to himself in particular (I Cor. 4:6). He
seeks to stamp out the egotism by which members are puffed up
in favor of one apostle against another. It was their feeling of
superiority that caused the Corinthians to have such popularity
contests. Yet all that they have they received from the Lord.
Their boasting (in apostles) shows that they feel like proud
possessors rather than like recipients. At this point Paul resorts
to irony: "Now you have all you could wish; now you have become rich; without us you have become kings; to be sure, would
that you did become kings in order that we might rule as kings
with you" (I Cor. 4:8). In this irony Paul is striking out against
their deep-seated spiritual pride. They thought that they were
so rich in spiritual teaching that they could argue over which
teacher was the best. Paul did not believe this. But in commenting on their actions he phrases his remarks ironically. They were
rich. They were kings. Did not such independence and indifference to the feelings of their fellow-Christians show that they
thought they had arrived? Paul then adds: "If only it were true
that you ruled as kings." Then he and the other apostles would
be free from their suffering and oppression to reign also (see I
Cor. 4:9-13). Irony here shows the gulf between the imaginary
and the actual.

FIGURES INVOLVING FULLNESS OF THOUGHT

Pleonasm

In pleonasm the writer repeats an idea which has already been
expressed simply because he has the habit of repeating. Pleonasm
is rarely seen by the English reader because the translators feel
that it would only bring misunderstanding. The English reader
would see it as meaningless redundancy. When Luke reports
Jesus' instructions to the two disciples who went to prepare the
last supper, we see the pleonasm in Luke's style: "And you will
say *to the household master of the* house" (Luke 22:11). This is
not carelessness on Luke's part, but a characteristic of his style
with certain words or ideas.[15]

Luke in commenting on II Samuel 7:12-16 declares "that God
swore with an oath [lit. took an oath with an oath] to him
[David] that one from the fruit of his loins would sit upon his
throne" (Acts 4:30). Here the verb by itself is sufficient and the

15 Blass-Debrunner-Funk, paragraph 484.

noun adds nothing. Yet this is a style which Luke follows because he wants to stress how energetically God entered into a living relationship with David and his descendants.

Epanadiplosis or Epizeuxis

This term describes a situation where an important word is repeated for emphasis.[16] There are two occurrences of the same expression in the book of Revelation that illustrate well this kind of repetition. An angel announces the doom of Babylon, the great civil power opposed to God: "Babylon, the Great *has fallen, has fallen* who caused all nations to drink from the wine of her passionate immorality" (Rev. 14:8; cf. 18:2). The rhythmic repetition of the verb "fall" in the aorist tense is very moving. A different example of epanadiplosis on the positive side is found in the refrain of the four living creatures (4:8): "*Holy, Holy, Holy* is the Lord God, the Almighty—the one who was and the one who is and the coming one." Here the language from the created beings who surround God's throne is reminiscent of the throne scene in Isaiah 6:1-5, especially vs. 3. Although there may be trinitarian implications in this three-fold repetition (epizeuxis), Isaiah's main purpose in this figure (and John's as well) was to drive home the holiness of God. Isaiah's stress is on the character of God rather than on the form and manifestation of his ontological essence.

Climax

In climax, a series of qualities, characteristics, or actions are listed. First, the quality is stated. Then this quality is specifically said to give birth to or to be followed by another quality. By the use of climax each quality, characteristic, or action is mentioned twice. Paul in Romans 5 says: ". . . we are boasting in *afflictions* because we know that *the affliction* produces *endurance,* and *the endurance* produces character [the quality of being approved, often with the implication of approved by test], and *the character* produces *hope,* and *the hope* does not disappoint . . ." (Rom. 5:3-5).

In II Peter 1 there is a similar example of climax. "And in reference to this very thing [the believers becoming sharers in the divine nature and their flight from the corruption in the world in the sphere of evil desire], having made every effort, provide in your *faith, moral excellence;* and in your *moral excellence, knowledge;* and in *your knowledge, self-control;* and in *your self*

16 *Ibid.,* 493(1).

control, endurance; and in *your endurance, love of the brothers;* and in *your love of the brothers, love"* (II Pet. 1:5-7). Repeating the list of qualities (climax) emphasizes the activity of the believer. This is clearly seen in vss. 8-10 where the believer who is doing this is never idle or unfruitful. But the believer who is not doing these things is so short-sighted that he is blind. His failure means that he forgets his cleansing from his former sins. It is no wonder that Peter concludes: "Wherefore rather, brothers, make every effort to confirm your calling and election, because if you do these things you will not be lost" (II Pet. 1:10). The actions listed are a confirmation of one's calling and election.

INTERROGATION

Rhetorical questions are far more than a teaching technique. Sometimes they are answered. At other times the answer is obvious and no explicit statement is necessary. But the question becomes a means of focussing the thought upon a central idea.

When discussing Abraham's faith being reckoned for righteousness, Paul speaks of what a blessed thing this is: "This blessedness then, was it toward the circumcision or toward the uncircumcision? Now we answer: 'Faith was reckoned to Abraham for righteousness.' How then was it reckoned? While he was in circumcision or in uncircumcision? Not in circumcision but in uncircumcision [it was reckoned]" (Rom. 4:9-10). These questions and answers indicated to any reader conversant with Judaism that the Jewish pride in a ceremonial rite was misplaced. Abraham came into a covenant relation before such rites were begun. The relationship of faith was central. To Paul, the rite of circumcision was peripheral—merely a sign of the faith that Abraham had before he thought of such a rite.

In another example Romans 8:31-36, with its numerous questions, prepares the way for the assertions of 8:37-39. The questions show the reader that God and Christ are *for us.* Paul considers the past and present action of God and Christ as proof that they are for us. He concludes by asserting that believers are winning a glorious victory over all obstacles. No external opponent can stop the believer or separate him from the love of God which is in Christ Jesus. The list of opponents is formidable. But the power of the one who loved us is the secret of the believer's victory.

DISTINGUISHING FIGURATIVE FROM LITERAL

Figurative language is a pervasive feature of human discourse. It lends vivacity to expression and adds depth of meaning. In order to understand any figure, one must of course first recognize the literal meaning and then, by reflecting on the relevant points of similarity, interpret the significance of the figure. Fortunately it is usually easy to recognize a figurative expression and to make the necessary distinctions. The brief classification and description given above should provide additional help. The student will soon learn that the penetration of a figure to reach an idea is a stimulating adventure.

IX Opaque Figures of Speech

Many seemingly obscure statements of the Bible can be brought into focus by seeing their context, language, and historical-cultural background. But there are other passages where genuine obscurity exists, and which cannot be interpreted by the foregoing methods. Sometimes the original writer may not have intended to puzzle his contemporary readers, but did so anyway. At other times the obscurity is no doubt intentional. In neither case should we simply pass over such materials. Rather, they are a challenge to any interpreter. If he cannot explain what is enigmatic, he at least knows why it should remain obscure! We begin with the figures which are intentionally obscure.

RIDDLES

A riddle is a concise saying which is intentionally formulated to tax the ingenuity of the hearer or reader when he tries to explain it.

Secular Riddles

Samson's riddle in Judges 14:12-20 comes in a period in Israel's history when every man did that which was right in his own eyes (cf. Judges 17:6; 21:25). This was true of the Judges as well as the common people. Samson decided that he wanted to marry a Philistine woman. In one of his travels to Timnah, the home of the girl, he killed a lion. Later he was able to get some honey out of the skeleton of the slain beast. During the pre-nuptial festivities he incorporated these two incidents into a riddle which he propounded to the thirty friends of the bridegroom who were provided for him by the Timnathites. If they correctly answered his riddle, he would give them thirty changes of clothing. But if they failed, they would owe him thirty changes of clothing. Samson was sure that they could not guess the answer since he had not even told his parents about the killing of the lion or about getting honey later from the skeleton. Samson's riddle has the concise language typical of riddles: "Out of the eater came forth food, and out of the strong came forth sweetness" (Judges 14:14). This is a typical secular riddle.

What began in fun and festivity ended in tragedy. The thirty friends of Samson threatened the girl and her father's house with burning if she did not find out for them the answer to Samson's riddle. By a persistent deluge of tears she finally extracted the answer from Samson. Just as the wedding feast was being consummated, when Samson was about to take his bride, the thirty friends of the bridegroom gave him the answer to his riddle. Samson exploded in anger. He knew at once how they had gotten the answer. So off he went twenty miles or so to Ashkelon where he killed thirty Philistines. He turned over their clothing to the men who had "solved" his riddle and went home. His Philistine wife was given to the best man. When Samson returned and found his wife had been given to another, he took revenge upon the Philistines. He burned their standing grain, the grain shocks, and olive yards by putting burning brands in foxes' tails, one brand tied to two fox tails, and by letting these pairs of foxes loose in the cultivated fields and olive yards. The Philistines, admitting that Samson had a just cause, slew the father and daughter who had wrongly treated Samson. But Samson then slew more Philistines "with a great slaughter" because they had put to death the girl and her father (Judges 15:8).

Note how this riddle is intertwined with the hostility between Israel and the Philistines. It caused the outbreak of hostilities and exploits on the part of Samson. For this reason it was remembered. Riddles were no doubt frequent among the Israelites and surrounding peoples during this period. It is important for the interpreter to observe: (1) the reason for the riddle; (2) the content of the riddle; and (3) the outcome of the riddle. Such observations make clear the existential orientation of history. Samson as a one-man army is certainly exceptional. Yet the military activities of Israel during the time of the Judges, of the united kingdom, and of the divided kingdom are not cold factual records. They involve human decisions, human weaknesses and failures, and human destiny.

Sacred Riddles

In Revelation 13:18 is a famous riddle. John describes the beast from the sea who makes war with the saints (13:1-10). Then he describes the beast from the earth who causes the earth and its inhabitants to worship the first beast (13:11-18). This second beast makes an image of the first beast. He gives breath to the image and enacts laws stating that as many as refuse to worship the image of the beast should be killed. (This false prophet —cf. 16:13; 19:20; 20:10—brings results similar to those recorded in Daniel 3 when charges were brought against Daniel's three friends for not worshipping Nebuchadnezzar's image. The account in Daniel does not state how many other Jews did not worship the image. Yet God delivered Daniel's three friends and all the other Jews as well.) Economic boycott is used. Without the mark or stamp of the beast no one is able to buy or sell. The stamp may be either the name of the beast or the number of his name. Then comes John's riddle: "Here is wisdom. Whoever has understanding, let him calculate the number of the beast. Now it is the number of a man. And his number is 666" (Rev. 13:18).[1]

Many attempts have been made to solve this riddle, but no one can claim that he has "the solution." By the phrase "number of a man" John means the numerical value of a man's name. This kind of numerology was well known in ancient times. There were no arabic numerals, so each letter of the Greek and Hebrew alphabet had numerical value. In Greek three obsolete letters (vau or digamma, koppa, and sampi) were employed with the regular letters of the alphabet.[2] For example, alpha = 1; beta = 2; gamma = 3; delta = 4; epsilon = 5; vau or digamma = 6; zeta = 7 etc. The name Jesus, by way of illustration, is composed of the letters: Iota, ēta, sigma, omicron, upsilon, and sigma *(Iēsous)*. They have the following numerical value: Iota = 10; ēta = 8; sigma = 200; omicron = 70; upsilon = 400; sigma = 200. Adding, one finds that the total numerical value of the name of Jesus is 888. John's original readers were those who read his letter in Greek. All speculation about the name being in Hebrew or Aramaic letters is weighed down by the complexity of transliteration from one language to another. In Aramaic, for example, the name Jesus may have two possible

[1] For the meaning here see Oskar Rühle, *"arithmeō, arithmos," TWNT,* I, 461-64. Henry Barclay Swete, *The Apocalypse of St. John* (1909), pp. 172-76. G. R. Beasley-Murray, "Revelation," *The New Bible Commentary* (1956), pp. 1185-86.

[2] See Goodwin and Gulick, *op. cit.,* paragraphs 3, 429, 446.

forms: *yēshua"* with a numerical value of 386 and *yᵉhoshua"* with a numerical value of 397. So whatever form of the name one selects in Aramaic for Jesus, it has less than half of the numerical value that the same name has in Greek.

The Greek name Teitan, for example, has the numerical value of 666, but this shows only that one can put together many combinations of Greek letters that will give the desired numerical total. When known "beasts" (political rulers) in the first century have their names or titles (or both) analyzed, the results are far from convincing. Nero Caesar in Hebrew letters comes out right if the consonants are NRWN QSR. But in the Talmud the word Caesar is spelled QYSR. If this is adopted, the total numerical value comes to 676. In Greek, of course, no form of Nero Caesar comes to 666.

Apparently this religious riddle is meant to be ambiguous. The activities, power, and influence of the antichrist are far more important than this numerical clue in his name. However, the riddle does emphasize the fact that specific persons will play key roles in opposing God and the people of God. The *purpose* of the riddle is to focus attention upon the antichrist. The *content* of the riddle, dealing as it does with the numerical value of the name, uses a common means of designating a person whom the writer did not or could not explicitly name. The *outcome* of the riddle is that the time of the antichrist's appearance is freed from all specific time settings since no one in ancient times clearly met the numerical description.

FABLES

A fable is a fictitious story meant to teach a moral lesson. The characters are often members of the animal or vegetable kingdoms whose actions, being contrary to the natural activities of animals or trees, depict the vagaries, emotions, and failures of human beings.

Jotham's Fable Against Political Tyranny

In Judges 9:1-21 is the account of how the men of Shechem revolted against the house of Jerubbaal (i.e. Gideon) and how they were reproved. After Gideon's death, Abimelech, who was Gideon's son by his concubine in Shechem, went to the men of Shechem and proposed that he be made their ruler. In order to make this operation less complex after the men of Shechem agreed to it, Abimelech hired some ruffians to slay 70 members of Gideon's family. Only Jotham, Gideon's youngest son, escaped. Soon after Abimelech was installed as ruler, Jotham emerged momentarily from hiding. Standing on the top of Mt. Gerizim, he proclaimed judgment against the men of Shechem by means of a fable.

One must read the fable to appreciate its beauty and effectiveness (see Judges 9:8-15; Jotham interprets and applies the fable in 9:16-20). The trees go out to choose a king. In order of preference they nominate the olive tree, the fig-tree, the vine, and finally the thorn bush (bramble or buckthorn). The first three decline because their task is so important that the waving to and fro over the other trees has no appeal for them. But the thorn bush feels differently. If he is anointed king, all the other trees will come and take refuge in his shade. If they do not come and enjoy the blessing of the thorn bush's shade, fire will proceed from the thorn bush and devour the cedars of Lebanon. What pictorial imagery! A thorn bush boasts in its shade! A thorn bush sets on fire the lofty cedars and burns them to charred and blackened ruins!

Jotham then applies the fable. If the men of Shechem have done right toward Gideon's household, and if they have done well in making Abimelech king, there should be mutual rejoicing between the people and their new king. But if they have not done right (to which the mass murder of seventy persons testified), then Jotham solemnly calls for fire to come out from Abimelech (the thorn bush) and devour the men of Shechem, and for fire to come from the men of Shechem and devour Abimelech. With this fateful word Jotham went into exile to Beersheba to escape Abimelech. The moral lesson in this fable was clear and was driven home with compelling effectiveness.

Jehoash's Fable Against Belligerent Meddling

There is another fable in II Kings 14:9. Amaziah, the king of Judah, had just returned from an impressive victory over the Edomites (II Kings 14:7). Now, as if playing a game, he wanted to see what his military forces could do against his northern neighbor, Israel. So he sent messengers to Jehoash, king of Israel, announcing that he would open a military campaign against him: "Come, let us measure our strength, one against the other" (II Kings 14:8).

Jehoash, aware of Judah's successes in the South, tried to deter Amaziah by telling him a short fable. A brier bush in Lebanon demanded that the lofty cedar tree give his daughter in marriage to the son of the brier bush. But before the brier bush could press home his demands a wild beast came through the area where it was growing and trampled it down. Jehoash then applied the fable by telling Amaziah that he was proud of his victory over Edom. He wryly suggests that he ought to enjoy his honor by staying at home. "Why should you engage in strife at the cost of misery? Both you will fall and Judah with you" (II Kings 14:10). Amaziah ignored his advice. Entering into battle at Bethshemesh, he was soundly defeated. Jerusalem was invaded. Part of its wall was knocked down. Gold, silver, and vessels were taken from the king's house and from the house of the Lord. The fable must not be allegorized to make every part of it refer to Amaziah and Jehoash, e.g. that Amaziah is the brier bush, Jehoash the cedar, and the wild animal who trampled down the brier the army of Jehoash. All that the fable says is that human pride is quickly brushed aside by the relentless events of life.

Ezekiel's Parabolic Fable Against Alliance with Egypt

Ezekiel 17 is divided into three parts: (1) The prophet's riddle and parable (really an allegory and fable), vss. 1-10; (2) Meaning of the story about the eagles and the vine, vss. 11-21; (3) The final planting of Jehovah when he establishes his Messiah as head over all, vss. 22-24.

In vs. 2 two different Hebrew expressions are used to describe the story which the prophet Ezekiel will use. He is "to put forth a riddle"—*chud chiydah*. The noun translated "riddle" can refer to "a dark, obscure utterance," or what we would call a riddle today, and to "perplexing questions."[3] He is also "to speak or use a parable"—*meshol mashal*. The noun translated "parable" has the meanings of: "proverbial saying," "by-word," "figurative prophetic discourse," "similitude," "poem" like an ode, and "sentences of ethical wisdom."[4] The Hebrew terms do not have a specific technical designation. The story which Ezekiel told in vss. 1-10 was a fable because it involves members of the animal and vegetable kingdoms doing things which no member of their species do as part of their natural activities.

A great eagle comes into Lebanon and crops off the top of the cedar. He takes it away to a city of commerce and merchants. He takes a seed of the land and plants it in surroundings which are conducive for growth. He plants it as a willow tree is planted, and it comes up a low spreading vine. He wanted this

3 BDB, p. 295.
4 BDB, p. 605.

vine to spread forth its branches and turn them towards him.

However, another eagle appears on the scene, and the vine turns towards this eagle instead. Even before the story is finished the Lord Jehovah asks whether this vine that inclined away from the eagle that planted it and turned towards another will prosper. The answer is that it will utterly wither.

In vss. 11-21 the prophet unfolds the meaning of the story, and it becomes obvious that this story is also an allegory. The story is composed to use several key elements as metaphors. The first eagle stands for the king of Babylon. The top of the cedar designates Jehoiachin and the princes who were carried away to Babylon. The seed of the land which was planted as a willow and came up as a low spreading vine refers to Zedekiah and the people who were left in the land. The other eagle to whom Zedekiah and the people inclined was Egypt. In turning to Egypt, Zedekiah broke his covenant with Nebuchadnezzar. This covenant had been confirmed with an oath. Such solemn statements and affirmations in ancient times involved the deity which a king claimed he served. In this case Zedekiah would have entered into this solemn agreement with Nebuchadnezzar by calling upon his God—Jehovah—as a witness. In 17:18-19 God declares that it is "my oath" and "my covenant" that Zedekiah has despised and broken. Unbeknown to Zedekiah, his covenant and oath with Nebuchadnezzar involved God. Jehovah was no mere formula in its ratification. Hence God pronounces judgment upon Zedekiah. He will be caught for his treachery and brought to Babylon. His army will be scattered, and he will come to utter defeat.

Against this dark background Ezekiel turns to a brighter picture. Instead of Nebuchadnezzar, the Lord Jehovah will take a young, tender twig (cf. Isa. 11:1; 53:2) from the top of the cedar and he will plant it upon a high and lofty mountain (cf. Isa. 2:2-4; Micah 4:1-5). Here it is the Messiah himself rather than the Messianic nation. This tree will bear fruit and be a goodly cedar. Here is the influence of the Messiah. All the birds come and dwell in its branches. Here is the response to the Messiah of all the peoples looked upon individually. All the trees know that it is Jehovah who has done this. He has brought down the high tree; he has exalted the low tree; he has dried up the green tree; and he has made the dry tree to flourish. The trees seem to represent the nations. The high tree and the green tree stand for those who, at any particular moment in history, seem to be flourishing. The low tree and the dry tree seem to represent those which have no significance. The destiny of individuals and peoples is controlled by Jehovah and is related to their response to the Messiah: " . . . I Jehovah have spoken and I will act"[5] (Ezek. 17:24).

Procedures for Interpreting Fables

1. Understand the contemporary situation in which the speaker resorted to a fable.

2. Note whether the fable is simple or complex, i.e., is the fable trying to teach a lesson by stressing one point or several points?

3. Observe the influence of the fable on the hearers and the immediate response or comment of the one who told the fable—words, attitude, or action of both hearers and of the propounder of the fable are significant.

4. State why the lesson taught in the fable is pertinent to modern man and in what other ways the same lesson can be brought to the modern reader's attention.

ENIGMATIC SAYINGS

These consist of statements which are so highly saturated with meaning that the hearer is perplexed because of his own unpreparedness for that meaning. Sometimes the modern reader is able to uncover more teachings to illuminate these sayings, thereby reducing the element of enigma. On the other hand, today's reader cannot stand in the original situation where the saying was given and may be puzzled now by elements which were clear when they were first uttered but are now unknown. The basic cause for the obscurity of these sayings is the condition of the hearers and the profoundness of the message.

Obscurity in Old Testament Revelation

In Numbers 12:6-8 there is a contrast between the manner in which God revealed himself to the prophets (by a vision and by a dream, *bammar'eh, bachᵃlōm*) and the way he revealed himself

---

[5] With a *waw* consecutive the tone is generally on the ultima (see Gesenius-Kautzsch-Cowley, 49h). But the shifting forward of the tone to the ultima is not consistently carried out. It is omitted regularly in the *lamed hē* verbs if the vowel of the second syllable is *i* except in *Qal* (only Lev. 24:5 before *aleph*) (GKC 49i, k [c]) . The verb *wᵉᵉ″asiythi* is a *Qal* form. Yet verbs both *primae gutturalis* and *lamed hē* have *Qal* forms which are identical with the *hiphil* (See GKC, 75r). Since this form differs from a *hiphil* only by virtue of the absence of a preformative, the *i* it seems could indicate a *waw* consecutive as a possibility instead of the *waw* conjunctive which the accent in the Kittel text favors.

to Moses. In this context Moses is in a class by himself. God spoke to Moses face to face (lit. mouth to mouth) in direct appearance or personal presence.[6] Contrasted to this is the phrase, "but not *in enigmatic sayings*" i.e. in dark or obscure utterance.[7] Hence God's revelation in and through the prophets by means of visions and dreams (inward intuition)[8] is pictured as being enigmatic. Such "obscure" revelation is contrasted to that presented to Moses by God's appearing to him in a direct personal way. To the biblical writers obscurity and enigmatic sayings do not prove that they failed in verbal expression. Rather the reasons lie deeper. Enigmatic statements are inherent in certain kinds of revelation. The way God reveals himself affects the content of that revelation. By way of summary, then, note three elements in enigmatic discourse: (1) condition of the hearers, (2) profoundness of the message, and (3) media through which revelation came to those who proclaimed it.

In Psalm 49:4 (Heb. text, vs. 5) the psalmist declares: "I will incline my ear [to receive revelation][9] with reference to a poem; I will propound[10] my enigmatical discourse with the help of a harp." The idea of some translators that the psalmist is talking about a proverb and the solving of a riddle[11] is not supported by the rest of the psalm. Where are the proverbs (in the technical sense)? Where are the riddles (in a technical sense)? The context indicates that the poet uttered a didactic psalm and that some enigmatic sayings are included in his poetic meditation.

Likewise the psalmist in Psalm 78:2 prefaces an historical psalm with the words: "I will open my mouth in a poetic discourse; I will pour forth enigmatical sayings derived from ancient times." The word for "poetic discourse" in the Hebrew is the word *mashal* which also means parable. The word for "enigmatical saying" *(chiydah)* also means riddle. By this language the psalmist simply means that his poetic discourse will teach a lesson and that some of the enigmatic features of his people's history will emerge in his recitation as he contrasts the acts of God with the actions and responses of God's people.

It is apparent that obscurity is not all of the same type. Whenever the cause for the obscurity is irremovable (involving either

6 BDB, *mar'eh,* 1.b., p. 909.

7 BDB, *chiydah,* 1., 295.

8 C. F. Keil and F. Delitzsch, *Biblical Commentary on the Old Testament: The Pentateuch,* tr. James Martin (1885), III, 80-81.

9 BDB, *natah,* Hiphil, 3. e., p. 641.

10 BDB, p. 295.

11 RSV. See *chiydah,* KB, p. 292.

the hearer, the message, or the medium through which revelation came), the interpreter can go only so far. By a wise use of the theme of promise and fulfillment, he may shed light on some enigmas. But he must be faithful to the enigmatic saying itself. He must not claim that when he has provided some light, he has told the whole story. The Old Testament as a whole without the New Testament would be an enigma for the Christian interpreter. There would be promise and no fulfillment. There would be a God who acted but who no longer acts (for Christians the Holy Spirit plays a very important part under the New Covenant). The Christian with his New Testament has the God who acted in the Old Testament, who acted in Christ and in the Church of Christ's apostles, and who has been active ever since through his Holy Spirit. Christ puts all that is enigmatic in a new light.

Obscurity in New Testament Revelation

Paroimia in John's Gospel. This word occurs four times in John's Gospel. It means *"dark saying, figure of speech* in which especially lofty ideas are concealed."[12] *"Paroimia* in John means *the concealed, dark speech* or *language* which obscures the meaning."[13] In John 10:6 the allegory of the good shepherd is designated "this concealed language." John adds: "But they did not know what the things were which he was speaking to them" (i.e. the Pharisees, cf. 9:40). It is true that the attitude and condition of the Pharisees would make the plainest language opaque. But this cannot be said of John 16:25a,b, 29 where Jesus talked to his disciples alone just before his arrest, trial, and death. "I have spoken these things to you in *dark sayings [concealed language].* The time is coming when no longer will I speak to you in *dark sayings [concealed language],* but I will announce to you plainly concerning the Father" (John 16:25). Although Jesus may be referring directly to these last discourses with them, his words are applicable to much of what he had taught. "Jesus' manner of speech generally until his departure from the disciples is designated as obscure language which is only able to express the supernatural truth imperfectly by hinting at it in human words."[14] Westcott shows why this is true when he says: "The description applies in fact to all the earthly teaching of the Lord. The necessity which veiled His teaching to the multitudes (Matt. 13:11ff) influenced, in other ways, His teaching to the disciples.

12 Bauer, p. 634.
13 Friedrich Hauck, *"paroimia," TWNT,* V, 854.
14 *Ibid.*

He spoke as they could bear, and under figures of human limitation."[15] The time when Jesus will announce to them plainly
concerning the Father is not explicitly stated. But in the light of
John 16:12-16 it would seem that Jesus had in mind his speaking
to the disciples through the Spirit. That time would be after
Pentecost.

Christ talks about the disciples asking in his name (vs. 26). He
speaks of his Father's love for the disciples because of their love
for Christ and their belief that he came forth from God. Then
very concisely Jesus summarizes his whole redemptive ministry
(16:28): "I came forth from the Father [mission], and I have
come into the world [nativity], again I am leaving the world
[passion], and I am proceeding to the Father [ascension]."[16] This
word brings an immediate response from the disciples: "Lo now,
you are speaking plainly and you are uttering *no concealed
language*" (16:29). They feel that this last statement is a sample
of the clearer elements of revelation which lie ahead and which
Jesus had just promised to them.

Hence concealed language is a reality. The interpreter must
not make this an excuse for skipping over difficult sayings. On
the other hand, he should beware of pronouncing *ex cathedra* the
one final meaning which makes all further discussion unnecessary.

Sententious sayings in the synoptics. There are many of these
which need careful thought and meditation. In Luke 11:33-36,
Jesus points to the common experience of lighting a lamp. When
the lamp is lit, no one puts it into a secret place or under a
grain measure. Rather he places it upon a lampstand. Then
Jesus employs the lamp in a metaphor. "The lamp of the body
is the eye" (11:34). Whenever the eye is sound or healthy, the
whole body is full of light. But whenever the eye is sick (in poor
condition), the whole body is full of darkness. The next saying
of Jesus is enigmatic: "Consider whether the light which is in
you is darkness" (11:35). Here Jesus seems to have changed to a
metaphorical use of "eye." The term is not used literally for
a part of the body but for the "eye" of the soul.[17] When the
inward person is sick morally and spiritually the eye of the soul
cannot transmit spiritual light. Only darkness then comes
through this channel. Jesus concludes his statements by more
metaphor plus a simile: "Now if your whole body is full of
light, having not any portion dark, the whole body will be

---

15 B. F. Westcott, *The Gospel According to St. John* (1908), II, 233.
16 *Ibid.*, p. 235.
17 Cf. Alfred Plummer, *A Critical and Exegetical Commentary on the
Gospel of Luke* (1914), p. 308.

wholly full of light just as whenever a lamp illuminates you by its beam" (11:36). In this metaphorical portion "the whole body" seems to stand for the whole person. "His being full of light" seems to refer to the spiritual soundness of this person. Not any portion of his inward being is dark. Hence the amount of light within is like the amount of light outside when the beam of a lamp completely illuminates the person. Conciseness and shifts from the literal to the metaphorical are the cause for the obscurity here. The profoundness of thought is undeniable. What we are controls what we "see."

Following this section in Luke, Jesus is invited to dine in the house of a Pharisee (Luke 11:37). He entered and reclined. This disturbed the Pharisee since Jesus had not first prepared himself for dinner by engaging in the Jewish ritual washings. Sensing how the Pharisee felt, Jesus pointed out that although they (the Pharisees) were cleansing the outside of the cup and the dish (external things) their own inward part (their soul) was full of greediness and wickedness (11:39). Then he addressed all the Pharisees: "Foolish men, the One who made the outside [external things] made also the inside [things of the soul], did he not? Moreover, give the things within [your vessels] as a donation to the poor, and behold all things are clean to you" (11:40-41). Here Jesus pictures God as the creator of the material universe and of the soul of man with all of its inward characteristics. The form of the question showed that Jesus knew that the Pharisees would agree with him on the matter of God as the creator of the material and spiritual. It is Jesus' conclusion that is so profound. In slightly veiled language Jesus maintains that a true sense of values makes all preoccupation with ceremonial matters to be impossible. If the contents of the dishes (the food) were given to the poor, and if all the needs of starving people were cared for, this would so occupy the mind of the Pharisees that they would not have time to be fastidious about ceremonial washings. All things would be clean to them. This was an outlook foreign to the Pharisees' thought because their outlook was colored by what they were within—a preoccupation with themselves and how well they were carrying out their own refinements of the law. This kind of self-centeredness left little room for an outgoing concern for those in deep need.

Procedures for Interpreting Enigmatic Sayings

1. Remove all the superficial ambiguities. Check the lexical meaning of words. Observe carefully the syntactical connections.
2. Pay careful attention to the context so that you can see how

the thought flows along *before, through,* and *after* the enigmatic portion.

3. Watch for quick shifts from the literal to the metaphorical. The use of a figurative meaning for that which has just been used literally is a frequent occurrence in enigmatic sayings where metaphor plays a basic role.

4. Check good commentaries after you have done firsthand careful exegesis for yourself. Where enigmatic materials occur, the interpreter who consults commentaries too soon becomes so occupied with possible solutions that he never grapples with the obscurity.

5. Write down a tentative statement (in your own words) of what you believe the meaning of the enigmatic statement(s) to be. Keep such a notation. Then you will be able to come back to it later and build upon your previous reflection. The next time you may take a different approach and may see angles that were not apparent the first time. This may lead you to a different conclusion. Yet even the first formulation will force you to bring together all the known elements into a statement that you hope would have been meaningful to those who first heard the saying. Revision is an important key to a deepening penetration of meaning.

X Extended Figures of Speech

The study of syntax revealed that clauses—larger grammatical elements—function as nouns, verbs, or adverbs. Likewise, extended figures of speech often function similarly to some of the short figures of speech. Whether the thinking be in Hebrew, Aramaic, or Greek, these extended figures of speech are not altered by the language vehicle. They have the same purpose and the same effect.

SIMILITUDES AND PARABLES

Definitions

A similitude or a parable is often an extended simile. An allegory, on the other hand, is an extended metaphor. Examples make this clear. Let us begin with the *simile*: "He was led as a *sheep* to the slaughter; and *as a lamb* before his shearer is dumb, so he openeth not his mouth" (Acts 8:32; Isa. 53:7). Next, here is a *metaphor* which makes use of the same animal: "Behold *the Lamb* of God who takes away the sin of the world" (John 1:29. The *similitude* is illustrated by the longer account of the lost sheep in Luke 15:4-7: "Which man from you having one hundred sheep and having lost one from them, he leaves the ninety and nine in the desert does he not and proceeds to the one which has been lost until he find it?" (Luke 15:4). In the same context of Luke is the *parable* of the lost son (Luke 15:11-32): " . . . Because this my son was dead and he became alive, he was lost and has been found . . ." (Luke 15:24). The allegory of the door for the sheep and the good shepherd is found in John 10:1-

212

16: "I am the door for the sheep . . . I am the good shepherd . . ." (John 10:7,11).

The chart below shows the main characteristics of the simile, the similitude, and the parable. Note that the similitude and the parable are almost identical. Hence throughout the rest of the discussion the word *parable* will be used in a general way to cover both the similitude and what is technically called a parable.

Simile	*Similitude*	*Parable*
1. One main verb	1. Plurality of main verbs in present tense	1. Plurality of main verbs in past tense
2. Formal comparison	2. Formal comparison	2. Formal comparison
3. Words used literally	3. Words used literally	3. Words used literally
	4. One chief point of comparison	4. One chief point of comparison
	5. Customary habit, almost a timeless truth	5. Particular example, a specific occurrence
	6. Imagery kept distinct from the thing signified	6. Imagery kept distinct from the thing signified
	7. Story true to the facts and experiences of life	7. Story true to the facts and experiences of life
	8. Explained by telling what the imagery stands for in the light of the main point of the story	8. Explained by telling what the imagery stands for in the light of the main point of the story

Parables by their very nature are the opposite of abstractions. Therefore any abstract definition of a parable is a paradox and is as ineffective as an abstract definition of an apple pie. Yet we need to learn all we can about parables. One of the old classics on the subject was written by A. B. Bruce in 1884.[1] Archibald M. Hunter has prepared an up-to-date summary of how parables have been interpreted.[2] It covers the history of the interpretation of parables from the New Testament times to the present. For a long time parables and their details were allegorized to a fantastic degree. At the end of the nineteenth century Jülicher effectively discouraged such a waste of intel-

---

[1] Alexander B. Bruce, *The Parabolic Teaching of Christ* (1884).
[2] Archibald M. Hunter, *Interpreting the Parables* (1960), pp. 21-41.

lectual energy by insisting that the interpreter concentrate on the *one* essential point of likeness.[3] Yet Jülicher himself said that the main point of a parable was some general moral truth. After citing the general moral truths which Jülicher regarded as the main thrusts of certain parables, Hunter rightly insists that the message cannot be divorced from Jesus himself.

> Yet the Man who went about Galilee drawing these innocuous morals was eventually spiked to a Cross. There is something far wrong here. Would men have crucified a Galilean Tusitala who told picturesque stories to enforce prudential platitudes? Of course they would not! For all his merits Jülicher had left the task of interpretation half done.[4]

When the parables are tied to the Christ of the Gospels and his message—the breaking in of the reign of God, they become vehicles not of a moral rearmament but of a radical revolution. This radical revolution begins with the individual; it forms new societies or communities (churches) within existing social structures; yet it contemplates the total transformation of all human society with Jesus Christ reigning as supreme king (Rev. 11:15; 19:11-16: I Cor. 15:23-28). C. H. Dodd was among the first to see this basic emphasis of Jesus' message (the breaking in of the reign of God) and to tie the parables to the central thrust of Jesus' message.[5] Dodd's book appeared in the middle of the 1930's when New Testament scholarship was bogged down in mechanical, historical-critical concerns. Dodd's volume on the parables helped to show that there were far more important things to do than to decide how many chapters there were in the original Q document! In Germany a decade or so later Jeremias gave his support to the soundness of Dodd's approach in observing carefully the settings of the parables in the teaching of Jesus.[6] Scholars today are sometimes sidetracked into debating how extensively the early Church adapted the parables to their own needs and situations. In so doing they can easily forget to put the parables into the large and powerful dimensions of Jesus' message. The time between Jesus' resurrection and our written Gospels was too short for the early Christians to revise the earlier opinions of the closeness of the harvest or consummation of the age (Matt. 13:49). The parables of Jesus, as they were, met the needs of those who heard the messengers of the early Church just as they met the needs of those who first heard them from Jesus and responded to his claims and demands. The needs and op-

---

[3] Adolf Jülicher, *Die Gleichnisreden Jesu* (1910).
[4] Hunter, *op. cit.*, pp. 38-39.
[5] Charles Harold Dodd, *The Parables of the Kingdom* (1936).
[6] Joachim Jeremias, *The Parables of Jesus* (1954), pp. 20-28.

pressions of those original readers of the Gospels differed scarcely at all from the needs and oppressions of those who heard Jesus utter the parables. Obviously, the job of the Church was to transmit the message rather than to adjust the message. Of course there were some adjustments in the form of explanations. But perspective, meaning, interpretation of Jesus' death and resurrection brought growing understanding to the groups of Christians in their fellowship with the risen Christ, with the Father, and with the Spirit. In their fellowship together, they grew in understanding of these truths that God had just revealed to them. This gave them a genuine appreciation for the words of Jesus —words that they were increasingly convinced would never pass away (cf. Matt. 24:35, Mark 13:31, Luke 21:33).

Reasons for Use

Jesus used parables to teach spiritual truths. The condition of each hearer determines whether that aim is realized or not. But Jesus used the parables to throw light on the reign of God, on the demands of God, on the response of men to the demands of God, and the like. Friedrich Hauck points out the similarity between Jesus' parables and those of the rabbis: "As with the Rabbis his [i.e., Jesus'] parables were obviously intended to serve this purpose—to make more easily understandable the strongly marked spiritual ideas through perceptual comparisons derived from well-known spheres."[7] Jesus told stories that were true to life to make clear what life is really about.

Those who were helped by the parables were those who really saw, who really heard. They were far different from those who went through the motions of seeing but did not see, who went through the motions of hearing but did not hear. Hauck points out: "The understanding of the parables presupposes hearers who are willing to go along with the ideas of the speaker and who are capable of grasping the [point of] similarity between the image and the thing itself."[8] Some in the crowds were amazed at Jesus' teaching because Jesus "was teaching them as one having authority and not as the scribes" (Mark 1:22; cf. Matt. 7:29). Not only did Jesus reveal authority in how he taught, but also in what he did: his miracles were samples of the reign of God which he came to declare (Matt. 12:28; Luke 11:20). However, the religious leaders resisted the authority of Christ's teaching and the authority of Christ's action. When they were told how Christ taught—"At no time did

---

[7] Friedrich Hauck, *"parabolē," TWNT,* V, 753.
[8] *Ibid.*

a man speak in such a way as this man is speaking" (John 7:46), they claimed that they had a solid front of opposition among their own kind, and the crowd who didn't know the law (as they did) was simply accursed by not sharing their inspired interpretation (cf. John 7:47-49) ! When Nicodemus suggested that they really "hear" Jesus first and that they "know" what he was doing, the religious leaders fell back on their expert knowledge of prophecy while at the same time they reminded him that Jesus came from Galilee—a despised section of the country: "Search and behold, no prophet arises from Galilee" (John 7:52). When it came to Jesus' works—the authority of his action—the Pharisees "explained" these by pronouncing Jesus to be in league with Beelzebub, the prince of the demons (cf. Matt. 12:24; Luke 11:15).

For people with this mind-set, the parable could clarify nothing. And for those who were under the influence of such people, the parables would appear as obscure riddles. Hauck declares: "The parable may be fruitless because an individual lacks the spiritual power to grasp the kernel; it may also be fruitless because the revelation about God which the parable contains is rejected."9

Between the parable of the soils (Matt. 13:1-9, Mark 4:1-9, Luke 8:4-8) and the explanation of the parable (Matt. 13:18-23, Mark 4:13-20, Luke 8:11-15), there is in all three Gospels a short section (Matt. 13:10-17, Mark 4:10-12, Luke 8:9-10) contrasting the crowd with the small group to whom it was given to know the secrets of the kingdom of God. Those outside (Mark) got information in parables only for the purpose that they should not see, or hear, or understand, that they should not return and it be forgiven them (Mark 4:12). This section has always been difficult. Mark and Luke stress the matter of purpose while Matthew puts the stress on cause. For Matthew, Christ spoke in parables because he had hearers who, although they saw, they did not see, although they heard, they did not hear or understand (Matt. 13:13). He applies Isaiah 6:9-10 to the contemporary generation. But he makes the quotation from the Septuagint, which by the use of the active voice shows why judicial hardening came to the generation of Isaiah's day: "And they closed their eyes" (Isa. 6:10; Matt. 13:15; Acts 28:27). Matthew obviously thought that the same thing was true of the generation of Jesus' day.

The present form of Matthew's, Mark's, and Luke's accounts concerning why Jesus spoke in parables (Matt. 13:10) discloses two main emphases: Jesus spoke in parables *because* many had

9 *Ibid.*

shut their eyes and closed their ears (Matthew); and, Jesus spoke in parables *for the purpose* that many would have an external acquaintance with his teaching but no internal relationship to it (Mark and Luke). Hunter presents three approaches to Mark 4:10-13:[10] (1) C. H. Dodd and many continental scholars declare that this passage is not from Jesus but a later construction. Jeremias, on the other hand, amasses some striking evidence for the genuineness of 4:11-12.[11] The preceding verse—Mark 4:10—shows the interest of all Christ's disciples ("those around him with the twelve") in the meaning conveyed through parabolic discourse. (2) T. W. Manson considers the section authentic but sees no purpose element at all in the Aramaic form in which Jesus presented the material. Manson astutely observes that the quotation made from Isaiah 6:10 is not from the LXX or from the Hebrew text but from the Targum, a paraphrase type of translation used in the Synagogue. He suggests that the Greek word *hina* (first word in Mark 4:12) was a *diy* in Aramaic. Although this Aramaic word may convey the idea of purpose, it also is a relative with the meaning "who." Hence Manson would translate vss. 11b-12: " ... but all things come in parables to those outside *who* see indeed but do not know, and hear indeed but do not understand lest they should repent and receive forgiveness."[12] Jeremias, who notes Manson's substitution of "who" for purpose, retains the purpose idea here himself but removes the negative purpose in the "lest" at the end of vs. 12 *(mē pote)*. The Aramaic expression *diy lᵉmah* behind *mē pote* does express negative purpose, but Jeremias prefers here one of its other meanings: "unless." If we adopt Manson's translation with Jeremias' ending,[13] we have this result: " ... but all things come in parables to those outside *who* see indeed but do not know, and hear indeed but do not understand *unless* they should repent and receive forgiveness." (3) Jeremias, who has already been referred to, regards this passage in Mark as coming from Jesus but as referring to all of Jesus' teaching. Instead of translating the last part of vs. 11 "everything is in parables" (RSV), Jeremias would translate the phrase: "But for those who are without *all things are obscure.*"[14] Therefore, his conclusion is:

---

[10] Hunter, *op. cit.*, pp. 110-112.

[11] Jeremias, *op. cit.*, pp. 12-13.

[12] Hunter, *op. cit.*, p. 112.

[13] Jeremias, *op. cit.*, p. 15.

[14] *Ibid.*, p. 15. See n. 23 where Jeremias shows how the formula *ginesthai en* followed by a noun is the equivalent for the verb "to be" and an adjective. He cites such examples as: "to be sorrowful" (I Macc. 1:27), "to be ecstatic" (Acts 22:17), "to be glorious" (II Cor. 3:7), etc.

Hence we conclude that the logion [saying] is not concerned with the parables of Jesus, but with his preaching in general. The secret of the present Kingdom is disclosed to the disciples, but to the outsiders the words of Jesus remain obscure because they do not recognize his mission or repent. Thus for them the terrible oracle of Isa. 6:10 is fulfilled. Yet a hope still remains: 'If they repent God will forgive them.' The last words afford a glimpse of God's forgiving mercy.[15]

This section in Mark 4:10-12 (cf. parallels in Matt. 13:10-17; Luke 8:9-10) illustrates the obstacles faced by the message of Jesus. No matter in what form Jesus' teaching was cast, there would be hindrances to prevent his hearers from understanding the message. This section shows that Jesus was under no illusions that his widespread popular acclaim represented a popular understanding of his good news about the reign of God. The "you" of Mark represents all of Jesus' disciples—the inner circle or twelve plus the larger group of those who faithfully followed him (cf. Acts 1:21-22). Those outside were spectators but not followers, hearers but not learners, professors but not doers (cf. Luke 6:46). Both groups heard parables. Both groups observed what Jesus did. Both groups heard Jesus answer questions put to him in public. God granted to one of these groups the knowledge of the secrets of the reign of God. To the other he did not. The reasons for God's action are not explicitly stated in this section, but the rest of the life of Christ shows why certain things were hidden from the wise and intelligent and revealed to infants (cf. Matt. 11:25-27; Luke 10:21-22).

Hence this section of Mark (4:10-12) treats of the parable— one of the main vehicles of Jesus' teaching—as representative of all of Jesus' teaching. Men's response to it is controlled by the action of God (Mark and Luke) and by the attitude of men themselves (Matthew). The scholarly investigations of Manson and Jeremias on the underlying Aramaic original show why Matthew and Mark have differing emphases. But both divine sovereignty ("it has been granted," *dedotai*, Matt. 13:11; Mark 4:11; Luke 8:10) and human response (seeing, hearing, closing the eyes) influence decisively the understanding of the parables. We are left with the staggering fact that although parables are a very clear form of teaching, the nature of Jesus' teaching and the condition of his hearers left his teaching in parabolic form to be obscure. *For obscurity of this kind no amount of hermeneutical technique can bring clarity.*

[15] *Ibid.,* p. 15.

Source of Parabolic Imagery

The content for the parables, like that of the Short Figures of Speech,[16] is taken from the surroundings and everyday life of the hearer. It shows Jesus' interest in agriculture and food production. Many parables center in domestic and family life. Trees and their fruit are pictured. Other parables come from the sphere of business, some dealing with employment practices and others with capital investments. Political life is not neglected. Civil law, personal property, the social structure and social concerns—all become an integral part of Jesus' parables. Even the weather serves as a basis for teaching. One reason that Jesus' parables are timeless is that he took the imagery for his teaching from that which was familiar to his hearers. He used these familiar facets to point to that which should have been familiar but in reality was not. A man should figure the cost of discipleship in the same way as one figures the cost of building a tower (Luke 14:28-30). The problems of building capital resources are as familiar today as they were in Jesus' day. Jesus made everyday experiences teach spiritual truths.

Settings for the Parables

Many modern writings on the parables emphasize a double historical setting: (1) The original historical setting(s) in some specific situation(s) in Jesus' ministry; (2) the setting in the primitive Church which controlled the written form of the parable and the literary setting for the parable.[17] But this twofold category is not as simple as it seems. Jesus undoubtedly told his parables in more than one "original" historical setting. Hence, those to whom he directed the parable and his purpose for employing the parable are more important than *the* original setting. The writers of the Gospels certainly were aware of the use of the parables in the oral proclamation of Jesus' teachings. Yet each evangelist selected certain materials and arranged them in his Gospel according to two principles—a chronological pattern and a topical pattern. This enabled the writers to set before their readers the basic emphases of Jesus' teaching and to show why the one who taught in this way was put to death by the Romans at the instigation of his own people. This anointed one who rose triumphant on the third day was the one whose actions and teachings brought men and women into the presence of God. Consequently, the literary setting of the ma-

16 See above, Chapter 6.
17 Dodd, *op. cit.*, p. 111. Cf. also Jeremias, *op. cit.*, p. 20.

terials is to make clear the various facets of Jesus' message, to unite the proclamation of Jesus with the person of Jesus. The Gospels are far more than an anthology of Jesus' words and works. They are authoritative summaries of his message, and they also provide further assertions about the meaning of his person.

The parable of the lost sheep is found in two places in the synoptic Gospels. In Luke 15:1-7 this parable is addressed to the Pharisees and scribes. These religious leaders were murmuring because Christ received sinners and ate with them. Christ's answer to their criticism is expressed in the parable of the lost sheep. The man with one hundred sheep, if he should lose one, leaves the ninety-nine and searches for the lost one. When he finds it he brings it home on his shoulder as he rejoices all the way. At home he extends an invitation to his friends and neighbors to rejoice with him because he has found the lost sheep. The point that Christ stresses is the joy over the recovery of that which was lost. Similarly, there is joy in heaven over one sinner who repents. Thus Christ tells his critics: I receive sinners and eat with them because their response to my message and my presence will bring a change of mind on their part and the corresponding forgiveness of sins. God rejoices over those who come back to him. Christ acted as he did toward sinners in order that they would know the way back to God.

The same parable of the lost sheep in Matthew (18:12-14) is addressed to the disciples. In the opening verse of chapter 18 the disciples ask Jesus who is the greatest in the kingdom of heaven. In vss. 2-4 Christ takes a child, places it in the midst of his disciples and makes it an example of humility. To receive one such child in Christ's name is to receive him (vs. 5). Christ then turns to the influence of adults on children. "Whoever causes one of these children who believe in me to sin," would be better off dead (vs. 6). The disciple must beware that no member of his body is instrumental in causing him to sin—hand, foot, eye (vss. 7-9). The disciples as a group are not to despise one of the believing children (vs. 10). Instead they are to be concerned about their welfare. "What seems best to you disciples?" (vs. 12). At this point is inserted the parable of the lost sheep. Look at the concern of the man who left the ninety and nine and sought the sheep who was wandering (vs. 12). If he finds the sheep, he rejoices more over it than over the other ninety and nine who did not wander (vs. 13). Then Jesus indicates the main point of the parable: "In this fashion it is not the will of my Father who is in heaven that one of these children perish" (Matt. 18:14). Here the stress is on the concern of the Father for little ones who may wander and perish. The disciples are to be as concerned for these as God the Father is.

The parable in Luke answers Christ's critics. The same parable in Matthew is addressed to Christ's disciples. In Luke the stress is on God's joy over the repentant sinner. In Matthew the stress is on God's will that no believing child wander and perish. The occasion in Luke seems to have been the original situation. In Matthew there is another application of the parable. Yet both passages teach basic truth about God. God has compassion toward sinners (Luke). God has concern for believers—in this case, children who in their young and tender age believe on him (Matthew). A study of the setting is always essential in finding the main point of the parable.

Conclusions to the Parables

As certain parables are brought to a close, the reader finds a terse, hortatory saying. These generalizing conclusions[18] are of such a nature that they may be found in several places in Jesus' teaching. Or if the conclusion is found only once, it tends to broaden out the more specific or confined emphasis of the parable.

The parable of the workers in the vineyard closes with the saying: "In this fashion the last ones will be first and the first ones last" (Matt. 20:16). In the parable itself, however, the stress is not on reversal of rank but rather on the goodness or kindness of God. Certain workers agree to work for the current rate of a day's wages. They are hired at 6 A.M. Then at 9 A.M., 12 noon, 3 P.M., and 5 P.M., additional workers are hired. At the close of the day's work (i.e., about 6 P.M., since the laborers worked a twelve hour day) the owner paid them all a day's wages and sent them home. The emphasis in the parable is on the goodness of the owner. On this particular day he paid full wages to all of his workers so that each would have enough money to support himself and his family. The application points to the goodness of God to all. The idea that those who were hired first should have also received some special indication of bountiful kindness from their employer because they worked a full day for the agreed wages is foreign to the whole thought of the parable. The stress is on the goodness of the owner to those who needed work, who at first could not find it, and then who found it at various times during the day. If the scribes and the Pharisees are represented by the

18 See Hunter, *op. cit.*, pp. 119-120.

protesters who felt that they should have been paid more because they completed a whole day's work, then the conclusion about the first and the last interchanging positions suggests that the current religious leaders would lose divine favor and those who believed the good news of the gospel would experience God's favor. Those who believed were certainly among the lower elements of society as far as the Pharisees were concerned. This concluding statement is a popular statement of Jesus. It is adaptable to many different strains of thought.

After Jesus commented on the rich young ruler and the special difficulty that the rich have in entering the kingdom of God, he summarized what the disciples had done in following him. They had left their near of kin for the sake of Jesus and the gospel. He said that those who had left all and had suffered persecution would receive back what they had left. In the age to come they will inherit eternal life. Then the saying appears again: "But many first ones will be last and last ones first" (Matt. 19:30, Mark 10:31). It is to be noted that the saying here differs from what it was in the parable of the workers in the vineyard. In the parable of the vineyard the stress lay on the last being first. In the section on the rich young ruler in Matthew and Mark the initial stress of the saying is on the first being last.

In Luke 13:22-30 Jesus is asked whether the number of those being saved is few. He does not answer the question directly but rather takes up the need for earnest endeavor and faithful obedience. There will be great consternation when his present hearers see Abraham, Isaac, and Jacob in the kingdom of God together with all the prophets but find themselves excluded. At the same time those who do recline in the kingdom of God will come from all parts of the world—east, west, north, and south. It is in this context that the saying occurs again: "And lo, there are last ones who will be first and there are first ones who will be last" (Luke 13:30).

In the parable of the talents (Matt. 25:14-30) Jesus tells the story of the man who, just before he went on a journey, called in his slaves and gave them some money to invest. He gave to one slave five talents, to another two talents, and to a third one talent. This apportionment of the money was on the basis of the ability of each. After much time the master returned and checked up on how well each of these slaves had invested his money. The one who had received five talents had gained another five talents. Similarly the one who had received two talents had doubled what he had initially received. The one who had received one talent simply returned it to his owner.

His excuse was that he was afraid of his master. He had hid the talent and now gave it back to its owner. His master rebuked him for not making use of the bankers so that he would have some interest to show. The master's stern rebuke concludes with the command to take the talent from the slothful slave and give it to the most productive of the three. The unworthy slave is to be cast out into the farthest darkness where the weeping and grinding of teeth indicate that his punishment was beyond remedy. In this conclusion another saying is recorded which is found in several other places: "Now to everyone who has it shall be given and he will abound; but from the one not having, even what he has will be taken from him" (Matt. 25:29).

This same saying is found in the section on parables in Mark and Luke where Jesus warns his hearers to be alert about what they hear (Mark 4:24; Luke 8:18). In this context, "hearing" is equated with "obeying." The reason for care as to what we "hear" (or obey) is found in this saying about giving to the one who has and taking away from the one who has not (cf. Mark 4:25, Luke 8:18). The saying is also found in Matthew's section on the reasons for parables. Those who have will be given more (i.e., they will know the secrets of the kingdom). But those who have not (those who only hear parables but do not enter into their meaning), even what they have will be taken from them (Matt. 13:12).

In the parable of the talents the unworthy slave who hid his talent probably stands for the Pharisee who took all the truth of God and kept it unto himself. Instead of imparting the truth of God to mankind, he built a hedge around the law so that others could hardly see what was there. If this be true, then the little phrase "even what he has" (Matt. 25:29) is pregnant with meaning. Since this emphasis is found elsewhere, one must conclude that Jesus often stressed the great difference between the individual who was growing in the things of God and the one who was static. "Even what he has" would describe a static fund of information rather than living, growing truth which was a part of an individual. The generalizing conclusion in this parable is a truth that has a pertinent application to this parable but is of such a nature that the theme enters into many other aspects of Jesus' teaching.

Sometimes what appears to be a conclusion to a parable or two parables is really a conclusion to a section in which the parables only re-enforce the main assertion. Consider Christ's parables of the tower builder and the strategy of the warring king. These are found in a context (see Luke 14:25-35) where

Christ is stressing the importance of counting the cost. For
one to come to Christ he must hate (conscious hyperbole) whoever or whatever might draw from him a greater response than
that which rightfully belongs to Christ. Christ's formula is
simple. The disciple must have an undivided allegiance to
Christ and a dedicated active bearing of the cross which God
puts upon him. The parables illustrate the need for a calcu-
lated awareness of the demands of discipleship. The tower
builder knows precisely what is the cost before he starts. The
king revises his strategy before he enters into active warfare.
The conclusion is: "In this manner, therefore, everyone from
you who does not renounce all of his own possessions is not
able to be my disciple" (Luke 14:33). This conclusion springs
from the whole narrative Christ has stressed: (1) There can be
no personal loyalties which consign him to a second place; (2)
There must be complete awareness of what is involved in discipleship. This conclusion adds the further qualification that
there must be no attachment to things. Counting the cost means
renunciation of materialistic considerations. A person cannot
be tied to his possessions and also be devoted to the Saviour.
Such an attitude is comparable to salt which loses its seasoning
power. The salt would be useless. Likewise the disciple who is
wrapped up with things is useless as a functioning follower of
Jesus. He is simply not a disciple.

Focus of Parables

In the definition of a parable we pointed out that parables
have one chief point of comparison. This is the focus of the
parable. It is important for us to relate the basic emphasis of
each parable to the central idea in Jesus' message.[19] The message of Jesus centered in and revolved around the reign of God.
The Greek word *basileia,* which designates the royal reign or
kingdom of God, appears over one hundred times in the Gospels.[20] Hence the parables serve to illustrate and unfold various
aspects of the reign of God.

Presence of the Reign of God. The main point of the parable of the tares is that heaven's reign or God's reign[21] is present but is not absolute. There is good seed and there are tares.
The tares are not to be rooted out now lest there be damage

19 See Hunter, *op. cit.,* pp. 42-91.

20 See Bauer, *op. cit.,* 3, pp. 134-35; Moulton & Geden, pp. 141-42.

21 For the evidence that "the reign of heaven" and "the reign of God"
are synonymous, see Bauer, p. 134; Karl Ludwig Schmidt, *"Basileia," Bible
Key Words,* II, Book iii, 37-54.

to the wheat. "Allow them both to grow together until the harvest" (Matt. 13:30). In the harvest time the bundles of tares will be for the fire and the wheat will go into the storehouse. The reign of God becomes absolute in the time of the harvest although discordant elements are now present within God's kingship or reign.

In Jesus' explanation of the parable of the tares (Matt. 13:36-43), the parable is treated as an allegory, and the meaning of various features is presented point by point. Matthew pictures this as a private session of Jesus with his disciples. The disciples want a further explanation. The sower is the Son of Man. The field is the world. The good seed refers to the sons of the kingdom. The tares are the sons of the evil one. The one who sowed the tares is the devil. The harvest is the consummation of the age. The reapers are the angels. Following this point-by-point application (vss. 37-39), there is a brief description of the consummation when the reign of God will be total. "The Son of Man *will send* his angels and they *will gather* from his kingdom everything that is offensive and those who are guilty of lawlessness and they *will cast* them into the furnace of fire. There *will be* the weeping and grinding of teeth. Then the righteous *will shine forth* as the sun in the kingdom of their father" (Matt. 13:41-43).[22]

This explanation accentuates the reign of God. The sons of the kingdom or reign are the good seed. The reign or kingdom then is present. The future aspect of the kingdom simply points to the universal sway of God's reign. The discordant elements are removed. The righteous will shine forth in the kingship or reign of their father. The kingship or reign of the Son of Man (vs. 41) is paralleled by the kingship or reign of the Father in

---

[22] Jeremias in his volume *The Parables of Jesus*, pp. 64-68, argues that the explanation of the parable of the tares is the work of Matthew. He finds different emphases in the explanation from the major thrust made in the parable itself. He notes linguistic expressions which, so far as he knows, had no Aramaic equivalents in the time of Jesus. He notes other expressions which he thinks are unusual for Jesus. Finally, he finds linguistic and stylistic characteristics of Matthew. Yet as one looks carefully at the data which are amassed (see footnotes, pp. 65-66), he finds that although there may be a higher frequency of the selected expressions in Matthew, they are not all confined to Matthew. A few expressions are. But these only show Matthew as the author of his Gospel; they do not prove that he was the creator of the explanation. That Jesus should talk with his disciples in private about the things which he taught in public was very natural. Further, that such explanations should show the characteristics and style of others besides Jesus is also natural. The lesson became a part of the learners. As they handed it down, the stamp of the hearers as well as the teacher is bound to become apparent.

vs. 43. This future stress in the explanation takes into account a far broader sweep of Jesus' teaching than does the parable itself. The parable points up the nature of God's reign prior to the climax. The climax is mentioned but is not developed. Yet the present dimension of the reign of God as well as the future dimension have one common source: what Jesus taught about this all-important theme.

When Jesus performed miracles, the Pharisees found themselves in a difficult position. They could not deny what was obvious to themselves as well as to the rest of the people, so they had to invent an explanation. They said that Jesus did these things by Beelzebub, the prince of the demons (Matt. 12:24, Mark 3:22). Jesus' reply to this explanation was a series of parables (Mark 3:23). A divided kingdom, a divided city, or a divided house cannot abide. It will be taken over by someone who will bring unity. The fact that Satan's kingdom is still abiding is proof that Satan does not cast out Satan. Hence the Pharisees' "explanation" is invalid. Jesus then told the parable of the difficulty of plundering the goods of the strong man unless one first binds the strong man. Then one can plunder his house thoroughly. This parable focuses in Jesus' miraculous deeds as proof of his power to bind the strong man, namely Satan, and all of his forces. Here again Christ underscores the presence of the reign of God: "But since I by the Spirit of God cast out demons, then as a result the reign or kingship of God has come upon you" (Matt. 12:28). The miracles of Jesus are samples of Christ's power and what the reign of God will be in its fullness. They testify that Jesus has the power to bind the strong man. They show that the reign of God was present.

Role of grace in the response to the reign of God. The parable of the two sons (Matt. 21:28-32), who were asked to work in the vineyard by their father, contrasts their initial response and their final action. The first son said that he would go but he did not carry out his promise. The second son said that he did not want to go but afterwards he changed his mind and went off to work. When Jesus asked which son did the will of his father, the religious leaders answered that it was the second son. Because of their response, these outcasts of society *were going* (present tense) before the Pharisees (represented by first son in parable) into the kingdom or reign of God. They had believed John and what he said. But the religious leaders were indifferent to John. They did not repent as a preparation for believing John. Both sons had the same invitation to work in the vineyard. Grace provided both sons with the opportunity of demonstrating their willingness to do the will of their father.

The disparity between the response of the two sons to the command shows the difference in attitude towards God and his gracious demands.

In the parable of the lost sheep as found in Luke (Luke 15:1-7; see above, "Settings for the Parables") we see the role of grace in the action of the shepherd who goes out to seek his lost sheep. He takes the initiative and looks for the lost sheep *until he finds it.* God's joy at the response to grace only highlights the grace that was extended.

Loyal adherents to the reign of God. The parable of the tower builder and the strategy of the warring king (see above, "Conclusions to the Parables") shows that those who are disciples of the king and adherents to the reign of God have taken into account all that is involved in such an allegiance (see Luke 14:25-35).

As Jesus concludes the Sermon on the Mount he compares the one who practices his sayings to a man who built his house upon the rock. No amount of adverse weather was able to shake or destroy the house because it had a foundation of rock. The one who listens but does not practice Jesus' sayings is likened to a foolish man who built his house upon the sand. When adverse weather came, the house collapsed (Matt. 7:24-27; Luke 6:47-49). The loyal adherent to the reign of God has prepared himself against the storms by faithful obedience to all that Jesus taught. But the one who was only a casual spectator will be swept away by the cataclysms of life. These contrasts leave an indelible impression on the reader.

Crises in the reign of God. The parable of the unfaithful husbandmen and their rejection of the owner's son (Matt. 21:33-46, Mark 12:1-12, Luke 20:9-19) comes out of Jesus' last days in Jerusalem. A man planted a vineyard. After providing all the equipment necessary for successful operation, he leased it to husbandmen. He himself lived some distance from this investment, so at a fixed time he sent his slaves to obtain his share of the fruit of the vineyard. The first slave came, but he was turned aside. A succeeding parade of representatives of the owner were treated in shameful fashion. Matthew says (after spelling out in detail the kind of reception they received): "One they beat, one they killed, one they stoned" (Matt. 21:35). A second round of representatives fared no better. The owner finally decided to send his son. Surely, he thought, they would respect him. But seeing him as the heir, they killed him so that they could dispossess the owner of his inheritance. Christ asks what the lord of the vineyard would do in such a case. The answer is simple. He will destroy them and give the vineyard to others. Mark and Luke record Christ as answering his own question. Matthew depicts the hearers as drawing the conclusion: "He will put the evil doers to a miserable death and lease out the vineyard to other husbandmen who will give back to him the fruit at their proper times" (Matt. 21:41). All three Gospels close the parable with the quotation from Psalm 118:22 about the stone repudiated by the builders which became the cornerstone. Such a turn of events is the Lord's doing and is remarkable in the eyes of those who behold it. The focal point of the parable centers on the killing of the son by the tenants (husbandmen), their punishment, and the giving of the vineyard to others. Matthew records an immediate application: "Because of this I say to you that the kingship or reign of God will be taken away from you and will be given to a nation (= people) making the fruits which belong to such a reign" (Matt. 21:43). All three accounts indicate that the religious leaders recognized this parable as being addressed to them. Their antipathy was so great that they wanted to seize Christ at that very hour (Luke 20:19), but one thing deterred them—their fear of the crowds (Matt. 21:46, Mark 12:12, Luke 20:19) who regarded Jesus as a prophet (Matt. 21:46). This is one of the great parables of crisis. It portrays concisely and forcefully the response and action of men together with the response and action of God. What this crisis would mean for the reign of God is not stated, but Luke says that the religious leaders exclaimed after the statement that the owner would give the vineyard to others: "May it not be" (Luke 20:16, mē genoito: "by no means," "far from it," "God forbid").

The parable of the ten virgins is also a parable of crisis (Matt. 25:1-13). The crisis is the return of Jesus to complete his messianic work. The parable teaches alertness and readiness for the Second Coming. Hunter thinks that the parable originally taught readiness for the crisis which resulted in Jesus' crucifixion and the changes which took place after Jesus' resurrection.[23] But there is nothing in the language of the parable

---

[23] Hunter, op. cit., pp. 86-87. Jeremias, Parables of Jesus, pp. 41-43, takes a similar point of view and tries to marshal all available evidence. But his case has numerous subjective elements. For example, the parable, he maintains, stresses the failure of the foolish virgins to provide oil, but Matthew (25:13) puts the stress on watchfulness, because the wise as well as the foolish virgins fell asleep. Yet certainly alertness or watchfulness does not demand a "go without sleep marathon"! Preparation for a coming crisis demands alertness for known demands; it does not mean abandoning basic human needs: food, water, or sleep. Jeremias is also subjective in his confidence that Jesus could never have created the metaphor of the bridegroom (Parables of Jesus, pp. 41-42; Joachim Jeremias, "numphē, numphios," TWNT, IV, 1094-97).

to suggest this; rather, the crisis occurs in a setting of joy. Hence it seems that Matthew is correctly reporting to us Jesus' description of a future time of joy. Jesus' use of a wedding feast to describe this time illustrates his creativity.[24] The crisis concerns Jesus' future reunion with his people.

Principles for Interpreting Parables

1. Seek to understand "the earthly details" of the parables as well as the original hearers did.

2. Note the attitude and spiritual condition of the original hearers.

3. If possible, note the reason which prompted Jesus to employ the parable. Such effort will show that parables were a part of Jesus' method of presenting fresh, living truths to audiences who were opposed to what they regarded as his innovations, who failed to see that he was putting new wine into new wineskins, or who needed instruction as to what the reign or kingship of God really involved.

4. State concisely the main point of the parable. Give reasons for your selection.

5. Try to relate the main point of the parable to the basic aspects of Jesus' teaching. Keep in mind the centrality of the reign of God in all that Jesus said and did.

6. Observe whether any generalizing sayings have come into the parabolic narrative. Their presence adds a hortatory note which may be central or peripheral to the main teaching of the parable.

7. Where most of the details of a parable are explained, try even harder to uncover the main emphasis. The fact that occa-

---

24 See Ethelbert Stauffer, "gameō, gamos," TWNT, I, 652. "Jesus expressed himself entirely in the circle of ideas of his fellow countrymen when he brought into view the meaning and the glory of the Messianic time in the pictures of the wedding and of the wedding banquet. The bridesmaids wait for the bridegroom until the late hour of the evening in order with their lanterns to give the escort for the bridal pair into the house of the wedding, where with a brilliantly illuminated table the seven-day wedding celebration begins: 'And those who were ready entered in with him into the wedding banquet.' Thus the primitive church must be ready at all times to wait in expectation for the advent of Christ: 'Be alert, therefore, because you do not know the day or the hour' (Matt. 25:10ff). This point, which is the same as in Luke 12:36ff, is certainly the main point. However, the sphere of reference of the parabolic imagery is consciously chosen. Mark 2:19 and parallels proves this assertion since here Jesus designates himself as the bridegroom. Here (Mark 2:19; see also John 3:29) the days of the wedding joy occur in the lifetime of Jesus; in contrast in Matthew 25:1ff they take place only at the time of his return—a very significant extension."

sionally traits of allegory should be blended in with a parable is natural since the function and purpose of the two may disclose a common objective. Relate the main emphasis to present-day readers. Remember that their situation may be quite different from those of the original hearers.

ALLEGORIES

Definition

At the beginning of this chapter it was made clear that a parable is usually a more extensive form of the simile while the allegory is a more extensive form of the metaphor. The following table will show the characteristics of the metaphor and the allegory. These characteristics should be compared with the earlier description of the characteristics of the simile, similitude, and parable.

Metaphor	*Allegory*
1. One main verb	1. Plurality of main verbs and mixture of tenses
2. Direct comparison	2. Direct comparison
3. Words used figuratively	3. Words used figuratively
	4. Plurality of points of comparison
	5. Emphasis usually on timeless truths
	6. Imagery identified with specific thing signified
	7. Story blends factual experience with non-factual experience to enable the narrative to teach specific truths
	8. Explained by showing why the imagery is identified with the reality and what specific truths are being taught

An allegory is a story put together with several points of comparison. For example, in the allegory of the good shepherd the story is told for the specific purpose of having the door represent Christ, of having the shepherd represent Christ, of having the sheep as those for whom Christ laid down his life, and of having the flock represent the union of all believers under the one shepherd, regardless of their cultural, national, or religious lineage (cf. John 10:1-16). This point by point comparison is true of most allegories. Often there is some ambiguity as to how many points in this complex comparison are there to convey specific teaching. Should we try to identify the hireling who flees (John 10:12) with the religious leaders of the day or is the detail just a part of the story to bring out the true concern of the shepherd? The writer would favor the latter opinion.

Allegory, a very legitimate way of teaching truth, should not be confused with allegorizing, which takes a narrative that was not meant to teach truth by identification. By a point by point comparison, allegorizing makes the narrative convey ideas different from those intended by the original author. Thus allegorizing is an arbitrary way of handling any narrative.

Paul's allegorizing in Galatians 4:21-31 is significant because this type of interpretaton is so rare in the New Testament. The apostle takes the historical narrative of Hagar and Ishmael, Sarah and Isaac, and the relations between the two offspring as historical facts that also have allegorical significance. Hagar as the bondmaid represents the Old Covenant and the present Jerusalem. Sarah as the free woman represents the New Covenant and the Jerusalem which is from above. The child of Hagar was born according to the flesh. Isaac in contrast is a child of promise. The persecution between the two sons of Abraham represents the conflict between legalistic Judaism (Christian or anti-Christian forms) and Christianity with its stress on salvation by grace. The separation of Hagar and her child from Sarah and her child depicts the clean break which must be made between Judaism and Christianity. This type of argument shows Paul making use of the allegorical method to heighten the contrast for his readers between bondage (Gal. 4:24-25) and freedom (Gal. 4:26-31). Paul's explicit indication that he was allegorizing shows that this was a conscious literary device to which he resorted only on rare occasions. Here such a procedure illustrates well the ideas which Paul was seeking to get across. Yet the Old Testament narrative itself, which provides the illustration, was in no way talking about an earthly Jerusalem and a heavenly Jerusalem.

Extensiveness of Their Use

Allegories appear in both the Old and New Testaments, usually with accompanying explanations but not always. They may be identified readily by consulting the characteristics of allegories listed on the preceding page.

In the Old Testament, Psalm 80 (vss. 8-15) portrays Israel as a vine from Egypt. Proverbs (5:15-18) extols marital fidelity by urging that a man drink from his own cistern and no one else's; the context shows how forceful this allegory is (see vss. 19-23). Another brilliant allegory, whose import is made clear by the context, occurs in Ecclesiastes 12:3-7: the man who lives for sensual pleasure will surely be disappointed in his old age. Finally, the false prophets are described unforgettably in Ezekiel (13:8-16) as men who build a wall and try to hold it together with whitewash.

In the New Testament there are such passages as the weapons of offense and defense in the Christian armour (Eph. 6:11-17), the good shepherd (John 10:1-16), and others. Though examples of allegory are relatively infrequent in the New Testament, when they do appear they convey a thought of notable importance.

Context for Each Allegory

By examining carefully the context, the interpreter can often determine who were the original hearers of the allegory, the reason the original speaker (writer) used the allegory, the meaning he assigned to each of the basic points of comparison, and finally, the role of the allegory in developing the total thought being presented. If the interpreter does not consider carefully the context, it is almost impossible to avoid bringing his own ideas into the allegorical imagery.

Focal Points of an Allegory

One allegory from the Gospels and one from the Epistles will illustrate the several points of comparison found in this type of figure. That the allegory is simply an extended metaphor becomes evident when the basic emphases are singled out for study.

John 15:1-10 is the allegory of the vine and the branches. There are three main points of comparison: (1) the true vine = Christ (15:1,5); (2) the vinedresser = the Father (15:1); and (3) the branches = disciples, believers (15:5). Let us consider the matters stressed around each of these focal points.

The whole passage stresses the central importance of the vine (Christ). A mutual relationship between the vine and the branch enables the disciple to bear much fruit (15:5b). "Be-

cause apart from me you [plural] are able to do nothing"
(15:5c). Separated from Christ the disciple can accomplish
nothing. The word "vine" occurs three times in the passage.
The pronouns "I," "my," "me," "in me," are found twenty-two
times in these ten verses. The details support the centrality of
Christ in the passage.

In the second point of comparison the emphasis is on the
action of the vinedresser (the Father). A branch that does not
bear fruit, although it is in vital union with the vine ("in me"),
the vinedresser cuts off (15:2a). The branches bearing fruit are
pruned for the purpose that they may bear more fruit (15:2b).
Here the Father is pictured as being concerned with fruitbearing. He takes decisive action to eliminate fruitless branches
and to bring to maximum production the branches that are attached to the vine.

Finally, the action of the branches (disciples) themselves is
considered. This illustrates the point that allegory combines
factual experience with elements that do not occur in the
earthly reality that is being used for metaphorical purposes. In
nature branches do not "act" at all. They may wave in the
breeze. They may dry up and wither. But the branches never
act on their own—they are simply a part of a tree or vine. In
this allegory, however, they "act" volitionally. The disciples are
told to "abide [totality of action] in me" (15:4a). Action is also
made clear by direct comparison: "As the branch is not able
to bear fruit by itself except it constantly abide [pres. tense] in
the vine, so neither you [plural] except you [plural] constantly
abide [pres. tense] in me" (15:4b). The literal branch abides by
being there "positionally." The disciples abide by being
there "relationally." In the allegory Jesus warns of the outcome if the disciple does not actively respond: "If anyone
does not abide [pres. tense, linear action] in me, he is thrown
away [gnomic aorist][25] as the branch, and it withers and they
gather them and cast them into the fire and they are being
burned" (John 15:6). Obviously Jesus was not thinking of a
mechanical connection. A vital relationship demands a constant
activity. Answers to prayer depend on this vital, active relationship (15:7). Fruitbearing, as a sign of this vital relationship,
brings glory to God and shows that the one so producing will
be Christ's disciple in the future as well as in the present (15:8).
In conclusion, obeying Christ's commandments is pictured as
evidence that the disciple is abiding in Christ's love (15:9-10).
This allegory dynamically portrays to the reader why he must

25 Bauer, 1. b. p. 130: "the aor. emphasizes the certainty of the result
and is gnomic [B1-D., paragraph 333; Rob., p. 836f]."

maintain a fresh, living relationship to Jesus Christ and his Father. This is what discipleship means.

Paul unfolds an allegory in I Corinthians 3:10-15. It may be called the allegory of the foundation and the superstructure, although it has several elements. In the context Paul speaks of the Corinthians as belonging to the realm of the flesh. As proof he cites their party spirit—one declares an allegiance to Paul while another is loyal to Apollos (I Cor. 3:5). In reality Paul and Apollos were simply ministers through whom the Corinthians believed. Paul may have planted. Apollos may have watered. But it was God who gave the increase (I Cor. 5:6). Both Apollos and Paul were God's fellow workers. The Church at Corinth was God's cultivated land and God's building.

At this point Paul introduces the allegory to emphasize the responsibility of all leaders in the Church. It has the following basic elements: the master-builder = Paul (I Cor. 3:10); the foundation = Jesus Christ (I Cor. 3:11); each builder = other teachers and leaders working among the Corinthians (I Cor. 3:5-6,10,12-15); materials built upon the foundation = teachings and persons taught, teachings which transform persons and persons transformed by the appropriation of teachings (I Cor. 3:9 [you are God's building]; I Cor. 3:6-8, 12-14 [a qualitative product which can be revealed and tested]); and the work = total result of the life activity of the teachers (I Cor. 3:13-14).

Most of these elements are self-explanatory. Two kinds of materials are built upon the foundation: that which is superior and that which is inferior. The Corinthians are said to be God's building (I Cor. 3:9). Paul earlier uses the metaphors of milk and solid food—figurative descriptions of teachings (I Cor. 3:1-2). Thus it seems that the materials stand both for teachings and for individuals who either are transformed by the teachings or use them merely to increase their fund of information. Teachers whose work is in the latter category find that it does not abide the testing fires of judgment. The teacher himself attains salvation. Yet because his work does not stand up under the probing examination of judgment, he feels that he has reached salvation as if he himself had passed through the fire.

Principles for Interpreting Allegories

1. Be able to state explicitly who were the original hearers or readers. This will enable you to see the allegory as a living vehicle of teaching rather than a literary form in an ancient narrative.

2. If possible, note why the allegory was told in the first place.

3. Search out the basic points of comparison stressed by the original speaker or writer. The allegory itself usually makes these clear by the emphasis put upon particular elements in the story. To find out what these stand for, look for explicit identification ("I am the true vine and my father is the vinedresser," John 15:1) or implicit identification from things said in the context (materials built upon the foundation, see I Cor. 3:1-2, 4-5, 6-8, 9, 12-14).

4. After listing the basic points of comparison and the things for which they stand, state in as simple a manner as possible why these truths were essential for the original hearers or readers and why they are essential for us today.

BIBLIOGRAPHY

Bruce, Alexander Balmain, *The Parabolic Teaching of Christ* (1884).
Dodd, Charles Harold, *The Parables of the Kingdom* (1936).
Hauck, Friedrich, *"parabolē," Theologisches Wörterbuch zum Neuen Testament*, V (1954).
Hunter, Archibald M., *Interpreting the Parables* (1960).
Jeremias, Joachim, *The Parables of Jesus*, tr. S. H. Hooke (1954).
Jülicher, Adolf, *Die Gleichnisreden Jesu* (1910).

XI Typology

No area of biblical interpretation needs more careful definition than typology. Some people associate typology with bizarre, fanciful meanings. To them typology and allegorizing are in the same class—worthless procedures for trying to find meaning in written documents. This is far from true. Allegorizing and typology have only one thing in common. They are both figurative methods of interpretation. But here the resemblance ends. They have a different background, a different attitude toward history, and a different way of handling meaning.

NATURE OF TYPOLOGY

In a single chapter we can touch only upon the most important aspects of typology. Much has been written on this subject in the last few years.[1] But with a clear picture of the

[1] Here are just a few of the works: G. W. H. Lampe, "The Reasonableness of Typology," and K. J. Woolcombe, "The Biblical Origins and Patristic Development of Typology," *Essays on Typology* (1957). E. Earle Ellis, *Paul's Use of the Old Testament* (1957), pp. 51-54, 64-65, 66-67, 88-90, 90-92, 95-97, 108, 124-25, 125, 126-35, 135-47. Hans Walter Wolff, "Zur Hermeneutik des alten Testaments," *Probleme alttestamentlicher Hermeneutik* (1960), pp. 140-180. Walther Eichrodt, "Ist die typologische Exegese sachgemässe Exegese?" *Probleme alttestamentlicher Hermeneutik* (1960), pp. 205-226. Joseph Bonsirven, *Exégèse Rabbinique et Exégèse Paulinienne* (1938), pp. 267, 269, 270, 275, 301-308, 311, 324, 327-30, 353, 356. Leonhard Goppelt, *Typos: Die Deutung des Alten Testaments im Neuen* (1939). A. Berkeley Mickelsen, "Methods of Interpretation in the Epistle to the Hebrews" (Unpublished Ph.D. dissertation, Department of New Testament and Early Christian Literature, University of Chicago, 1950). Henri de Lubac, "Typologie et Allegorisme," *Recherches de Science Religieuse*, XXXIV (1947), 180-226.

main aspects of typology, we can study the examples with understanding and discernment.

Definition

In typology the interpreter finds a correspondence in one or more respects between a person, event, or thing in the Old Testament and a person, event, or thing closer to or contemporaneous with a New Testament writer. It is this *correspondence* that determines the meaning in the Old Testament narrative that is stressed by a later speaker or writer. The correspondence is present because God controls history, and this control of God over history is axiomatic with the New Testament writers. It is God who causes earlier individuals, groups, experiences, institutions, etc., to embody characteristics which later he will cause to reappear.

In the desert, when the children of Israel were bitten by serpents, Moses was commanded to make a serpent (presumably out of brass) and set it up on a standard. Everyone bitten by a serpent was to look up to the elevated model of a serpent. When he did so, he lived. This Old Testament event is considered typical of the New Testament event of Christ's death upon a cross: "And just as Moses lifted up the serpent in the wilderness, in this fashion, it is necessary that the Son of Man be lifted up, that everyone believing in him might have eternal life" (John 3:14-15). The points of correspondence are: (1) the lifting up of the serpent and of Christ; (2) life for those who respond to the object lifted up. The need of those responding is implicit. In these two points of correspondence it is clear that typology involves a higher application of meaning. Both the brass serpent and Jesus were lifted up. Yet the meaning of the "lifting up" is infinitely greater in the latter case. The same is true of the response. In the case of the type, those who looked at the brass serpent "lived," i.e., they did not die of snake bite but continued their physical life. In the case of the antitype, those who commit themselves to Christ who was lifted up on a cross have "eternal life," i.e., they are transformed and energized within by a new kind (qualitatively) of life both now and in the life to come. This meaning of life is infinitely greater than the former. Even so, it is still proper to speak of a higher application of meaning. The points of correspondence are historical in both events.

Typology and allegory need to be contrasted. Woolcombe defines typology as: "The establishment of historical connections between certain events, persons or things in the Old Testament,

and similar events, persons or things in the New Testament."[2]
Typology in this definition is considered to be a method of
exegesis. Abraham's offering of Isaac (his only son) could be
considered as a type of God's offering of Christ (his only begotten Son) (cf. Heb. 11:17-19). To point out this connection is to
use typology as a method of exegesis. Considered as a method
of writing, typology is defined by Woolcombe as: "The description of an event, person, or thing in the New Testament in
terms borrowed from the description of its prototypal counterpart in the Old Testament."[3] When Paul, speaking of the immorality in Corinth (I Cor. 5:1-8), calls malice and wickedness
a leaven, he uses the term "leaven" in the same derogatory sense
that it had during the Passover festival (Exod. 12:15) when all
leaven was to be scrupulously removed from the houses of the
Israelites. This use of leaven is typology as a method of writing.
The point of correspondence lies in that which is to be removed from the life of a people. Under the Old Covenant it
was a material substance. Under the New Covenant it was every
kind of evil. Typology as a method of exegesis is "the search
for linkages between events, persons or things *within the historical framework of revelation,* whereas allegorism is the search
for secondary and hidden meaning underlying the primary and
obvious meanings of a narrative."[4] The allegorist takes any narrative (even though the original author gives no indication of
having his assertions stand for something else) and after ignoring the primary or obvious meaning, he arbitrarily attaches
to the narrative the meaning he wants it to convey. In practice
he treats the narrative in such a way as almost to deny its historicity, although in theory he may stoutly defend its historicity.

Typology is historically oriented. Allegory rests "on a particular quasi-Platonist doctrine of the relation of the literal
sense of Scripture—the outward form or 'letter' of the sacred
writings—to eternal spiritual reality concealed, as it were, beneath the literal sense."[5] This eternal spiritual reality supposedly concealed within the narrative belongs to an integrated body
of knowledge. The allegorist, by a purely subjective response
independent of what is objectively written, endeavors to bring
forth certain aspects of this idealistic system of spiritual truth.
The story of Herod's slaughter of the infants of Bethlehem is
allegorized in a sermon included among the *spuria* of Chrysostom. Lampe summarizes it as follows: "The fact that only the

2 K. J. Woolcombe, *op. cit.,* p. 39.
3 *Ibid.,* pp. 39-40.
4 *Ibid.,* p. 40.
5 Lampe, *op. cit.,* p. 30.

children of two years old and under were murdered while those
of three presumably escaped is meant to teach us that those who
hold the Trinitarian faith will be saved whereas Binitarians
and Unitarians will undoubtedly perish."[6] Such are the phan-
tasies that arise from allegorizing.

The Greek word for "type," *tupos*, occurs fourteen times in
the New Testament. Although it has several meanings, the
word has only two basic ideas: (1) pattern, (2) that which is
produced from the pattern, i.e., a product. *Tupos* is used of
the *mark* (or pattern) of the nails (John 20:25). It is also used
of that which is formed, an *image* or *statue* (Acts 7:43). The
word *tupos* describes a *pattern* of teaching (Rom. 6:17). It also
stands for the *content* or *text* of a letter (Acts 23:25). It is used
technically of an *archetype, model,* or *pattern* both by Stephen
and by the writer of Hebrews (Acts 7:44; Heb. 8:5). It is most
frequently used of an *example* or *pattern* in the moral life
(Phil. 3:17; I Thess. 1:7; II Thess. 3:9; I Tim. 4:12; Tit. 2:7;
I Pet. 5:3). Finally, it is used of *types* given by God as an indication of the future, in the form of persons or things (Rom.
5:14; I Cor. 10:6).[7] Adam was the type of the one who was about
to be, namely Jesus Christ, the head of the new humanity (Rom.
5:12). Certain evil actions of the children of Israel and what
resulted are typical warnings of what will befall Christians if
they follow a similar course (I Cor. 10:6,11). The episodes happened and are recorded in the Old Testament so that Christians
will not desire what is forbidden, or become idolaters, or practice immorality, or tempt the Lord, or murmur (I Cor. 10:6-11).
The Greek adjective *antitupos* (anti-type) has the meaning
"*corresponding to* something that has gone before. The *antitupos* is usually regarded as secondary to the *tupos* (cf. Exodus
25:40), but since *tupos* can mean both 'original' and 'copy' (see
tupos 2 and 5) *antitupos* is also ambiguous."[8]

Peter describes Noah and his family—eight persons—as being
brought safely through the water of the flood. He then adds (I
Pet. 3:21): "Which [water] also now saves you through the resurrection of Jesus Christ, baptism, a *fulfillment* [of the type]; it is
not a removal of the dirt of the body, but it is a pledge of a
good conscience towards God." Peter says that the deliverance
indicated in baptism corresponds to the deliverance experienced
in Noah's being brought safely through the flood. The higher
reality of baptism is foreshadowed by Noah's deliverance in the
flood. Baptism "fulfills" by involving the believer in a deliver-

ance that infinitely transcends Noah's deliverance in the flood. The correspondence is between a higher New Testament reality and a lower Old Testament experience. But *antitupos* can also designate a lower earthly reality which corresponds to the higher heavenly reality. "Now Christ did not enter into a sanctuary made with hands, a [mere] *copy* of the true [sanctuary], but into heaven itself, now to be made manifest to the face of God on behalf of us" (Heb. 9:24). Hebrews states that the earthly sanctuary of the temple is a mere copy of the true sanctuary in heaven. The earthly is secondary to the heavenly, whereas in the flood-baptism typology, deliverance in the flood is secondary to the deliverance of baptism.

God and His People in History

To understand typology, the interpreter must come face to face with one of the great truths of the Bible. To both Old and New Testament writers, God is not an abstraction. He is not a central idea for an ethical way of life or the *raison d'être* for the various cultic aspects of worship. He is a God who acts. He is a God who reveals himself. He is a God who builds upon what he has said and done before. He is known by his people, through his people, among his people. This relationship with his people opens up fellowship with God himself. Thus the people of God are always the divinely chosen means for acquiring a fully developed knowledge of God.[9]

Israel was the people of God in the Old Testament. But in the New Testament, God brought into being a new people of God who are freed from nationalistic restrictions. The New Testament use of the word *laos* (people) shows great variety.[10] Strathmann summarizes the occurrences of the word in the New Testament. He notes its common meanings of "crowd," "population," and "people." He touches briefly upon the national use of the word where it refers to a nation or nations. He sketches out carefully the uses of *laos* where the word refers to Israel. But his most significant contribution comes where *laos* refers to Christians, i.e., the Christian Church. He develops the main thrust of such passages as Acts 15:14; 18:10; Romans 9:25-26; II Corinthians 6:14-16; Titus 2:14; I Peter 2:9-10; Hebrews 4:9; 13:12; Revelation 18:4; 21:3. He shows why it is significant that many peoples have been blended or melted into one new people. What is decisive for this new people is the creative, redemptive

---

9 Cf. Wolff, *op. cit.*, pp. 175-76.
10 See Bauer, *op. cit.*, pp. 467-468.

act of God in sending Christ, and the people's faith or commitment to Christ.[11] The oneness and finality of this new people of God, who were brought into existence through Christ, sets the stage for the whole typological view of correspondence.

The unity of the New Testament people of God with those who preceded, while at the same time maintaining their separate identity in ways of approaching God, is part of the logic of promise and fulfillment. Strathmann summarizes the situation in this way:

> The carrying over of the title of honor *laos* (supply *theou*) — the people of God—from Israel to the Christian church is only one form alongside of others, wherein the certainty of early Christianity is revealed to possess and to be the fulfillment of the Old Testament promise, the realization of that to which the religion of Israel aimed, the essential reality over against the shadowy, previous representation. Christ is the fulfillment of that towards which the law and the prophets aimed: thus his church is the true *laos* (supply *theou*), as it is the true Israel of God (Gal. 6:16; I Cor. 10:18; Rom. 9:6), the true seed of Abraham (Gal. 3:29; cf. Rom. 9:7f), the true circumcision (Phil. 3:3), the true Temple (I Cor. 3:16), the true q^ehal *yhwh* [congregation of Jehovah] (see *ekklēsia*). It is the true *laos* in whose midst God dwells and which has access to him, because it [the true people] is holy as that which has been sanctified by Christ. In all such formulas a firmness expresses itself in an uncomparable tightness by which the Christian church with its religious historical possession is bound so firmly with the Old Testament community while at the same time it differentiates itself upon the ground of the redemptive act of God in Christ from the rudiments (of the Old Testament community) now left behind.[12]

The oneness of the people of God consists in their receiving God's promises and experiencing their fulfillment. The newness of the people of God is in the power, task, and activity of the Messianic community which is tied to Jesus Christ. Being bound to him, the Messianic community saw all of the shadowy representations replaced by direct access to God, by a final sacrifice, and by a demonstration (or proof) of the Spirit and of power (cf. I Cor. 2:4-5). The Church consists of those upon whom the end of the ages had come (I Cor. 10:11).[13] Therefore, in these last days[14] God speaks in a Son (cf. Heb. 1:2). God is weaving the

11 Strathmann, *"laos," TWNT,* IV, 49-57.
12 *Ibid.,* pp. 56-57.
13 See *aiōn:* Bauer, p. 27; Hermann Sasse, *TWNT,* I, 203. The interchange of singular and plural in the word "age" is often purely formal. See Blass-Debrunner-Funk, paragraph 141(1).
14 Cf. Bauer, *"eschatos,"* 3.b., p. 314; *"hēmera,"* 4.b., p. 348.

pattern of history: what he does earlier may give intimations of what he will do later. Not every divine work is prefigured, but enough to help us understand the later work (with its higher meaning) because we have already experienced the earlier. The key to the understanding of typology lies in the interpreter's whole-hearted entering into the concept of the people of God shared by the early Church. Paul has made this concept perfectly clear in the allegory of the olive tree and the branches (Romans 11:17-24).[15] An understanding of this passage makes it much easier to comprehend the true significance of typology.

Validity of Typology as a Method of Interpretation

No one has framed the question more pointedly than Walther Eichrodt in his article: "Is Typological Exegesis Relevant Exegesis?"[16] By relevant exegesis Eichrodt means pertinent for the present-day student. "Is current-day exegesis able to classify typology among its basic hermeneutical principles or must it exclude it from these?"[17] In the course of the article Eichrodt shows that typology has a place and unfolds just what that place is.

Eichrodt acknowledges in forthright fashion the basic assumptions which affect his approach to typology. These include the conviction that both the Old and New Testament display a qualitative homogeneity in their revelation of God, in contrast to every other religion known in history. On the basis of this

[15] See Johannes Schneider, "klados," TWNT, II, 720-21. Schneider contrasts the Jewish view of the redemptive community [people of God] with Paul's view. "For Jewish thought the idea of the redemptive community stands in a most confined relation with the fact of the blood-related connection of the physical descendants of Abraham. In Jewish thought the equation redeemed people = people of Israel is quite self-evident. Paul destroyed this equation through the procedure by which he set up the proposition: the promise which Abraham received on the basis of his faith has value for 'the seed' (Gal. 3:16), i.e. Christ. So that the men of faith who belong to Christ and are 'one' in him (Gal. 3:28), are the heirs of the promise of Abraham. The equation has no meaning any longer with Paul: redemptive community = Israel according to the flesh, but on the contrary, redemptive community = Israel according to the Spirit. Paul completely preserves the continuity of the redemptive community, but the structure of the same has become with him an entirely different thing. Now there belongs to the redemptive community of God only those Jews who believe as Abraham. Belief means, however, in the situation of Christ: to recognize Jesus as the Messiah and to affirm his sacrifice as the valid redemptive act of God for men. Whoever does not do that has no further right in the redemptive community of God" (p. 720).

[16] Cf. Note 1 of this chapter.

[17] Eichrodt, op. cit., p. 212.

presupposition Eichrodt sees a line running through the Old Testament which has its perspective goal in Jesus Christ.[18]

Eichrodt next discusses whether the modern historical understanding of the Old Testament makes the typological approach impossible. He answers, no. Yet to use the typological approach is to reveal immediately its difference from the grammatical-historical approach, which focusses attention on only one period or setting and employs a narrow conception of historical fact. According to Friedrich Baumgärtel,[19] facts for modern historiography consist only of a related chain of experiences which can be empirically demonstrated. Past events, of course, cannot be demonstrated directly. Yet if they are to be classified as "facts," they must be of the same *sort* as could be observed in a laboratory. The phenomena may be unique or ordinary, but they must stand within the stream of human existence and must originate from forces confined to this stream.[20]

Eichrodt does not share this view of "fact." He charges Baumgärtel with ignoring an important reality—namely that the kerygma of Israel has many allusions to earlier events that cannot be well-documented in a multiplicity of historical sources. But the earlier event gave rise to the historical fact of the kerygmatic assertion.[21] The exodus is a case in point. In later years Israel was frequently reminded of God's mighty deeds when he took them out of the land of Egypt. This proclamation, for Eichrodt, is "a further reflection of historical events in the faith of Israel which has to be evaluated in itself as historical fact and as such must be taken seriously."[22] It would be preposterous to insist that we cannot believe in the exodus unless we find an Egyptian account that enumerates the ten plagues and tells how the Egyptians felt when they lost their slave labor. Neither ancient nor modern people have been known to be very talkative about their defeats. Nor is all historical evidence of the same kind. Eichrodt points out that certain pieces of evidence are ignored. "It is not perceived why this testimony [material in the prophetic kerygma and elsewhere] which Baumgärtel himself designates in one place 'an inner fact' must not be allowed to be utilized as a subsequent description of redemptive history."[23]

The central good, namely salvation, is the same under both

---

18 *Ibid.*
19 Friedrich Baumgärtel, "Das hermeneutische Problem des Alten Testaments," *Probleme alttestamentlicher Hermeneutik* (1960), pp. 114-139.
20 *Ibid.*
21 Eichrodt, *op. cit.*, pp. 217-18.
22 *Ibid.*
23 *Ibid.*, p. 218.

covenants. In the Old Testament it is the rulership of God over Israel and the peoples. This rulership involves the earth. Likewise the eternal life of the glorified individual in the New Testament, as Eichrodt sees it, "does not stand . . . in a heavenly kingdom . . . but on the contrary the rulership of God likewise is upon a renewed earth."[24] The historically-oriented character of both the Old and the New Testament gives to typology its strength and explains its frequency. Eichrodt calls attention to the rule of God in history as a central feature of salvation.

The only way to discover the proper relationship of the Old Testament message to the New Testament is for the investigator himself to be "deeply stirred by the word of God in Christ."[25] Such an "intimate contact with the salvation appearing in Christ"[26] causes the Old Testament to open its deepest meaning to the investigator. This opening is a subjective presupposition. Yet Eichrodt is encouraged by the fact that investigators who have different approaches and assumptions are united "in the recognition of this rule of faith as a presupposition of all theological investigative work."[27] He contrasts the attitude with which Old Testament specialists greeted such a statement about the rule of faith in 1928 with the attitude which he found thirty years later. Optimistically, he feels that "we must recognize here a hopeful change of great bearing."[28] When it comes to exegesis, Eichrodt wants no oversimplification. The exegete must have not only conviction of faith but also an awareness of the whole circumference of his task. "The complicated catchwords of a pneumatic, christological, theological, typological exegesis are able to disappear in order to make place for a simple, relevant exegesis, i.e. an exegesis which knows that its subjective presupposition is in the decision of faith of the investigator and recognizes the whole circumference of its task."[29]

Typology should by no means become the ruling concept in Old Testament exegesis. New Testament usage shows that the use of typology must be confined. Wherever typology is employed, there should be an essential correspondence involving central Old Testament historical facts. These should be related to the basic characteristics of the New Testament message about salvation. Eichrodt's final conclusion is: "Typology must play only a subordinate role; but to be relevant exegesis in this situ-

24 *Ibid.*, p. 219.
25 *Ibid.*, p. 223.
26 *Ibid.*
27 *Ibid.*, p. 224.
28 *Ibid.*
29 *Ibid.*

ation [or role] is not unworthy for it."[30] Eichrodt rightly insists that one does not employ typology chapter after chapter as he goes through an Old Testament book—Genesis, for example. But in his exegesis of a book of the Old Testament, the interpreter may find correspondences between earlier and later actions of God or experiences of the people of God which indicate that typology can be used to bring out the full significance of these correspondences.

Essential Characteristics of Typology

In listing the characteristics of typology the word "type" will refer to what occurred earlier in history, and the word "antitype" to what occurred later. The things compared are always placed by the biblical writers within the sphere of history. To call this "redemptive history" is somewhat misleading. History does not redeem. It is God who redeems. Since the people of God are participants in or witnesses of certain kinds of action, the combination of God's actions and the actions of God's people may make the title "redemptive history" seem appropriate. But it is dangerous to make "redemptive history" some category separate from the ongoing stream of total history. God does select a people, a place, a time for his actions and for the actions and activities which he assigns to his people. But he does not select a history. He is Lord of History. He comes *into* history. He works *within* history through his people and through anything else he chooses to use. Redemptive actions and events together with the disclosures of redemptive meaning to actions and events have eternal significance. If the expression "redemptive history" highlights this significance, it is useful. But if this redemptive history seems to be removed from the rough and tumble of man's everyday existence, then the gospel has been distorted. Paul was sure that King Agrippa was "acquainted with" or "knew about" the redemptive events of the incarnation. Why? "Because I cannot bring myself to believe that any of these things has escaped his notice; for this thing has not been done in a corner" (Acts 26:26). Hence when typological comparisons are drawn, they come out of the living stream of human existence.

Types and antitypes disclose the following characteristics: (1) Some notable point of resemblance or analogy must exist between the type and the antitype. The *particular point* must be worthy of notice. This does not mean that the type itself, in all

[30] *Ibid.*, p. 226.

that it was, must be outstanding in the Old Testament. But the point or comparison stands out. (2) Even though a person, event, or thing in the Old Testament is typical, it does not mean that the contemporaries of the particular person, event, or thing recognized it as typical. To the wilderness generation the brazen serpent was a means of deliverance from snake bite. It did not show them that the second member of the Godhead would die on a cross as God's eternal sacrifice for sin. (3) The point of correspondence is important for later generations because they can see that God's earlier action became significant in his later action. A right perspective on both the type and the antitype is essential if the interpreter is to appreciate their full force.

EXAMPLES OF TYPOLOGY

Persons

Solomon. In II Samuel 7:14 God tells David that his son Solomon will build a house for him. Solomon is not mentioned by name. He is referred to as David's seed. God promises: "I will establish *his* kingdom" (II Sam. 7:12). The throne of his kingdom is said to be established forever (II Sam. 7:13). Of this one who will build a house for God's name, God declares: "I will be his father, and he shall be my son" (II Sam. 7:14a). God will not take his lovingkindness from Solomon as he took it from Saul, but this does not mean that God will be indifferent to his sin: "If he commit iniquity, I will chasten him with the rod of men, and with the stripes of the children of men" (II Sam. 7:14b). Solomon's apostasy resulted in God's punishment (see I Kings 11). Solomon's actions are all the more tragic as we realize that God had brought him into a living relationship with himself: "I will be his father, and he will be my son."

The writer of Hebrews takes this statement of God to Solomon and applies it to Christ: "Now to whom of the angels did he ever say: 'You are my son, today I have begotten you.' Or again, 'I will be to him for a father and he will be to me for a son'?" (Heb. 1:5). The point of correspondence is the father-son relationship. It is obvious that the writer of Hebrews makes a higher application of meaning. The nature of sonship in the type differs from that found in the antitype. This is true in all examples of typology. The interpreter must note the differences as well as the likenesses. Yet although there is a qualitative difference between the two father-son relationships, Solomon did enter into one kind of father-son relationship with Jehovah (Yahweh). God did put him upon the throne of his father

David. Jesus was not only eternally related to his father but during the days of his flesh he carried out perfectly the will of his father. Consequently, Solomon as a person and Solomon as a king in this relationship is typical of Christ.

After seeing the New Heaven and the New Earth, and after describing some of the characteristics of the New Jerusalem, John declares: "The one who is victorious will inherit these things, and I will be his God and he will be my son" (Rev. 21:7). Although the exact form of the quotation is somewhat modified, the reader has no difficulty recognizing that John is making use of II Samuel 7:14. But here the father-son relationship originally used of Solomon and God is now applied to the victorious believer in his eternal fellowship with God. There are differences; nevertheless the point of correspondence, that of an actual, historic, and living relationship to God, is certainly suitable for typological application. The whole concept of the father-son relationship is profound. It is basic because it is rooted in the being of God. It stirs man in the depths of his being because he knows that he is no longer an orphan in the universe; God has created him for a destiny beyond his fondest dreams. Being a son, he belongs to the One who made him and redeemed him.

David. There is a good deal of skepticism in some quarters today about the genuineness of much of the Davidic materials in the Psalter. Be that as it may—and this writer does not share the negative skepticism concerning psalm titles per se—each psalm does have an author or authors. The problems of authorship are not highly pertinent to a discussion of typology. In the Psalter Hebrew poets do express the struggles of their own souls. They register the heights and depths of their beings. They declare the truths that they knew about God. Their writings show the comfort they had received from these truths and why their knowledge of God had made them conscious of their sins. Their experiences and expressions are admirably suited for typological application.

Psalm 69 (68 LXX) is ascribed to David in the psalm title. It is the cry of one who is in deep distress. Many are his enemies and foes. He feels that he will be overwhelmed. God knows about his foolishness; his wrong doings are not hidden from God. He pleads for God to act. On behalf of God he has been reproached and has borne shame. He has become estranged from his brothers and alienated from his relatives. Yet he has been faithful to God. "For the zeal of thy house hath eaten me up; and the reproaches of them that reproach thee are fallen upon me" (Ps. 69:9 [vs. 10 in Hebrew; 68:10 LXX]). When the psalm-

ist gave outward expression of his repentance and his need for
God, he became the subject of slanderous remarks and songs.
Therefore he seeks deliverance from God.

This is the setting for the passage quoted above. (1) The
psalmist has a real zeal for the place where God is worshipped.
(2) He himself has borne the reproaches of those who reproach
God. His actions and experiences are designated in the New
Testament as typical of Christ's experiences. Early in his Gospel
John reports Jesus' cleansing of the temple. After getting the
business men and their products out of the temple area, Jesus
told them to stop making his Father's house a house of merchan-
dise (cf. John 2:16). Then John records: "His disciples remembered that it had been written: 'The zeal of your house will eat
me up' " (John 2:17). Both Jesus and the psalmist had a zeal for
the place where God was worshipped. The Old Testament passage records the fact of the zeal but does not tell how this zeal
was manifested. In the antitype the evidence for the zeal is
given first. Then the quotation from the Old Testament is introduced to explain why Jesus did what he did.

In the opening verses of Romans 15, Paul asks those who have
a strong standard for their consciences to bear with the over-
conscientious scruples of those who are not mature or strong in
the faith. They are not to please themselves. Each is to please
his neighbor so that his neighbor may become strong. He then
adds: "Now Christ also did not please himself, but just as it
has been written: 'The reproaches of those reproaching you fell
upon me' " (Rom. 15:3). Christ's bearing of reproach is evidence
that he did not please himself. The "me" in the Romans passage is distinctly Christ, whereas in the Psalms, the psalmist is
noting his own experience. Both the type and the antitype
experienced reproach for God. The nature and intensity of that
reproach differs; the fact and the reality of the reproach is firmly
imprinted both upon the minds of the psalmist and the Saviour.

Isaiah. In the eighth chapter of Isaiah, the prophet tells how
the name of his son is descriptive of the plundering raids of the
king of Assyria. Before the child can cry "my father" or "my
mother" Syria and the Northern kingdom will taste defeat in
war. With such dreadful events just over the horizon Isaiah is
to bind up the testimony and seal the law among the disciples
of Jehovah (Isa. 8:16, Hebrew text). The prophet then describes
his own situation: " . . . I will wait for God who turns away his
face from the house of Jacob and I shall have placed my confidence in him. Behold, I and the children whom God gave to
me, they will be both for signs and wonders in the house of

Israel from the Lord, Sabaoth, who dwells in mount Zion" (Isa. 8:17-18 LXX).

The writer of Hebrews, for whom the Septuagint is the Bible, quotes these two verses from Isaiah (see Heb. 2:13). He applies them to Christ. It is Christ whose confidence is firmly rooted in God. It is Christ and the children whom God gave to him who are brought together and share a common bond of humanity. He does not develop the comparison further, but his reasoning indicates that just as Isaiah and his physical children were signs and wonders to their contemporaries, so Christ and his spiritual children are signs and wonders to later generations. The common bond of humanity which Isaiah shared with his children was also shared by Christ with "his children." Such typological comparisons, when fully understood, illuminate the thought which the writer of Hebrews is seeking to convey.

Melchizedek. In the Old Testament, Melchizedek is mentioned in only two passages: Genesis 14:17-20 and Psalm 110:4. In the Genesis record the following facts are listed about Melchizedek: (1) He was king of Salem (earlier name of Jerusalem); (2) He brought forth bread and wine; (3) He was a priest of God Most High; (4) He blessed Abraham on behalf of the Most High God; (5) He ascribed blessing to God for the victory which he granted to Abraham; (6) Abraham gave to him the tenth part of the spoil. In Psalm 110 the one addressed as Lord (vs. 1) is designated a priest forever after the order of Melchizedek (vs. 4).[31] This is a declaration of Jehovah himself, re-enforced by an oath to make clear that he in no way intends to alter this assertion.

The writer of Hebrews discusses the Genesis passage in Hebrews 7:1-10. The quotation from Psalm 110:4 is frequent (cf. 5:6,10; 6:20; 7:11,17,21). Every aspect of the quotation is stressed: "The Lord swore and he will not repent, 'You are a priest for ever according to the order of Melchizedek'" (Ps. 110:4 [109:4,LXX]). Sometimes the writer of Hebrews puts the stress on the oath, at other times on the fact that God will not repent, or on the priesthood, or on the "forever," or on "the order of Melchizedek." The latter is prominent because the writer of Hebrews contrasts the Levitical priesthood with the Melchizedek priesthood. The writer of Hebrews does not discuss all the details of the Genesis narrative. He does not mention the bringing forth of bread and wine or Melchizedek's blessing God. He confines himself to the details that show the impor-

---

[31] Gunkel argues for the antiquity of the psalm and for the historicity of Melchizedek. See Hermann Gunkel, *Die Psalmen. Göttinger Handkommentar zum Alten Testament* (1926), p. 485.

tance of Melchizedek and his priesthood. Therefore, he emphasizes in the Genesis narrative (1) the name and title of this ancient figure; (2) his being a priest of God Most High; (3) his blessing of Abraham; (4) and Abraham's giving of the tenth to Melchizedek. The writer of Hebrews interprets literally these details in the Genesis narrative. He does argue one point from the silence of the narrative (no mention is made in Genesis of Melchizedek's father, mother, genealogy, birth or death), but his main emphasis is on the action and position of Melchizedek as recorded in Genesis. That Melchizedek is a type of Christ is seen in that the writer of Hebrews draws one basic conclusion from the silence of the Old Testament narrative. With no mention of birth, death, parents or genealogy, Melchizedek simply lives as far as the narrative of the Old Testament is concerned. "Having been made similar or like to the Son of God, he [Melchizedek] abides a priest forever [in the O.T. account]" (Heb. 7:3). The "being made similar to the Son of God" indicates that Melchizedek is a type. For the writer of Hebrews the points of correspondence consist in Melchizedek's superiority as a priest, his independence from all earthly relations, and the absence of any allusion to his death. Quantitatively, however, the writer of Hebrews places far more stress on Christ's being similar to Melchizedek. This is because he is arguing historically. Two priesthoods are referred to in the Old Testament. Christ resembles the Melchizedek priesthood rather than the Levitical priesthood. Unlike moderns in their historical interest, the writer of Hebrews is content with the Old Testament narrative as it is. It serves his argument well. Of course, Melchizedek, a true believer in God, a Canaanite priest-king who ruled in Jerusalem, died and passed from the earthly scene. But all of these details were omitted. From the Old Testament we know nothing as to how Isaiah died or what caused the death of Zechariah, the son of Berechiah. But nothing is made of this from the typological standpoint. But in Melchizedek's case the omission is made use of by the writer of Hebrews. Therefore, the typical character of Melchizedek is controlled by a twofold selection: (1) The picture of his life as given in the Old Testament; (2) The underlining of certain details which bring the correspondence into clear focus.

Events

Events or experiences, rather than the persons who participate in them, are also utilized in typology. Here the comparison is from event to event rather than from person to person.

Rest. In Genesis 2:2-3, God is said to rest on the seventh day from all of his work. In Psalm 95:7-11 (94:7-11,LXX) the psalmist appeals to his people to fall down and worship before Jehovah their maker. He is their God and they are the people of his pasture and the sheep of his hand. He pleads with them to hear God's voice and he warns them about hardening their hearts. The wilderness generation is used as an example of those who hardened their hearts and tempted Jehovah. Jehovah felt a loathing against that generation for forty years. Because of their estrangement, he swore in his wrath that they would not enter into his rest, i.e., the land of Canaan.

The writer of Hebrews quotes the passage from the Psalms in Hebrew 3:7-11. He first gives a word of admonition (Heb. 3:12-14). Then he interprets the passage literally (Heb. 3:15-19). But in the next chapter (4:1-11) he takes the idea of rest found both in the Psalms and in Genesis and uses it to designate an eternal state of perfect fellowship with God. This sabbath rest remains for the people of God (4:9). They are to give diligence to enter into this final resting where they will rest from their tasks just as God rested from his tasks after creation (Heb. 4:10-11). This typological correspondence is again historically oriented. Canaan as a land of rest denoted the place of God's appointment for the people of Israel. Eternal fellowship with God as God's rest for his people also denotes the place of God's appointment for his people. In the bliss of full fellowship with God his people share his rest.

Grief. In Jeremiah 31 the prophet paints a picture of a future time of joy. Virgins, young men, and old men will rejoice in the dance. Vineyards will again be planted on the mountains of Samaria. God will turn mourning into joy. He will comfort. He will make them rejoice from their sorrow (Jer. 31:15). Rachel, the mother of Joseph and Benjamin and therefore the mother of the Northern tribes, weeps for the ten tribes which were carried away into captivity to Assyria. The slaughter which accompanies military defeat and the deportation of a whole people are adequate reason for uncontrollable outbursts of grief. Rachel, the favorite wife of Jacob, who died in the birth of her second son, is aptly chosen by Jeremiah to express grief over the slaughter and devastating defeat of the Northern kingdom. As Judah stands on the brink of a similar defeat, the picture of future prosperity illustrates the role of prophecy to comfort when the external surroundings yield only darkness and pessimism.

In Matthew 2:17-18 the word of Jeremiah 31:15 about Rachel weeping for her children, and refusing comfort because her children are not, is applied to the women of Bethlehem. Those living in Bethlehem and the surrounding borders were cruelly victimized by Herod the Great. He commanded that all infants in this area two years and younger should be killed. By this means he hoped to make sure that no one would take away his political power. In such an application of the text from Jeremiah, Matthew employs typology. The point of correspondence is the grief displayed in the face of tragedy. In Jeremiah's day, the grief was for national tragedy. During Jesus' infancy the grief was for local tragedy—the brutal and perverse slaying of helpless infants. The expression of grief was fulfilled in the sense that it received a new application of the meaning. Unlike allegorizing, typology makes no new addition of meaning.

Called out of Egypt. In Hosea the prophet tells of Israel's waywardness, backslidings, and indifference to God. Yet God still loved Israel. "When Israel was a child, then I loved him and I called my son out of Egypt" (Hosea 11:1).

Matthew takes this statement and applies it typologically to God's call of the young Jesus from Egypt to return with his parents to the land of Palestine: "From Egypt I have called my son" (Matt. 2:15). The oscillation in Hebrew thought between the individual and the group is a common shift.[32] The point of correspondence is the coming out of Egypt. In the case of the type it was the nation. In the case of the antitype, it was the young child Jesus. There is a different application of meaning, but there is no arbitrary assertion of meaning.

Passover. In Exodus 12 the ordinance of the passover is set forth to the people. The killing of the paschal lamb and the part that the blood of this animal would play in their deliverance is carefully explained (cf. Exod. 12:21-23). Christ is not only called the lamb of God (John 1:29)—a metaphor, but in Paul we read: "Now, indeed, our paschal lamb [or passover lamb] was killed [or was sacrificed]" (I Cor. 5:7). This is typology because the killing of the passover lamb in the Old Testament is made to depict metaphorically the death of Christ. This higher application of meaning obviously transcends the earlier counterpart. But the death of the sacrifice is the point of correspondence. The difference lies in the nature of what was sacrificed. The superiority of Christ's sacrifice because of who he is and what he did is the theme of Hebrews 9:1-10:18. The fact that Christ's sacrifice is of infinitely greater worth than that of all of the passover lambs supports Paul's plea in I Corinthians 5-6 for a holy life.

---

[32] See Russell Shedd, *Man in Community* (1958), pp. 3-89.

Things

Other cases of typology refer to some kind of thing, either tangible or intangible. We will give two examples, pertaining to *instruction* and to the *temple*.

Instruction. In Psalm 78:2 the psalmist declares: "I will open my mouth in a parable" (ASV). The Hebrew word *mashal* has a variety of meanings: "proverb, parable, proverbial saying, byword, similitude, prophetic figurative discourse, poem, sentences of ethical wisdom."[33] In this particular context the word *mashal* means didactic poetry: "I will open my mouth in didactic poetry." The rest of the psalm, which illustrates from history the unfaithfulness of the people of Israel, shows that "didactic poetry" is the exact meaning that *mashal* is carrying here. The Greek word *parabolē* has almost as great variety: "juxtaposition, comparison, illustration, analogy, parable, type, by-word, proverb, and objection."[34] So the psalmist proclaims at the beginning of his psalm that he is going to instruct his readers, the people of Israel.

Matthew quotes this verse (Matt. 13:35) from Psalm 78 as indicating the form of instruction that Jesus would use in instructing the multitudes. His teaching would be in parables. But here the word parable designates a technical form of literary expression. Both the Hebrew and Greek words are used to designate this kind of literary expression. This is one particular meaning which the words have. They have some other meanings that are equally particular and still other meanings that are more general. But most of the meanings, whether they are particular or general, have a didactic flavor. It is this matter of instruction which is the point of correspondence. For the psalmist, the instruction consisted in recounting some of the high points in the history of the people of Israel. For Matthew the instruction consisted in a technical literary form (see Chapter 10) by which Jesus conveyed truth. This is a more specialized meaning than the psalmist had in mind. Yet both the didactic psalm and the technical literary form known as the "parable" have one purpose: to teach the readers or hearers what the writer or speaker wants them to know or, in the case of the parables, what he wants them to hear. Hearing was not always followed by understanding because of the attitude and condition of the hearer. Here then is typological correspondence between two things.

Temple. From Solomon to the Exile, from the period of

---

[33] BDB, p. 605.
[34] Liddell and Scott, p. 1305.

restoration to A.D. 70, the temple held an important place in the religious life of Israel. For example, the psalmist declares: "Because of your temple *(heykal / naos)* at Jerusalem, kings will bring gifts to you" (Ps. 68:29 [vs. 30 in Hebrew; 67:30, LXX]). The temple stood at Jerusalem not only as a place where Jehovah dwelt and was worshipped but also as a symbol that God was in the midst of his people to strengthen them (cf. Ps. 68:28, 35). The temple was a focal place in Israelitish worship.

In the New Testament, although the old meaning also occurs, a new, higher application of the word "temple" is found. Observe what Paul says to the Corinthians: "You [pl.] know, do you [pl.] not, that you [pl.] are *temple* of God [they were not all there was of God's temple; there were other churches, but they were qualitatively a part of the temple], and the Spirit of God is dwelling in you [pl.]? If anyone destroys the *temple* of God [the one just mentioned], God will destroy this one, because the *temple* of God is holy, which [members of the temple] you [pl.] are" (I Cor. 3:16-17). In his second epistle Paul again develops this same theme: "What agreement has [the] *temple* of God [no article in Greek; stress is on the qualitative aspect of noun] with idols? Because we are *temple* of [the] living God just as God said: 'I will dwell in them and will move [or walk] among them, and I will be their God, and they shall be my people'" (II Cor. 6:16). Here an assembly of believers is called God's temple. The people of God or the Church is God's temple. The householders of God (i.e., members of God's household) are a temple. They are God's habitation. All of this is made very clear in Ephesians 2:19-22:

> Therefore, then you [pl., Gentiles] are no longer strangers and foreigners, but you [pl.] are fellow citizens of the saints and householders of God, having been built upon the foundation of the apostles and prophets, Jesus Christ himself being the cornerstone, on which [foundation and cornerstone] every building [every particular assembly of believers] being fitted or joined together [with every other group] is growing into a holy *temple* in the Lord, on which you [pl.] also are being built together by the Spirit for a dwelling place of God.

The temple as a place of worship in the Old Testament is replaced by a new structure of worship in the New Testament. This new structure is the Church of God composed of churches. It is the household of God composed of householders. It is the people of God composed of believers. This is a higher application of meaning. There is typology here in the sense that the Old Testament reader is made aware of a *place* of worship while the reader in the New Testament sees a *sphere* of worship. The latter centers more clearly in persons. Yet the Old Testament place of worship also centered in persons. By the collective idea of "temple" all that is involved in the "place of worship" or "sphere of worship" is brought together. The nature of the latter "totality" is far greater than that of the earlier "totality."

INTERPRETATION OF THE OLD TESTAMENT IN NEW TESTAMENT QUOTATIONS AND ALLUSIONS

Because examples of typology in the New Testament are so profuse, we might wonder if typology was the only method used in the New Testament to interpret the Old Testament. The answer is no. We have room here for only a brief summary of the ways that the Old Testament is treated in the New Testament. These categories are not mutually exclusive; sometimes an Old Testament passage is treated in more than one way in the same context. The variety shows the large place that the Old Testament held in the thinking of the New Testament writers. Some quotations are from the Hebrew text; many more are from the Septuagint; others differ from both either because the writer was using some other written text (such as a targum or another Greek version), or oral tradition, or was quoting from memory and was not trying to be exact, or was altering the original statement to make it adapt more easily to his particular train of thought.

Literal Interpretation

On many occasions the New Testament writers interpret the Old Testament literally. A writer like the author of Hebrews, who uses only the Septuagint, will interpret this particular version literally. If the LXX and the Hebrew text agree, one may just speak of the Old Testament being interpreted literally. Numbers 12:7 speaks of Moses as being faithful in the whole of God's household. The writer of Hebrews interprets this passage literally in Hebrews 3:2,5. For other examples of "simple literalism" in Hebrews see 6:13-14 (quoting Gen. 22:16-17), 8:5 (quoting Exod. 25:40), 11:18 (quoting Gen. 21:12), etc. Where the Hebrew text and the Septuagint do not agree, then a Septuagint literalism in Hebrews means only that the Greek text is being interpreted literally. In Hebrews 1:7 the writer quotes the Septuagint rendering: "Who makes his angels winds, and his ministers flaming fire" (Ps. 103:4,LXX; 104:4, Hebrew text). His interpretation is literal based upon the Septuagint rendering. In other passages the writer interprets the Septuagint literally but adapts it to his purpose.

The student who can use only English has a hard time checking on Old Testament quotations. Even if the Old Testament is being interpreted literally, the polished translation of the Old Testament into English from Hebrew may not coincide with an equally polished translation of the New Testament into English from Greek. This is one of the many places where the knowledge of the original languages is indispensable.

Typological Interpretation

The preceding pages have made clear that typological interpretation is very frequent in the New Testament. This higher application of meaning, whether from person to person, from experience (event) to experience (event), or from thing to thing, is rooted in the history both of the type and of the antitype. The point of correspondence has significant meaning in both contexts. But since the whole (of which the point of correspondence is a part) has far greater significance in the antitype than in the type, there is no doubt that typological interpretation is an example of figurative language. The points of dissimilarity show that there is a distinct difference between literal interpretation and typological interpretation. Both kinds of interpretation make important contributions to the New Testament's use of the Old Testament.

Quotation with Interpretive Alteration—Midrash Pesher[35]

Another procedure followed by New Testament writers in their interpretation of the Old Testament is the adapting of certain words or phrases for their own purposes. These adaptations may occur because the writer is quoting from memory and blends ideas from two or more passages. These adaptations may involve the substitution of one thing, such as a pronoun, for another, or perhaps the addition of a word or phrase. A series of quotations in II Corinthians 6:16-18 illustrates very well this matter of interpretive alteration.

Paul	Leviticus 26:11-12	Ezekiel 37:27
vs. 16 "Just as God said"		
[Pauline formula] "I will dwell in them"	"I will place my covenant among you [pl.]" (LXX)	"My dwelling place will be among them" (LXX)

[35] For the term "Midrash Pesher"—"explanatory interpretation"—and its role as a method in Pauline interpretation see Ellis, *op. cit.*, pp. 20, 27, 43ff., 139-47.

and   "I will place my tab-   "My dwelling place
                    ernacle in the midst   will be over them"
                    of you [pl.]" (M.T.   (M.T.)
                    = Massoretic text)

"I will walk around   "And I will walk
among them   around among you
                      [pl.]" (LXX)

and   "And I will walk
                      about in the midst of
                      you [pl.]" (M.T.)

"I will be *their* God   "And I will be your
and *they* will be my   [pl.] God and you   "And I will be their
people"   [pl.] shall be my   God and they shall be
                         people" (LXX)   my people" (LXX)

Paul	*Isaiah 52:11-12*

vs. 17 "*Wherefore,* come out from   "Come out from *thence*" (LXX)
the midst of *them*"   [First expression of LXX in series
                                        of those from Isa. 52:11 adapted
                                        by Paul]

                                        "Come out from *there*" (M.T.)

                                        "Come out from the midst of
                                        her" (LXX) [Third expression of
                                        those adapted by Paul]

                                        "Come out from the midst of her"
                                        (M.T.)

and

"Be separate" [See opposite col-   "Be separate" (LXX) [Fourth ex-
umn for change of order of   pression of LXX in series of those
phrases from Isaiah 52:11]   utilized by Paul]

"Says the Lord" [Pauline for-   "Purify yourselves" (M.T.)
mula]

and

"Stop touching the unclean thing"   "Stop touching the unclean thing"
[Note change of order in opposite   (LXX) [Second expression in se-
column]   ries of those utilized by Paul]

                                    "Do not touch the unclean thing"
                                    (M.T.)

Ezekiel 20:34

"And I will receive you,"

"And I will receive you from the countries where you were scattered among them" (LXX)

"And I will gather you together from the lands where you were scattered among them" (M.T.)

II Samuel 7:14,8

vs. 18 "And I will be *to you* [pl.] for a father and *you* [pl.] will be to me for son*s* and *daughters* says the Lord, Almighty."

"I will be *to him* for a father and *he* will be to me for a son" (LXX and M.T.)

"The Lord, Almighty, says the following things" (LXX)

"... Thus says, Jehovah of hosts ..." (M.T.)

In this section (II Cor. 6:14-7:1) Paul is contrasting Christians and pagans. The Greek word *apistos* means "faithless," "unbelieving."[36] In I Corinthians in both the singular and plural it is used as a technical term for "heathen" or "pagan(s)" —see I Cor. 6:6; 7:15; 10:27; 14:22-24, cf. I Tim. 5:8; Tit. 1:15. The contrasts are sharply drawn: righteousness and lawlessness, light and darkness, Christ and Belial (name for the devil), a Christian believer and a pagan unbeliever, and the temple of God and idols. These contrasts are always essential, but they were particularly needed in an environment such as that in Corinth.[37] Hence to be unevenly yoked with pagans could bring disaster to any Christian group.[38]

---

[36] Bauer, p. 85.

[37] See E. B. Allo, *Saint Paul: Seconde Épitre aux Corinthiens* (1956), pp. 185-187. Of this section in second Corinthians Allo says in part: "This present admonition is directed against the demoralizing contact with the pagans themselves who had carried back little by little paganism's injurious influence. Such expressions as 'infidel,' 'lawlessness,' 'darkness,' 'idols' remove all equivocation upon this point.

"To seek to remove the distinction between Christians and pagans in the affairs of everyday living is to desire to institute an illegitimate world, enormous in deceptions and ruin as the ill matched marriages of families. ... Paganism and its customs to which it is necessary to conform are under the domination of the 'prince of this world,' of Belial, to whom Paul several times in this epistle gives a distinct existence as the indomitable

Paul chooses passages from the Old Testament which emphasize the distinctive holy character of Christians. In vs. 16
he uses two Old Testament passages, Leviticus 26:11-12 and
Ezekiel 37:27, yet altering them to show that Christians are
God's own people and thereby distinct from pagans. The phrase
"I will dwell in them," though somewhat like Ezekiel 37:27,
is a Pauline formulation of the Old Testament language. The
Leviticus passage speaks of God's walking around among his
people, but the pronoun is "you" (pl.) while Paul uses the third
person pronoun, plural "them." The concluding phrase in this
verse of "their God" and "they will be my people" uses the
exact language of Ezekiel 37:27.

In vs. 17 Paul uses Isaiah 52:11-12 and Ezekiel 20:34, drawing most heavily upon Isaiah 52:11. Four phrases are taken
from this one verse, but they are used in an order to suit the
apostle's thesis that the Christians in Corinth should avoid the
wrong kind of associations with their pagan neighbors. Thus
the "her" of Isaiah referring to Babylon is replaced by "them,"
which in Paul's thought refers to the pagans. The phrase "I will
receive you" taken from Ezekiel 20:34 means in Paul: "I will enter into active fellowship with you," as the quotation in the
next verse indicates. In the original passage it referred to the
bringing back of the Israelites from their dispersion among the
nations.

In vs. 18 Paul quotes II Samuel 7:14,8, but he makes interpretive alterations to adapt it to the situation in Corinth. The
"him" and the "he" which originally applied to Solomon are
changed into the "you" (pl.) which refers to the Corinthian
Christians. The making of the word "son" into a plural and the
addition of the word "daughters" also fits well the situation in

enemy who especially lays a trap for the readers. The Christians, on the
contrary, considered in the collectivity of the church as regenerate in each
of their individual souls are 'the temple of God' (see I Cor., our comment
at 3:16f; 6:19; Eph. 2:21). Good common sense says that no basic accord is
possible.

"...In a city like Corinth the dangers of the re-paganization of con-
verts must have been continually reappearing, and the long absence of
Paul, in spite of his letters, would have allowed the poorly consolidated
steadfastness of Christians to decline further. It was urgent that he [Paul]
make use of all his authority" (p. 186).

38 Karl Heinrich Rengstorf, *"heterozugeō,"* TWNT, II, 904: "In 2 Cor.
6:14 the word ['to be unevenly yoked'] serves for a figurative description of
the abnormal situation which emerges at any time when Christians follow
in their behaviour the precepts of the world which knows nothing of that
which has been given to the church.... Paul leaves no doubt therein that
where this happens, the church as the church of Jesus comes to its
end ... "

Corinth. This idea may have been suggested to Paul by such a passage as Isaiah 43:6.

Not only does this passage in II Corinthians illustrate interpretive alterations but it is also another example of the multiple use of typology. Each of the passages exemplifies a typology of persons. The Leviticus passage is directed originally to the obedient in Israel while Ezekiel 37:27 is proclaimed to the unified Judah and Israel gathered from among the nations. In Corinthians Paul applies the material, with his own interpretive adaptations, to the Christians in Corinth. Isaiah 52:11-12, which is spoken to the exiles who return from Babylon, Paul applies also to the Christians in Corinth. Ezekiel 20:34 describes Israel gathered from the nations, but Paul applies it to the Christians in Corinth. Finally, II Samuel 7:8,14, is spoken to David about Solomon but here Paul applies and adapts it to the Christians in Corinth.

It is important to note in these interpretive alterations that the main thrust of the original passage is left intact. Pronouns may be changed, the order may be altered, and tense additions may occur, but the basic meaning of the passage is preserved. In typology a statement may be applied to a higher level, but such a transference does not obscure the correspondence or the identity of meaning preserved in the comparison.

Old Testament Language in a New Train of Thought

Occasionally (but not often) the New Testament writers use an Old Testament passage in a way that differs radically from the meaning it had in its Old Testament Hebrew setting. In these instances the main thrust of the passage is changed.

For example, compare Romans 10:6-8 with Deuteronomy 30:12-14. For Paul, what is in the heart and in the mouth is the declaration of faith, while in Deuteronomy it is the commandment of God which is in the heart and in the mouth.

In Hebrews 10:37-38 the author quotes from the LXX of Habakuk 2:3-4. There are important differences between the Greek translation and the Hebrew original in Habakuk. Our knowledge of this Hebrew original has been enhanced by the Habakuk commentary found among the Dead Sea Scrolls. This commentary presents us with a very early form of the Hebrew text, which is very similar to the Massoretic text. There are also differences between the LXX text and that used by the writer of Hebrews. A study of these differences will show that while the Hebrew text is concerned with a Chaldean whose soul is puffed up within him, the Greek text deals with one who shrinks back. The Hebrew text speaks of a vision which is surely coming. The Greek text has an individual who is coming and will not delay. The writer of Hebrews, of course, in his customary fashion follows the Greek text, but he rearranges the phraseology to suit his purpose. Certainly the Old Testament language has been transposed into a new train of thought.

In Romans 11:26-27 Paul quotes from two passages: Isaiah 59:20-21, with one clause from Isaiah 27:9. There is only one major change, but this change is of such a nature that the whole direction of the action in the original passage is altered. In the Hebrew text of Isaiah 59:20 "a redeemer comes *to Zion.*" In the LXX the deliverer comes *for the sake of Zion.* But Paul in Romans has the deliverer come *out of Zion.* He uses the passage eschatologically. At the time when all Israel will be saved, the deliverer comes out of Zion. At that time he will turn away ungodliness from Jacob. The actor remains the same whether he comes "to" or "out of." Therefore, the changes are not as great in this example as the two preceding. But still one is puzzled at a deliverer who will come *out of* a sinful nation to turn away their impiety (i.e., the impiety of the people). Certainly the clearer idea is that of the deliverer coming *to* a sinful nation to turn the nation away from its sin. This is the stress of Isaiah. To retain Isaiah's stress with Paul's emphasis —a redeemer coming *to* and *from*—makes the most sense in an eschatological passage. Yet the Romans passage makes only the one assertion: "The deliverer will come *out of* Zion" (Rom. 11:26).

Allegorical Interpretation

This kind of interpretation has already been defined as the arbitrary assigning of meaning to the words of the Old Testament. This added meaning is foreign to the ideas conveyed by the words in the Old Testament context. By this procedure, statements in the Old Testament carry a meaning given to them by the writer of the New Testament who employs them in an allegorical sense. Very little allegory—if allegory is defined in the way it has just been done—is found in the New Testament. One passage is clearly allegorical, however, since Paul says so explicitly. This is his interpretation of Hagar and Sarah in Galatians 4:21-31. Some have also detected a note of allegory in I Cor. 9:9-12.[39] Paul does not deny the historicity of the command about oxen being unmuzzled when they work, but his explanation seems to indicate that he did not consider the his-

[39] K. J. Woolcombe, *op. cit.,* p. 55.

torical meaning to be significant. The main thrust of the command, according to Paul, is to show that ministers who proclaim the gospel have a right to live from the gospel (cf. I Cor. 9:14). There surely seems to be some allegory here, but both the example in Galatians and this one in Corinthians are mainly illustrations derived from Old Testament experiences. These illustrations, like typology and unlike allegory proper, are firmly rooted in history. Yet the added meaning rather than the higher application of meaning is certainly present. Hence allegorical interpretation is the best heading under which to classify these passages.

Procedures for Interpreting Typology

1. Note the specific point or points of correspondence between the type and the antitype. These should be examined carefully in the light of the historical context of both. The New Testament person, event, or thing as well as that of the Old Testament is viewed historically by the author who makes use of typology. The interpreter must see the type and the antitype as specific, concrete realities that men encountered and to which men responded.

2. Note also the points of difference and contrast between the type and the antitype. This not only develops the historical picture but also removes the artificialities that are fatal to all true typology. The uncovering of differences does not minimize the true significance of the point or points of correspondence.

3. The New Testament picture of the unity of the people of God should be grasped in its full significance. This gives a valuable perspective on the matter of typology. Full understanding of typology is dependent on our position in history. During some periods there has been such an exaggerated emphasis on typology that the true nature of typology has been tragically obscured. During other periods the study of "types" was looked upon as highly suspicious. Typology was in the same category as magic. This prejudice also prevents understanding. History indicates that it is difficult to maintain a balance in typology. Where the interpreter shares the biblical emphasis on God and his people in history, he finds it much easier to maintain a proper balance in typology and to appreciate the true worth of the typological approach.

The question is often asked: "But how about the Old Testament materials which are not specifically used in the New Testament as types? May not the present day interpreter follow the example of the New Testament writers and point out the typical significance of other things in the Old Testament?" There are more genuine correspondences than the New Testament writers drew. If treated properly, these could be instructive. But often typology becomes an excuse for sensationalism in interpretation. Such sensationalism must be firmly repudiated by every honest interpreter. But if an interpreter, fully aware of the unity of the people of God, can show historical correlations while being aware of the differences between the type and the antitype, he certainly may observe such historical parallels. In such an activity the interpreter must discipline himself severely. Here are some rigorous guide rules:

(a) A potential type must show a similarity in some *basic quality* or *element*.

(b) The *basic quality* or *element* of this potential type should exhibit God's purpose in the historical context of the *type* and also God's purpose in the historical context of the *antitype*. God's purpose may not be the same, but the point of correspondence will have the same meaning. In the application of this meaning in the antitype there may be an infinitely higher significance. But there is oneness of meaning.

(c) That which is taught by typological correspondence must also be taught by direct assertion. By a typological procedure of comparison, Christ is said to be creator in Hebrews 1:10-12. The writer quotes Psalm 102:25-27 (Eng. txt.) and applies it specifically to Christ. In this Old Testament psalm the psalmist attributes creation to Jehovah. What is said of God the Father is applied to Christ the Son. But typology is not the only source for the idea of Christ as creator. Christ's role in creation is directly asserted in Colossians 1:16. The bold assertions in the prologue of John are also pertinent: "All things were created through him and apart from him not one thing was created which has been created" (John 1:3). All things were created *in* him, *through* him, and *for* him (cf. Col. 1:16). The use of direct assertion as a check on typological correspondence is essential for anyone looking for genuine typological parallels. Awareness of direct assertion will help to make sure that there is genuine correspondence in one particular point of comparison between a potential type and its possible antitype.

No one should launch out on a career of finding more types until he has carefully studied all of the New Testament examples of typology first. A thorough understanding of these will take time and effort. But the understanding gained in such an undertaking is well worth that effort. In the New Testament, typology was used to make prominent the message of God's grace in Christ—not to exalt the teacher. Interpreters who are faithful to the New Testament can only do the same thing. Any typology which is farfetched or artificial will only hinder the proclamation of the gospel. Hence care in the employment of typology will always be essential.

BIBLIOGRAPHY

Bonsirven, Joseph, *Exégèse Rabbinique et Exégèse Paulinienne* (1938).
Eichrodt, Walther, "Ist die typologische Exegese sachgemässe Exegese?" *Probleme alttestamentlicher Hermeneutik,* ed. Claus Westermann (1960).
Ellis, Earle. *Paul's Use of the Old Testament* (1957).
Lampe, G. W. H. and Woolcombe, J. J., *Essays on Typology* (1957).

XII Symbols and Symbolical Actions

NATURE OF BIBLICAL SYMBOLS

A symbol is a sign which suggests meaning rather than stating it. For example, God established the rainbow as a sign, pledge, or symbol *('ōth)* that he would not bring another flood to destroy mankind. This particular symbol, like many others, requires explanation.

Where symbols are not explained or are explained only briefly, ambiguity may result. The interpreter is forced to be subjective. Even when an explanation accompanies the symbol, he may read more into the symbol than the explanation warrants. Consequently it is highly important in interpreting symbols to control this subjectivity through a broad acquaintance with all of the biblical symbols. The interpreter must thoroughly understand the cultural situation in which the symbol originally appeared, and avoid forcing symbols into a maze of complex theological speculations. Simplicity should be the norm.

A summary of the characteristics of symbols may make them easier to understand. (1) *The symbol itself is a literal object.* It may be a boiling pot, a collection of good and bad figs, a ram and a he-goat, or riders on horseback. In each instance, the writer describes an actual pot, or animal, or men on horseback. (2) *The symbol is used to convey some lesson or truth.* The two baskets of good and bad figs (Jer. 24) stood for two groups in Judah. The good figs indicated those who had been carried away captive to Babylon. The bad figs stood for the rest of the people of Judah—Zedekiah, his princes, those who remained in Jerusalem and southern Palestine, and those in Egypt. Restoration is promised to those represented by the good figs. Divine judgment remains for those represented by the bad figs. As a result of these judgments, none of these people will be left in the land that God gave to their fathers. (3) *The connection between the literal object and the lesson it teaches becomes clearer when we learn what the one who used the symbol meant to convey by it.* Symbols have a self-authenticating credibility when their import is known. As long as the one who puts forth a symbol explains it, the interpreter faces no great difficulty. But where the explanation is lacking or is only partial, the interpreter must strive to find what the symbol originally was meant to teach. Many times the original speaker or writer probably felt that the context was sufficient, needing no supplementation by explicit statement. This caused no great hardship to the hearers of his own time.

Later readers, however, do not fare so well. Nor does a comparison of symbols always help, since the same or similar act could have diverse meanings. For example, Moses was commanded to strike the rock (Exod. 17:1-7) on one occasion and to speak to the rock (Numbers 20:8,10-13) on a later occasion. The immediate purpose for both the striking and the speaking was to obtain water for the people of Israel, who on both occasions were at the point of revolt because they lacked water. Were God's orders merely to test Moses' obedience and self-control in the midst of a difficult situation? Or was the rock a symbol of something else? Is the meaning the same on both occasions? Is there a progression from the overt act to a verbal request? The disobedience of Moses is explicitly said to involve a lack of trust in Jehovah and a failure to treat him as holy. But there is nothing explicit about the rock in the Old Testament, and comparing the two incidents is hardly sufficient to determine whether the rock has symbolic significance. Paul in I Corinthians 10:3-4 speaks of "spiritual food," "spiritual drink," and a "spiritually accompanying rock," but how the spiritual is related to the physical he does not elucidate. He suggests that Christ was to Israel what the rock was. But does this mean that Christ was also the spiritual food and drink? If so, such participation did not deter divine judgment (see I Cor. 10:5-12). Recognizing these characteristics of symbols and the problems of meaning, let us turn to some examples.

CLASSIFICATION AND EXAMPLES OF SYMBOLS

External Miraculous Symbols

Many modern students allow no place in their thinking for miracles. They agree that the writers of the Old and the New

Testament believed in miracles, but add: "These people belonged to a prescientific age. Since we now know that cause and effect prevail, we cannot admit to the kind of miraculous phenomena reported in the Bible."

Such an approach is based on preconceived ideas of how the universe must operate. Further, it underestimates the people of biblical times. Miracles were meaningful to these people precisely because they did believe in the regularity of nature. The mighty acts of God were mighty because they showed his control over this pattern of nature. He changed the pattern only rarely, and for purposes which he may or may not have disclosed. But the change in the pattern, whether or not God revealed the full significance of the change, convinced the people of God that their God was alive, that he acted and was concerned about them. Such beliefs were a contrast to those of other ancient people, who believed in gods that did nothing (cf. Elijah's taunt, I Kings 18:26-27). A god who is imprisoned within a pattern laid down by nature, who does not and cannot act apart from it, could hardly be considered a Supreme Being. The God known to the people of the Bible was both a God of order and a God of freedom. The regularity of nature testified to God's order, the miracles to his freedom.

There are very few external miraculous symbols. The cherubim and the flaming sword placed at the East of Eden (Gen. 3:24) testified to the rupture of fellowship between man and God. The burning bush at Horeb (Exod. 3:2) awakened Moses to a realization of the presence of God and to his awe-inspiring holiness. The pillar of cloud and fire which went before the Israelites day and night (Exod. 13:21-22) symbolized God's presence among his people and his guidance of them. Jehovah went before them in (b^e) these external phenomena. These last two symbols are ordinary objects of nature transformed to help both Moses and the people realize that God was not merely an idea but a reality. The individual who encountered God as a particular fact through the symbol of the burning bush or through a luminous cloud standing over the camp at night could either respond in faith or remain indifferent and self-centered. Moses certainly responded in faith. But most of those who witnessed the fiery cloud died in the wilderness because of unbelief. How versatile God is in making himself known! What resistance men present to all of God's versatility! Modern men may express their resistance by shutting God up to channels of action which are acceptable to their own unalterable laws. Another form this resistance takes is to rewrite history so that only human actions are considered relevant. Those who are under the illusion that God can be confined by such means should think seriously about the blindness that sin imposes on the intellect (cf. II Cor. 4:4).

Visional Symbols

In the next chapter a brief section will discuss how prophets came to know the things which they proclaimed. One common means was that of the vision. We see this in the heading to the book of Isaiah: "The vision of Isaiah which he saw" (Isa. 1:1), or the phrase: "the words of Amos which he saw" (Amos 1:15; cf. Mic. 1:1; Hab. 1:1).

A visional symbol consists of those things which were seen by the prophet when all of his mental powers were brought to new heights of perception. The symbol seen in the vision involved a common object from everyday life although it stood for something else. Because of its role in the vision, this object stands for a reality which the prophet must press home to his hearers.

The Lord showed Amos a basket of summer fruit. He asked him what he saw. The prophet replied: "A basket of summer fruit." Next the Lord answered: "The end is come unto my people Israel; I will proceed no longer to overlook them" (see Amos 8:1-12). In this section there is a play on two similar sounding Hebrew words: *qayitz* (summer fruit) and *qētz* (end). This is an understandable symbol among an agricultural people. A ripe basket of fruit at the close of summer is either consumed by eating, or if left uneaten, it is consumed by spoiling. Just as the basket of fruit speedily comes to its end, so the Lord will bring his people Israel to the end which he has appointed for them. He will no longer overlook their sin. He will act in judgment (Amos 8:3). This is a vivid symbol.

Another example of a visional symbol is the golden candlestick with a bowl on the top from which seven pipes brought oil for seven lamps. Beside this candlestick were two olive trees, one to the right of the bowl and one to the left which supplied the oil to the bowl (Zech. 4:1-14). Zechariah himself was puzzled by the two olive trees. Twice he asked what or who these stood for (vss. 11,12). The angel's reply after Zechariah's twice-repeated question suggests that the answer should have been self-evident to Zechariah. Hence the angel's answer is slightly enigmatic: "These are the two sons of fresh oil [i.e., the two anointed ones] who stand before the Lord of the whole earth" (vs. 14). Throughout Israelitish history the candlestick played a prominent part in tabernacle and temple worship. The candlestick apparently symbolizes the people of God as God's lights in the world. The only thing unusual about this candlestick in Zechariah is how it was supplied with oil. The oil came directly from the two olive trees. Since the angel thought that their identity should be self-evident to the prophet, the two olive trees must stand for Zerubbabel, the head of the civil government of the Jews who returned to Palestine, and for Joshua, the high priest who endeavored to get the priesthood functioning again. Obviously these symbols promise an abundance of oil to bring abundance of light. The kind of oil which the people of God need is the energizing of God's Spirit. The kind of light which they must send forth should also come from this source. This Old Testament symbol seems to point beyond the days of the return of the Jews from the exile to the Pentecost of the Christian Church when God's Spirit was poured out upon his people. But its immediate thrust concerned the power and the light needed by the people of God who had returned to their own land. They faced all sorts of obstacles. God would empower his two chosen leaders—Zerubbabel and Joshua—to be the channels through whom this power and light would come to a needy people. This symbol is difficult because there is no explicit explanation. Yet if we carefully study the book itself and the language of the passage, and if we are aware of the role that the prophets saw as God's calling for his people, then certain emphases begin to emerge in this symbolic picture. In the interpretation of a symbol like this, no honest interpreter dares be dogmatic. Neither does he need be apologetic for a meaning which satisfies the demands of the context.

This symbol in Zechariah served as the basis for a second visional symbol many years later. John in Revelation has two witnesses or prophets whose ministry extends for three and one half years (Rev. 11:3-12). He designates these two prophets as "the two olive trees and the two lampstands [candlesticks] who stand before the Lord of the earth" (Rev. 11:4). It is obvious that he has modified the picture of Zechariah. Here each prophet is symbolized by a lampstand and by an olive tree. By such symbols John tries to show that these two prophets are divinely empowered for their task. They are supplied with oil or with power. The light which they emit will involve not only truth but the power of judgment. Fire from their mouth will devour their enemies. The two prophets may withhold rain. They can turn the waters into blood, and they can smite the earth with a plague as often as they wish. When they have finished their prophetic ministry, the beast who comes from the abyss overcomes them and kills them. Their bodies lie unburied

in the streets of Jerusalem for three and one half days. The
pagans who were harassed by the prophetic ministry of these
two prophets and rejected it rejoice and celebrate over the
death of their tormentors (Rev. 11:10). After three and one half
days the two prophets are resurrected and ascend to heaven in
the presence of their enemies (Rev. 11:11-12). These two Christian prophets play an important role. John's description so
emphasizes the aspect of judgment that the interpreter can
evaluate fairly their character and enduement only if he takes
seriously into account the symbols of the two lampstands and
the two olive trees. These point unmistakably to their Spirit-
filled life and power. They proclaimed the light of truth as
well as the fire of judgment.

For other visional symbols see: Jeremiah 1:13; chap. 24;
Ezekiel 37:1-14; Daniel 2:31-35,36-45; 7:1-8; 8; Zechariah 1:10;
1:18-19; 5:1-11; 6:1-8.

Material Symbols

In contrast to visional symbols, material symbols consist of
things which can be seen, touched, felt, and used by chosen
representatives of the people of God or by all the people. These
are actual objects which convey a meaning beyond their material use.

One common material symbol of both the Old and New Covenants is that of blood. Rites involving blood are found among
many ancient peoples and are found currently among many
primitive religions. Therefore, it is important to find out what
the people of God in the Old Testament understood by this
symbol. Why were there prohibitions against eating blood?
Why was the blood so important in the sacrifices? The first question is answered clearly in Deuteronomy 12:23-25.

> Only be sure that you do not eat the blood because *the blood is
> the living being [life]*, and you shall not eat *the living being [life]*
> *with the flesh.* You shall not eat it; you shall pour it out upon
> the earth like water. You shall not eat it in order that it may go
> well for you and for your sons after you, because you shall do
> that which is right [pleasing] in the eyes of Jehovah.

Here the life itself is identified with blood. Thus the living
being is not to be eaten with the flesh. The flesh itself is not
to be regarded as sacred, but the life or living being is. When
it comes to the role of blood in the sacrifices, Leviticus 17:11
makes it clear that the blood itself is a complex. There is that
within the blood which plays a role in atonement.

Because the *living being [life] of the flesh, it is in the blood*. And
I have given it [the blood] to you upon the altar for the purpose
of making atonement on behalf of [for the sake of, for] your persons; *because it is the blood with the living being [life] that makes
atonement*.

The blood with the life makes atonement—not the blood by
itself. The blood considered apart from the life is in the same
category as the flesh. Yet the blood can be separated from the
flesh. But the life or living being is not so easily identifiable.
Hence the blood (with which life is associated) is used to make
atonement. What really matters is the life or living being. This
explanation of the symbol still leaves many questions unan-
swered. But enough is said to show that a profound concept of
blood was held by the people of God in the Old Testament. It
stood for a living being or life poured out. Sin which robs men
of life is atoned for by the pouring out of life. The New Testament accepts this formula, but makes one important clarifica-
tion. The life which is poured out must be that of the being
of God (see Heb. 1:3; 7:16; 9:14; 13:20). Christ offered himself,
his life for sinners (see Heb. 9:22-28).

Another material symbol found in visions is the cherub or
cherubim. This word (in Hebrew, *kᵉruv*) is found over ninety
times in the Old Testament. It is found only once in the New
Testament (Heb. 9:5). The appearance and function of the
cherubim in the visional symbols would seem to indicate an
order of angelic beings. Ezekiel provides enough material to
show the complexity of the symbol (see Ezek. 1:5-28; 9:3;
10:1-20; 11:22; 28:14-16). They have four faces, four wings, and
four wheels—one for each face. There is a vital relation between
the wheels and the living creatures (see Ezek. 1).

But the material cherubim are much simpler. They were
found in the tabernacle and temple in the Most Holy Place.
There they faced each other and overshadowed the mercy seat
with their wings. Jehovah of hosts was enthroned on the cherubim (I Sam. 4:4; II Sam. 6:2 = I Chron. 13:6; II Kings 19:15
= Isa. 37:16; Ps. 80:2; 99:1). The glory of the Lord appeared
by the cherubim and from this area he spoke (Exod. 25:18-22;
37:7-9; Num. 7:89). These cherubim were made of gold.

Other images of the cherubim were carved on the gold-plated
cedar planks in the inner walls of the temple and on the olive
wood doors (I Kings 6:29-35; II Chron. 3:7).[1] As material symbols they stand for the holiness of God. By their location they
also connote his inaccessibility (cf. Heb. 9:8). Here are sym-

---

[1] BDB, p. 500.

bols of creatures who have an immediate and intimate relation with God. This symbol conveyed to the Israelites the exalted character of God. It helped the Israelites to be filled with awe at the contemplation of God. It is significant that the meaning of the symbol became fixed in the thinking of the Israelites. Never did they worship the cherubim, although on many occasions they lapsed into idolatrous practices. With this symbol they could only think of the true God. When they departed from God, they also turned aside from the symbol.

Of course there are many other material symbols: the tabernacle as a whole, the Holy and Most Holy Place, the furniture in these two compartments, the altar of burnt offering and the laver of brass—these are only a few. In studying any material symbol, the interpreter should note carefully what is associated with the particular symbol, how it functions, any explicit statements about its purpose, and the extent and frequency of its occurrence. When giving a meaning to the symbol on the basis of these considerations, we must not introduce ideas that would have puzzled those who actually viewed the symbol. Material symbols do not constitute an opportunity for inventive genius. Rather they stand for basic elements in the relationship between man and God.

Emblematic Numbers, Names, Colors, Metals and Jewels

We can rarely be sure that particular examples of this category carry any symbolism. The primary function of numbers is to indicate measurement of time, space, quantity, etc. Colors are usually a means of aesthetic expression. Metals have utilitarian qualities that dictate their use. Jewels are often introduced because of their beauty and splendor. Names are usually routine appellatives to pinpoint persons and places. Yet there are instances when the interpreter wonders if a symbolical meaning is not co-existent with the literal meaning. In other places this is clearly the case. And in still other occurrences these emblematic expressions are purely symbolical. But to insist that any of these elements is solely symbolical and consistently means a certain thing takes careful study. The evidence rarely supports a consistent symbolic meaning in some dogmatic scheme of classification.

Numbers. Any symbolic meaning given to numbers must be based on an inductive study. Take, e.g., the number twelve. In the Old Testament there are the twelve tribes of Israel. In the New Testament there are the twelve disciples (Matt. 10:1), the twelve apostles (Matt. 10:2), and the number twelve by itself—

"He was seen of Cephas, then of the twelve" (I Cor. 15:5). In the book of Revelation the number twelve plays a large role.[2] There are twelve thousand sealed from each of the twelve tribes of Israel (7:4-8). The woman clothed with the sun has a crown of twelve stars on her head (12:1). The New Jerusalem has twelve gates and at the gates twelve angels (21:12). Inscribed on the gates are the names of the twelve tribes of Israel (21:12). The city has twelve foundations and inscribed on them are the names of the twelve apostles of the lamb (21:14). The city is laid out as a square with the dimensions of 12,000 stadia, apparently on each side. If this be true, the city would have 1500 miles on each side (21:16). The height of the wall is 144 cubits (12 $\times$ 12, just as the 144,000 was 12,000 $\times$ 12)—cf. 7:4 with 21:17. The foundations of the walls consist of twelve costly jewels (21:19-20). The twelve gates are twelve pearls. The trees of life ("tree" in Rev. 22:2 is a collective noun) are on each side of the river which proceeds out of the throne of God. These trees yield twelve kinds of fruit, yielding their fruit each month (22:2). With this background of usage, one can see why Rengstorf takes the number 144,000 symbolically. He speaks of the twelve tribes in the words of Kraemer as "the typical number of the unbrokenness, of the irreducible completeness of the theocratic people, of the people for God's own possession."[3]

Rengstorf proceeds further:

If the language is of a sealing of 12,000 out of the 12 tribes, there is asserted by this that the number of those sealed is determined through the counsel of God and that the community (church) built out of them bears the characteristic of absolute completeness; further, indeed that this community (church) is to be of a vast magnitude. The expression "the twelve" is useful for the stress on the divine will, which at the same time is always a redemptive will and is revealed also here as a redemptive will. The expression "the thousands" is useful for calling attention to the magnitude of the community (church). The uniform origin of the twelve thousand out of the individual tribes is useful for recognition of the regularity of the divine action and for the completeness of its results. The attestation to the absolute unity of the sealed ones is their concentration in the number, 144,000. The whole is nothing other than the resolute and confident acknowledgement of God as the Lord of his community (church) who attains his goal in it [the church], within its history. Any other interpretation necessarily leads the wrong way.... The author of the Apocalypse thus speaks

[2] See Karl Heinrich Rengstorf, "dōdeka," "(hekaton tesserakonta tessares)," "dodekatos," "dōdekaphulon," TWNT, II, 321-328, especially pp. 323-325.
[3] Ibid., p. 323.

here, as in similar contexts of the true Israel of Paul, which Jesus brought into reality in the church (or the community).[4]

Others may put the point differently. Nevertheless, since the author of the Apocalypse has already asserted the unity of the people of God by his use of the words *laos* (people), *hagios* (saints), and *doulos* (servants, slaves), his use of the number twelve only re-enforces this concept of unity. Even the structural layout of the New Jerusalem seems to confirm this connection of the number with the people of God. The tree(s) of life and the twelve fruits as well as the leaves stand for the imperishable goods of eternal life.[5] These are shared by his servants who serve him (Rev. 22:3).

There are many other numbers which the Bible student can study carefully: one, three, four, seven, ten, forty, seventy, etc. The apocalyptic expressions "time, times and half a time," "1260 days," and "forty-two months" all designate a period of three and one half years. This expression has both a temporal as well as a symbolic import.[6]

Names. These may also be used as symbols. Not only names of places but also the name of an institution can be radically modified by a qualifying genitive. John, the author of the book of Revelation, had a real antipathy for national Judaism which had turned away from his Messiah and Lord. He speaks of the blasphemy of those who say that they themselves are Jews. "On the contrary they are not but are of the synagogue of Satan" (Rev. 2:9; cf. also 3:9). For John, true Jews must be Christians. Otherwise, they have no right to the title "Jew" *(Ioudaios).* Their place of worship is no longer God's synagogue, but the synagogue of Satan. The term "synagogue" then becomes a symbol of Satanic opposition to the good news of Jesus Christ.

John's antipathy to Judaism is also seen in the symbolical names he gives to the Jewish capitol, Jerusalem. He calls the city "Sodom" and "Egypt." This startling identification is made certain beyond any contradiction by the modifying local clause "where our Lord was crucified" (Rev. 11:8). The book of Revelation does make use of Jewish language and terminology. Nevertheless the book is definitely a Christian book. The Judaism out of which Christianity came is viewed as having all of the characteristics of "Sodom" and "Egypt." Judaism and paganism had joined hands to stamp out Christianity, but very

[4] *Ibid.*, pp. 324-25.

[5] See Johannes Schneider, *"meros,"* TWNT, IV, 601.

[6] See Henry Barclay Swete, *The Apocalypse of St. John* (1951 [reprint]), pp. 131-32.

likely the early Christians felt that the Jewish antagonism was sharper. These symbolical epithets show how deeply first century Christianity was wounded by Jewish hatred. Paul's picture of Judaism in the middle of the first century (I Thess. 2:14-16) seems to be equally applicable to the Judaism at the close of the century. A little meditation on the significance of symbolical names opens up large vistas of new ideas. Consider for example "Babylon" and "the New Jerusalem" in the book of Revelation.

Colors. As with numbers, any symbolic import of colors comes from association. Ancient colors were not nearly so distinct as ours. Hence the modern interpreter must see the colors as the ancients saw them rather than as a whole host of distinctly graduated colors. Such colors as blue, purple and scarlet, white, black, red, etc., are prominent. The opening of the first four seals (Rev. 6:1-8) shows us colors in a particular context. There is a rider on a white horse, a red horse, a black horse, and a yellowish green or pale horse. From what they do, these riders seem to represent a conqueror, active combat in war, famine, and finally sickness, death, and Hades. Whether there is a symbolic correlation between color and the idea represented will always be a subjective decision. An alignment of color and idea will help each reader make his own test:

White Horse = A military conqueror
Red Horse = Active combat in war
Black Horse = Famine
Yellowish green or pale Horse = Sickness, death, and Hades

We can be sure that these first four seals depict vividly the total effects of war which will prepare the world for the final period of crisis that precedes the second coming of Christ.

Metals and Jewels. Of all the emblematic elements, metals and jewels are most difficult. They are usually found in lists. Whether they have symbolic import either totally (where more than one occurs) or individually is not easy to determine. In Daniel 2:31-45 the vision of the king shows the monetary value of metals. The order goes from the highest to the lowest: gold, silver, brass or bronze, iron, and mixture of iron and clay. Inherent worth seems to be a clue which points to a re-enforcing symbolic meaning. As already indicated, the twelve foundations of the wall of the New Jerusalem consist of twelve different gems. These are all specifically listed (Rev. 21:14,19,20). The twelve gates are said to be of pearl (Rev. 21:21). The symbolic import of the twelve gems—an interpreter has every right to doubt that there is any—seems to be a collective one. Some of the gems listed are difficult to identify. But the thrust of the total is to picture the beauty, worth, magnificence, and finality of the eternal city.

Emblematic Actions

Sometimes action symbolizes or suggests an idea that lives vividly in the minds of those who observe it or who participate in the action. Emblematic action in Scripture is drama at its best. The actor not only conveys a message to himself and to others, but he is living his own life, not that of another. He and what he does become the symbol.

Both Ezekiel (Ezek. 2:8-3:3) and John in Revelation (10:2, 8-11) were commanded to take a roll or scroll and eat it. In Ezekiel this is part of the prophet's call or commission. In Revelation the symbolic action is described in a section in which John's call is reaffirmed. He is told that his ministry as a prophet is not yet finished. The content of the book which Ezekiel was to eat contained lamentations, mourning and woe —like much of the message which he brought to his people. The book which John took and ate seems to have contained a picture of the climax in which God will take his great power and will reign. It is a climax in which the people of God will experience suffering and unparalleled blessing, and those who are opposed to God will know judgment and banishment from his presence. As in Ezekiel, the rest of the book of Revelation (chaps. 11-22) sets forth the themes covered as the mystery of God is brought to completion (Rev. 10:7). But the symbolic action, both for Ezekiel and for John, is focused in the act of eating the book. In the case of John equal attention is given to the result of the digestive process. Ezekiel says that the roll was in his mouth as honey for sweetness (3:3). John is told of a twofold effect: in the mouth it will be as sweet as honey but in the stomach it will be bitter. When John actually carried out the command, the results were exactly as the angel had said. What does all this mean? The symbol seems to be saying that the prophet's message must be a part of him. He is not reading a prepared script, as a radio or television announcer reads a commercial. The message enters into his whole being. The stress on sweetness (both Ezekiel and Revelation) indicates the privilege and joy of proclaiming God's message. The bitterness which John knew may symbolize the psychological impact of identifying himself with his readers and taking seriously what God says. The possibilities for good or evil both in the present and in the future are staggering. When we add to these possibilities the reality of God, what he has done, what he is doing, and what he intends to do, then the tragedy of human sin makes the man who is spiritually sensitive sick at heart. When he contemplates the result of human sin in a particular life, he thinks of how different the outcome would have been if the individual had substituted righteousness for unrighteousness. A prophet who is attuned to the message of God and who is aware of the tragedy of sin would certainly suffer the extremes of joy and bitterness.

The lives of Old Testament prophets are studded with examples of emblematic action. In Ezekiel 4-5 the prophet builds a model of a besieged city (4:1-3). He lay on his left side for a long time and on his right side for a shorter time (4:4-8). He lived on a weighed diet and used cow dung to cook his food (4:9-17). He shaved his hair and beard, dividing the hair into three parts (5:1-4). All these are emblematic actions. Jeremiah's experience in going to the house of the potter is one of his famous symbols (18:1-6), yet many of his other emblematic actions are also instructive (see Jer. 13:1-11; 19:1-2; 27:1-15; 43:8-13). One of the most moving accounts of emblematic actions of the prophets is Hosea's obedience to God in marrying a harlot. His own family experiences depicted the relation between Jehovah and his people Israel (see Hos. 1-3).

Emblematic Ordinances

In the New Testament, baptism and the Lord's supper involve (1) common material elements, (2) the action of men, and (3) the action of God. Since both material and action are prominent, these two ordinances or sacraments merit a separate category among symbols. Unfortunately, both of these emblems have long been the source of controversy. Yet what is needed today on the part of individual Christians is a fresh study of all the passages in the New Testament pertaining to what White calls "the biblical doctrine of initiation"[7] (baptism), and those pertaining to the consecrated cup (the believer's participation in the blood of Christ) and the broken bread (the believer's participation in the body of Christ) (I Cor. 10:16-17). Every earnest effort to take seriously what the New Testament says brings a far greater depth of meaning to these emblems. Thousands of Christians have been cut off or have cut themselves off from great spiritual blessing and growth because they take too lightly Christian Baptism and Christian Communion. In study-

---

[7] R. E. O. White, *The Biblical Doctrine of Initiation* (1960).

ing these emblems the student must look at more than the passages where "baptism," "baptize," or the formal language of the institution of the Lord's supper are found. He must look at the synonyms for baptism as well.[8] He should study everything discussed in connection with the Lord's supper. He should understand carefully the Johannine language of feeding upon Christ and what bearing this has upon the believer's attitude at the Communion table. Spiritual revival can be the result of a new awareness of the meaning of the sacred ordinances. Whether one uses the terms "emblems," "sacraments," or "ordinances" is not the important thing. What is important is how one responds to the meaning that God has given to these sacred rites. These are not mechanical rituals. They are God-given expressions of grace, of what God has done, is doing, and will do in Christ.

PRINCIPLES FOR INTERPRETING SYMBOLS

1. Note the qualities of the literal object denoted by the symbol.

2. Try to discover from the context the purpose for using a symbol.

3. Use any explanation given in the context to connect the symbol and the truth it teaches. If the symbol is not explained, then use every clue found in the immediate context or in any part of the book where the figure occurs. Try to state why the symbol was effective for the first hearers or readers.

4. If a symbol which was clear to the initial readers is not clear to modern readers, state explicitly what the barrier is for the modern reader. Where there is uncertainty of meaning, the interpreter should proceed from those factors of which he is the most sure. Only the man who is wise in his own judgment (cf. Rom. 12:16) has all the answers on symbols. We should always strive to improve our understanding of symbols where uncertainty prevails and where our decision as to meaning is tentative.

5. Observe the frequency and distribution of a symbol (how often and where found), but allow each context to control the meaning. Do not force symbols into preconceived schemes of uniformity.

---

[8] See Albrecht Oepke, *"louō," "apolouō," "loutron"* ["wash," "wash away," "place of washing" ("water for washing," "the bath")], *TWNT*, IV, 304-08.

6. Think or meditate upon your results. The reason Paul could glory or boast in the cross of Christ (Gal. 6:14) is that he knew what this symbol stood for. Meditation always precedes such a response.

XIII Prophecy

A prophet is a spokesman for God who declares God's will to the people. Prophets play a prominent role both in the Old Testament and in the New Testament. In the lists of gifts or offices (I Cor. 12:27-30; cf. Eph. 4:11-13) the Bible student finds "prophets" listed immediately after "apostles." How familiar is the language: "And God appointed some in the church, first apostles, second prophets, third teachers..." (I Cor. 12:28). In addition, men like Daniel and Paul, who are not officially listed among the prophets, added the prophet's duties to their other assigned tasks. John is likewise said to "prophesy to or about[1] peoples and nations and languages and many kings" (Rev. 10:11). We encounter prophets and prophecy throughout the Bible. So it is imperative that we interpret the prophetic materials aright. But before we can do this we may need to correct some erroneous ideas. We need an approach that will read nothing into prophecy that is not there, that will make clear all that the prophet said or wrote to his own people, and that will make the correctly interpreted message of the prophet relevant to our own times. This is no small task.

SOURCE OF THE PROPHETIC MESSAGE

One question is basic: where did the prophet obtain his materials? The Scriptures take full cognizance of the false prophets who prophesy lies and speak from the deceit of their own heart (see Jer. 14:14-15). These prophets created their own

---

[1] Bauer, II, l. b., *delta*, p. 287.

material without any genuine relationship to Jehovah. In one sense, the true prophets created their own material too, for each one's individual style is stamped upon his message or writing, but they did not originate their messages. They stood in a vital relationship to God, and it was he who spoke as well as they. Hence the ways through which the message came to the prophets are important to the interpreter.

Dreams or Night Visions

Dreams or night visions as media of acquiring knowledge on the part of the prophets have some use,[2] but they should not be regarded as a main method. A classic text which refers to this method is Numbers 12:6: "If your prophet be [a prophet] of Jehovah [better, following Marti,[3] "If your prophet be from Jehovah"], I will make myself known unto him in a vision; I will speak in [with] him by means of a dream." A true prophet who is of Jehovah or from Jehovah will have God speaking in him or with him. The dream or vision seems to be the ordinary dream of the night, with the power to retain what was dreamed (the Hebrew word *chazōn*, which indicates a higher kind of vision experience, is not employed here). God here uses a common experience to convey truth to the prophets. It does not follow, of course, that our dreams are revelations of God. The dream happens to be one of the manners in which God spoke to the fathers in (by) the prophets (Heb. 1:1). Since he has now spoken in a Son, such ways are no longer needed (Heb. 1:2).

Ecstatic Visions

A much more common source of information for a prophet is what he saw in an ecstatic state. Such an ecstatic state was not a self-induced excitement in which the prophet jumped around in an irrational manner, but the state was one in which the prophet had all of his mental and spiritual faculties raised to a new level of performance. The prophet Habakkuk tells of taking his stand upon a rampart. He looks forth closely *to see* what God will speak with (in) him (Hab. 2:1). Here is his alertness and preparation for God, so that he can lay hold of what God is going to reveal to him. These vision forms or experiences were occasionally in the night (cf. Isa. 29:7; Job 4:13; 20:8; 33:15; 7:14). However, most of them occurred during the

---

2 See BDB, *chalōm*, p. 321; *mar'ah, mar'eh*, p. 909.
3 Gesenius-Kautzsch-Cowley, paragraph 128, d.

day when God brought to the mind of the prophet the content which the prophet was later to proclaim. The prophet is said *to see the word or message of Jehovah* (Isa. 2:1; Micah 1:1). Note the opening words of Amos: *"The words* of Amos... *which he saw* (Amos 1:1). Prophets *saw a vision* (Isa. 1:1; Ezek. 12:27; 13:16, etc.), *an utterance, oracle* or *revelation* (Isa. 13:1; Hab. 1:1). The false prophets *see visions of emptiness* (Lam. 2:14), just plain *emptiness of speech* (Ezek. 13:6,9,21; 21:34; 22:28; Lam. 2:14), *deception* or *falsehood* (Ezek. 13:8; Zech. 10:2). It is obvious that the vision experience is content-centered. Jeremiah commands his readers not to listen to the words of the prophets who prophesy to them. These cause them to become vain, i.e., they fill the people with vain hopes. They *speak a vision* of their heart and not from the mouth of Jehovah (Jer. 23:16). Sometimes negative statements help us to formulate the positive. Note *what Jehovah did not do* for the false prophet. By reversing this, the interpreter will see what Jehovah did do for the true prophet:

> And Jehovah said unto me: "The prophets prophesy in my name;
> I did not send them, and I did not command them, and I did not
> speak unto them. They prophesy to you a vision of falsehood and
> divination, and worthlessness, and the deceit of their heart" (Jer.
> 14:14).

The true prophet prophesies a vision of truth. He both spoke and wrote the truth of the vision. Written truth is stressed in Habakkuk 2:2. So content-centered is the idea of a vision for the Hebrews that the word "vision" is used as a title of a book of prophecy (see Isa. 1:1; Nahum 1:1; Obad. 1).

Direct Encounter with God

In dreams and visions the prophet sees or hears in a manner roughly similar to closed circuit television. But in direct encounter, God himself is present to the prophet as he makes his disclosures through word, speech, or declaration. The phrase, "the word of the Lord came unto,"[4] frequently refers to a prophet who conveys the message to a king or to a nation as a whole. In II Kings 20:1-6 we see God directly communicating with his prophet. Hezekiah, the king, was at the point of death. Isaiah came to him with an authoritative message from the Lord making it clear that the king should set his house in order because he was going to die (vs. 1). This news caused Hezekiah to pray fervently and to ask the Lord to remember his faithful

4 See Chapter 4, pp. 84-85.

dedication to the things of God (vss. 2-3). Isaiah had left the immediate presence of the king, but while he was on the way out of the palace, God met with him ("And before Isaiah had gone out of the middle court, the word of the Lord came to him," RSV). Isaiah is to turn around. He is to tell Hezekiah that God has heard his prayers and seen his tears. God will heal him and add fifteen years to his life. God will deliver Hezekiah and Jerusalem out of the hand of the king of Assyria. God will defend the city for his own sake and for that of his servant David (vss. 4-6). Isaiah did not see a vision or have an "instant" variety of dream. He had a direct message from God which he immediately conveyed to Hezekiah, the king. This message reversed the preceding one, so Isaiah certainly would have to be very sure of God's disclosure to make such a drastic change. Here is a prophet fully alert and active, returning with a fresh word for the king. It is no wonder that there was a note of confident certainty in the prophet's messages.

Interaction with Events Followed by Revelation from God

Earthly interaction followed by divine revelation is a more frequent form of direct encounter with God. It differs from the others in that a specific historical event brings the prophet into a relationship with God, because of which the prophet has an authoritative message from God to deliver. For example, Zedekiah sent two of his lieutenants to Jeremiah to ask him to inquire of Jehovah about Nebuchadnezzar, the king of Babylon, who was making war against the people of Judah. Zedekiah knew Nebuchadnezzar's intentions. So did Jeremiah and all of the rest of the people (Jer. 21:1-2). In this ominous situation, Jeremiah gave one of his darkest pronouncements. He had a "thus saith the Lord" which pointed only to defeat, death, and dispersion. When the city of Jerusalem was surrounded, the only course of action that could prevent complete annihilation was for the people to flee to the Chaldeans. In the days just before this great national disaster, Jeremiah was pleading for justice and the deliverance of the downtrodden from the hand of the oppressor (see Jer. 21:3-14).

Again, it was in a time of crisis that the king Jehoiakim burned up the scroll produced by Jeremiah and his secretary, Baruch. The king gave orders for Jeremiah and Baruch to be taken prisoners, but Jehovah hid them (see Jer. 36:1-26). At this time the word of the Lord again came to the prophet. Jeremiah was to prepare another scroll like the one Jehoiakim had burned. As far as the indifferent king was concerned, he would be slain, and he would not even have the honor of being buried. Jeremiah carried out God's orders. He reproduced the first book and added many like words (Jer. 36:27-32).

In the stirring days after the deportation of many of the leaders of Judah to Babylon, the king of Babylon appointed Gedaliah to govern the people remaining in the land of Palestine. In the factional strife that later arose in Palestine, Gedaliah was murdered. The remaining leaders feared that his murder would lead to severe reprisals. Therefore, they asked Jeremiah to ask Jehovah what they should do. They promised in advance that they would do whatever the Lord said (Jer. 42:6). This time Jeremiah had to wait ten days (Jer. 42:7). But the answer was crystal clear. If they would stay in the land of Palestine, God would establish them. If they went to Egypt, sword, famine, and pestilence would blot out every one of them (Jer. 42:7-22). As Jeremiah was completing the picture of these two alternatives, he sensed that his hearers already had made up their minds what they were going to do. His reactions were correct, for they all fled to Egypt. They also took along Jeremiah and Baruch (Jer. 43:1-7).

Each of these examples shows the prophet as personally involved in the crises of his people.

Life Situation of the Prophet

Even though the prophet may not have been personally involved in the event, his life situation often put him in personal proximity to all that was going on about him. After Hezekiah recovered from his near-fatal illness, he received letters and a present from Merodachbaladan, the son of Baladan, king of Babylon. Hezekiah was flattered that a distant ruler should treat him with such respect. The messengers who brought the letters and the gift were given a royal tour of all the splendors and material possessions in Hezekiah's palace. After their departure, Isaiah came to see Hezekiah. He asked about the messengers, where they had come from, and what they had seen. The king let the prophet know how honored he felt that he should be recognized by so distant a ruler. Then Isaiah declared to Hezekiah the word of Jehovah of hosts. All of Hezekiah's treasures would some day go to Babylon. His descendants would be carried away to Babylon. Hezekiah, showing his spiritual immaturity, rejoices that this lies beyond his times, and in his days there will be peace and truth (see Isa. 39:1-8; II Kings 20:12-19).

This private exchange of diplomatic amenities did not involve Isaiah, but the prophet still gave to the king the authoritative significance of these events. The king had gained fifteen more years of life, but he did not gain wisdom to evaluate realistically Judah's dubious position in the pathway of advancing empires. His possessions seem to have been his standard of value.

When it comes to a prophet like Isaiah, the *Sitz im Leben,* i.e., his life situation, enabled him to respond at any time, and his own existential milieu thereby played a prominent role in his message. He had his own existence among a particular people during a particular epoch. He spoke from God, but he spoke as a man within a people to a people.

The various ways in which the prophet obtained his message show how simple and direct is the relationship of the prophet to the Lord and to his people. All mechanistic and artificial approaches to the prophet and his message are conspicuously absent.

NATURE OF THE PROPHETIC MESSAGE

The nature of the prophetic message is related to the even broader question of the nature of prophecy. We have already touched upon some of the basic ways in which the prophet obtained his message. Now we must examine that message as well as the one who gave it. Because of the breadth of the subject,[5]

[5] For a comprehensive summary of the extensive scope covered by prophecy see Helmut Krämer, Otto Rendtorff, Rudolf Meyer, and Gerhard Friedrich, *"Prophētēs," "prophētis," "prophēteuo," "prophēteia," "prophētikos," "pseudoprophētes," TWNT,* VI, 781-863. Here is an outline of the article: "A. The word group in secular Greek citations [Helmut Krämer, pp. 781-796]: I. Linguistic Usage; II. Pertinent varieties of usage: 1. Prophetic oracles; 2. The poet as *prophētēs;* 3. The wider usage; 4. Synopsis. —B. *naviy'* in the Old Testament [Otto Rendtorff, pp. 796-813]: I. The derivation of the word; II. The Verb: 1. The older texts; 2. The prophetic books; III. The noun: 1. Groups of prophets; 2. Individual characteristics; 3. The transfer of the designation to older figures; 4. *naviy'* in the prophetic books; 5. The true and the false prophet in Deuteronomy; 6. *naviy'* in the other writings; IV. Other designations for the prophets: 1. *'iysh ᵉlōhiym;* 2. *ro'eh;* 3. *chozeh;* V. Forms and content of the prophetic proclamation; VI. The language usage of the Septuagint.—C. Prophecy and prophets in the Judaism of the Hellenistic Roman period [Rudolf Meyer, pp. 813-828]: I. The problem of contemporary prophecy: 1. The non-canonical rabbinical accounts; 2. The rabbinical tradition; II. The historical outward forms: 1. The prophetic event according to Palestinian sources; 2. Prophecy in the light of Alexandrian theology; 3. Seers and prophets; 4. The ruler with the threefold office; 5. The messianic prophets; III. The Apocalyptic Literature; IV. The end or destruction of prophecy. —D. Prophets and prophesying in the New Testament [Gerhard Friedrich,

only basic issues can be considered. The purpose of this discussion is to prepare the way for a statement of principles to be followed in interpreting prophecy.

Role of a Prophet

The prophet is a spokesman for God who declares God's will to the people. Two possible etymological meanings are both supported by usage: "to call, proclaim" ("caller," "proclaimer"), or "to appoint" ("the appointed one").[6] Yet since "prophecy embraces such a variety of phenomena that it appears almost impossible to bring it together under one common aspect,"[7] we must turn to what the prophets did to understand their role. They were certainly superb proclaimers or messengers of the word of God. They set forth this word both in promise and warning. They dealt with many aspects of the life of their people and of things in the future. They were used of the Lord to examine, prove, or test the people (Jer. 6:27). They proclaimed inevitable judgment as well as judgment to be avoided. They acted both as watchmen and intercessors. They spoke to and out of many kinds of life situations.[8]

The role of the prophets in the New Testament had much in common with the Old Testament role, although there were some differences. Peter views prophecy as coming upon all age groups (Acts 2:16-18) in fulfillment of the words of Joel. Paul encourages the Christians at Corinth to strive for prophecy (I Cor. 14:1,5,12,39). Thus Friedrich observes: "It is not a gift for select individuals, but, on the contrary, it can fall to the share of each one, though naturally, practically it also remained confined to a comparatively fixed circle."[9] A prophet was involved in the life of a community. In the Old Testament, the com-

---

pp. 829-858]: I. The occurrence and word meanings; II. The Old Testament prophets; III. Prophets before Christ [in the N.T.]; IV. John the Baptist; V. Jesus; VI. Church prophets: 1. The essence of early Christian prophecy; 2. Comparison with the Old Testament prophets; 3. The most important charisma; 4. Ecstasy and prophecy; 5. Speaking with tongues and prophecy; 6. Prayer and prophecy; 7. Revelation and prophecy; 8. Gnosis and prophecy; 9. Teaching and prophecy; 10. The Gospel and prophecy; VII. False prophets.—E. Prophets in the ancient church [Gerhard Friedrich, pp. 858-863]: I. The Old Testament prophets; II. Jesus as a prophet; III. Church prophets; IV. False prophets."

[6] See Otto Rendtorff, *ibid.*, p. 796; Koehler-Baumgartner, pp. 586-588.

[7] Rendtorff, *ibid.*

[8] *Ibid.*, pp. 810-812.

[9] Gerhard Friedrich, "Comparison [of N.T.] with Old Testament Prophets," *Ibid.*, p. 850.

munity was the theocracy of Israel, the people of God in the covenant nation. In the New Testament, the community is the Church, the people of God of the new covenant. The prophet spoke *from* God *to* the community *about* the community, *about* the nations round about, and *about* the world at large. The prophets had a message commensurate with the greatness of the one who appointed them.

Aspects of the Prophet's Message

In declaring God's will to the people, the prophet may touch upon the past, the present, or the future. But whatever the temporal orientation, Amos captures the heart of the prophetic message in his terse exclamation: "Prepare to meet thy God, O Israel" (Amos 4:5). In this chapter (4) Amos refers both to the past, telling of God's various judgments—which had no effect on the people—and to the future, since God will continue his judgment. In Chapter 5 Amos continues the discussion about seeking Jehovah. The attitude of the people towards good and evil shows whether they actually are seeking Jehovah. For those who despise justice and righteousness, the day of the Lord (i.e., the day when God acts) will be a day of darkness and not of light. As the chapter closes, Amos turns his attention from Israel's apostasy to its future captivity (Amos 5:25-27). But whether he is discussing the past, present, or future, the prophet is seeking to make God the most genuine reality that men can know and experience.

Unfortunately, many do not see the wholeness in the prophet's message. They ignore those parts dealing with past and present, and focus all their attention on the future elements still unrealized. The more distant the elements on the prophet's prophetic horizon, the better. Lo, the prophet might have been talking about jet airplanes and such a prediction would only show how far ahead of his time the prophet was! This type of thinking is ludicrous but tragic, for it discloses confusion piled on confusion concerning the nature of the prophet's message.

Prophecy does have a future aspect. But the prediction of God's doings was given to a particular historical people, to awaken and stir them. They might not grasp all the meaning of the message, but the message—with the disclosure of future things—was given to influence the present action. The only way a description of a jet airplane could have influenced a man's action during some period of Israelite history would have been to increase his agelong desire to fly as a bird, or to increase his fears of the military prospects of such increased mobility. The future aspect of prophecy was not given to satisfy man's curiosity about the future. When interpreters force prophecy to function in this way, prophecy is being turned aside from its real purpose.

The two aspects of prophecy have been called "forthtelling" and "foretelling." By forthtelling is meant exhortation, reproof, correction, and instruction. By foretelling is meant prediction of events to come—some immediate, some more distant, and some very distant. As long as these distinctions are regarded as aspects of one message given by one prophet to one people they help to emphasize the Judaic-Christian concept that history is going somewhere. It is basic to Judaic-Christian thought that there are to be many crises followed by a mighty climax when the age to come will break through in its totality. God will then reign supreme. His will is to be done on earth as it is in heaven (Matt. 6:10). Completing his plan for this earth, God will create new heavens and a new earth. The former things shall not be remembered, nor come into mind (Isa. 65:17). Death, mourning, crying and pain will be no more, "because the first things have passed away" (Rev. 21:4). Yet this distinction between "forthtelling" and "foretelling" can also lead to an artificial analysis of a prophet's message. The instruction, reproof, correction, and exhortation may be neglected in favor of an occult pursuing of future mysteries. But even the future aspect of the prophet's message was meant to instruct, to reprove, to correct, and to encourage by exhortation. Such eschatological expressions as "behold, the days are coming," "and it will happen in that day," "at that time," "in those days" are not intended to whet the appetite of the curious who want to penetrate the future. Rather they are to show that God's program will move forward according to his schedule. He is going to act, and what he will do affects what the hearers are doing now. If they will take into account his future activity, they will live differently from those who ignore the reality of God.

Hence the message of the prophet was meant to induce holy living and a spontaneous, loving obedience to God. To differentiate the various elements in the message, to see what stretched out far beyond the original hearers, is proper as long as the totality of the message is not lost sight of in the process. But to lose sight of the original hearers and to focus our attention on what may tickle the fancy of the curious-minded in the present day is to lose sight of the very reason for the message. This results in a tragic distortion of the purpose behind prophecy.

Prophecy and History

Regarding the relationship between prophecy and history, two erroneous views have gained a surprising number of adherents: (1) Prophecy (future aspect = apocalypticism) is a more vivid way of writing history after the event has occurred. (2) Prophecy is simply history written beforehand. Let us consider each of these approaches.

The entire predictive aspect of prophecy came under attack when naturalistic rationalism argued that real prediction is impossible in a universe governed wholly by cause and effect. Furthermore, God never revealed objective truths about himself; he simply revealed himself in events which would mean nothing to a person lacking faith. But the rationalists had to do something with the biblical claims to predictive prophecy, and with the large amount of material which appears to the average prudent man to be predictive prophecy. This was their answer: most of the apparently-predictive materials were written after the events which they predict. Since history is rather dull to many readers, the prophetic style livens up the narrative and makes it more readable. Earlier interpreters who did not perceive "this method" were either naive or unenlightened. If a certain passage could not be dismissed by this strategy, its message was generalized and called a brilliant insight by one whose mind refused to be shut up within the confines of Hebrew daily life.

But prophecy is not history written after the event. Ordinary historical writing in the Bible lacks the enigmatic character of prophecy. It is characterized by a treatment of details and their subordination to basic events in some type of chronological pattern. This is in contrast to the prophetic narratives which deal with future realities. These realities are set forth as important particulars, but subordinate details are not presented in developed time sequences or consistent trains of thought. Any man who could write history in the form of Hebrew prophecy would have to forget half of what he knew in order to give the appearance of being a prophet. But the artificiality of such a tactic would surely show through.

The other erroneous approach to prophecy consists in the belief that prophecy is history written beforehand. But this is also impossible, because prophecy never gives as complete a picture of an event as does an historian's account. The historian must provide some account of the antecedents to an event, of the event itself, and of its consequences. He must, in other words, supply many particulars. Let us imagine that the circle below contains all the elements needed to give an adequate picture of a definite historical event. The elements will be represented by a number of x's.

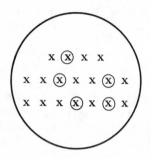

Some of the x's are circled; these represent factors in an historical event which were revealed beforehand to and by the prophet. It is obvious that these *alone* would give a very inadequate picture. But if prophecy were history written beforehand, all of the x's would be circled and the enigmatic character of predictive prophecy would disappear.

In Matthew 4:12 the evangelist tells of Jesus withdrawing into Galilee after he heard that John was handed over to be put into prison. He notes that Jesus did not make Nazareth his headquarters for his Galilean ministry, but rather he dwelt in Capernaum along the sea of Galilee in the ancient territories of Zebulun and Naphtali (Matt. 4:13). Matthew asserts that this Galilean ministry is a fulfillment of Isaiah 9:1-2 (Heb. txt. Isa. 8:23-9:1). Here is a literal translation of the section:

> Because gloom will not be to her who was in distress. At the former time he treated with contempt the land, Zebulun, and the land, Naphtali, but in the latter time he has caused them to be honored, the way by the sea, beyond the Jordan, the district [or Galilee] of the Gentiles. The people who walked in the darkness saw a great light. Those dwelling in the land of deep shadow [same word as in Ps. 23:4], light has shone upon them.

The phrase "the way of (to) the sea" designates the ancient caravan route which ran from Damascus to the Mediterranean (Accho as the seaport).[10] The next phrase, "beyond the Jordan," refers to East Jordan, i.e., the land on the east side of the Jor-

---

[10] R. B. Y. Scott, "Isaiah: Chapters 1-39," *The Interpreter's Bible*, V, 230.

dan and the sea of Galilee. The last phrase in the first of these two verses Procksch would translate: "from the land beyond Jordan to Galilee of the nations."[11] These descriptive phrases mark out a rather extensive geographical territory: (1) From Damascus to the Mediterranean, especially the western borders of Palestine; (2) The country east of Jordan; (3) The northern borders of Israel. From the east of Jordan to Galilee of the Gentiles marked out a piece of land in Isaiah's day that was largely inhabited by Gentiles and showed degrading heathen influence. The western borders of Palestine were also Gentile territory with a few Jews scattered here and there. Isaiah's words point out that gloom will no longer be in the land which was in distress. Upper and lower Galilee are singled out as that part of the land which had especially been dishonored, but at the latter time they will be honored. A people whose course of action was in darkness will see great light. For the dwellers in the land of the deep shadow, light will shine upon them.

These words were fulfilled during the ministry of Jesus. But we must read the New Testament to see just where Jesus carried on his ministry in Galilee. He went to the lost sheep of the house of Israel. Most of his ministry in Galilee, therefore, was confined to the immediate environs of the Sea of Galilee and the territory west of the sea. Very little was recorded of Jesus' ministry in the territory east and north of the Sea of Galilee, because there were few Jews there. Jesus did journey to the borders of Tyre and Sidon (Mark 7:24). He healed the daughter of the Syrophoenician woman (Mark 7:24-30). He healed a deaf and dumb man in the territories of Decapolis (Mark 7:31-37). The setting for Peter's confession was in Caesarea Philippi (Matt. 16:13-20, Mark 8:27-30, Luke 9:18-21). If Mt. Hermon was the mount of transfiguration, this would represent the northern and eastern limits of Jesus' travels. But even the events of the transfiguration (Matt. 16:28-17:13, Mark 9:1-13, Luke 9:27-36) and the healing of the epileptic boy possessed of a demon (Matt. 17:14-20, Mark 9:14-29, Luke 9:37-43a) do not represent a widespread ministry. The Gospel records show that the Galilean ministry of Jesus was largely limited to his own Jewish people. He was the light which shone so brightly in the darkness of his own people. During Jesus' earthly ministry only a few Gentiles came into contact with him. Through the ministry of the early Church many Gentiles came to see a great light which illuminated their darkness as well. But the prophecy of Isaiah which was fulfilled in the Galilean ministry of Jesus was hardly a

---

[11] Otto Procksch, *Jesaia I,* p. 144 quoted in Scott, *op. cit.,* p. 230.

history written beforehand. Likewise, the Gospel records are far from a complete history. Yet in their incompleteness they tell us more about the Galilean ministry than Isaiah does. The materials which are in the Gospels do enable us to see where Jesus travelled in Galilee, why he spent much time there and went down to Jerusalem for specific occasions. Prophecy cannot be history written beforehand because God does not disclose major and minor elements that are essential for even an incomplete historical picture. What God makes known as well as what he withholds are both a part of the total plan of redemption. As history moves on, the full-orbed picture emerges. Earlier intimations of what is to come serve to remind the people that the totality of history is in God's sovereign control.

Progressive Character of Prophecy

On many subjects prophecy is an unfolding, expanding kind of treatment. The prophets deal with the basic questions of how man and God can come into fellowship with each other—what God requires, what God will do, and what man must do. Prophecy is progressive in the sense that later revelation is based upon earlier revelation. In many portions (here is the fragmentary aspect of revelation) and in many ways God spoke to the fathers in the prophets (Hebrews 1:1). In the last of the days he speaks in a Son (Heb. 1:2). Later revelation is climactic. Not only is the One through whom God speaks much more than a prophet, but the content of the gospel and the truths it reveals surpass anything revealed up to this time.

This progressive element is also present in predictive prophecy. Later revelation often discloses elements omitted from earlier revelation. Even so the sum total of what God discloses does not comprise a complete picture. The progressive character of prophecy gives us more materials. Yet ambiguity and enigma are not eliminated by greater quantity. It is true that the more we have to meditate upon, the easier it is to see dominant characteristics emerging. Consider, for example, the antichrist. He is the final enemy of God and of the people of God just before God takes his great power and reigns. The picture of this enemy develops slowly. When we have marshalled all of the evidence, the picture becomes clearer but there are still many uncertain features. The little horn of Daniel 7:8,21 carries out his activities until the saints of the Most High possess the kingdom. The horn has the eyes of a man and a mouth which speaks great things. He makes war with the saints and prevails against them. The picture seems to indicate an imperial

leader and an imperial government opposed to God and his
people. The abomination of desolation or the detested thing
causing horror is found three times in Daniel (9:27; 11:31;
12:11). It is also mentioned in Matthew 24:15 and Mark 13:14.
The horror-causer in Daniel seems to involve some gross sacrilege in a holy place. But the sacrilege, whatever it may be, is
perpetrated by some person. Hence person and thing are inter-
mingled in the imagery. In the Gospel accounts exactly the same
thing occurs. In Matthew the abomination is described as a
thing which stands in a holy place (24:15). But in Mark a
neuter noun ("abomination") is modified by a masculine participle. This strange grammatical shift shows that for Mark the
abomination is a person who stands where he ought not to
stand (Mark 13:14). The man of lawlessness in II Thessalonians
2 is clearly an individual. He opposes and exalts himself against
all that is called God or is worshipped. He arrogates to himself
the prerogatives of deity. He sits in the temple of God and proclaims that he himself is God (II Thess. 2:4). This lawless one
is the offshoot or product of the mystery of lawlessness which is
continually operating. But while the mystery of lawlessness is
operating, the restraining or hindering principle is also in effect.
Just as the mystery of lawlessness takes form in a man, so the
restraining or hindering principle appears in a person. When
this restraint is removed, i.e. ceases to exercise its hindering
function, the man of lawlessness is revealed. Many interpreters
have conjectured as to who this personal manifestation of the
restraining principle is. But nothing in the context enables the
interpreter to make a positive identification.[12] Christ will destroy this lawless one by the manifestation or appearance of his
coming. In the epistles of John, antichrists are viewed as already
present. These deceivers hold false views of the person of Christ.
In this way they are against Christ and all that he stands for. In
Revelation 13 the beast from the sea has all of the characteristics
of the little horn of Daniel 7. The beast seems to represent an
imperial leader and an imperial government bent upon the
destruction of the people of God. The destruction of this leader
is described vividly in Revelation 19:20. There is remarkable
agreement in the pictures of John and Paul of the destruction
of this final great opponent of the people of God at the second
coming of Christ.

Here we have an example of the progressive character of predictive prophecy. But we also see the enigmatic features that
resist all attempts to draw clear lines of connection. This char-

12 See Hermann Hanse, "katechō," TWNT, II, 829-30.

acteristic of prophecy must be recognized by all interpreters. Where it is forgotten, an unhealthy dogmatism prevents further progress. It is just as dangerous to put more on the map than God put there as it is to remove any of that which he did unfold. On some subjects, the extensive quantity of the material itself prevents an easy correlation. Progress does come as we amass the total elements for study. But no one should try to work out an integration of the material too quickly. Those who do often depend solely on the work of someone else. Having committed themselves to the premises of someone else, they merely check the logic. Instead, we must always test the basic premises to see whether they actually agree with what Paul, for example, or John taught. This testing of premises (both of our own and of others) takes time. But the results are so important that we dare not do less.

Restricted Perspective of Prophet

In dealing with the predictive aspect of prophecy, we must remember that when God spoke to and through his servants, he did not give them unlimited vision. Instead they were confined within a divinely limited perspective. On no subject is this more apparent than on the second coming of Christ. Most of the writers of the New Testament indicate clearly that they believe that Christ may come in their lifetime. John in Revelation leaves no doubt on this matter as far as he is concerned. In 3:11 Christ declares: "I am coming at once [without delay];[13] hold fast what you have in order that no one take away your crown." In chapter 22 this is a constant refrain: "And behold I am coming at once [without delay]: blessed is the one who is observing the words of the prophecy of this book" (vs. 7). "Behold, I am coming at once [without delay], and my reward is with me to give to each as his work is" (vs. 12). "The one declaring these things says: 'Yes, I am coming at once [without delay]' " (vs. 20).

Some will respond: "Two thousand years have gone by; we can no longer operate in such a framework." But the quantitative passage of time does not change the qualitative issues which confront men in every generation. The conviction that the consummation of history, with the return of Christ, may occur in our lifetime makes us alive to the qualitative issues confronting

---

[13] This Greek adverb *tachu* might also be translated "soon," "in a short time"—cf. Bauer, pp. 814-815—but this translation only reduces the sense of urgency without changing the meaning. The context in Revelation demands a stress on a strong personal sense of urgency on the part of each one who reads these words.

mankind. The New Testament belief in the second coming of Christ is no form of escapism. The New Testament writers believed that Christ was returning to this earth to do something to it. His presence would make it possible for men to live. He rules with a rod of iron to break the hold that sin has on men. The resurrection of the saints and the judging of those who follow the beast are only individual parts of a great picture: "The kingdom of this world becomes the kingdom of our Lord and of his Christ, and he will reign for ever and for ever" (Rev. 11:15). Direct divine rule in the affairs of men will be a true revolution. This revolution, like all revolutions, will have many new and unexpected elements. But the scriptural data is sufficient to convince all those who take it seriously that this period is well worth waiting for. Men can reject this framework only if they have abandoned or greatly altered the biblical idea of consummation.

LANGUAGE OF THE PROPHETIC MESSAGE

We are using the word "language" in a very broad sense to cover not only linguistic expressions but also imagery, customs, and descriptive terminology. The language of the prophet is colored by all of his present and past surroundings. He speaks to his people in their language, in their thought patterns. He makes use of the customs which they know. When he refers to transportation, he talks about horses, chariots, camels, small ships, larger grain boats. When he speaks about armaments, he mentions spears, shields, swords, etc. When he discusses the means and manner of worship, he may refer to the temple and sacrifices. His outlook upon the world of his day is in terms of the nations that pressured his people: Philistia, Moab, Syria, Ethiopia, Egypt, Edom, Arabia, Babylon, etc., all have oracles directed to them. These people, in their indifference to God and in their hostility to Israel, are for the prophet more than national enemies. They are God's enemies. Thus the prophet's message is deeply colored by the times in which he lives and the people to whom he ministers.

This affects the predictive aspect of his message. Some of his predictions dealt with the immediate future. But others of his statements, often unknown to himself, stretched far down the corridors of time. He looked for the imminent consummation of the present order and the introduction of the age to come; but his limited perspective, into which God had placed him, was for the purpose of having a God-centered prophet and people. A time-centered, history-centered approach that puts God in the background and events in the foreground makes life revolve around events or persons and not about God. This is either actual or incipient idolatry. In dealing with prophecy whose fulfillment is distant in time from the prophet there are at least three possible approaches:

(1) The interpreter may insist upon *a literal fulfillment of all details*. If the prophet mentions horses and bridles, there will be horses and bridles. If the prophet mentions shields, bucklers, bows and arrows, handstaves, spears (cf. Ezek. 39:9), these exact weapons will be utilized. Those who follow this procedure have lost sight of the perspective of the prophet and the people to whom he ministered. When they thought of transportation, horses and bridles or camels were the common means of travel. When they thought of weapons, shields and spears came immediately to mind. Had a prophet talked about anything else, even if God had broadened his perspective and disclosed other kinds of transportation and armaments, they would have been meaningless to the people. Because of the perspective of the prophet and the situation of the people, this kind of language is inevitable.

(2) In contrast to the literalist, another interpreter may insist on *the symbolic meaning of an entire prophecy*. Finding elements which belong to a past epoch, the interpreter proceeds to make every aspect of the prophecy simply a picture of the ideal hopes of Ezekiel and his contemporaries for a better life,[14] or he may apply a prophetic picture to the Christian Church and have it cover the rather extensive period from the beginning of the Church to the new Jerusalem of Revelation 21-22.[15]

(3) A third way of approaching such prophecy is *in terms of equivalents, analogy, or correspondence*. The transportation (chariots for example) of the prophet's day will have a corresponding equivalent in the time of its fulfillment. Likewise the weapons mentioned by the prophet will have the counterparts of the time of fulfillment. The enemies of the people of God in one period will be replaced by later enemies. The details of worship of God's people at an earlier period will be replaced by the means laid down by God during the period of fulfillment.

A good test of *fulfillment by equivalency* may be illustrated in Ezekiel 40-48. First let us look carefully at a condensed outline of the book which shows the setting and main content of these chapters:

---

[14] Typical of rationalistic interpreters.

[15] On Ezekiel 40-48 see for example the older work of Carl F. Keil, *Biblical Commentary on the Prophecies of Ezekiel* (1876), II, 416-434.

The last chapters (40-48) treat in detail the temple, the priesthood, the temple ritual, and the allocation and distribution of the land. Following the principle of *equivalency* laid down above, the interpreter must first understand why Ezekiel gave these sketches to his first hearers. In exile with no temple, priesthood, or land, these descriptions taught that the worship of God was not a thing of the past. Yet from Ezekiel's time to Christ the restored worship did not assume these lines and the land was not distributed according to this pattern. The picture of the glory of the Lord filling the house (43:1-5) and the relationship which these chapters describe between the Lord and his people did not occur. Consequently there seems to be no reason why Ezekiel's description may not depict the worship of God by his people in the time of the consummation. Because of what God did in Christ, there will be no return to the shadows, but rather there will be the worship of God on a transcendently higher level. Holding to the one people of God in the New Testament consisting of Jew and Gentile (see Rom. 11; the words *laos, oikos, doulos, hagios*; Matt. 21:43 and I Pet. 2:9-10; Eph. 2:1-3:6), an interpreter should apply these materials to the worship of God in the time of consummation. The twelve tribes stand for the unity of the people of God. If the interpreter keeps *a literal base* (e.g. worship = worship; Palestine = Palestine)

16 The late R. H. Pfeiffer, unfortunately, had a consistent, naturalistic outlook on the Old Testament. Hence his reconstruction of sources, authors, and dates of original writing is controlled by rationalistic presuppositions. But in outlining the Old Testament books, he strives very hard to bring all the materials before the reader. This condensation does not do justice to Pfeiffer's love of detail and his ability to combine the broad sweep with a careful preservation of the particular parts. On Ezekiel see R. H. Pfeiffer, *Introduction to the Old Testament* (1941), pp. 518-525.

while at the same time he makes use of *the principles of correspondence and analogy* (People of God = Jew and Gentile in Christ, cf. Ezek. 43:7-9 which speaks of God's dwelling [*shaken*] in the midst of the children of Israel for ever, with Rev. 7:9,15 which speaks of God's dwelling [*skēnoō*] with those from all nations and tribes and peoples and tongues; Rev. 21:3 which speaks of the tabernacle of God being *with men:* "And He will dwell [*skēnoō*] *with them*), he will achieve very satisfactory results. He may look upon this worship as occurring in the land of Palestine beginning in the period just prior to Christ's coming (cf. Rev. 11:1; 14:6-20; note how the saints are defined in Rev. 14:12-13 and extending on through the early reign of Christ to the New Heavens and the New Earth). Ezekiel 40-48 treats of the worship of God in evidence before the return of the King and during his eternal reign (see Rev. 11:15). Whatever the outward forms of worship involve, they will have this in common with the ancient ritual—that of bringing an active response on the part of men as they enter into a vital, outward fellowship with God.

To suppose that the ancient ritual will be restored should be abhorrent to everyone who takes seriously the message of the book of Hebrews. The law was merely a shadow of the good things about to be (Heb. 10:1). With Christ as a priest coming out of the tribe of Judah (not Levi), there is a change of both priesthood and law (Heb. 7:12-14). This change is dramatic and far-reaching. The commandment about the priesthood has been annulled (Heb. 7:18). The law with its priesthood perfected nothing, but the bringing in of the better hope did bring perfection (Heb. 7:19). Hence when the writer of Hebrews wrote his epistle, the first covenant was in a state of being old. It was in the process of being treated as obsolete while growing older all the time. It was near to disappearance (Heb. 8:13). God took away the first—the whole order of sacrifices (Heb. 10:5-8), in order to establish the second—his will which consists in the offering (cf. Rev. 11:1; 14:6-20; note how the saints are defined in 10:14-18). The temple, priesthood, and ritual connected therewith were the shadow of which Jesus Christ was the reality. *Hence the worship of God in the future will not return to the shadow but will exalt the reality.* It will make real and vital all that Christ accomplished during his first coming. At his second coming Christ will legislate just how this can best be done. His people just prior to his coming may in some way anticipate this legislation by forms of worship which will help keep them faithful to God as they endure great pressures from the wrath of Satan (Rev. 12:12) and from the wrath of the nations or pagan peoples (Rev. 11:18). The worship of God in heaven (pictured so magnificently in the Apocalypse) when brought to earth will make this earth a different place. To conceive of earthly worship directed by the Son of God himself is to enter anew into the meaning of those profound words: "Thy kingdom come, thy will be done on earth as it is in heaven" (Matt. 6:10). Therefore, Ezekiel here (chaps. 40-48) had his mind focussed by God on a great reality. He used the language of his day to make this reality understandable to his people. Those of us who have this language plus all of the New Testament can still see only dimly how glorious this reality will be. But by making use of correspondence, analogy, and equivalency together with the truths of the New Testament expressed in a great variety of ways, we can grasp a little more of this reality. A growing understanding in this realm (beauty of worship in the future fellowship with God) is evidence of Christian growth.

PROCEDURES FOR INTERPRETING THE PROPHETIC MESSAGE

In order to simplify the method by which we make a valid approach to prophecy, we will list six areas. With each one a basic principle will be enunciated and explained.

General Hermeneutics

1. Make a careful grammatical-historical-contextual analysis of the passage. This is fundamental and is the first task of the interpreter. He must understand the meaning of the words and the exact relationship which the words have to each other. He should know the historical background of the prophet and the people to whom the prophet ministers. He should note the context that precedes the passage and the context that follows the passage. The flow of thought from the preceding passage and on to that which follows should be clear in the interpreter's mind. Any parallel passages that may shed some light should be consulted. But in comparing passages he must be sure to treat each from the grammatical-historical-contextual approach *before* comparisons are drawn. If we study a number of contexts, we will soon see that the contents of prophetic passages are not arranged in a systematic, topical order!

Focusing of Particular Message

2. State explicitly to whom or to what the statement or passage refers. Is the passage addressed to the hearers or readers

while also being about them? Or is it proclaimed to them but about someone else? Here is a good place to observe whether a passage is predictive or didactic. If it is predictive, we must observe whether any conditions are attached. Jonah feared that Jehovah might attach some qualifications or conditions to his clear-cut message of a coming destruction. This is why the prophet was reluctant to go to Nineveh. Again, if the passage is predictive, we must observe whether it is fulfilled or unfulfilled. If the prediction was fulfilled, we need to study all the materials that illuminate that fulfillment. A multiple fulfillment is a better descriptive label than "double sense." Double sense would imply two meanings for a statement. Multiple fulfillment refers to one meaning applied in two or more ways. An example of multiple fulfillment may be seen in the language describing Antiochus Epiphanes which may also characterize accurately the man of sin (the final Antichrist). The descriptive language of Jesus concerning the fall of Jerusalem (fulfilled in A.D. 70) may also serve to describe the military situation in Palestine and Jerusalem at the time when Christ returns.

Kinds of Prediction

3. Where fulfillment of prophecy is found in the New Testament, differentiate for the sake of clarity between direct and typological prediction. Both are equally valuable. Direct prediction consists of an Old Testament prophetic statement which refers to nothing prior to New Testament times and which has its fulfillment solely in New Testament times. The birth of Christ at Bethlehem is an example of this kind of prediction (Matt. 2:5-6; Micah 5:2 [5:1 in Hebrew]). A typological prediction is an Old Testament prophetic statement that does refer to something prior to New Testament times although it finds its highest application of meaning in the events, people, or message of the New Testament. The betrayal of Christ for thirty pieces of silver is an example of this kind of prediction (Matt. 27:9-10; Zech. 11:12-13). In Zechariah it was the prophet himself, acting as a shepherd for his people in Jehovah's place, who was evaluated for thirty pieces of silver. Since Zechariah was Jehovah's representative, this was also the value which the people of Israel put upon God himself. Stephen's words show why what happened to Zechariah was applicable to Jesus: "As your fathers did, so do ye" (Acts 7:51 ASV). Typological prediction is very common and is extensively distributed throughout the New Testament. To interpret it properly we must become involved in the Old Testament context and application as well

as in the New Testament context and application. This brings a greater depth of understanding to the interpreter's exegesis and exposition of the basic truth(s) set forth in the prophecy.

Christological Orientation

4. Let the finality of God's revelation in Christ color all earlier revelations. This is not a reversal of the first principle which centered in the grammatical-historical-contextual approach. Rather it is simply the acknowledgement that Christians are Christians when they interpret the Old Testament. Christ speaks of the one flock and one shepherd at the climax of his earthly ministry (John 10:16).[17] The New Testament unfolds the significance of the new people of God, the body of Christ, his Church. Any treatment of prophecy which ignores what Jesus Christ did in breaking down the barrier between Jews and Gentiles or tries to reconstruct that barrier has dismissed one of the key effects of Jesus' atoning death. The house or household of God is a structure of great importance.[18] Because it is living and growing and tied to Jesus Christ, it covers both covenants and reflects the great destiny God has for his people. The New Testament does not simply add additional facets to the Old Testament concept of God and his people. It transforms the whole concept. It shows that the being of God consists in the Father, the Son, and the Holy Spirit. It makes clear that the people of God are those who have been reconciled to God through the death of his Son and who as a people for God's own

[17] For the oneness of the people of God developing out of the usage of *laos* ("people") see Chapter 11, above, pp. 240-242.

[18] Otto Michel, "6. 'The House of God' as an early Christian Figurative Expression for the Church," *TWNT*, V, 128-131. "In a midrash of Numbers 12:7LXX: *ouch houtos ho therapōn mou Mousēs en holōi tōi oikōi mou pisteōs estin* Hebrews 3:1-6 explains that Moses was a true servant 'in the whole of God's house,' that Christ, however, as the Son was placed 'over God's house' *(en holōi tōi oikōi autou,* 3:2,6; 10:21: *epi ton oikon tou theou).* Indeed, it was in the Old Testament with the expression 'my house' that Israel itself was thought of, yet the New Testament exegesis calls attention to the equation of 'God's house' and the church; to be sure, our midrash actually presupposes theologically this language usage that the church is 'God's house.' According to Hebrews 3:3 the honor of the servant Moses is related to that of the Son, Christ, as the 'honor' of the house is related to that of the builder of the house. Not through the Old Testament text, but perhaps through the Hellenistic tradition which easily connected the concept of the house with that of the builder of the house, the comparison, Moses = Christ, is further expanded in this meaning. *Kataskeuazein* is very suitable as a verb in the sense of 'to erect a building.' Christ is thus esteemed in his office as 'Son' *(huios)* and 'Lord' *(kurios)* as builder of the Old Testament community of God *(oikos tou theou,* 3:3). He is placed as Son 'over the house' (3:6), and we are permitted ourselves

to glory to be 'God's house' if we under other circumstances preserve the confidence and the boasting in our hope until the end. This circle of ideas shows on the one hand how self-evidently the equation is made use of: Church = God's house, and on the other hand what a developed Christology Hebrews unfolds. The conception that the church is 'God's house' is clearly connected together with the old proclamation, that the church is God's 'temple' (I Cor. 3:16; 6:19), and it grows out of it. Also here it is quite important to recognize, that the N.T. does not subscribe as Philo to an individualistic piety in which the individual pure soul becomes 'God's house,' but on the contrary the New Testament gives first of all to the church as such the predicate, 'God's house' or for example 'God's temple.' In Ephesians and in I Peter the old motif of the new spiritual temple is taken up and is worked out with similar characteristics: 'You are fellow citizens of the saints and householders of God, a building built upon the foundation of the apostles and prophets, in which Jesus Christ is the cornerstone; in him the whole building joined firmly together grows into the holy temple in the Lord; in him also ye were built for a lodging (dwelling, house) of God in the Spirit' (Eph. 2:19-22). 'Approaching to him (=Christ), to the living stone, which was rejected to be sure by men but with God he is elect and precious, and he built you yourselves as living stones into a spiritual house for a holy priesthood for the purpose of presenting spiritual sacrifices which are acceptable to God through Jesus Christ' (I Pet. 2:3ff). How self-evident the concept 'house' is in its reference to the church, I Peter 4:17 teaches: 'For it is time, that judgment begin in the house of God' and I Tim. 3:15: 'In that case, however, that my coming must be delayed, you must know, how the conduct ought to be in "God's house," that is in the church of the living God, which is the pillar and bulwark of the truth.' One probably must be permitted to say that this piece of tradition is joined firmly to the early Christian *kērugma*. The motif *oikos tou theou* is referred to the church, but it is not properly referred to the picture of a family of God, but on the contrary *oikos* remains really 'house,' spiritual, super-earthly in contrast to the stone temple in Jerusalem and to the sanctuaries of the heathen. Christ then is the 'living stone' (*lithos zōn*, I Pet. 2:4), who on the one hand is explained as a precious cornerstone to the foundation of the whole building (Isa. 28:16; Ps. 118:22; Mark 12:10), but on the other hand he can also become a stone of stumbling and a rock of offence (Isa. 8:14; Rom. 9:33). The Christians are fitted in as 'living stones' (*lithoi zōntes*) in the building (I Pet. 2:4f; Eph. 2:22); indeed, the picture is able to change and it is able to embrace with reference to the Old Testament the priesthood as well as also the holy people (I Pet. 2:5,9; Heb. 13:15f). This way of looking at things: heavenly temple, holy priesthood, sacrifice pleasing to God connects, blends, and gets the mastery of the train of thought although it is derived out of various roots and builds no real unity. The sentence I Pet. 4:17 takes up an Old Testament prophetic idea (Jer. 25[32]: 29; Ezek. 9:6): the plagues and the judgment of God strike the 'Sanctuary' and the 'city' first in order to purify and sanctify them; in this way they are a fragment of eschatological design. The reminder, I Tim. 3:15, wishes to clearly impress a firm catechetical truth: the church is 'God's house,' a pillar and support of the truth. Although in Greek *oikos* can be used not only of a local gathering but also of a religious association, one is reminded first of all also in our passage of the spiritual edifice which draws similar pictures (*stulos, hedraiōma*). The church is 'God's house,' 'pillar,' and 'bulwark' as a reference to the Spirit dwelling in it, to the revelation borne to it, to the tradition proclaimed by it."

possession (Tit. 2:14; I Pet. 2:9; cf. Exod. 19:5-6) will have God dwelling together with them (Rev. 21:3) and will serve him (Rev. 22:3-4).

Apocalyptic Imagery

The apocalyptic motif in the Scriptures is that of judgment followed by triumph and glory. Many books, either in isolated portions or in extended portions, have this type of theme. Daniel, Zechariah, and Revelation are prominent examples. The imagery in these books is often hard for the interpreter to understand or to clarify to others.

5. For apocalyptic imagery, follow the principles given at the close of the chapter on symbols.[19] Make sure that your interpretation of such imagery would be entirely clear to the original author. In evaluating commentaries in this regard note how far the commentator has been able to enter into the thought of the original writer. When a commentator fills apocalyptic imagery with his own ideas, he disqualifies himself as a true interpreter. It is much better to say: "I do not know what this means" than to force a meaning upon the imagery which it was not meant to carry.

Proportion of Literal and Figurative Elements

6. Remember that interpretive analysis must precede a decision on the exact relationship between the literal and figurative in any passage. Deciding what is literal and what is figurative must be based upon grammar (meaning of words and relationship of words), history, culture, context, and convictions of the original writer himself. Sometimes the original writer expresses his convictions very clearly, as John does in the book of Revelation on national Judaism (Rev. 2:9; 3:9; 11:8)[20] where he denies to the unbelievers among the Jewish people the right to the name "Jews." At other times a writer's convictions are seen in what he does. Paul's second letter to Timothy shows his conviction that death was very close and that he would not live to Christ's second coming (II Tim. 4:6-8). Yet the reality of the second coming is as bright as ever to him (4:8). In other instances convictions grow out of the developing thought of the early Church. Such a consensus was hammered out only through the persecutions, trials, and difficulties that the Church experienced. The unity of the people of God is one such concept. The

19 See Chapter 12, p. 278.
20 See Chapter 12, pp. 274-75.

Jewish people cut themselves off from any active relationship with God by their unbelief and their fierce opposition to the gospel. All who did believe—Jews and Gentiles—were in active relationship with God and came forth as the people of God. Hence both by experience and by revelation basic convictions came to be a part of the New Testament writers.

The literal meaning—the customary and socially acknowledged meaning which carries with it the ideas of actual and earthly[21]—must become the base for figurative meanings. Upon this base they depend. If an interpreter declares that a certain expression is figurative, he must give reasons for assigning a figurative meaning. These reasons must rise from an objective study of all factors and must show why the figurative meaning is needed. Sometimes interpreters insist that elements are figurative because their system of eschatology requires it, not because the Scriptures and objective factors demand it. It is surprising how figurative some adherents to extreme literalistic schools can be![22] On the other hand Swete, in order to maintain an amillennialist point of view, feels he must take the expressions "first resurrection" and "lived" *(ezēsan)* to be figurative (Rev. 20:4-5). These are spiritual and not corporeal.[23] To take them as referring to a bodily resurrection might give further grounds for taking the phrase "for a thousand years" (Rev. 20:2,3,4,5,6,7) as an actual period of time of a long, extensive duration. Since the interpreter does not want to do this, he spiritualizes "the first resurrection" and "live." Yet all the basic works support a future living and a bodily resurrection.[24] Before launching out on the thin ice of groundless allegorizing to get some spiritual lesson, the interpreter should consult basic lexical works. Where there are compelling grounds for figurative meanings, they should be adopted. A careful interpreter will interpret both

---

[21] Bernard Ramm, *Protestant Biblical Interpretation* (1956), pp. 220-25. Ramm, to promote clarity of thought, shows the various meanings attached to the following expressions: (1) Literal, (2) Spiritual, (3) Mystical, (4) Allegorical, (5) Typological. The word "literal" can mean real or actual in contrast to fictional. In this sense the new Jerusalem is a literal city but not an earthly one. Yet the literal meaning usually conveys the earthly, visible, and concrete. Figurative meanings are based on this kind of literal meaning.

[22] Alexander Reese takes W. Kelly and A. C. Gaebelein to task for their figurative interpretation of Daniel 12:1-3. See *The Approaching Advent of Christ* (1936), pp. 41-42, 264.

[23] H. B. Swete, *The Apocalypse of St. John*, pp. 263-267.

[24] On "the first resurrection" see Bauer, 2. b., p. 60; Albrecht Oepke, *"anastaśis," TWNT*, I, 372; Johannes Schneider, *"meros," TWNT*, IV, 601. On "lived" *(zaō)*, see Bauer, p. 336; and even Rudolf Bultmann leaves no doubt as to what John means, *TWNT*, II, 367.

literally and figuratively because the passage he is interpreting demands these procedures. Labels suggesting that a man is either a completely literal interpreter or a completely figurative interpreter are foolish. If they were true, they would indicate that the individual thus designated would be totally unable to grapple with meanings and ideas. Such people usually do not try to interpret. Therefore, a careless tossing around of labels should be avoided at all costs. The well-balanced interpreter has objective reasons for both literal and figurative meanings.

BIBLIOGRAPHY

Krämer, Helmut; Rendtorff, Rudolf; Meyer, Rudolf; and Friedrich, Gerhard: "Prophētēs," "prophētis," "prophēteuō," "prophēteia," "prophētikos," "pseudoprophētēs," Theologisches Wörterbuch zum Neuen Testament, VI (1959).

XIV Descriptive Language of Creation and Climax

The biblical accounts of creation and climax have been extensively discussed throughout the current century and it is likely that the discussion will continue for some time to come. Most certainly the oft-recurring question as to how God created the world and how he intends to consummate human history is one of wide and intense interest. However, if we are looking for a play-by-play account of either of these divine activities, we will search the Bible in vain. Much is said in Scripture about the fact of creation and God's vital association with all that took place. Enough is said about climax in the New Testament so that by the time the reader has completed I Corinthians he knows that all things will be in subjection to God. When the reader has completed the book of Revelation, he knows that separation from God or fellowship with God are the two possible destinies before mankind. The return of Christ, the earthly reign of Christ, the judgment of all men by Christ are some basic topics about climax dealt with in the Bible. Yet such questions as the age of the universe, the nature of light, the time and procedures by which God prepared the earth for habitation of man are not touched upon at all. Nor are the equally interesting questions of the relationship between heaven and earth during the earthly reign of Christ, the exact timing of the disappearance of the heavens and earth with a roar when the elemental substances being consumed by heat break up into their component parts (II Pet. 3:10), or just how God is going to bring into existence new heavens and a new earth (II Pet. 3:13) touched upon. Yet it is important that we consider the language used to convey to us what God has revealed about creation and climax. Interestingly enough, we find that the same kind of language is employed to describe the beginnings and endings of history.

COMPLEX BLENDING OF LITERAL AND FIGURATIVE ELEMENTS

As has been mentioned many times through this book, "literal" and "figurative" interpretation are not even vaguely synonymous with "proper" and "improper." To call something literal which is figurative is just as erroneous as to make something figurative which is literal. "Literal" refers to the customary and socially acknowledged meaning in an actual, ordinary, earthly situation. "Figurative" refers to the transfer of the literal, ordinary meaning from one sphere to another so as to convey by analogy or comparison a different or deeper or higher truth. "The animal *devoured* his meal" is a literal statement. "The flames *devoured* an old landmark" is a figurative statement. The figurative is certainly based on the literal, but the action is transfered into an entirely different sphere. Both of these spheres are in the earthly realm. When an animal devours a meal, he chews it, swallows it, and digests it. Flames have no teeth, mouth, or digestive process. Nevertheless, they "devour" anything combustible which lies before them. The figurative meaning in this case has to do with the removal of what lies before the consuming quality of fire. But whether it be food that is devoured or an old building, both realities are removed from the scene. One is not imaginary and the other real. Both occurrences are actual experiences.

So it is in the accounts of creation and climax. To say that certain language is figurative does not mean that the event is unreal. In fact, when the language of the earthly realm as we have known it for the last five thousand years is used to describe the beginnings of all that exists and the climax of all that exists, the figurative language best conveys that which is most real, abiding, and certain. Earthly language from a known sphere of existence is used to describe what took place or will take place in a sphere of existence that no mere human creature has ever entered. God must attest to that which took place in creation and that which will take place in the climax. Furthermore, the people to whom he first disclosed these things were surrounded by polytheism and had made only the most rudimentary observations of the world of nature. God disclosed his truths in language taken from the life experiences of the Hebrews and the early Christians to describe for them that which far transcended all that they ever knew. What took place in creation and what will take place in climax also transcends all that we know. Because we know more about the universe (or universes) through empirical observation, we may be able to ask more intelligent questions about the "how." Surely scientific knowledge (another name for the classified record of empirical observation and evaluation) ought to help us to appreciate the power and might of God to bring into existence and to maintain all that exists.

Interpreters who come to the biblical accounts of creation and climax must note carefully the following facts: (1) The language of these accounts is directed to those who knew nothing of the vastness of space, the world of the microscope, or of the intricacies of physical organisms. The vast majority of mankind still knows very little about these things. (2) Any pride that rests in the completeness of our superior knowledge is ridiculous because of the vast amount of data of which we know nothing. (3) The biblical narratives center their attention upon God as the ultimate cause and do not concern themselves with the chain of secondary causes and effects. (4) The discussion of creation and climax centers on God and man rather than on nature and events. In the biblical accounts men are confronted with God rather than with some statistical norm as to how he holds some aspects of his creation together.

With these facts in mind, we would expect the accounts of creation and climax to blend the figurative and literal aspects of language. When we consider the materials in the light of all that the Scriptures have revealed about God, we are impressed even more with the use of figurative language. Without it, little or nothing could have been disclosed. With it God was able to indicate how much more there is yet to be known. Man now knows in part. Because the whole is so much greater than the part, the honest interpreter abandons all pretense of being able to present the whole picture. But the part which he has is meaningful and he endeavors to interpret and explain this segment so as to benefit fully from what it has to say to the contemporary reader.

LANGUAGE OF THE CREATION OF MAN (GENESIS 2:7-8)

Rather than survey all of the biblical materials on creation (a subject on which one could write more than one volume!), we will consider one sample passage—the account of the creation of man (exclusive of woman) in Genesis 2—to observe carefully the kind of language employed. Just how is this particular creative action of God described?

"And Jehovah God formed the man"

Metaphor of molding. The Hebrew word *yatzar* means to form or fashion.[1] It is used of a potter who forms a vessel out of clay (cf. Jer. 18:4,6). The vessel of a potter or the clay of the potter represents the product or the material which is produced or worked on by the potter. By the skillful manipulation of his hands he forms or fashions some decoration or useful object.

When this word is used of God, the figurative meaning at once becomes apparent. God does not literally have hands like the potter to manipulate clay. The verb "form" is a synonym of the verb "create." Yet it is a more concrete word than "create." The word "form" or "fashion" connotes immediacy and the care and effort required to bring something new into existence. The word "create," while it stresses that something new is brought into existence, conveys nothing of the involvement on the part of the creator. To speak of a dress designer creating a new style does not make the hearer aware of the effort involved. He thinks only of the result. Consequently, in Genesis the word "form" or "fashion" show God's involvement in creation.

Objects of molding in Genesis 2. In vss. 7-8 it is the man whom God molds, forms, or fashions. In vs. 19 it is every beast of the field and every bird of the heavens that God forms or fashions. The first chapter records that on the fifth day God commands that birds are to fly over the earth, upon the face of the expanse of the heavens (1:20). On the sixth day God commands the earth to bring forth living creatures. God is said to make the beasts of the earth after their kind (1:24-25). On this same day a very terse summary is given of the creation of man: "Let us make man in our image, after our likeness, and let them have dominion over. . . . And God created man in his own image, in the image of God created he him; male and female created he them" (1:26-27). But the picture of God *forming* man, birds of the heavens, and beasts of the field in Chapter 2 shows that creation was not some impersonal activity. God is involved as a potter is involved in his work. It is also to be noted that man, birds, animals were all "formed" or "fashioned" of the same material—out of the ground (vs. 19). Man was made to have dominion (Gen. 1:26) over the birds and the beasts whom God also molded. Man's superiority does not lie in his material makeup, but rather in the fact that he was made in the image and likeness of God (Gen. 1:26).

---

[1] BDB, p. 427.

Molding of Israel as a people. To understand better the significance of God's activity of "forming" or "fashioning" in Genesis 2, one should see how the expression is used of God in other contexts. The theme that God "formed" Israel as a people is a prominent one. God "formed" the nation from the womb (Isa. 44:1,2,24). The analogy of God as the potter and Israel as the clay is explicitly asserted in Isaiah 45:9,11 and 64:8 (vs. 7 in Hebrew). "Thus saith Jehovah, the Holy One of Israel, even the one forming him . . ." (Isa. 45:11). "But now Jehovah, you [sg.] are our father and we are the clay, and you [sg.] are the one forming us, and all of us are the work of your hand" (Isa. 64:8 [vs. 7 in Hebrew txt.]). The word "form" in the preceding two references is a Qal, active participle. The active participle in Hebrew "indicates a person or thing conceived as being in the continual uninterrupted exercise of an activity."[2] This indicates that God did not bring Israel into existence as a nation by one instantaneous act. Rather in Isaiah's day he was still fashioning the nation even though more than a millennium had passed since he had first called Abraham to be the father of a great multitude. The whole nation is viewed as Jehovah's servant whom he formed (Isa. 44:21). He had formed this people for the purpose that they should set forth his praise (Isa. 43:21). The word "form" is used as a parallel expression for the word "make" in Isaiah 27:11 and for the word "create" in Isaiah 43:1. In the latter reference the words "form" and "create" are both participles. If they were to be regarded as substantives—they seem to be adjectives modifying Jehovah—they would illustrate the principle that "the participle construed as a *noun* . . . indicates repeated, enduring, or commonly occurring acts, occupations, and thoughts." [3] As adjectives they show the enduring effect of God's action.

Molding of individual persons. In the servant passages of Isaiah, the individual servant is the one whom Jehovah formed from the womb to be his servant (Isa. 49:5). God's individual sons and daughters are each created, formed, and made (Isa. 43:7). Before God formed Jeremiah in the womb, he knew him; before he came forth from the womb, God sanctified him and appointed him to be a prophet to the nations (Jer. 1:5). The control of God over the life of Jeremiah is vividly pictured as going back before his birth. God fashioned him for the job he was to carry out. This again shows God's involvement in the life of an individual. The forming involves a process in the life of the individual.

[2] Gesenius, Kautzsch, Cowley, paragraph 116 a.
[3] *Ibid.*, 116 f.

Molding of individual things. The figurative meaning of "forming" or "fashioning" impresses us when we read of Jehovah as the one who formed the eye. If he could do this, will he not see (Ps. 94:9)? The word "to form" is also used to show Jehovah's influence on the process of insect reproduction. God was forming locusts at the beginning of the shooting forth of the crop, i.e., the spring crop after the mowing of the king (Amos 7:1). When these locusts descended upon the land, they ate up the herbage. But because of the request of the prophet, this judgment was turned aside, so that there was a chance for things to grow again. The closeness of "form" to "create" is seen in the description of the sea with all its various kinds of life. Singled out for special attention is the leviathan (whale?)[4] whom Jehovah formed to play in the great sea with its large expanse of water (Ps. 104:26).

Molding of the physical earth. In Psalm 95:5 after stating that the sea belongs to God, the psalmist speaks of Jehovah's hands as having formed the dry land. Isaiah too speaks of God who formed the earth. He is said to have formed it to be inhabited and not to be a chaos or desolation (Isa. 45:18). God is the one who formed the mountains and created the wind (Amos 4:13). Here again the figurative language is apparent. In the psalm passage, anthropomorphic language makes the picture vivid: Jehovah has hands and he employs them to form or fashion the dry land. Here again God is a creator, but not by remote control. He was personally involved in the processes or methods by which he fashioned the earth to be an inhabitable environment for living creatures. He is personally present when he makes changes in any process, when he introduces a new process, or as he continues a process already in existence. God is not a prisoner in a mechanistic universe. Nor is he a watchmaker who checks to see that the spring is functioning properly. He himself is the spring, but he is not the watch! Only a pantheist would identify God with his creation.

Molding of all that exists. Jeremiah pictures God both in creation and providence (Jer. 10:12-16). God *made* the earth by his power. He *established* the world by his wisdom. He *stretched out* the heavens by his understanding. Providentially, he brings a tumult of waters in the heavens *at the uttering of his voice.* He *causeth vapors to ascend* from the ends of the earth. He *makes lightnings* for the rain and *brings forth the wind* out of his treasuries. Yet mankind plunges into idolatry although idols are simply vanity and falsehood. "The portion of Jacob is not like these idols because *He is the one who fashions the sum-*

4 BDB, *liwyathan*, p. 531.

total of all that exists[5] (Jer. 10:16a). The context here indicates that the molding or forming of God includes both creation and providence. God's relationship to the totality is the same as his relation to any part of that totality. He has a personal, not a mere mechanistic relationship, to any and all aspects of his creation. Yet his personal involvement in the thunderstorm does not take away the process from the combination of secondary factors involved in thunder, lightning, and rain.

"Of the dust from the ground"

In Genesis 2:7 the student should note a double accusative construction. The direct object of the verb "to form" is "the man." This is the accusative of the person. Immediately after "the man" the accusative of the thing is found which indicates that of which the man is made.[6] More intensive study of the word "dust" or "dry earth" is needed to see just what it means. For example in Genesis 3:14 a curse is put upon the serpent. His manner of movement will tie him very close to the ground. As part of the curse it is said that he will eat dust all the days of his life. He will search for food along the surface of the ground. Out of the dust or loose earth he will uncover his food. Dust indicates the general sphere of the serpent's activities. But there are a number of passages (including Gen. 2:7) where the word "dust" stands for the basic material elements of which man is composed. The biblical narrative in these instances oscillates in the use of the word "dust" between its meaning as elements in atomistic independence and these same elements being formed in a physical totality of a living creature. Sin creates a world of instability so that quickly one may go from the physical totality of a creature to atomistic independence. The simplicity of Genesis 3:19 on this subject is remarkable. The picture cannot be improved upon. The existential reality of man's physical disintegration strikes home with a compelling urgency.

From material elements to physical organism. Both man and animals are composed of "dust" or "earth." Man was formed

---

[5] BDB, *kōl*, 2. b. with article, *hakkōl*, (b), p. 482: "In a wider sense, *all*, whether all mankind or of all living things, the universe (*to pan*), of all the circumstances of life (chiefly late), Jer. 10:16 = 51:19."

[6] Gesenius, Kautzsch, Cowley, paragraph 117, hh. "Expressions which mean *to make, to form, to build something out of* something; in such cases besides the accusative of the object proper, another accusative is used for the material of which the thing is made, e.g. Gen. 2:7 . . . *and the Lord formed man of the dust of the ground.*"

from the dust of the ground (Gen. 2:7). God formed the beasts from the earth or ground (*ᵃdamah;* Gen. 2:19). The actual meaning here seems to be that God arranged the material elements in man, beast, and bird so that when he introduced life into this arrangement, the physical organism or totality was just exactly what he wanted—a bird, a beast, or a man. All are basically composed of the same materials, but in their physical forms one does not confuse a man with an eagle or with a horse. Today we may note many similarities and differences which Genesis never intended to mention. The main thing that Genesis clarifies is that the *physical* elements of man, birds, and beasts have a common base.

From physical organism to material elements. After sin entered the world, God informed Adam that in the sweat of his face he would eat bread until a certain time (Gen. 3:19). The body (or physical organism) in its present form will return to the ground or earth because from it (i.e., from these basic elements) man was taken. Then a very solemn statement is made: "Because dust you [sg.] are and you will return unto dust" (Gen. 3:19). The phrase "dust you are" is a noun clause in Hebrew with the predicate put first for emphasis.[7] Noun clauses with a substantive as predicate "represent something *fixed, a state* or in short *a being* so and so."[8] The physical totality of the human body as an organism must not obscure from man that he is composed of the basic materials of the ground. As a physical being he is still dust. True, this dust is arranged into a complex functioning organism. But this physical organism will come to an end. "You will return to dust." Note that the "you" is identified with this physical organism. Paul also does this where he asserts that we not only have a body but that we are a body (Rom. 6:12-13). But the New Testament also emphasizes that man is more than a body. He is a person who can live apart from the body and be at home with the Lord (II Cor. 5:8; cf. Phil. 1:21-24). As such, he is a deprived person—a man deprived of a body. But with the resurrection he again will be a unified person, no more to suffer dissolution.

A number of Old Testament passages point to the reversible equation: from physical organism to material elements. In Ecclesiastes 3:19-21 the equation makes no distinction between man and beasts. The writer of Ecclesiastes is viewing life from a perspective of man under the sun and is therefore pessimistic. All is vanity and a striving after wind (cf. 2:11). But some of

[7] *Ibid.,* paragraph 141, 1.
[8] *Ibid.,* paragraph 141, e.

his pessimism may be a realism derived from empiricial observation. He notes that both man and beast die. He assumes that they all have one breath or spirit. Physically all go to one place. "All are of the dust, and all turn to dust again" (Eccles. 3:20). Job asks God to remember that God made him as clay and asks the question: "And wilt thou bring me into dust again?" (Job 10:9). The psalmist said: "For he knoweth our frame; He remembereth that we are dust" (Ps. 103:14). In the next psalm, a number of living creatures are mentioned. When God takes away their breath, "they die and return to their dust" (Ps. 104:29). The Old Testament views the physical organism as a complex arrangement of dust—this is incisively stated with reference to man (Gen. 3:19). God put the physical organism together. Life is in his sovereign hands. When he takes life away, the physical totality returns to basic materials. There is a profound simplicity in this concept. There are no complex chemical formulae. There is no philosophical speculation about substance and attributes. Rather what is observable to every person becomes the common denominator of physical being (ground, dust, earth). God arranged matter and brought in the additional factor of life. How God did this is not discussed. The fact that God brought life is clear, but the how (in a scientific sense) receives no attention from the biblical writer.

"And he breathed breath of life into his nostrils"

Life and breath in the human sphere are obvious, observable characteristics. Genesis says that man received this breath by the action of God. We turn then to observe "breath" in God and breath in his creatures.

Breath of God. God has no lungs. He does not expel air. Hence to say that God breathes or to talk about his breath is a figurative way of making the living character of God real to man. To say that God is "alive" is a somewhat abstract way of describing the only independent living being in existence. But to talk about the breath of God makes man aware of God as moving and acting. To breathe the breath of life into man's nostrils is to recount vividly that God imparted life to the man. Philosophers who dislike anthropomorphisms may say that some unthinking person might conceive of God as a man on his knees testing his lung capacity. But such dangers are worth the risk because the gain made possible by this use of figurative language far outweighs any such possible loss. God made man alive by imparting life from himself to man. God made the creatures under man alive also by imparting life to them. In the case of man there is greater stress on the arrangement of the material elements. Then this being, planned according to God's dimensions, has breath come into his nostrils by God so that he can give evidence of God's breath (imparted life) by breathing in and out through his own nostrils. Again in this non-philosophical picture we see awesome simplicity.

God's breath is pictured as a hot wind kindling a flame (Isa. 30:33), as a destroying wind (II Sam. 22:16 = Ps. 18:16), as a cold wind producing ice (Job 37:10), and as that which gives man understanding and life (Job 32:8; 33:4). Here is God in action. The action has varying consequences. But of the decisiveness of that action there is no doubt.

Breath of man. God is the one who gives breath to the people of the earth (Isa. 42:5). Job maintains that he will not be guilty of falsehood nor will he utter deceit as long as his breath is in him (Job 27:3). The widow with whom Elijah was staying had a son. He became ill, and his sickness was so severe "that there was no breath left in him" (I Kings 17:17). In each of the above references breath obviously symbolizes life. In Daniel 10:17 there is a double figure when the prophet describes the psychological effects of his visions: "As for me, straightway there remained no strength in me, neither was there breath left in me." Daniel does not mean that he could not breathe or that he died. Rather he tells of his being "left breathless" by the vision. He was exhausted emotionally and psychologically.

Breath in man is also used to indicate finiteness: "Cease for yourselves from man who has breath in his nostrils, since at what value is he to be esteemed?" (Isa. 2:22). Set against a background of haughtiness, idolatry, and judgment, the answer is that man in his finiteness is not worth very much. He has no independent breath. It is merely in his nostrils and may cease at any time. What man is by himself and what he becomes by being rightly related to God are two contrasting pictures. Here is where the uniqueness of Christianity stands out. A Christian is one who has joined himself to the Lord (I Cor. 6:17) and who is in Christ. Being tied to Christ he shares his life and Christ lives in him (Gal. 2:20). Christ is his life (cf. Col. 3:4). It still may be said of a Christian that his breath is in his nostrils, but one cannot stop there; the Christian's life has been hidden with Christ in God (Col. 3:3). The Christian has become what he is because of the One to whom he is bound.

Breath of physical creatures living on land. In the summary of the effects of the flood, the writer states that the flood brought about the death of land animals and man (Gen. 7:21). The narrative discloses further: "All in whose nostrils was the breath of the spirit of life, of all who were on dry ground died" (Gen. 7:22). Life or breath ceased for these because of the judgment of God. Here breath is considered a common characteristic of many of God's creatures.

"And the man became a living creature"

This expression indicates that by direct action God brought life to his own arrangement of material elements in man (Gen. 2:7) and to animals as well (see Gen. 2:19). The Hebrew term *nefesh chayyah* (living creature or living being) is used frequently in Genesis.

Living creature in Genesis 1. In the opening chapter of Genesis, "living creature" is used of all the creatures which abound in the waters (vss. 20-21). It also describes the living creatures on land such as cattle, creeping things, and beasts of various kinds (vs. 24). Plants or green herbs are mentioned as the staple diet for living creatures, i.e., for the various kinds of animals and birds (vs. 30). However, the term "living creature" is not applied to man in the first chapter as it is in the second.

Living creature in Genesis 2. In vs. 7 man becomes a living creature. In the King James Version, ASV, and RSV the Hebrew words *nefesh chayyah* are translated "living soul" or "living being." However, the Hebrew phrase is exactly the same as that used in Genesis 1:20,21,24,30 and Genesis 9:12,15. In vs. 19 God brought the beasts and the birds to Adam to name them: "And whatsoever the man called every living creature, that was the name thereof." In this chapter the term "living creature" is used of both man and animals. It is clear in this context that the term refers to physical life.

Living creature in Genesis 9. The Noahic covenant with the sign of the bow is drawn up with specific parties. True to the biblical pattern, the covenant is laid down and is not worked out by any mutual collective bargaining. God promises that the waters will never destroy life in the way that Noah's contemporaries experienced destruction. The covenant is made "with every living creature" (vs. 10). This term includes man, birds, cattle, and every beast of the earth. The pre-eminence of man is seen in the fact that God uses the language of "me and you and every living creature" (vss. 12,15). Yet the universal comprehensive usage of man and all physical creatures predominates in verse 16. When God sees his bow, he will remember the everlasting covenant between himself "*and every living creature of all flesh* that is upon the earth" (vs. 16). Creatures having physical life were made partners with God in a covenant that he laid down. He made known his future course of action toward them.

Meaning Conveyed by the Language of Creation

Genesis 2:7-8 exhibits the forcefulness of the complex blending of literal and figurative language. The term "Jehovah God" specifically (i.e., literally) designates the creator of heaven and earth who entered into a covenant relationship with his people. The verb "formed" is a figurative expression which describes God as being personally involved in all of his activities of creation and providence. The noun "man" stands literally for an individual who later received a wife and conceived children. The phrase "dust from the ground" is figurative and stands for the basic material elements of which man is composed. Whether "dust" in each of its uses is designed or undesigned metaphor—i.e., intentional or unintentional figurative language—cannot be determined from this vantage point. The material elements in man, beast, or bird are structured and arranged by God—molded or fashioned by him—into the form which he planned or willed. Hence the total phrase concerning the forming of man from the dust of the ground puts the emphasis on God's personal execution of his own plan. The phrase "and He breathed breath of life into his nostrils" is figurative and depicts God's personal activity in creating and communicating physical life to man. Any phase of the personal activity of a unique being such as God may have some things in common with the personal activity of man, his creature. But the infinite variety of possibilities that God has for his personal activity allows for great differences as well. Breath is put into man's nostrils in the sense that anyone can observe breathing. The nostrils themselves are the nose (literally) through which breath, the indication of life, comes in and out. "Breath" and "breathing" are concrete expressions for life. The literal element "nose" or "nostrils" in no way makes the whole statement literal. Such a misinterpretation would have God dependent upon oxygen for life (if he breathes in and out). He would become a man, as many idolators have conceived him to be. The last phrase describes the results of God's activity: "And man became (or came into being) a living creature." Literally and actually an individual man came into being as a result of God's creative activity. God placed, put, or set this individual in a garden. By God's activity he became a living creature among other living creatures. He stands forth as a physical creature in God's creation. The phrase "living creature" shows man's identity with the rest of creation. The fact that man was made in the image and likeness of God (Gen. 1:26-27) shows man's distinctiveness in all of creation.

LANGUAGE OF FINAL JUDGMENT AND DESTINY
(REVELATION 20:11-15)

In this area, too, there is a blending of figurative and literal language to enable the reader to grasp a reality which has not yet occurred and the full nature of which has not been made known. But what is made known is clarified by the type of language employed.

Appearance of God (Revelation 20:11)

God is described as one who is seated on a great white throne. From his face the heaven and the earth "flee," i.e., vanish or disappear. In the book of Revelation the author speaks of the throne of God and of the lamb (Rev. 22:1,3). But wherever the throne is mentioned by itself, although Christ may be mentioned in the context, the same context makes clear that the throne is the throne of God [the Father] (see Rev. 4:10 [twice]; 5:1,7,13; 7:9-10, 15 [twice]; 19:4,5). In the light of the assertion of the Gospel of John that the Father has given all judgment to the Son (John 5:22, cf. vss. 22-30), some might want to infer that the one seated on the throne is Christ. However, the picture and language found in Revelation 19:4-5 seems to make God the one who receives the attention of the seer in this vision. Yet the very language of God "being seated" is figurative language. His occupying a throne is a way of describing his majesty. Use of the phrase "from whose face" helps to show that the God of revelation is a personal being. By this figurative language the actual, objective being of God confronts the reader. Such figurative language is very effective. One could, of course, draw false inferences because of the presence of this kind of figurative language. God does not "sit down" because he is tired. When he is occupied with the activities around his throne, he is not ignorant of the fact that the earth and the heaven have disappeared.[9] "His face" does not point in only one direction. The error of such ideas can be easily corrected. What is more important is the fact that through this kind of language the reality of God is brought home to the simplest

---

[9] See Bauer, *pheugō*, 5. *vanish, disappear*, p. 863.

reader. If he will listen, God's truth will break through into his being. God is the reality whom he will face in judgment.

Records of Judgment and Life (Revelation 20:12, 15)

The dead, the great and the small, stand before the throne of God. Books are opened. The dead are judged according to their works from the records—the things written in the books. In addition to these many books there is another book that plays a prominent role in the judgment. This is the book of life. Anyone who is not registered in the book of life will be cast into the lake of fire.

The word "book" here refers to a scroll.[10] The phrase "the books are opened" refers to a scroll being unrolled.[11] This, too, is figurative language. Scrolls with men's deeds recorded and a scroll with their names recorded upon this register of life convey the idea that God knows well the doings of men and the destiny of men. Past deeds are not forgotten. The writer of Ecclesiastes believed that God would bring every work into judgment (Eccles. 12:14). The picture of scrolls helps us grasp this reality. If God were to impart the same revelation to a prophet in modern times, some kind of electronic computer might provide the figurative language or metaphor to picture God's records of judgment. But neither scrolls nor electronic computers are necessary adjuncts for God's judgment. God's decisions are unfathomable; his ways are inscrutable. We cannot know how God is going to confront each individual man with his thought, words, and deeds. God does not need a tape to play them back. But however he does it, there will be one result: men will answer to God for what they are, for what they have thought and for what they have done. Yet the opening of books and the registrations in the book of life have played an invaluable role in describing God's knowledge of each individual's character and future state. In no other way could this reality be stated except by this kind of figurative language.

Death and Hades in the Lake of Fire (Revelation 20:14)

Death in the New Testament is looked upon as an enemy. It is the last enemy to be wiped out or abolished (I Cor. 15:26, 54-55). When death is treated as an enemy, it is being personified. Hades in the New Testament, with the meaning "the un-

---

[10] Gottlob Schrenk "biblion," TWNT, I, 617.

[11] Bauer, anoigō, l. c., p. 70: "open a book in scroll form . . . Rev. 5:2ff; 10:2,8; . . . 20:12."

derworld," is viewed as the place of the dead. It is also a place of punishment (cf. Luke 16:23). Hades and death are both personified in Revelation 6:8; 20:13-14. Hence it is clear that death itself, the place where the dead go, and the place of torment for some (the usual word for place of punishment is Gehenna, *geenna*) are all pictured as being banished from God's universe and from his presence. The lake of fire is defined as the second death (Rev. 20:14). The first death brings a separation of a person from his body. The Christian, though separated from his body, is in the presence of his Lord (cf. II Cor. 5:6-8; Phil. 1:21-24). The non-Christian in Hades or Gehenna is separated both from his body and from God. The outcome of resurrection is either a resurrection unto life or a resurrection unto condemnation and punishment which is preceded by judgment[12] (John 5:28-29). Hence physical death is the only separation that a Christian can experience. But for the man who will not commit his life to Jesus Christ and turns away from his redemption, physical death is a prelude to final separation from God. There are just three steps: (1) physical death; (2) Hades or Gehenna—separation from God before judgment; (3) lake of fire (preceded by resurrection) or the second death—separation from God after judgment. Death and Hades are looked upon as being put into the lake of fire because when God creates new heavens and a new earth, all will be in harmonious fellowship with him except those who are condemned to final separation from God. With "Death" and "Hades" banished—the great captors of men (note personification) —there remain two great unities: the unity of all that revolves around the being of God and the unity of all that is separated from him.

Persons in the Lake of Fire (Revelation 20:13,15)

In the preceding discussion of death and Hades in the lake of fire, we noted that the lake of fire is the second death. It is the final place of separation from God for those who want God to stay out of their lives and to leave them alone. To show that separation from God is torment, the figurative language of "lake of fire" is employed. Everyone shrinks back from a volcano of burning lava. Hence the lake of fire becomes an analogy of something far worse. When Jesus Christ was made sin for us (II Cor. 5:21) he experienced separation from God. His words: "My God, my God, why hast thou forsaken me?"

---

12 Bauer *"krisis,"* 1. a. beta, p. 453.

(Matt. 27:46; Mark 15:34) lay bare the torture of his own soul at being cut off from God. He bore man's separation that man might not be separated. Yet for those who trample under foot (treat with disdain) the Son of God and count his atonement to be unclean or profane, there can only be separation—"a certain fearful expectation of judgment and fiery zeal [literally, zeal of fire] which is about to consume the adversaries of God" (Heb. 10:27). But since the noblest of saints have experienced only an infinitesimal fragment of what full fellowship with God can mean, the opposite of complete separation from God is exceedingly difficult for man to comprehend. Separation involves persons. It involves a place. And the absence of God denotes punishment. Further details about this punishment are impossible since we know very little about the nature of the resurrected body or of the range of its emotional and intellectual responses.

Meaning Conveyed by the Language of Final Consummation

The basic picture is clear. Individually, each man will appear before God and will be judged by God. The figurative language of God *being seated* on a *great white throne* with heaven and earth disappearing *from before his face* is chosen by the seer or prophet in Revelation to make his readers conscious of the reality of the Judge. The Judge is no abstraction; he is the Living God.

In driving home the reality of the judgment, John depicts *the books being unrolled,* and then another book, distinct from these—*the book of life*—is also *unfolded.* Such figurative language shows men that God knows their deeds and will decide their destiny.

To make sure that the reality of punishment penetrates the consciousness of his readers, John speaks of *Death* and *Hades* in the *lake of fire* and of the end of the individual who is not found written in the book of life as being cast into *the lake of fire.* Death and Hades are personified. No more will they hold men captive. Separation from God is described in the figurative language of the second death or the lake of fire. This language also is chosen to show men the wretchedness of being banished from the presence of God. Christ condensed the terrors of eternity into a few moments of time, but no man except Christ has experienced just what separation from God really means. This carefully chosen language gives the readers some glimpses, but the actual reality defies description. To be without God for eternity is the picture of a man beyond hope and beyond help. These statements have the ring of eternal defeat and doom. That such a destiny involves man's own decision as well as God's (II Thess. 2:10-12) underlines the seriousness of man's response.

ATTITUDE AND APPROACH NECESSARY TO UNDERSTAND DESCRIPTIVE LANGUAGE

1. We must recognize that figurative language is indispensable in conveying to us realities beyond empirical experience. If God in revelation had not chosen to use such language, our ignorance would be total. Now we know in part. Though the part may be small, it is extremely valuable and meaningful.

2. The realities described by the figurative language of creation and climax are crucial for men to understand, for we are deeply involved in them (results of creation) or will soon be the active participants in them (judgment, blessing, punishment). As created beings, it is imperative that we understand as fully as possible the demands and purposes of God. Neither God nor man whom he made in his own image are in any sense figurative. Yet to describe the nature of God and the nature of man and the relationships between God and man exhausts human language. Such realities demand the use of combinations of figurative and literal language to give us every possible insight.

3. We should interpret figurative language so as to make its full impact fall upon our contemporaries. The vast majority of people in the world today are occupied with trivia. They delude themselves into thinking that this pattern of life is normal. This is part of the deceitfulness of sin. The language of Scripture—in this case the figurative language of creation and climax—can penetrate man even in his dull and blind obsession with unreal "things" if he will respond to it. Creation and climax speak to men about *their* destiny. We must use these biblical emphases and the genuine meaning given to them to confront men with *their* creator, *their* redeemer, and *their* judge.

4. Such language and the truths conveyed by it were not given to satisfy our scientific curiosity but to assure us about the "whence" and the "whither" of our existence. To let our ignorance of what we do not know become a battleground among Christians while we lose sight of what we do know is most tragic. The urgent message of creation and climax must be heard at all costs and nothing should be allowed to obscure it.

XV Poetry

Poetry has its own way of reaching into the hearts and minds of men. No formal list of principles, no careful analysis of the mechanics involved in poetry can tell why it impresses so deeply. Yet some analysis must be provided, especially of Old Testament poetry. The New Testament contains some poetry (for example the songs in the book of Revelation), and some of the sayings of Jesus may have been cast into poetic form, but the vast bulk of the poetry of the Bible is in Hebrew. It is to this kind of poetry that we turn our attention.

EXTENT OF POETRY

Those who have studied the King James Version or even the excellent American Standard Version (1901) were not made aware of how extensive poetry is in the Old Testament. One of the merits of the Revised Standard Version (1946-1952) is the printing of poetry as poetry. This innovation not only made Psalms, Proverbs, and Job stand out in all of their poetic grandeur, but it made many readers aware for the first time of how much poetry there was in other Old Testament books. The Song of Solomon, a song about the dignity, purity, and intensity of human love with its emphasis on the propriety of physical beauty, is entirely in poetry. Most of Isaiah and Jeremiah are poetry. There is some poetry in Ezekiel. Hosea is mostly poetry, as are Joel and Amos. In the book of Jonah, the prophet's prayer from the belly of the fish is in poetry. Obadiah and Micah are entirely poetry except for the introductory titles. All but a few verses in Nahum are in poetry. Habakkuk is entirely poetry. All of Zephaniah is poetry except for the first verse. Two sections of Zechariah—9:1-11:3 and 13:7-9—are poetry. Throughout the Pentateuch and the historical books there are scattered portions of poetry. Lamentations is entirely poetry. From the standpoint of quantity alone, this is an extensive body of literature. Years ago Milton S. Terry showed that one could not emphasize too strongly the fact that some structural form is essential to all poetry.[1] When poetry is laid out as poetry, the student has a base from which he can examine many aspects of poetic structure. One must know Hebrew to enter into all the intricacies of Hebrew poetry. Some of its features, however, can be conveyed through English translations. An understanding of some of these features will help the interpreter to enter into the meaning of the original author.

POETIC FORM

Although form is essential for the full effect of poetry, translations made for extensive distribution and for ease of reading cannot point up all features of Hebrew poetry. This would require too much space and the excessive markings required would disturb those unacquainted with the fundamental rudiments of Hebrew poetry.

Parallelism and Stressed Units: Definitions

In many languages, both ancient and modern, poetry consists in a balance of *sound,* i.e. in *phonetic* rhythm. Nursery rhymes are a simple form of this balance of sound. Many people enjoy making up rhyming couplets, although they are quick to acknowledge that this does not make them poets! Yet they tend to identify true poets with masters of this balance of sound. But in Hebrew and Akkadian (as well as in such languages as Egyptian and Chinese), poetry consists in a balance of *thought,* i.e., in *logical* rhythm. The poet follows one assertion by another line of thought parallel to the first. A verse then consists of at least two parts in which the second part is parallel to the first. Parallelism is one of the main features of Hebrew poetry.[2]

[1] Milton S. Terry, *Biblical Hermeneutics,* pp. 92-94.

[2] On parallelism and other aspects of Hebrew poetry the interpreter will find the following works instructive (even though some are only by way of historical development): Robert Lowth, *Lectures on the Sacred Poetry of the Hebrews* (1829). George Buchanan Gray, *The Forms of Hebrew Poetry* (1915). Theodore Henry Robinson, *The Poetry of the Old Testament* (1947). W. O. E. Oesterley and Theodore H. Robinson, *An Introduc-*

Two lines (distich) usually constitute a verse, but there are three line (tristich) verses, four line (tetrastich) verses and even five line (pentastich) verses. In the last two types, the interpreter must be sure that what looks like a four line (tetrastich) verse is not actually two two-line verses (distichs) and that a five line (pentastich) is not in reality a distich and a tristich. This balance of thought between two or more lines also involves a certain number of stressed units in each line. In the usual two-line verse (distich) there may be three stressed units in each line (3:3).

Not-according-to-our-sins   / did-he-act   / toward-us
Nor-according-to-our-iniquities / did-he-deal-fully / against-us.
(Ps. 103:10)

There are all sorts of other combinations such as 2:2, 3:2, 2:3, 3:3:3, 2:2:2, and 2:2:3. These cover two- and three-line verses. The various kinds of stress are interwoven with the various kinds of parallelism.

Complete Parallelism

Synonymous parallelism. Assuming that the poet is using a two-line verse (distich), synonymous parallelism occurs where the second line expresses an identical or similar thought to the first line. Observe that the metre or stressed units in the following example is 3:3.

Who-forgives / all / your-iniquity
Who-heals   / all / your-diseases.
(Ps. 103:3)

Antithetic parallelism. In a similar distich, antithetic parallelism occurs when the second line expresses a thought which is in sharp contrast to that which was declared in the first line.

The metre here is also 3:3.

A-gentle-answer   / turns-away / rage
But-a-word-that-hurts / stirs-up   / anger.
(Prov. 15:1)

tion to the Books of the Old Testament, "The Forms of Hebrew Poetry" (1934), pp. 139-149. Edward J. Young, *An Introduction to the Old Testament*, "The Characteristics of Hebrew Poetry" (1949), pp. 281-286. F. F. Bruce, "The Poetry of the Old Testament," *The New Bible Commentary* (1956), pp. 39-41. Charles Franklin Kraft, *The Strophic Structure of Hebrew Poetry* (1938). W. McClellan, "The Elements of Old Testament Poetry," *Catholic Biblical Quarterly*, III (1941), 203-213; 321-336.

Synthetic parallelism. This is a category formulated by Bishop Lowth but in reality is not true parallelism. The meaning continues but the balance of thought is lost. The thought is extended—it flows on—but the stress and balance of true parallelism is not there.

> And-now / my-head / is-lifted-up
> Over / my-enemies / round-about-me.
> (Ps. 27:6a)

Emblematic parallelism. In this kind of parallelism one member or line makes a statement figuratively while the other member makes an assertion in a literal manner.

> As-a-hart / longs / for-flowing-streams
> So-my-soul / longs / for-thee-O-God.
> (Ps. 42:1)

Stairlike parallelism. Here is a fascinating kind of parallelism which utilizes meaningful repetition to the utmost. A part of the first line is repeated while the newer elements build up to a climax. In the following example, note that the parallelism is complete except for one unit.

> Ascribe / to-the-Lord / O-Sons-of-God (angels) /
> Ascribe / to-the-Lord / / glory-and-strength
> Ascribe / to-the-Lord / / the-glory-of-his-name.
> (Ps. 29:1-2a)

Introverted parallelism. In this type, two lines stand closely together, and they are balanced off against two other lines. In a strophe or stanza consisting of eight lines, introverted parallelism is found when lines 1-2 correspond to lines 7-8, and lines 3-4 correspond with lines 5-6. This kind of parallelism between two lines against another two lines is called *external parallelism.* The previous examples exemplify *internal parallelism*—the balance between two parts of a distich (the two lines in a two-line verse). In the following example, the parallelism is complete except for one unit.

> Unto-thee, O-Jehovah / I-was-crying
> Unto-the-Lord / I-was-imploring-favor.
>   What-is-the-profit / in-my-blood?
> / in-my-going-down / unto-the-pit?
>   Will-the-dust / praise-thee?
>   Will-it-make-known / thy-truth?
> Hear, O-Jehovah / and-be-gracious-to-me,
> Be-a-helper / for-me.
> (Ps. 30:8-10; M.T. vss. 9-11).

Incomplete Parallelism

Where every stressed unit in one line has a counterpart in the next line, the parallelism is complete. But where this is not the case, the student finds incomplete parallelism. There are two kinds of incomplete parallelism.

Incomplete parallelism with compensation. In this kind of parallelism there are the same number of stressed units in each line, but they are not exact counterparts. For example in a 3:3 metre, one stressed unit will have an exact counterpart. The other two stressed units in one line will have two other stressed units in the next line as a compensation but not as corresponding counterparts. The following example of this kind of parallelism is taken from the Psalms. The pattern is given first in letters to make clear how the thought is balanced.

```
            a.     b.     c.
                   c′.    d.     e.
```

As-for-man / his-days / are-as-the-green-grass
           / As-the-flower-of-the-field / so / he-blossoms.
                              (Ps. 103:15)

Incomplete parallelism without compensation. This type of parallelism is incomplete because there are stressed units in one line which have no exact counterpart in the next line. Further, there is not even a compensating unit to maintain the same number of stressed units (even though they do not all correspond exactly) in successive lines. In the following example the pattern in letters shows clearly what is parallel and what is not.

```
        a.              b.     c.
        a′.             b′.
        a″.     d.      e.
                                f.      g.
                                f′.     g′.
```

One-thing /   /   /I-have-/from-the-Lord
                                      asked
That   /   /   /I-will- /
                                      seek
My-dwelling/in-the-house-/all-the-days-/   / / to-look /   on-the-
    of-the-Lord   of-my-life   delightfulness-
                                                             of-Jehovah
                                      / /to-contem-/   in-his-
                                            plate   temple

                              (Psalm 27:4)

Parallelism is a fascinating characteristic of Hebrew poetry. Those who can study the poetic material in the Old Testament only in an English translation will find that some of these categories are very clear in the English text, e.g., synonymous, antithetic, emblematic, and stairlike parallelism. On the other hand, metre involving the number of stressed units in each line, whether the parallelism is complete or incomplete, and the nature of the parallelism demand a study of the Hebrew text. A student with even one year of Hebrew can enter into many of these elements and feel firsthand the forcefulness of Hebrew poetry. Even the person who reads only English translations, however, will profit from knowing something about the nature and structure of such poetry. Through poetry, prophets and psalmists opened their hearts and poured forth their anguish, their personal concerns and their concerns for their people, their joys, their expectations from God, and their awareness of the qualities in the being of God. Often in this kind of poetry we see the individual servant of God transformed into an instrument of rare quality. His surroundings may be dark, his personal situation may be desperate; but what he says has a ring of genuineness found only in those who stand face to face with God on the brink of eternity. A man in this situation stands between two worlds. His poetry reflects the urgency of such a crisis.

Stanzas or Strophes

Since the last half of the nineteenth century there has been prolonged discussion as to how the lines in Hebrew poetry are grouped together to form stanzas. To divide a poem into paragraphs on the basis of thought *gives* a stanza structure to the poem, but this in no way establishes a strophic arrangement by the original author. Scholars at first laid down exact patterns for stanzas. They said that each stanza did not need to have the same number of lines, but when there was variety, there should always be two stanzas of the same number of lines unless one stanza acted as a pivot:[3] $2 + 3 + 4 + 4 + 3 + 2$, or $2 + 3 + 4 + 2 + 3 + 4$, or $2 + 3 + 4 + 5 + 4 + 3 + 2$. From such complicated schemes other scholars turned to the suggestion that all strophes of a poem must have the same number of lines. This in turn led to artificial reconstructions so that such evenness could be maintained. It now seems best to allow two, three, or four lines to stand as a stanza where

[3] Oesterley and Robinson, *op. cit.,* p. 147.

the meaning supports such a unit. To insist that these units must have equal lines or must be balanced according to some pattern is to set up artificial standards that may have been foreign to the thinking of the original author. He may indicate his desire to have stanzas by a constantly recurring refrain: "For his steadfast love [mercy, lovingkindness] endures forever" (Ps. 136). Or some mechanical device may be employed such as beginning one line, two lines, or groups of lines with the first letter of the alphabet followed by the next letter throughout the poem. Such poems are called acrostics. In Psalm 119 there are eight consecutive lines with each letter. Apart from such indications, length and thought breaks are the only criteria available to the interpreter.

Obviously there is subjectivity in laying out stanzas of Hebrew poetry. Oesterley and Robinson emphasize both length of lines and division in thought:

> It may be repeated that there are two essential conditions for the recognition of strophic arrangement. The first is regularity in length—probably even uniformity; and the second is a clear division in thought at the end of each strophe. Only where these are fulfilled, are we safe in describing the structure of a given poem as strophic.[4]

Thought breaks as a basis give a poetic paragraphing and an increased clarity. But to uncover equal lined sense sections in an extended series of poetic passages is almost impossible. Hence, what appears to be a carefully worked out strophic arrangement of the poetic materials in modern English translations is in reality poetic paragraphing. The translator has exercised the powers of an editor. In both poetry and in prose such divisions of larger sections of thought make it much easier for the reader to grasp and to follow the flow of thought of the writer. But the reader should be aware that a large number of these do not satisfy the criteria of Oesterley and Robinson given above.

Word Order and Arrangement of Words

In word order and arrangements, Hebrew poetry has certain features in common with poetry of other languages. The first of these is *anacrusis*—a word often appears at the beginning of a line which stands outside the metre. These words are usually interjections, conjunctions, or pronouns. In Lamentations the word "how" exemplifies this construction in 1:1; 2:1;

---

4 *Ibid.*, p. 149.

4:1. In Jeremiah 12:1-2 the word "wherefore" (maddua"), by virtue of its standing outside of the stressed units, emphasizes the urgency of the poet's question: " ... Wherefore, does the way of the wicked prosper? ... Near art thou in their mouth but far from their affections."

Acrostics or alphabetical poems have already been mentioned. Psalm 119 is the most famous of these. In these poems each verse or group of lines has a particular letter at the beginning. The order is from the beginning of the alphabet to the end. Not always is there a single letter for each line. Sometimes the poet goes on to the next letter every half line or the first part of a distich (cf. Pss. 111, 112). On the other hand Psalms 25, 34, 145, Proverbs 31:10-31, Lamentations 1-2 make the shift every verse from one letter to the next. Psalm 119 makes the shift from letter to letter every strophe or stanza. To say that acrostics are artificial and therefore dull is to show one's prejudice against a mechanical structural formula. Although acrostics do not favor spontaneity, one has only to read Lamentations 1-4 to see how moving this kind of literature can be.

Assonance in Hebrew poetry consists in words which sound alike. For example, in a highly metaphorical piece (Gen. 49:17) Dan is called a serpent (nachash) upon the way ... who bites (hanoshek) the horse's heels. Alliteration is found in Hebrew just as it is in other languages. This occurs where two or more words in the same context begin with the same letter (in Hebrew this means with the same consonant). "My eye ("eyniy) is wasted ("ashshah) from grief, it grows old and weak ("athaqah)[5] because of my foes" (Ps. 6:7 [vs. 8 in M.T.]).

PERSONAL DIMENSION IN POETRY

The very essence of poetry is destroyed if we are absorbed in the mechanics of it. For it is not the mechanical aspects of poetry but the poet himself who makes a deep impression upon us. It is this personal dimension in the Psalms that attracts so many day after day to this great body of literature. For an experience of entering into this personal dimension in poetry a person should read through the book of Lamentations at one sitting. The one who does will see that the calamity that has befallen a nation and a people presses hard upon the prophet and poet. He expresses not only his own sorrows and sufferings, but he enters into the experiences of his people, individually

[5] In each of these examples the Hebrew word begins with an Ayin (Hebrew letter) indicated in the transliteration by the double quotation marks (").

and collectively. It is difficult to give examples here because in quoting even the well-known verses apart from their context we lose much of the meaning. In Lamentations 3:22,23 the poet has just referred to his own bitterness and how his soul is bowed down within him when he rises to exclaim:

It is the steadfast love of Jehovah,
> that we do not come to an end;
> that his mercies do not fail.
> They are new every morning;
Great is thy faithfulness.

Immersed in all of the travail of existence, the poet, nevertheless, is focused on the being of God. This personal dimension brings in the depths of human expression. Here man stands face to face with reality because he stands face to face with God.

POETIC IMAGERY

Figurative language in poetry because of the stressed units of thought seems to have even greater effectiveness than in prose. Consider, for example, the comparative imagery of Isaiah 1. The heavens and the earth are personified. They are asked to listen to the charge of the Lord (vs. 2). The sons which he has reared have rebelled against him. The ox and the ass know their owner and master, but not so God's people (vss. 2-3). He has smitten them, yet they continue to rebel. Their head is sick, their heart faint; from the top of their head to the bottom of their feet there are bruises, sores, and bleeding wounds. No healing aids have been applied to these wounds (vss. 5-6). Desolation has come upon their country and cities. Yet the daughter of Zion survives "*like* a booth in a vineyard, *like* a lodge in a cucumber field, *like* a besieged city" (vs. 8). The original readers could "see" in these images the seriousness of their plight. If the Lord had not left a few survivors, their end would have been *like* Sodom and *like* Gomorrah (vs. 9). Although they have not been blotted out in such a way, in metaphor the prophet addresses the leaders as "rulers of Sodom" and the people as "people of Gomorrah" (vs. 10). All of their religious activities are only a burden to the Lord because their hands are full of blood (vs. 15). What a picture this is of a people far from God!

What is the way back? The people are to wash themselves and make themselves clean (vs. 16). They are to present their arguments before the Lord and enter into dialogue with him. Yet if they will come before him and talk with him, it is he who will change them. Note the comparative imagery (simile) in the following statements: "though your sins are *like* scarlet, they shall be as white *as* snow; though they are red *like* crimson, they shall become *like* wool" (vs. 18). Willingness and obedience will bring blessing; obstinacy and rebellion will bring destruction by the sword (vss. 19,20).

The faithful city is said to have become a harlot (vs. 21). The people's silver has become dross; their wine is mixed with water. The princes have become rebels. They are the associates of thieves. Hence God will act in wrath. He will melt away the dross of his people and remove their alloy (vss. 24-25). During this period of judgment the people of the faithful city will be *"like* an oak whose leaf withers, and *like* a garden without water. And the strong shall become tow [that which is shaken off from the flax when it is beaten], and his work a *spark"* (vss. 30-31). Observe how this imagery comes out of the daily life of the people. The last words of the chapter (vss. 29-31) describe vividly the places of idolatry (vs. 29), the decline of the people from their beauty and freshness (vs. 30), and the fact that the work of idolatry becomes the spark which destroys both the idolater and his idol (vs. 31). This conflagration "burns" its way into the minds of the readers. There is a compelling forcefulness in poetic imagery which demands the attention of the reader. The longer he gives his attention, the deeper the content of the poetic imagery imprints itself upon him.

ESSENTIAL FACTORS INFLUENCING MEANING IN POETRY

In the Psalms

The Psalms are a magnificent collection of poetic materials. Parts of the Psalter extend from the formative times of the Hebrew people to the period beyond the exile, the Persian epoch. Among the Psalms are all of the characteristics of poetry we have thus far discussed. Correct interpretation demands that we be aware of these characteristics. But there are also other factors that the interpreter should consider.

1. Seek out the historical occasion for the particular psalm. To do this, we must make use of the contents of the psalm and the individual psalm title. It is true that the psalm titles as a whole were not composed by the original authors but represent the opinion of later editors and collectors. However, these titles are not to be dismissed as the work of later hero worshippers who wanted to increase the fame of an ancient celebrity. The content of the psalm and the psalm title often shed light as to

the historical situation of the original writer and such light often makes parts of the psalm more significant. It is better, however, to admit ignorance of the particular context than arbitrarily to assign a psalm to a particular historical occasion if there is not enough evidence to justify such a classification.

2. From the contents of each psalm note the attitude, the outlook, the psychological mood, and the emotional tone of the poet when he composed the psalm. Calvin called the book of Psalms "an anatomy of all the parts of the soul."[6] The interpreter should seek to understand the personality of the poet.

3. Observe the basic convictions of the poet about the being of God. It is to these that he returns as he feels the mounting pressures of life.

4. In the Messianic psalms note the typical elements and any elements that seem to apply only to the Messiah. The richness of the poetic imagery in these psalms may make them harder to interpret, but their sheer beauty of expression must be appreciated in terms of an historical perspective rightly focused on the period of their composition.

5. In dealing with the imprecatory elements in the Psalms, the interpreter should regard them as the poetic expressions of individuals who were incensed at the tyranny of evil, yet whose attitude towards retribution is so colored by their sense of being wronged or of the blasphemy committed that they speak out in language (cf. Pss. 109,137) far removed from the teaching that one should leave judgment to God, or from Jesus' statements on the treatment of enemies.[7] Of course, no Old Testament poet knew the teachings of Jesus! But the revelation of God in the Old Testament did speak about vengeance: "Thou shalt not take vengeance, nor bear any grudge against the children of thy people; but thou shalt love thy neighbor as thyself: I am Jehovah" (Lev. 19:18). The word in Deuteronomy about "vengeance is mine, and recompense" (32:35) is formally quoted in Romans 12:19 and Hebrews 10:30. Fathers are not to be put to death for the children or children for the father (Deut. 24:16). Further, "the son shall not bear the iniquity of the father, neither shall the father bear the iniquity of the son" (Ezek. 18:20). For the right attitude towards enemies see Proverbs 24:17; 25:21. The intensity of the poet's feelings are certainly the product of his experiences.

[6] John Calvin, *Commentary on the Book of Psalms* (1845), I, xxxvi.
[7] See C. S. Lewis, "The Cursings," *Reflections on the Psalms* (1958), pp. 20-33.

In Proverbs

To distinguish rigidly between secular and religious proverbs is only to reflect a modern thought pattern. Proverbs consist of short, sagacious sayings taken from everyday life. Some of them involve God and wisdom. Others are concerned with many other aspects of man's existence. These proverbial sayings among the Hebrews came from a people who since the time of the Exodus had believed that God was the God of the whole earth who exercised authority in every aspect of life. Idolatry—the setting up of other gods which could be felt, handled, and seen—was a constant temptation. But the isolation of religion into a domain separate from the rest of life was not the attitude of the ancient Hebrews. The terminology of "secular" and "religious" proverbs conveys this idea to many modern readers. Proverbs concern man in his relationship to God, to other men, to self, to things or possessions, and to the specific qualities of moral excellence. One might speak of (1) personal proverbs, (2) interpersonal proverbs, (3) proverbs referring to God, (4) proverbs referring to possessions, and (5) proverbs referring to moral principles.

Regardless of the subject matter of the proverbs, this collection of proverbs is poetry from beginning to the end.

> Proverbs is written in poetic style. That is, each verse is characterized by the parallelism of its members, or stichs, and by a certain number of beats or accents—usually three or four—in those stichs. Paronomasia [a play upon words which sound alike but usually have a different sense] also plays an important role in the literary structure of the book. The couplet, composed of two stichs, is the most common form of the proverb.[8]

Once we recognize the poetic character of the proverbs, a sound approach to these maxims or epigrammatic sayings involves certain considerations.

1. Determine whether the proverb involves any of the short figures of speech (see Chapter 8).

2. Ascertain the character of the proverb, its scope and bearing by studying carefully its content. Because the proverbs are brief, this often takes much time and effort. Although we rarely can know the situation out of which the proverb came, we are helped to see the main point by the polished smoothness that came from its constant repetition.

[8] Charles T. Fritsch, "The Book of Proverbs," *The Interpreter's Bible,* IV, 776.

3. See if the context into which the editor has placed the particular proverb sheds any light on its meaning. Often this context is of no help, but sometimes proverbs are so grouped together that a common theme or parallel theme is developed.

4. Do not explain the obvious in proverbs. Interpretation should center on what is obscure. If the obscurity cannot be removed, this should be stated at the outset. A discussion on the technicalities of why a proverb is obscure can be helpful. But one should not arouse expectations that cannot be fulfilled in the course of the discussion.

In Job

The prologue and the epilogue in the book of Job are in prose. The prologue (1:1-2:13) gives the setting for the book: the faithfulness of the man Job, the council in the court of heaven, the misfortunes of Job, and the visit of his three friends. The epilogue (42:7-17) briefly describes the restoration of Job.

The rest of the book of Job (3:1-42:6) is written in poetry. The poet wrestles not only with the question as to why the righteous suffer but with such questions as the nature and approach to God, the meaning of existence, and the meaning of faith.[9] To handle such themes the writer conveys his ideas in a masterful exhibition of poetic skill.

> The literary mastery of the poet is unsurpassed in the Old Testament, and his stylistic versatility, vigor, conciseness, and elegance are probably superior to those of any other Hebrew poet. . . .
> As dramatic poet, he was the Shakespeare of the Old Testament; as a theological poet, he was brother of the Hebrew prophets. . . .
> *The Necessity of a Christ.*—Comfortless solitude among men leads at times to a solitude with God, but Job is alone even before God. Yet a luminous thread runs through the drab canvas. Any one of the details taken separately may be of little significance, but viewed together they reveal the authenticity of the poet's inspiration as well as the height of his literary genius. . . .
> The hero himself, within his flesh, and not as a stranger, will contemplate with his own eyes the fullness of the Divine [Job. 19:25-27]. Not a word is now hinted about God's recognition of his innocence. He expects now neither reward nor clearance. The vision of God is enough. The age long repugnance to lift the veil of death is broken, but only for the sake of communing with the Deity. This is not a belief in the natural immortality of the soul, nor is it the hope that man is able by his own power to find

[9] Samuel Terrien, "The Book of Job," *The Interpreter's Bible,* III, 897.

access to God: Job now surrenders all claim and trusts solely in the power of a heavenly high priest to present him before the holy of holies.[10]

Keeping in mind all that one knows about Hebrew poetry, the interpreter should pay attention to the various speakers who take part in a most fascinating poetic dialogue.

1. Study the complete utterances of the main characters: Job, Eliphaz, Bildad, Zophar, and Elihu. Observe what they say and evaluate the soundness of their declarations on the basis of what appears to you to be their basic assumption or assumptions.

2. Study the declarations of God. Note why there is such a stress on Job's ignorance and how this is related to the self-assuredness of the other speakers.

3. Note the recurring themes and how these are developed.

4. Pay attention to the answers that are unfolded rather than searching for answers to questions which the author did not choose to discuss. Because of the profoundness of the topics dealt with, the discussion must be confined to certain aspects of the themes. Careful study will uncover a great deal of illumination to the real questions which are raised. This illumination is of the searchlight variety, however, with many aspects of the topic still in the dark. Yet this in no way detracts from the message of Job. Job himself had to find out that it was not information he needed so much as he needed God himself. Perhaps we who interpret also need to learn the same lesson: "I had heard of thee by the hearing of the ear; but now mine eye seeth thee" (Job 42:5).

In the Prophets

The extent of the poetry in the prophets has already been set forth. A few principles will help the interpreter as he interprets particular poetic passages.

1. Note how much of the particular prophetic book is in poetry.

2. In the particular passage apply sound techniques and procedures from the areas of context, language, history and culture.

3. Observe all of the figures of speech employed.

4. Keep in mind the role of parallelism to convey and reenforce meaning.

---

[10] *Ibid.*, pp. 892, 893, 900, 901. See Terrien's excellent discussion of the poetry of Job: "V. Language and Poetic Structure," pp. 892-896. See also "VII. Theological Significance," pp. 897-902.

5. Note how the personal dimension and the poetic imagery helps to make the reader contemporaneous with the prophet. By studying these factors we can enter both into the prophet's experiences and his message, into the situation of his people, and into God's actions towards prophet and people. In all of this the prophet becomes a real person with a genuine message from God.

BIBLIOGRAPHY

Bruce, F. F., "The Poetry of the Old Testament," *The New Bible Commentary,* eds. F. Davidson, A. M. Stibbs, and E. F. Kevan (1956).

Gray, George Buchman, *The Forms of Hebrew Poetry* (1915).

Gottwald, N. K., "Poetry, Hebrew," *The Interpreter's Dictionary of the Bible* (1962).

Kraft, Charles Franklin, *The Strophic Structure of Hebrew Poetry* (1938).

Oesterley, W. O. E. and Robinson, Theodore H., *An Introduction to the Books of the Old Testament* (1934).

Robinson, Theodore Henry, *The Poetry of the Old Testament* (1947).

Young, Edward J., *An Introduction to the Old Testament* (1949).

XVI Doctrinal Teachings

No area in the Christian Church stands more in need of re-vitalization than that of doctrinal teaching or theology. Some may object saying, "But look at all the manuals, handbooks, independent books, and multiple-volume works on theology that have appeared since the close of World War II." True, there has been a great literary production of material. But how well does the average church member know the basic truths of Christianity and how well can he show the biblical basis for such beliefs? Many people consider doctrine to be an abstract formulation that is either hard to understand or is somewhat like the multiplication table—useful for mental activity but uninteresting.

Some ministers and church leaders veer away from doctrinal teaching because they believe that it leads to division among Christians. Unfortunately, however, ignorance concerning the great truths of Christianity often leads to an even greater peril—an outward appearance of godliness with no power (cf. II Tim. 3:5). If Christian truth and Christian living are brought to-gether (as they are in the New Testament), and if the basis for both is thoroughly understood by sound theological interpreta-tion in the Old and New Testament, a new power and a new unity will appear among Christians even though they are sep-arated organizationally along denominational lines.

When we remove doctrinal teaching from its biblical-histori-cal context, we open the door to rationalistic manipulations in theology. The cold hand of rationalism knows no boundaries. It can invade the doctrinal studies of those who are proud of their orthodoxy as well as those of a more liberal perspective. The only way to avoid the paralyzing hold of rationalism is to stay genuinely open to the message of Scripture *before, during,* and *after* one molds and formulates it into an organized structure. The trained or untrained theologian must then be diligent not to add or subtract from the essential emphases in formulating his doctrinal structure because of some plausible conjecture as to what the full picture must be. If God has revealed only a partial picture—and this is certainly what Paul declares in I Corinthians 13:9-13—then the arrangement of what has been revealed must not use rationally invented links to give an artificial wholeness. Instead of accepting a certain truth as part of God's revelation, interpreters are sometimes tempted to substitute something more in keeping with how they think God *should* work. When Peter tried this in connection with Christ's death, he received one of Jesus' sternest rebukes—"Get behind me, Satan" (see Matt. 16:21-23; Mark 8:31-33). Because Peter did not understand the things of God but only the things of men, he structured God's way in terms of man's thinking.

TEACHING MINISTRY OF THE CHURCH

In the King James Version the Greek noun *didaskalia* is always translated "doctrine"[1] and in the Pastorals where the adjective "sound" accompanies it (I Tim. 1:10; II Tim. 4:3; Titus 1:9; 2:1) the phrase "sound doctrine" may carry modern connotations that may not have been in the mind of the original writer. The word itself has both an active meaning and a passive meaning. In the active, *didaskalia* means the act of *teaching, instructing,* while in the passive it means that which is taught, i.e., *teaching.*[2] A brief survey of the use of the word points up the teaching ministry of the Church. It shows that doctrinal teaching is part of a larger whole, and that to narrow doctrinal teaching to certain topics viewed in an abstract setting can easily lead to philosophizing rather than to a proper understanding of Christian truth and Christian living.

The word *didaskalia* is used of human teachings. Jesus said that the Pharisees and scribes exemplified the words of Isaiah (29:13) by honoring God with their lips but with a heart far removed from him. In this state they worshipped God in vain "*teaching* as *teachings* the commandments of men" (Matt. 15:9; Mark 7:7). Hence the doctrine or teaching of the Pharisees was

---

[1] Cf. Young's *Analytical Concordance to the Bible,* p. 267.
[2] See Bauer, p. 190. Karl Heinrich Rengstorf, *"didaskalia," TWNT,* II, 163.

only human teaching tragically substituted for the commandments of God. In Colosse part of the philosophical speculation
concerned a legalistic asceticism that forbade eating, enjoying,
or consuming (KJ, "touch not, taste not, handle not") anything.
Paul designates such legalism as "in accord with the commandments and *teachings* of men" (Col. 2:22). It contributes to the
very indulgence of the flesh that it seeks to correct (Col. 2:23).
Ephesians pictures a contrast between the perfect or mature man
and the one who is immature, "tossed here and there by every
wind of *teaching,* in the trickery of men, in the craftiness with
respect to the deceitful scheming" Eph. 4:14). In these two passages human teaching is pictured as encouraging fleshly indulgence. The changeableness and shiftiness of human teaching,
springing from a deceitful heart, tosses the immature Christian
around while jeopardizing his whole standing and stability.

In contrast to human teaching, there is the teaching of demons. Men who withdraw from the faith cannot live in a
vacuum. They pay heed to deceitful spirits and to "*teachings* of
demons" (I Tim. 4:1). The minds of men are controlled either
by truth or error.

Teachers of truth hold an important office in the Church.
God appoints "first apostles, second prophets, third *teachers*
. . ." (I Cor. 12:28). In Ephesians there is a similar statement
except that the fourth group consists of pastors and *teachers*
(Eph. 4:11). In Romans 12 Paul speaks of the various gifts and
he encourages those who have these particular gifts to use them
in performing their appointed functions. "Whether the one
teaching, let him use the gift in his *instruction*" (Rom. 12:7).
Here is an active sense of the noun *didaskalia—instruction.* Such
instruction meant making known the details of Jesus' earthly
life, the meaning of his death and resurrection, the proper conduct of Christians who have been joined to Christ and who
share his life, and the climax of history which awaits the return
of Christ.

In the opening chapter of I Timothy there is a list of serious
moral offences and crimes. It is for these that the law has been
established. Then the writer adds: "And if there be any different
wrong doing opposed to *sound teaching*" (I Tim. 1:10). Sound
teaching then involves some "thou shalt nots." The "teaching"
referred to in this passage consists of norms for human conduct.
Today "sound teaching" often is limited to such topics as the
person of Christ, the doctrine of the Holy Spirit, etc., with such
teaching largely limited to abstract definitions, differentiation,
and discussions.

The New Testament describes the one who corrects false

asceticism as "being trained in the words of the faith and in *the noble teaching*" (I Tim. 4:6). In this case, doctrine or teaching is used to show that teaching of distinctions in foods and asceticism in marriage are false. To be trained in the true words of the faith and in the noble teaching the teacher must make the Christian message an inherent part of his life. Thus teaching is no mere dissemination of information. It is the verbal expression of what the teacher himself is experiencing.

Paul exhorts Timothy to give careful attention to teaching. The noun *didaskalia* here has an active sense: "Until I come apply yourself to [public] reading, to exhortation, to *instruction*" (I Tim. 4:13). The instructor is closely tied to his instruction. Hence in the same context is the exhortation: "Take pains with yourself and with *the instruction*" (I Tim. 4:16). It is apparent that the truths about the Christian faith were conveyed by instruction. This active teaching ministry demanded a great deal of the instructor. He was to fix his attention upon himself as well as upon his teaching.

The elders of the New Testament also are involved in teaching: "Let the elders who rule [or manage] well be counted worthy of double pay, especially those who toil in the message and in *the teaching*" (I Tim. 5:17). The message here seems to be the proclamation of good news, of reconciliation to God through commitment to Christ, while the teaching seems to refer to instruction in Christian living.[3] A restricted emphasis or meaning to *didaskalia* is rather rare. Much more common is the comprehensive meaning involving the Christian faith as a whole.

Slaves are urged to watch their conduct and to count their masters worthy of all honor "lest the name of God or *the teaching* be blasphemed" (I Tim. 6:1). The teaching obviously represents the essence of the Christian faith. Similarly God's name represents all that God is.

Teaching involves both the truths of what God did in Christ and also the teachings of the Old Testament. Paul was Timothy's spiritual father in regard to the truths of God which he taught Timothy both by speech and writing as well as by his life. II Timothy 3:10 reads: "You have followed as a rule *my teaching.* . . ." This is followed by a list of other aspects of Paul's life that Timothy also observed: "My conduct, my aim in life, my faith, my patience, my love, etc." These were to Timothy *exhibits* of what God did in Christ through Paul. The Old Testament is also a source of teaching or doctrine: "Every Scripture passage [by Scripture is meant the Old Testament] is

---

3 Rengstorf, *"didaskalia," TWNT*, II, 165.

inspired of God and is profitable for *instruction* . . . " (II Tim.
3:16). Here also instruction heads the list of those things for
which the scriptural passages are profitable. "Now as many
things as were written beforehand [the Old Testament] were
written for *our instruction* [or doctrine]" (Rom. 15:4). The
scope of the Old Testament is quite broad. Many facets of life
are touched upon. Consequently, "instruction" does not refer
to some narrow part of the whole but to the impact of the entire
Old Testament.

The book of Titus also stresses the central role of teaching.
After listing the qualities that a bishop should have, Paul concludes with a picture of the bishop "clinging to the trustworthy
message in accordance with *the teaching (tēn didachēn)* in order
that he might be able both to exhort in *the sound teaching (en
tēi didaskaliai tēi hugiainousēi)* and to reprove those who contradict" (Titus 1:9). The teaching is to serve as the basis for the
trustworthy message and for exhortation. With such a standard
the bishop can reprove those who contradict. Titus himself is
to be an example. He is to be a pattern of good works. As a
teacher he is to show integrity in the teaching, dignity, and
sound preaching that is beyond reproach (Titus 2:7-8). Such a
combination would produce a man whose influence is felt both
through what he does and what he says. This positive emphasis
removes all grounds of criticism for those hostile to the gospel.
Slaves are to exhibit reliability, that they may "adorn *the teaching* of God our Saviour in all respects" (Titus 2:9,10). The
teaching tells men how to live and the teaching itself is also a
part of men's daily lives. Christians can adorn "the doctrine"
by their conduct (Titus 2:10), or they can cause it to be blasphemed (I Tim. 6:1). In today's world the term "doctrine" often
has a narrower meaning. It sometimes refers to a body of
specific truths about God and man's relationship to God. This
body of specific truths may be couched in erudite, difficult language. Or it may be in simpler language which by its simplicity
confronts the reader with profound depths of meaning. But regardless of the form, we must remember that doctrine is for the
whole man, not only for his intellect. A study of *didaskalia* in
the New Testament shows that the whole individual is involved
in teaching. The teaching must become a part of us. When this
happens Christian lives become different from those who know
nothing of Christian truths or who merely know about these
truths. Classification and structuring of doctrinal truths ought
to have one main purpose: to make it easier for these truths to
become a part of us. Although a Christian may not grasp all
that is involved in each particular truth, he can still use it and

make it a part of himself. The fact of the return of Christ is written large in the New Testament. Differences about the "how" of this great event should in no way hinder the appropriation of the truth itself. Most people do not understand in detail how an internal combustion engine works, but this has not kept them from making the motor car a part of their daily lives. Doctrine must become a part of men's daily lives. It must be both "taught" and "walked." Forgiveness of sins is a doctrinal fact. Thankfulness and rejoicing are two responses to this fact. Where such responses are tied to the meaning of forgiveness of sins, the combination is an example of doctrine being "walked," i.e., consciously becoming a part of the Christian's daily activity.

HUMAN STRUCTURES FOR DOCTRINAL THOUGHT

Every theologian presents theological materials in his own way. If he accepts the canonical Scriptures of the Old and New Testament (without the Apocrypha) as the base for his theology, he must still select and arrange the theological materials to show their significance either in terms of individual parts of the Scriptures and historical periods or in terms of the whole. This has led to two main ways of structuring the relevant biblical materials. These ways are usually designated as biblical theology and systematic theology.

Biblical Theology, or the Historical Theology of the Old and New Testaments

The name "biblical theology" is rather unfortunate. Any theology which is not "biblical" has no right to the term theology but should be classified as a philosophy. What has been labeled "biblical theology" is more accurately the historical theology of the Old and New Testaments. Theological materials are arranged in terms of the same historical period, e.g. eighth century prophets,[4] of the same literary form, e.g. the Synoptic Gospels,[5] of the same author, e.g. the Pauline letters, or of in-

---

[4] Cf. J. Barton Payne, *The Theology of the Older Testament* (1962).

[5] Paul Feine, *Theologie des Neuen Testaments* (1951). Feine sets forth the theological materials of the New Testament in the following arrangement: I, The Teaching of Jesus according to the Presentation of the [Synoptic] Gospels; II, The Theological Views of the Early Church [Acts]; III, The Teaching of Paul; IV, The Teaching of John's Gospel and the Epistles of John; V, The Theological Views of the General Christian Writings, 1. The Apocalypse, 2. The Epistle to the Hebrews, 3. The Epistle of James, 4. The First Epistle of Peter, 5. The Epistle of Jude, 6. The Second Epistle of Peter; VI, The Main Ideas of New Testament Theology.

dividual writings which are more general either because of the geographical distribution of their recipients or because their contents do not generally pertain to one particular congregation.[6] But no matter how the material is grouped *biblical theology seeks to discover how the original author and original readers were influenced by their historical situation and how the message from God was peculiarly suited to that historical situation.* God's actions and God's self-revelation came to his servants in crisis and emergency, in victory and prosperity, in war and in peace. God's people may have been plunged into apostasy or may have been suffering under the brutal hand of the oppressor. All of these situations throb with life and meaning. And into these situations God came with new life and new meaning. Hence biblical theology is concerned with definite historical situations. Because of this the biblical theologian centers his attention upon: (1) the theological teachings in a particular canonical writing or closely related group of writings; (2) the specific period of the original writer(s) and readers; (3) distinct factors in the situation which influenced each writer, readers, and teaching.

In this approach the biblical theologian must be constantly aware of the biblical languages, all known historical factors, and the freshness of the message of God through his servant to men involved in a life and death struggle with dread realities. In recent years biblical theologians have turned more toward topical arrangements rather than historical categories. Yet their methodology is still historical. Most of the categories they employ are taken from the biblical materials.[7] The use of a topical arrangement does not make them systematic theologians. It is still the particular historical settings and the biblical language which determine the arrangements. Just how this material from another historical setting is to be applied to contemporary man is a question each theologian must answer for himself. How he answers it reveals whether he regards himself as having great

---

[6] *Ibid.* See Feine, Section V, pp. 373-401.

[7] Cf. Alan Richardson, *An Introduction to the Theology of the New Testament* (1958). The chapter divisions in Richardson's book show how he structures New Testament theology: I, Faith and Hearing; II, Knowledge and Revelation; III, The Power of God unto Salvation; IV, The Kingdom of God; V, The Holy Spirit; VI, The Reinterpreted Messiahship; VII, The Christology of the Apostolic Church; VIII, The Life of Christ; IX, The Resurrection, Ascension and Victory of Christ; X, The Atonement Wrought by Christ; XI, The Whole Christ; XII, The Israel of God; XIII, The Apostolic and Priestly Ministry; XIV, Ministries within the Church; XV, The Theology of Baptism; XVI, The Eucharistic Theology of the New Testament.

continuity with historic orthodoxy, some continuity with historic orthodoxy, or a minimal amount of continuity with historic orthodoxy.

Systematic Theology

Systematic theology among orthodox theologians is very biblical in the sense that it derives its subject matter from the Scriptures. It differs from biblical theology in that it treats the whole of the Bible (for Protestant theologians, the canonical Scriptures of the Old and New Testaments without the Apocrypha) rather than working through the parts in their historical framework. *A systematic theologian takes the theological materials from this comprehensive whole and arranges these in a logical framework which he himself has created.* The framework of thought may or may not represent an historical school of theological interpretation depending on the theologian who draws it up. But no matter how loyal a particular theologian is to a tradition or a school, each systematic arrangement has its own individual touch. The systematic theologian chooses and creates the framework that he believes best exhibits the major and minor emphases of the whole Bible.[8] These logical categories reflect the

8 Take for example Louis Berkhof, *Systematic Theology* (1949). Here are the main logical divisions and emphases: I. The Doctrine of God. A. The Being of God (Existence, Knowability, Being and Attributes, Names, Attributes in General, Incommunicable Attributes, Communicable Attributes, The Holy Trinity). B. The Works of God (Divine Decrees, Predestination, Creation in General, Creation of the Spiritual World, Creation of the Material World, Providence). II. The Doctrine of Man in Relation to God. A. Man in His original State (Origin, Constitutional Nature, Man as the Image of God, Man in the Covenant of Works). B. Man in the State of Sin (Origin of Sin, Essential Character of Sin, Transmission of Sin, Sin in the Human Race, The Punishment of Sin). C. Man in the Covenant of Grace (Name and Concept of the Covenant, The Covenant of Redemption, Nature of the Covenant of Grace, Dual Aspect of the Covenant, Different Dispensations of the Covenant). III. The Doctrine of the Person and Work of Christ. A. The Person of Christ (Doctrine of Christ in History, Names and Natures of Christ, Unipersonality of Christ). B. The States of Christ (State of Humiliation, The State of Exaltation). C. The Offices of Christ (Prophetic Office, Priestly Office, Cause and Necessity of Atonement, Nature of Atonement, Divergent Theories of the Atonement, Purpose and Extent of the Atonement, Intercessory Work of Christ, Kingly Office). IV. The Doctrine of the Application of the Work of Redemption (Soteriology in General, Operation of the Holy Spirit in General, Common Grace, Mystical Union, Calling in General and External Calling, Regeneration and Effectual Calling, Conversion, Faith, Justification, Sanctification, Perseverance of the Saints). V. The Doctrine of the Church and the Means of Grace. A. The Church (Scriptural Names of the Church and the Doctrine of the Church in History, Nature of the Church, Government of the

contemporaneous character of systematic theology, i.e., the biblical materials can be organized so as to answer current questions asked about the nature of God, the nature of man, etc. However, systematic theology often reflects instead the questions and philosophical emphases of a bygone epoch. When this occurs, the student finds discussions of issues that no longer occupy the minds of men or that have been modified and changed over the years. In such a situation the systematic theologian loses his opportunity to give the insights that would otherwise be possible as he unfolds the meaning of theological truths viewed from the perspective of the sum-total of all of revelation. Hence, systematic theologies, like translations of the Bible, must always be kept up to date. This does not mean that the basic Christian truths are changing but that the intellectual, social, and moral climate constantly changes. At the end of the nineteenth century many intellectuals were impressed with the goodness of man. In the last half of the twentieth century, with the threat of nuclear war hanging over mankind and with the memory of the holocaust of two world wars fresh in their minds, thinking men are confronted with the badness of man. In both periods the theologian had for his task the duty to point out the biblical emphasis that man is a sinner and to show what is involved in a sinner being restored to fellowship with God. But exactly how he formulates and expresses these doctrines of the nature of man and the salvation of man will be influenced by whether the thinking around him is optimistic or pessimistic.

Every theologian must be prepared to defend his reasons for emphasizing certain areas. Why are certain biblical statements given more weight than others? Does not his subordination of many elements under one heading minimize some important facts in these lesser elements? These are questions with which modern systematic theologies must grapple realistically. Systems are useful in bringing together large collections of material, but they are not self-authenticating. The system-maker must defend his arrangement. He must show us why he prefers his arrangement to other unifying patterns. If he is merely attracted by the logical coherency of the premises without testing the premises to see if they cover fairly all of the biblical evidence, he does not

Church, Power of the Church). B. The Means of Grace (Means of Grace in General, The Word as a Means of Grace, The Sacraments in General, Christian Baptism, The Lord's Supper). VI. The Doctrine of Last Things. A. Individual Eschatology (Introductory Chapter, Physical Death, Immortality of the Soul, Intermediate State). B. General Eschatology (Second Coming of Christ, Millennial Views, The Resurrection of the Dead, The Final Judgment, The Final State).

really know whether "the system" merits his confidence or not. This he must find out or he runs the risk of a serious disillusionment.

Teamwork on the Part of Theologians

Biblical theology and systematic theology are complementary disciplines. If we consider theological teachings only in terms of the historical background into which they came, we may have a history-centered theology. If we look at theological teachings only in terms of a logical system of thought, we may end up with an intellectual, idea-centered theology. God can be omitted from both approaches. Even when God is made central neither approach by itself is sufficient. Paul Tillich was right when he declared that "the Biblical source is made available to the systematic theologian through a critical and ultimately concerned biblical theology."[9] It is the duty of the biblical theologian to show how grammatical and historical factors influence theological teachings in particular writings from specific periods when God revealed himself. It is the duty of the systematic theologian to bring together all of the teachings on any particular subject—e.g. the atonement—and to show what is involved in the total meaning. Since the total picture will always be stated in contemporary language to people who live in a particular epoch, the wording or phraseology used by the systematic theologian to express this total meaning is crucial. Like the biblical theologian, he will employ biblical language, but since he covers a broader sphere, he must also use the language that best brings together all of the separate emphases and that says to the modern reader what the biblical writers would say to the modern reader if they could speak to him in his situation. This is no easy task. Hence Paul actually might not understand his own teaching on the kenōsis (Christ's emptying or depriving himself, Phil. 2:7) if he read some modern theology books!

Biblical theologians and systematic theologians must work together. Neither ought even to imply that the other is unnecessary. When both really work together, we will see a renaissance of the kind of theology that is relevant to the man of today. Theological topics are not simply for discussion and debate. They are meant to be guides for sound thinking and sound living. When they degenerate into mere controversy, then the common task of the biblical and systematic theologian has been forgotten: to make Christian truth meaningful to Christian people.

9 Paul Tillich, *Systematic Theology* (1951), I, 50.

ANALYTICAL THINKING IN DOCTRINAL STUDIES

In almost any volume on biblical theology or systematic theology, the theologian may discuss a particular biblical passage, but in so doing he focusses the reader's attention on whatever doctrinal theme he is discussing. If he should be developing the topic of the person of Christ, he might turn to the prologue of John's Gospel (John 1:1-18). Much of this would be relevant to his discussion. Yet the section on John the Baptist (John 1:6-8) very likely would be passed by unnoticed, since other assertions in this very same section would provide the theologian with the crucial elements that he needs. The analytical thinker must select what is pertinent to the subject at hand. He must analyze a passage for what it will say about a limited subject or theme. Whatever does not help develop that theme is omitted from this particular discussion. The theologian does not necessarily ignore what is omitted. Instead, he considers each passage as a whole and then omits what is not relevant. But the analytical thinker must also face the question: Can I by impartial reasons defend my choice of certain elements in any passage as the only ones relevant to a particular subject? Unless he can honestly answer yes, his analytical reasoning runs the risk of being turned into an artificial rationalism.

The more the systematic theologian knows about the context, grammar, and historical background of the passage, the greater will be his skill in making this analytical type of selection. The Protestant conviction that every believer should interpret the Bible for himself does not mean that every believer will interpret it equally well. Even among interpreters well-trained in all the skills necessary for valid analytical thinking about matters of doctrine, there are vast differences in actual performance. There is no room for pride on the part of interpreters. Analytical thinking is hard work. The chances of error by either omission or commission (i.e., the assertion of that which the passage does not say) are staggering. Here the biblical maxim is certainly applicable: "The one who thinks that he stands, let him take heed lest he fall" (I Cor. 10:12; in its original context the maxim is applied to the sins which befell the Israelites). Constant vigilance and practice are necessary for progress.

APPROACH TO DOCTRINAL MATERIAL IN PARTICULAR PASSAGES

What is involved on the part of an interpreter who endeavors to bring forth from a particular passage what it teaches upon a selected doctrinal theme? Some important considerations must be taken into account.

Attitude of the Interpreter

He must be a redeemed personality who knows the power of God's grace in his own heart and life. He must have a love for all Christian brothers who are joined to Christ by faith. It is bizarre for Christians to attack by their writings other believers who hold to different opinions on some particular doctrine. In oral discussion as well as in writing, two Christians sometimes act as if the other were an opponent to be run out of town as quickly as possible. The ultimate in fleshliness and pride comes when one Christian condemns another, maligns his character, and makes him the object of gossip because of some minute doctrinal difference. The person who does this often justifies his actions by claiming that "his opponent" is guilty of grave doctrinal dereliction. Paul reproved the Corinthians for their fleshliness when he said: "You are still those who belong to the realm of the flesh. Because where jealousy and strife are among you, you are fleshly, are you not, and you walk on a mere human plane, do you not?" (I Cor. 3:3). Doctrinal interpreters must exhibit the fruit of the Spirit. They must walk on a high plane, or they will not acquire a true understanding of the great theological truths of God.

Awareness of the Nature of Literal and Figurative Language

Throughout this book we have said that both literal and figurative language convey great and essential truths. We must be aware of the literal meaning in order to recognize the shift from the literal to the figurative meaning. Furthermore, the literal meaning is always related to the figurative meaning and must be understood if we are to see what the original author wanted his hearers to grasp.

In doctrinal interpretation we find both literal and figurative language. In Romans 8:20-23 Paul describes the physical creation—all the elements under man—as having been subjected to frustration. This creation will share the glorious freedom of the children of God. Together with the children of God, creation is in travail and in agony. Then Paul adds:

> And not only so, but we ourselves also, although we possess the first fruits of the Spirit, are groaning within ourselves as we are eagerly awaiting adoption, i.e., the redemption of our bodies (vs. 23).

This one verse provides material for the doctrine of the Spirit and for one aspect of eschatology—a study of what will happen to the believer's body. In both instances figurative language is used. Believers are said to have the first fruit, i.e., the Spirit, or (as in the above translation) the first fruits of the Spirit, the first fruits which the Spirit has poured out with more to come. In the one case the genitive is taken as appositional and in the other case the genitive is regarded as subjective (or possibly possessive). The flow of thought seems to favor the idea of the believer having the first fruits which the Spirit has poured out. Here is an agricultural term used figuratively to teach that the blessings of the Spirit which the believer now possesses are not the "whole harvest" but only the beginning. These blessings are a sample of the glorious things to come. Christians who have these blessings still feel the tensions of finiteness and the pressures of a world where sin still reigns. In this situation the believers eagerly await "adoption, the redemption of our bodies." Two figurative terms here indicate the prospects for the believer so far as his body is concerned. The term "adoption" is a legal term describing how one not born into a family becomes legally a part of the family. "Redemption" also is used figuratively, since it literally means the setting free of a slave or captive by the payment of a ransom. Those who are adopted into God's family still await one climactic experience of their adoption—the replacing of their imperfect, mortal bodies by immortal glorified bodies. This is a redemption because the believer's body was a slave to the frustrations of a sinful finiteness. In being transformed it will be set free and the believer then will know the glorious freedom of the sons of God. The word "body" is used literally. Redemption involves a transformation of the body, but the destiny of the believer still involves bodily existence. Thus we see that awareness of the nature of literal and figurative language can bring new depths of meaning to doctrinal interpretation.

Careful Employment of General Hermeneutics

A third principle in handling of doctrinal material is that the interpreter pay strict attention to general hermeneutics. The necessary procedures regarding context, language, history, and culture must be employed. For example, the kind of action in verbs or participles will show whether sanctification in any particular passage is a process, a state, or a decisive declaration or experience. Context will show whether a theme is concluded where a chapter ends or if it continues on into the next chapter (see I Thess. 4:13-5:11). Context, language, history, and culture are important for doctrine because every doctrinal assertion is colored by these factors. Usually only a few of the cultural-historical factors can be known, but there is little excuse for ignorance or neglect regarding context and language. To disregard contextual or linguistic factors suggests ignorance, carelessness, or an intentional omission of unwelcome data.

The "proof text" method in theology fell into disrepute because it notoriously neglected context. It often tended to confine itself to the revered King James Version whether the textual reading behind the King James Version had good manuscript support or not. However, there is nothing wrong with proof texts so long as context, language, history and culture are found to support what is being "proved." If an interpreter uses a list of verses to support some particular point of doctrine, he must first make a careful study to see exactly what point these verses illustrate and corroborate. If a reader or hearer looks up a passage and finds that it does not actually support the point that it was claimed to support, he will question the validity of the rest of the textual support. Nothing will harm doctrinal analysis more than carelessness in this particular area.

Precise Formulation of Exactly What the Passage Teaches

Some interpreters are so eager to compare one passage with another and to allow other passages to shed light on "problem" passages, that they never discipline themselves to state *first* in their own words precisely what the original "problem" passage teaches doctrinally. In reality, the relation of one passage to another is secondary. The primary element is the emphasis in the particular passage being studied. After the interpreter carefully phrases for himself exactly what he thinks the passage says (using the techniques and procedures of general hermeneutics), then he may compare the passage with other passages bearing on the same subject. Such comparisons may be helpful and profitable. But this should be done only *after* the interpreter has made himself state exactly what the passage affirms. Otherwise we tend to use other passages to "explain away" the unambiguous assertions of the so-called "problem" passages. Only by a willingness to be confronted with all the evidence, whether or not it agrees with our preconceived opinions, can we grow as faithful expositors of Christian doctrine.

Best Textual Readings as Base for Doctrinal Teaching

Students who read their New Testament in Greek know that

in the critical apparatus there are other readings besides those appearing in the text. To cite a verse like I John 5:7 (KJV) as supporting the doctrine of the Trinity is foolish. The verse in Greek form appeared in the third edition of Erasmus' Greek Testament. It has never been found in any Greek manuscript since Erasmus' day. Erasmus himself took the verse out of later editions of his own Greek Testament. But because the third edition (1522) became the basis for a standardized text, the King James translators, having this text before them, introduced this extraneous verse into the English Bible. No passage should be employed to support any doctrine until the interpreter has made sure that it is supported by good manuscripts and can, therefore, be regarded as what the original writer said. Most modern translations indicate in footnotes where the textual base is poor or where other readings are possible. Carefulness here marks the interpreter as an alert, dedicated student of the doctrinal materials. Sometimes the better text will strengthen the usefulness of a text for doctrinal purposes (cf. John 1:18, "the only-begotten God"—this reading is supported by the Alexandrian family of manuscripts, the Peshitta Syriac, Irenaeus, and Origen.)

FROM THE PART TO LARGER WHOLES

Having considered how an interpreter should approach the particular passage, we should also consider how the larger wholes of theology can be evaluated.

Limited Wholes of Biblical Theology

Regardless of how biblical theologians group materials in their historical approach to doctrinal truths, the interpreter is aware of distinctive emphases, of growth and development, of continuity between the Old Covenant and the New Covenant, and of discontinuity between some of the elements in the two covenants. Intense variety is apparent. Yet progressive revelation is also apparent if the interpreter understands the nature of the biblical idea of progress. When we feel for ourselves the fresh and powerful creativity of God's chosen servants, we begin to appreciate the methodology of biblical theology. The limited wholes are stepping stones. They unite and bring together a great deal of material. But they do not introduce artificial uniformity. Instead we feel a sense of true unity. This unity is found in God who reveals himself. Biblical theology confronts the theologian with a God who reveals himself in history. There is no need for some abstract, artificial unity. If the biblical theologian carefully amasses the many strands of theological teaching, he will be able to show how this material holds together. Let us be aware at the outset that all of the strands of the pattern are not to be found, because God did not choose to reveal everything which belongs to his counsel. This obvious limitation should deter anyone from trying to find in the totality a kind of "complete picture" which is not characteristic of any of the parts. From the total of all the parts there will certainly be more strands than any one part possessed. But the very fact that there are details that cannot be forced together declares that God did not intend these elements to be placed together without some other facets coming in between. When these "missing strands" are not to be found in any of the parts, then the interpreter ought to conclude that the action of God which discloses the limited way he reveals truth in any one period is representative of God during all of the periods of revelation. He revealed enough so that men would have a growing and sufficient rule for faith and practice. In the ages to come he is going to show or demonstrate more of the extraordinary riches of his grace in his kindness towards us in Christ Jesus (Eph. 2:7). But now, even with a complete summary of past revelation, we are definitely in a sphere where we know only in part.

Comprehensive Totality of Systematic Theology

We need a comprehensive handling such as is found in systematic theology to show the extensive amount of material available in Scripture on various doctrinal themes. The value of any particular systematic arrangement must be judged by the clarity of the presentation, by the simplicity of the organization, and by the completeness of the material collected. A good system will have the following characteristics.

Consistent presentation of valid theological inferences. The systematic theologian must take into account biblical theology with its presentation of the various emphases of the historical periods and groupings. He must also bring the materials together without forcing their alignment. In so doing, he can set forth sound theological conclusions that grow out of the evidence and are not imposed upon it.

Avoidance of invalid inferential reasoning. The systematic theologian must resist the temptation to package everything in artificially neat units. The drawing of extensive deductions from a well-established premise and the arranging of these deductions in a flawless pattern of argument has deceived many theologians into thinking that the results represent the very truth of God. Unless such deductive reasoning can be supported by inductive Scriptural evidence at every point it does not meet the qualification of Christian theology. It is certainly legitimate for Christians to philosophize. But such philosophy must be tested in the same crucibles as other philosophies. It must not be called pure theology and thus be given a status and authority that it does not possess.

Flexibility and adjustability of the framework. Every good system of theology must be a growing one. Flexibility and adjustability are characteristics of growth. Many systems of theology have come into disrepute because they have been brittle, unchanging systems that forced everything into preconceived molds. But every good theologian would rather discard his system (if it could not be changed!) than be guilty of forcing a fact to fit into a category rather than having the category provide a setting or place for the fact. The contrast is great between forcing feet into shoes and fitting feet with the right shoes.

Distinction between ideas and language of creedal formulations. In theology there are always iconoclasts who feel that creeds are outworn statements and therefore useless. One can almost hear them say: "What we need is something new to awaken the minds of those slumbering in the revered language of past epochs." But many of those who use creeds are far from being asleep. This is an unnecessary castigation. Creeds have great value. They testify to the care and earnestness with which earlier Christians endeavored to state basic Christian truths. Yet their language, although highly revered, should not be considered unalterable. If the idea behind the creedal statement can be rephrased so as to speak more clearly to modern man, then such a rephrasing should be carried out. Understanding is the key to communication. Here we are assuming that there is a valid biblical basis for the creedal statement. Unfortunately, this is not true of all creedal formulations. But certainly valid biblical truth must be communicated. No love for familiar, revered language of the past should obscure the need to communicate the truth in a form that can easily be understood. There is more than one way of doing this. But it must be done.

Awareness of the lessons of historical theology. No good system of theology ignores or disdains the theological struggles of the past. The errors and heretical aberrations of the past still reveal to us what should be avoided. We gain a valuable perspective by sensing that we are a part of a whole host of Christians who have labored and toiled throughout the centuries over the revelation of God. Fresh creativity must be tempered by an awareness of the failures and successes of others. This tempering will help today's theologian to produce works that will abide rather than fall by the wayside as ill-advised and hastily thought out speculations.

BIBLIOGRAPHY

Feine, Paul, *Theologie des Neuen Testaments* (1951).

Rengstorf, Karl Heinrich, *"didaskalia,"* *Theologisches Wörterbuch zum Neuen Testament*, II (1935).

Richardson, Alan, *An Introduction to the Theology of the New Testament* (1958).

Vos, Geerhardus, "The Nature and Method of Biblical Theology," Chapter I, *Biblical Theology: Old and New Testaments* (1948).

XVII Devotion and Conduct

What is the relation of doctrinal teaching to devotion and conduct? Perhaps the distinctions can be made clear by three simple questions. What should a man *know* about what God has done or revealed? The answer is found in *doctrine*. How should a man *respond* to God whom he knows by virtue of his experience of salvation? This is the concern of *devotion*. What should a man *do* in the existential situations of life? Here we face the problems of *conduct*. The purpose of this chapter is to set forth the proper use of the Bible in devotion and conduct.

Many individuals permit their use of the Bible in devotional activities and in the determination of their conduct to be ruled strictly by feeling. No matter how haphazard their approach and how erroneous their conclusions, they justify their actions by saying: "God told me this or that in my devotional reading." Yet it would seem logical that the more sacred and holy the experience, the more careful we should be to avoid anything unreliable or that would contribute to wrong conclusions. On the other hand, the individual Christian should not feel that he needs "a check list" to read the Bible properly for the edification of his own soul. Surely we want the maximum return from our day-to-day conduct. Such a return cannot be achieved by a careless indifference to our procedure or by an over-fastidious preoccupation with every detail of our method. Rather we must consider the main objectives of personal Bible study.

FELLOWSHIP WITH GOD THROUGH THE SCRIPTURES

When it comes to devotional Bible study and prayer, there is no ambiguity in the fact that prayer is concerned with what a believer has to say to God. But there is ambiguity in the statement that the believer studies the Bible to hear what God has to say to him. This is a valid statement, if we mean by it that a person studies the Scriptures on any particular occasion to discover what may be applied to his own life at that particular time. There are always two variables in personal, devotional Bible study. (1) The passage being read will change from day to day. (2) The needs of the individual will change from day to day. The same passage could be read ten times during a year. If the reader is filled with the Spirit and is walking in fellowship with God on each occasion, he may apply to himself different things on each occasion. Perhaps the passage is selected from Isaiah. This was originally written to the people of Israel. Or it may be taken from Philippians, originally written to the people of God, the believers in Philippi. Our personal applications may be different from those of the original readers. Personal application involves the working out from the passage *a principle* that is true for anyone who belongs to God or a principle for individuals in parallel situations. Legitimate application by the formulation of sound principles is in truth what God has to say to the individual Christian.

Many have read the statement of Isaiah when he saw the Lord high and lifted up: "Here am I; send me" (Isa. 6:8). Isaiah's response becomes their own by a simple identification. Yet in the original setting Isaiah's commission included going to a people to make them less responsive so that for them there could be no understanding or healing. Only in rare situations could we validly apply to ourselves this latter part of Isaiah's commission. Perhaps a faithful servant of God laboring in a place where he finds little or no response to his preaching might apply to himself the principle that lack of understanding, blindness of eyes, and dullness of heart on the part of his hearers was a judgment of God upon a particular group of people who, though often confronted with the truth, turned away from it. But he must be sure that there is a true parallel between himself and Isaiah, between the people to whom he is ministering and the people of Israel. Such a conviction is hard to get. In the fourth chapter of Paul's letter to the Philippians we find his earnest entreaty that Euodia and Syntyche live in harmony in the Lord (Phil. 4:2). He highly praises these women "as those who fought at his side in spreading the gospel" (Phil. 4:3). He encourages an unnamed individual, whom he calls "true yokefellow," to help these two women who were quarreling. Certainly, two Christians who are quarreling today—be they men or women—might well apply this statement about living in harmony to themselves. The principle, then, is that of believers living in harmony with one another. This is true even though today's Christians cannot—like those to whom Paul's statement first came—claim that they helped Paul the apostle in his ministry in Philippi. This obvious fact helps to make clear the confined or limited meaning in the passage as well as the universal possibilities of application of the principle of harmonious living.

God does speak through the Scriptures to men today. When an individual reads a scriptural passage, he must take full account of the differences between the Old Covenant and the New Covenant, between that pertaining only to the people to whom the passage first came and that which is pertinent to all peoples despite different geographical and temporal settings. Yet an individual's awareness of these things should be overshadowed by his sense of the reality and nearness of God. As he reads the scriptural narrative, he enters into the experience of Isaiah. He shares the experiences of those at Philippi as well as the content of Paul's letter to the Philippians. He may apply to himself the words first written to the Philippians: "Cease being anxious but in everything by means of prayer and entreaty with thanksgiving let your requests be made known to God. And the peace of God which surpasses all powers of thought will guard your hearts and minds in Christ Jesus" (Phil. 4:6-7). The "cease being anxious" was addressed to the whole group of Christians at Philippi. Each had to apply these words to himself. So today, the reader makes the shift from a command given to a group to himself as a member of the group. I am not to be anxious. I am to make my requests to God. My heart and mind will be guarded by God's peace. Both the original reader and the present day reader apply the Scriptures to themselves and have fellowship with God in this experience.

Response comes when the interpreter applies what he reads to himself and his own situation. If he remains indifferent, there has been no real application. If he is genuinely moved, action and response will follow. The reader must bring an active mind to his devotional study. He should ask himself *one* basic question that really consists of four parts. What in this passage applies to: (1) *a believer's relationship to God?* (2) *a believer's relationship to other believers?* (3) *a believer's relationship to unbelievers?* (4) *a believer's responsibility for himself—personal outlook, attitude, growth, endeavors to avoid defeat and to achieve maturity?* With such questions uppermost in his thinking, he will see results. No longer will he close his Bible with only some general idea of its contents or even with a precise listing of all that the passage said. Rather he will see those factors that affect his relationship to God, to believers, to unbelievers, and to himself. With an openness to God and to his Spirit he will become actively involved in being a Christian and becoming a saint (in the New Testament sense of the word).

DIRECTION FROM GOD FOR THE DECISIONS OF LIFE

Every devout Christian discovers that being a believer demands that all decisions be God-centered. More than that, he wants God's guidance in making the decision. Every day involves a host of minor decisions. The earnest Christian sometimes finds that what first seemed to be a minor decision actually had far-reaching, major implications. He also faces unavoidable major decisions that he knows are crucial. These decisions must be made and, once made, can rarely be reversed. Further, each Christian must make these decisions for himself. No one else can make them for him.

What role does the Bible play in these minor and major decisions? Does the Bible play an indispensable role in the matter of guidance? The Bible provides us with principles which will help us to make decisions. If we know God's will for other individuals, we *may conclude* that our situation is parallel and that this is God's will for us. For example, a Christian becomes ill with a chronic disease, e.g. heart trouble, diabetes, or asthma. He makes use of all the help that God has provided through modern medicine. At the same time he and his friends pray earnestly for healing and deliverance from the disease. He seeks to live a life which is pleasing to God. If God does not grant healing, the individual may conclude, as he reads II Corinthians 12:7-10, that God's will for him is like God's will for Paul—"my power is made perfect in weakness or sickness."[1] As he reads the passage he learns that Paul's afflic-

---

[1] The vocabulary and syntax of this passage makes it clear that Paul had a physical malady. He had a thorn in his body, i.e. an illness whose effects were as painful to him as a thorn. The only thing which is not clear is the exact kind of illness which bothered the great apostle. On the word "thorn" (*skolops* could also be translated "stake," "splinter") see Bauer (Arndt and Gingrich), p. 763: "Paul alludes to his illness . . . in . . . *there was given to me a thorn in the flesh*, 2 Cor. 12:7." On the word *kolaphizō* (KJV "buffet") see Bauer, pp. 441-42: " 'strike with the fist,' 'beat,' 'cuff,' someone. . . . 2. fig. of painful attacks of an illness described as a physical beating by a messenger of Satan, 2 Cor. 12:7, variously held to be: a. epilepsy . . . b. hysteria . . . c. periodic depression . . . d. head-

tion came to him because of the abundance of revelations which he had received. In this regard, Paul was different from any modern Christian. Yet Christians throughout all ages have experienced God's power energizing and strengthening them in physical afflictions of various sorts. Paul's response to God's will has been re-echoed by these saints: "Therefore, most gladly rather I will glory [boast] in afflictions [any kind of weakness except a moral or sinful kind] in order that the power of Christ may take up its abode over me" (II Cor. 12:9). The sense of Christ's power outbalanced the distress of affliction.

Such major decisions as choosing a life partner and the choice of a vocation or life work demand a thorough knowledge of the Bible. Of course, no specific text will tell the seeker whom to marry or what life work to pursue. But he will find much about the attitudes of husband and wife toward each other and toward God. Marriage is to be in the Lord and it is to be a holy relationship (cf. I Cor. 7:39; I Thess. 4:1-8 [RSV]). He will find Paul stressing the importance of work (II Thess. 3:10,12). He will find that whatever a believer does is to bring glory to God (I Cor. 10:31). Instead of *direct assertions* which constitute the divine guidance, the Christian who knows his Bible and who has made its principles a part of him will know *the principles* and the passages that bear upon any major or even minor decision.

Someone will reply: "But is this all there is to guidance?" No, it is not. Here are some further considerations. (1) *Guidance involves a self or personality who is centered upon God.* It is almost impossible for a man whose life revolves around himself to obtain guidance from God. God is not in the same category as a tax consultant whose services are sought only when things get too complicated. The man whose life revolves around himself may want God to straighten out his problem but not to straighten out his life. (2) *Guidance involves a careful awareness of how events and past experiences have prepared the way for the present.* How each of us has come to his present situation plays a part in what each one will do and just where he will go in future days. (3) *Further, guidance involves a complete openness to God as is demonstrated in our prayer life.* When Paul speaks of prayer and guidance, he talks of those praying with him as "contending along with me in your prayers on behalf of me toward God" (Rom. 15:30). Paul himself made three requests: To be delivered from the disobedient in

aches, severe eye trouble . . . e. malaria . . . f. leprosy . . . g. an impediment in his speech." See also Karl Ludwig Schmidt, "*kolaphizō*," *TWNT*, III, 818-21.

Judea; to have his collection or ministry be acceptable to the saints in Jerusalem; and to go with joy to the saints at Rome, *if God is willing*[2] (Rom. 15:32). Prayer is hard work because the person puts all that he is into the experience. (4) *Finally, guidance involves a quiet dependence upon the Holy Spirit or Helper to illuminate the believer's understanding.* With these qualities and a knowledge of the Bible, a Christian can enter realistically into all the known factors that must be assessed in making his decision. He must view all these factors from a higher perspective than that of himself, and this perspective comes only to the one whose inward man is centered upon God, who recognizes that God has already directed his steps, whose prayer life has resulted in a fellowship with God that testifies to the believer's being joined to God in Christ, and who is depending on the Holy Spirit to enlighten him. Guidance is never mechanical, but neither is true Bible study. Guidance involves the courage to act and a complete confidence in God. The believer who has God's guidance thinks of himself as being on God's side, as being one member of God's people. Because of a humble dependence upon God the believer never boasts in his guidance. He glories only in God. He does not testify long and loud about how God flashed a verse upon his mind and he instantly knew the will of God. Rather he shows what guidance means to him by his performance in the task that God guided him to undertake.

COMMANDS OF GOD FOR DAILY LIVING

Conduct involves not only guidance but obedience. The frequency of the imperative mood (or alternatives for the imperative) in both the Old and New Testaments is amazing. Some passages, such as I Thessalonians 5:13-22, list a series of imperatives. These touch upon many aspects of daily living. They are addressed to the Christian group in Thessalonica. Yet all of them are relevant for us today. Note the particular matters singled out for attention: (1) Esteem for spiritual leaders (vs. 13). (2) Group harmony—"keep the peace among yourselves" (vs. 13). (3) Handling of the disorderly, i.e., the idle or lazy—"admonish the disorderly" (vs. 14). (4) The fainthearted —"encourage the fainthearted" (vs. 14). (5) Morally weak—"help the morally weak" (vs. 14). (6) Attitude toward people—"be forbearing (patient) to all" (vs. 14). (7) Retaliation—"watch out lest any recompense evil in exchange for evil" (vs. 15). (8) Re-

2 See Bauer, *"dia,"* III, 1. d., p. 179: "to denote the efficient cause . . . *dia thelēmatos theou, if God is willing,* Rom. 15:32."

sponse to that which is morally right—"always strive for the good of one another and for all" (vs. 15). (9) Expression of joy —"rejoice at all times" (vs. 16). (10) Activity in prayer—"pray constantly [unceasingly]" (vs. 17). (11) Thanksgiving—"give thanks in everything; for this is God's will in Christ Jesus for you" (vs. 18). (12) Relation to the Spirit—"stop quenching [stifling, suppressing] the Spirit" (vs. 19). (13) Attitude toward prophecy—"stop rejecting with contempt the gift of prophecy" (vs. 20). (14) Discernment—"put to the test [examine] all things; hold fast to that which is noble [morally good]" (vs. 21). (15) Association with evil—"keep away from every kind of evil" (vs. 22). Such imperatives demand time for meditation. Often the language is familiar, so we read them six at a time. In a series such as the one above, the reader should read them all. This he should do rapidly and then go back and spend time on each one. But the time spent on meditation will be the most rewarding because it will drive home the contents of each one to the reader. Perhaps for the first time a preposition will leave its imprint—"give thanks *in* everything" is quite a different thing from giving thanks *for* everything. Or it may be the present tense. Believers are to cease from stifling the Spirit (vs. 19). How tragic that we should have any pattern of life that makes us suppress or quench the Spirit! Many observations like these will come to the one who will meditate upon the imperatives and the context in which they are found.

Some commands are for a particular man in a particular situation. When Timothy is encouraged to use a little wine for the sake of his stomach and his numerous times of weakness (I Tim. 5:23), the modern reader who also may have stomach trouble does not take this as a prescription for his own physical ills. He checks with his physician to find out what is the best thing for him to take. Throughout the Bible there are commands of this kind. An understanding of the historical and cultural background usually clears up matters like these. For instance, no one should try to dress or follow hair styles of ancient times. Yet propriety or quiet modesty (involving an absence of any sensational calling attention to oneself) is surely a principle that one must follow in matters of dress and appearance (I Pet. 3:3; I Tim. 2:9). No wife seriously calls her husband "lord," yet she does respect him. Love without respect indicates something seriously wrong with a marriage. Unless the downward course is checked, soon there will be no love or respect.

Sometimes Christians want specific commands on various kinds of recreation or amusement. What does the Bible say about skin-diving? Of course, the answer is nothing! But the *principles* of time or money involved, the aftereffects on the Christian's interest in the things of God, the help or hindrance in testifying for God, the effect on physical and emotional well-being—all of these principles and others which could be enumerated should not make it difficult for each individual Christian to decide for himself. One person might find that skin-diving took too much time, so he would not engage in the sport. Another might find that the exhilaration from the sport enabled him to function in a more efficient way for God. So he would decide that this would be a good thing for him to do. With God in the picture no one has to fear at all to leave such decisions in the hands of the individual believer and God. Obviously, the lack of specific commands in various areas is no hindrance. Often the only real hindrance is our unwillingness to "put to the test all things; hold fast to that which is morally good" (I Thess. 5:21).

Counsel of God for Personal Dialogue

Early in the Christian life Christians realize that they are witnesses for Christ—"You shall be witnesses of me both in Jerusalem and in all Judea and Samaria and unto the ends of the earth" (Acts 1:8). Christians are to exhort, encourage, and comfort one another. Witnessing, encouragement, comfort, and exhortation can be addressed to groups or can be on a man-to-man basis. The Christian Church should arise and with dedicated members move forward into the greatest campaign of personal dialogue ever launched.

Dialogue implies two people talking. Some individuals seem to think that witnessing is a one-man operation. I testify to another and he listens. However, since witnessing, exhortation, comfort, and encouragement involve *conversation,* then the absence of dialogue should be disturbing. What role does the Bible have in this kind of dialogue? It has a basic role to play, but the form in which the exact words of the Bible are presented will vary greatly. When a Christian talks with someone who knows little or nothing about the Bible—unfortunately there are millions of people like this—he must either quote the biblical language and then explain it, or he must present the biblical idea as clearly as he can without going through the two steps (quotation and explanation). The party with whom we are carrying on the dialogue must be encouraged to ask questions. If we are functioning as a counsellor we should help the one with whom we are counselling to formulate an answer to his own questions in the light of biblical teaching. Too often a counsellor is so busy trying to get his point across that instead of listening to the man with whom he is talking, he is planning what he will say next. Unless there is genuine listening and entering into the needs of the one with whom we speak, there will be little accomplished for God. Careful listening will enable us to choose the right biblical idea to help the person. As people open their hearts in this kind of dialogue, the counsellor cannot help being deeply moved by his responsibility and the great opportunity for spiritual good that lies before him.

When a Christian converses with a fellow Christian who has either a slight or an excellent knowledge of the Bible, he must assess carefully just what is his exact role. Does the man or woman need encouragement, consolation, or exhortation? In any case, the counsellor again must listen. Verbal prescriptions with an authoritarian finality will be of little or no value. We must be sure to use scriptural language with which the other person is familiar. With the numerous versions of the Bible now available in English this becomes more and more difficult! It is often helpful to try to bring to familiar words a new emphasis that has meant a lot to us but may have escaped the notice of our fellow Christian. What an uplift would come to the Church of Christ if Christians encouraged each other, comforted each other, and exhorted each other with a true sense of spiritual unity—identifying ourselves with each problem and difficulty, "considering ourselves, lest we also be tempted" (Gal. 6:1). This could change the whole image of the Christian Church. Once again the hallmark of the Christian Church would become: "Behold how they love one another." Where there is true love there is true listening. Then the Bible becomes a living book. Going on from the themes of sacred Scripture, the two participants in the dialogue will lose themselves in the being of God. This is the role of the Bible in personal dialogue: to bring men into a new awareness of God.

Message of God for Public Preaching

At first it seems superfluous to ask: "What role does the Bible play in public preaching?" But the answer may not be as simple as first appears. Preaching is concerned with doctrinal teaching, with devotion, and with conduct. It endeavors to proclaim to a group of people what they should *know*, how they should *respond* to God, and what they should *do*. These elements have already been discussed in this and preceding chapters. But we need to be reminded that from the reading of the text to the benediction, the message of God must be heard from the pulpit, and the people must be brought face to face with God. So often the listener hears only a collection of miscellany. Occasionally he notices the eloquence of the speaker and his polished arrangement of ideas. Or he may get a hurried arrangement of heterogeneous thoughts or the borrowed notions of great divines living or dead. The minister must take time to have fellowship with God through the Scriptures. When he experiences vital fellowship with God in Scripture and in prayer, the parishioners are much more likely to hear the word of God instead of some substitute.

Three main kinds of sermons are preached. A topical sermon is one in which a theme or subject is announced and then developed, e.g. "An effectual remedy for grief." The main points may come from various parts of the Scriptures. A text may also be used, but it is not the focal point of the sermon. In a textual sermon a particular text provides the main points, but the subpoints depend on the logical analysis by the minister of the subject and text. An expository sermon is one in which both the main points and the subpoints of the sermon are derived from the text or textual passage. The order and arrangement, however, is logical, and the minister does not pretend to preach on all of the details. For example, a sermon on "Ability to comfort as a by-product of affliction" could be either a textual or expository sermon based on II Corinthians 1:3-7.

The minister can confront his people with the message of God in all three kinds of sermons. But it is also true that in any service the hearer can listen attentively to the sermon, can acknowledge that a right response to affliction enables him to help others, can be convinced that genuine experience produces genuine awareness of others who are going through a similar experience, and yet never have a sense that he is hearing these truths *from God*. Instead, he hears them as coming only from the minister. Sometimes the fault lies entirely with the hearer. Every dedicated minister of Jesus Christ takes great care that the failure to hear truths from God does not lie with him. In his preparation and delivery he himself is aware of God, of the work of Christ, and of the work of the Spirit. This is not simply an intellectual acknowledgement on his part that God, Christ, and the Spirit are realities. Instead it involves a vital fellowship with God the Father, with Christ the Son, and with the indwelling Holy Spirit.

If he follows the principles of hermeneutics, the preacher will make a good bridge or connection between the biblical meaning and the modern application. But fellowship with God is the indispensable element in building this all-important bridge. Where application is incisive, the sermon preparation and delivery possess both the note of revelational historicity (faithfulness to the original context) and a recapitulative applicability (an application in modern context as pertinent as the application in the ancient setting). The hearer, sensing that the preacher has applied the truths he is speaking about to his own life, then makes the application to himself and enters into the riches of God's truth.

Such preaching has power. Scripture becomes alive for those hearing it, for it has already become alive to the minister who preaches it. Whether it becomes alive to everyone in exactly the same way does not matter. Both hearer and minister are aware of a power within. Paul speaks of the Romans "as abounding in hope by the power of the Holy Spirit" (Rom. 15:13). In Ephesians he speaks of believers "being strengthened with power through his Spirit in the inward man" (Eph. 3:16). God's word in man's language means that human symbols are employed and that these symbols make God's truth alive and applicable to the individual. As faithful servants of God, we will consistently try to bring our hearers into this experience. Otherwise we become noisy brass gongs and clashing cymbals (cf. I Cor. 13:1). The crucial question to ask oneself at the close of every sermon is: did the word (the proclaimed truth of God) become alive to me and to my hearers? The magnetic power of preaching where the word of God becomes alive is unmistakable. Such preaching has its own rewards. As we experience these rewards, we will strive harder for true, effective preaching. In such striving God is glorified. Preaching which brings no living message from God brings instead a sense of loss, both to the minister and to his hearers. Such emptiness need not be. *"Draw near* to God, and he will *draw near* to you" (James 4:7). "Now the law made nothing complete [perfect], but the introduction of the better hope [Christianity] did bring completion, through which hope *we are drawing near* to God" (Heb. 7:19). Closeness to God is essential for getting close to men and their needs.

Conclusion

XVIII Distortion through Artificial Assumptions

Every dedicated Christian wants to interpret the Bible according to sound principles. In fact, each to the best of his ability uses many sound principles. Most of the principles mentioned in this volume will not be new. The arrangement, the emphases, or the connections among the principles may constitute new insights to good interpretation. But even with the best principles, there is still at least one pitfall lurking beneath the steps of the interpreter. This is the danger of artificial assumptions that jeopardize his use of sound procedures.

NATURE OF ARTIFICIAL ASSUMPTIONS

It is impossible to compile a catalogue of artificial assumptions. Yet their nature may be clarified by some examples.

(1) An artificial assumption in biblical interpretation consists of any principle which is *foreign by its very nature* to the material which is being interpreted or is *unnecessary* to bring out and express the meaning of the biblical passage. For example, some people assume that later religious ideas are always much more developed than earlier ones. This is foreign to the biblical emphasis on the proneness of men to apostatize from God, to turn away from him. Religious ideas in such periods of revolt are *not* more developed than the earlier ideas when genuine faith and commitment were present.

(2) An artificial assumption in biblical interpretation consists in *any arbitrary application of legitimate principles* which implies that this principle leaves room for only one possible

369

meaning. For example, the grammatical interpreter might infer that a particular circumstantial participle must be causal. Yet it is the context that establishes the causal use of a circumstantial participle. In certain contexts the same participle might be interpreted as temporal or conditional or concessive or causal. The participle in Acts 19:2, having believed *(pisteusantes)*, is very likely temporal: "Did you receive the Holy Spirit *when* you believed?" Of course, if it were not for the context (which favors the temporal use), it could be causal: "Did you receive the Holy Spirit because you believed?" To say that the participle must be causal is an arbitrary application of a legitimate grammatical principle.

(3) An artificial assumption in biblical interpretation consists in *the importing of principles from the humanities or sciences into the biblical sphere* where they are not at home and for which they were not made. For example, an interpreter might assume that observable (secondary) causes are the sole concern of historians and any judgment which goes beyond these can have no standing since it represents unverified human opinion. See Chapter 1 under the heading "Valid and Invalid Principles."

(4) An artificial assumption in biblical interpretation consists in the use of *any principle which makes the passage say what the interpreter wants it to say* although the use of objective principles agreed on by interpreters of various persuasions show that such meaning for the passage is impossible. An example of this is the arbitrary declaration that the Greek word *apostasia* means "rapture" when it has no other meaning in the Koine writers than "rebellion" or "apostasy."[1]

(5) An artificial assumption in biblical interpretation consists in the use of *any principle that is contrary to any of the basic emphases of the New Testament.* This would include, for example, any proposition which denies the oneness of the people of God as taught in the New Testament.[2]

Assumptions like these distort the meaning which the interpreter draws from the passage. Excellent procedures of interpretation are tragically vitiated by such insidious assumptions. Often it is those assumptions which seem so harmless or even appear (before they are tested) to be so biblical that do the most damage. We must put to the test all things and hold fast to that which is good in reference to our interpretive procedures as well as to our conduct in general.

---

[1] See Bauer, p. 97. Heinrich Schlier, *"apostasia," TWNT*, I, 510-11. Liddell & Scott, p. 218.

[2] See Chapter 11, pp. 240-242; Chapter 13, pp. 301-303.

General Sources of Artificial Assumptions

One source of artificial assumptions lies in the fields of philosophy, theology, sociology, political science, psychology, etc. Competent specialists working in these areas usually reject in total the artificial assumption taken from their field into another area of learning, or they modify the principle for use in another area, and then, of course, the principle loses its artificial or synthetic character.[3]

Interpretation is also distorted if we become enamored with some minor element of the Bible and then see that element everywhere. If a sectarian emphasis dominates our interest, we can make any passage a prelude to our favorite theme. Therefore, any out-of-balance interest, even if it is in a major element of the Bible, harms the interpreter. He loses a true sense of perspective. Once lost, a balanced perspective is difficult to regain. Under the illusion of being exhaustive in our study, we "find" what we are looking for in places where no one else has ever seen it.

We are rarely aware of where our artificial assumptions come from even if we are conscious of their deleterious effects on our interpretation. We may know that someone taught this to us. We may be able to cite numerous works that teach the same thing, but this only proves that unsupported assumptions can be popularized almost as easily as sound ones. The best thing to do with artificial assumptions is forget them. To dwell upon their history accords them far more attention than they deserve. Nevertheless, they all have a history, and the number of those who have been deceived by their apparent plausibility is often appallingly large.

Areas Often Plagued by Artificial Assumptions

The three areas of general hermeneutics have all been invaded by synthetic or unnatural ways of treating the material. Works which claim to interpret the Bible often illustrate improper procedures in handling the biblical data in matters of context, language, or history and culture. Non-parallel material is introduced to override the clear demands of the context on the assumption that it "unfolds" the meaning. English ideas of time are sometimes introduced into Greek and Hebrew tenses although the particular forms in Greek or Hebrew deal with kind of action rather than time of action. Some interpreters

3 See Chapter 1, pp. 10-19.

assume that the Israelites borrowed certain practices and festivals from neighboring nations even though there may be no supporting evidence to establish such a connection. One example is the assumption that Israel had an enthronement festival *each* year to mark the anniversary of the ascension of the monarch to his throne. The pageantry of such an affair is said to explain some of the phenomena in the Psalms. Or the spread of idolatrous practices is claimed as an indication of the spread of other features of group and national life. But without clearcut evidence, such conjectures should never be elevated to controlling principles.

In the area of special hermeneutics all sorts of strange assumptions creep in. This is particularly true regarding extended figures of speech—especially parables, typology, prophecy, doctrinal teachings, and devotion and conduct. In any one of these, people who ride hobbies are almost certain to be absorbed in peculiar axioms or approaches. Unfortunately, sincerity and piety are no protection against poorly devised approaches. Every interpreter has a solemn duty diligently to free these areas from assumptions which would distort the meaning.

EXCLUSION OF ARTIFICIAL ASSUMPTIONS

Let us examine briefly one specific passage: I John 2:18-27. We will observe possible assumptions and conclusions working together to produce unsatisfactory interpretation of particular points in the passage. The passage deals with two main themes: those who deny the faith, and a clearcut differentiation between truth and falsehood.[4]

In verse 18 John addresses his readers as "children" and declares twice that it is the last hour. From the article in the English translation, where it certainly belongs, we might assume that the article is to be stressed: it is *the* last hour. But John did not want the article stressed. The article does not appear at all in Greek. The noun "hour" is modified by an adjective "last" which makes the noun definite. Further, this expression precedes the verb and this position preceding the verb "to be" may also indicate definiteness. But there is no stress here on individual identity or particularity. Such an emphasis would demand the article in the Greek text.[5] John

---

[4] Cf. Amos Niven Wilder, "The First, Second, and Third Epistles of John," *Interpreter's Bible*, XII, 242-250.

[5] For the distinctions between definiteness and individual identity or particularity see Dana and Mantey, pp. 137-153; A. T. Robertson, *A Grammar of the Greek New Testament in the Light of Historical Research*, p. 756. Note also the discussion of Blass, Debrunner, Funk, paragraph 273.

stresses the definiteness of the quality of the time: "[the] last hour [as far as the present age of the world's existence is concerned] it is." The material not in brackets is literally what John says. The material in the brackets is what the syntax shows that he means. The time in which John found himself had the qualitative earmarks of the consummation of the age. The presence of many antichrists was a definite indication. Another generation will also have the same qualitative signs that John saw and some that he did not see. At Christ's return it will indeed be "*the* last hour." Such value judgments—last hour and *the* last hour—can be made only from a perspective in history. Modern interpreters who make such distinctions do so because of their perspective and because of the basic New Testament belief in the return of Christ into history.

Someone might assume that "many" antichrists implies there is no personal, individual Antichrist. But this was not John's thought. His readers had been taught that the Antichrist is coming. This is what they heard. To show that this was no vague generality, John adds "even now many antichrists have come." He looks at the plurality of antichrists—those who deny that Jesus is the Messiah and thereby put themselves unequivocally against Christ—as proof of the eventual emergence of one supreme foe of Christ. *The* Antichrist who was already present and who was *the* liar was in his day much like the later model except that the latter will have greater power and destructiveness. In attitude they share the same outlook and make the same response.

In reading verse 20 in the King James Version the interpreter could assume that because the believer has an anointing from the Holy One—by anointing John certainly seems to mean the Holy Spirit—he knows all things. Taking this statement in its broadest possible meaning, John would be saying that the Christian has universal knowledge. Or limiting it somewhat, the Christian would know all things which pertain to the truth. But the best textual manuscripts (B, aleph) have a different reading which puts an entirely different light upon the passage: "And you have an anointing from the Holy One, and you all know [about this anointing]." Textual criticism must be utilized by the interpreter to prevent him from wrong assumptions drawn from the late Byzantine (Koine) text.

In historical-cultural studies it is possible to make generalizations such as that the Messiahship of Jesus was no longer important after the fall of Jerusalem. The letters of John were apparently written during the last ten or fifteen years of the first century. Yet verse 22 stresses the importance of confessing that Jesus is the Messiah. The one denying the Messiahship is the Antichrist. Hence it is an artificial assumption to say that after the fall of Jerusalem the Messiahship of Jesus was no longer important. Such an erroneous assumption could blind the interpreter to the full significance of I John 2:22.

Artificial assumptions can be avoided only by a growing awareness of the many factors that influence meaning in any passage. The fact that an assumption has been common for a long time does not make it valid. Distortion because of completely invalid principles, partly invalid principles, or even slightly invalid principles is still distortion. Because we are still erring and finite, distortion will dog our steps and discourage us. But we must be forever discontented with distortion. The One who set us free is worthy of our best, and to that goal we will bend all of our interpretive efforts.

XIX Balance through Care and Practice

This book is not meant to help its readers "grade" the interpreters they hear or read. *It is meant rather to help every reader train to become a better interpreter himself.* Any training program, whether in business, in recreation, or in interpretation, demands constant effort. Practice is essential for improvement.

THE MEANING OF BALANCE

An interpreter who has balance in interpretation is somewhat like the swimmer who has mastered the main swimming strokes. There is freedom and yet adherence to correct procedure.

The balanced interpreter is aware of all the elements that must be taken into account to interpret correctly. A working awareness of these elements comes slowly and painstakingly—long after we have intellectually accepted the fact of them. But we must still begin with a factual knowledge of the elements involved. The chapter titles under general and special hermeneutics provide a concise compendium of all these elements. The principles and techniques of each area vary. But all of these procedures have the same objective: *to unfold what the passage meant to the human author (as he was energized by God to convey a specific message) and original readers and what the passage means to us today.*

Balance involves not only an awareness of the elements but also a co-ordination of the elements. If I want to learn how to swim the various strokes correctly, I can sit down with a swimming manual and find out exactly what the arms and legs are supposed to do. But when I get into the water and try to co-or-

dinate all of my muscles so that I glide easily through the water,
I find that co-ordination is a skill to be mastered, not a series of
rules to be memorized. So it is in interpretation. It takes skill
to bring together all the elements needed to interpret any one
passage correctly. When we are preoccupied with one set of
factors, we may temporarily forget other equally basic procedures. With practice, however, correct procedures become a part
of us and coordination comes naturally.

With experience the interpreter who learns to coordinate all
of the elements also learns to judge the relative importance of
each of these elements. Language may not seem too important
to the Christian who has read his Bible in English. But when
he sees how language helps the interpreter to get at the meaning, he puts the knowledge of language high on the scale of
importance. When the interpreter becomes aware of the difference between literal and figurative language and why figurative
language is so indispensable in conveying the truths of God, his
respect grows for figurative language.

Context, language, history and culture, typology, symbols
and symbolical action as well as figurative language all play a
vital role in prophecy. Consequently, prophecy to the experienced interpreter becomes far more than forthtelling and foretelling. He sees it as a profoundly complex interweaving of
many factors. Because he knows what prophecy involves, it
ranks high on his scale of importance. He is not content,
however, with a pseudo-sophisticated approach to prophecy that
gives the illusion of organizing and arranging the interpretation of prophetic materials into a complete picture of God's
future course of action. He knows that such an approach is
built on artificial assumptions and feeds curiosity with an
event-centered watchfulness instead of a Christ-centered alertness. It is a Christ-centered alertness that produces Christians
who stand erect and lift up their heads when they begin to
see the signs of consummation because they know their redemption is drawing near (cf. Luke 21:28). For them the consummation of history is no abstract outline of events but a
period like all other periods in the world's history in which
Christians are to demonstrate their faithfulness to God. It will
be unlike all other periods because of the collision of forces involved (wrath of Satan [Rev. 12:12], wrath of the nations [Rev.
11:18], and wrath of God [Rev. 11:18]).

Coordination and true balance demand a personal appropriation of the principles. Hence no principles of biblical interpretation can ever be considered as mechanical rules. They can

never be applied the way factors are manipulated on a slide rule that will automatically give a correct answer. Rather the procedures are guides for active, alert minds to enter into a richer understanding of truths that have absorbed men for centuries. Hence the principles are to make possible the communicating of person (original writer) with person (reader), of God with his creatures and with those who are redeemed by his grace. There is no impersonal way of getting at meaning, but there are principles to help persons discover meaning. These principles become a part of the person (reader or interpreter). Consequently the result is that of person (biblical writer) meeting person (biblical interpreter), of true communication from one to the other.

CORRECTING BAD HABITS

The first step in correcting bad habits in our thinking process is to admit that we have such habits. This is not easy for any of us. It is characteristic of those who have great skill in any talent or profession to affirm their interest in increased effectiveness. They will observe very carefully any particular habit or motion which tends to make their performance ineffective. Interpreters should do likewise. We can all interpret better than we are doing right now.

Bad habits come from two sources: (1) faulty principles, or (2) ignoring good principles which the interpreter knows intellectually but has never bothered to practice. Many interpreters are not aware of the faulty principles they are following. They may be unable to judge whether they are interpreting well or poorly. Therefore, a knowledge of sound principles is essential to discover and root out bad habits. For example, to disregard context is a bad fault, but even well-trained interpreters occasionally find themselves doing this. If biblical phraseology can be used to drive home a certain point, many people will employ it for that purpose without stopping to ask whether this was the idea the biblical writer had in mind. In doing this, the interpreter may be using the authority of the Bible to put forth an idea that in reality finds no support in the Bible although it is expressed in biblical phraseology.

Bad habits must be recognized. Good habits must be faithfully practiced. Hence, will power is essential in correcting bad habits in interpretation. We must determine to so interpret the Bible that it is not our authority being unfolded but the authority of the biblical writer who proclaimed God's truth. As God's faithful servant he proclaimed God's message. Therefore, bad habits of interpretation often involve a subtle transfer of authority. Human miscellany is a poor substitute for a divine message.

FORMING GOOD HABITS

To cultivate good habits, we must begin by doing a thing the right way. The right way often seems at first to be more difficult than doing it some other way. But as soon as facility is gained the superiority of the right way becomes apparent.

In forming good habits of interpretation, we must constantly depend on the Holy Spirit. This does not mean that the Holy Spirit will point out our interpretive faults whether we are concerned about them or not. But a dependence on the Holy Spirit and an openness to his reproof will help our faltering will power. He will help us to discipline our thinking, to carry out the task of interpretation in a way that is honoring to God.

It often helps us to form good habits of interpreting the Bible if we talk over procedures with fellow Christians who come from different denominational backgrounds. If we talk only to those who interpret "our way," we begin to assume that "our way" is the correct way. We never get a chance to see a more excellent way in actual operation. The mutual exchange of ideas in the realm of interpretation may lead us to the use of a better atlas or a better bible dictionary than we have been using. Constant exchange of ideas provides a positive incentive for high quality interpretation.

THE ONE TO WHOM WE MUST GIVE ACCOUNT

Perhaps even interpreters forget that we must give an account for our interpretation. Jesus said that men will give account in the day of judgment for every idle or useless word (Matt. 12:36). Falsity in the realm of interpretation is not going to be ignored simply because the interpreter was sincere. Wrong interpretations often lead other Christians astray. Occasionally such error may indicate that the interpreter is not at peace with God and the interpretive deviation is an indication of a deeper and more fundamental disturbance. Interpreters need to remember the words of James: "Do not become many teachers, my brothers, because you know that we will receive the greater condemnation" (James 3:1). A teacher or interpreter stands at a peculiar point. Often he has the opportunity to open the Scripture in such a way that a fellow Christian can step out of shadows into great light. How tragic if he only leads his

Christian brother into some bypass where he becomes occupied with things of little eternal significance. How we handle the word of God at such points may influence not only the destiny of another person but also the fruit which this life can bring to God.

"All things," declares the writer of Hebrews, "are naked and laid bare to his eyes, with whom is our account" (Heb. 4:13). If I am aware that I must give account for how I interpret, then I will be thoroughly honest in my interpretation. Where I am not sure, I will so indicate. Where I am very sure, my assurance will rest not in any emotional feeling or reasoning but in a quiet survey of the objective factors upon which it rests. Dogmatism on subjects and matters where the evidence is not clear is out of place. The man who knows that he must give account for how he interprets has no time for a dogmatism on debatable questions. Rather he humbly and contritely bows himself before God and cries out with the psalmist: "Let the favor of the Lord our God be upon us, and establish thou the work of our hands upon us, yea, the work of our hands establish thou it" (Ps. 90:17). God must establish our interpretive word. Then this interpretive word can serve a useful purpose in extolling the word of the Lord which abides forever.

General Bibliography

General Bibliography*

Ahern, Barnabas M., Sullivan, Kathryn, and Heidt, William G., (eds.), *New Testament Reading Guide*. 14 vols. Collegeville, Minnesota: The Liturgical Press, 1960.

Aland, Kurt, *Kurzgefasste Liste der griechischen Handschriften des Neuen Testaments*. Vol. I: *Gesammtübersicht*. West Berlin: Walter de Gruyter & Co., 1961.

————, *Kurzgefasste Liste der griechischen Handschriften des Neuen Testaments*. Vol. II: *Einzelübersichten*. West Berlin: Walter de Gruyter & Co., to be published.

————, *Das Neue Testament auf Papyrus*, Vol. IV. West Berlin: Walter de Gruyter & Co., to be published.

Aland, Kurt and Rissenfeld, H., *Vollständige Konkordanz des griechischen Neuen Testaments*. Unter Zugrundlegung aller modernen kritischen Textausgaben und des textus receptus. Vol. III. West Berlin: Walter de Gruyter & Co., to be published.

Albright, William F., "The Old Testament World." *The Interpreter's Bible*, ed. George Arthur Buttrick *et al.*; Vol. I. New York and Nashville: Abingdon Press, 1951-57.

Allo, E. B., *Saint Paul: Seconde Épître aux Corinthiens*. Deuxième edition. J. Gabalda et Cie., 1956.

Anderson, B., *Understanding the Old Testament*. Englewood Cliffs, New Jersey: Prentice-Hall, 1957.

Barr, James, *Biblical Words for Time*, Studies in Biblical Theology series. Naperville, Illinois: Alec R. Allenson, Inc., 1962.

————, *The Semantics of Biblical Language*. London: Oxford University Press, 1961.

Bauer, H. and Leander, P., *Grammatik des Biblisch-Aramäisch*. Halle: Max Niemeyer, 1927.

Bauer, H. and Leander, F., *Historische Grammatik der hebräischen Sprache des Alten Testaments*. Halle: Max Niemeyer, 1929.

————, *Kurzgefasste biblisch-aramäische Grammatik*. Halle: Max Niemeyer, 1929.

---

* Inclusion of any book or article does not mean endorsement or agreement with all of its contents.

Bauer, Walter, *A Greek-English Lexicon of the New Testament*. Ed. and tr., William F. Arndt and F. Wilbur Gingrich. Chicago: The University of Chicago Press, 1957.

Baumgärtel, Friedrich, "Das hermeneutische Problem des Alten Testaments." *Probleme alttestamentlicher Hermeneutik*. Herausgegeben von Claus Westermann. München: Chr. Kaiser, 1960.

Beasley-Murray, G. R., "Revelation." *The New Bible Commentary*. Eds., F. Davidson, A. M. Stibbs, and E. F. Kevan. Grand Rapids: Wm. B. Eerdmans Publishing Co., 1956.

Benedict, Ruth, *Patterns of Culture*. New York: Houghton Mifflin (Mentor), 1934.

Berkhof, Louis, *Principles of Biblical Interpretation*. Grand Rapids: Baker Book House, 1950.

————, *Systematic Theology*. 4th revised and enlarged edition. Grand Rapids: Wm. B. Eerdmans Publishing Co., 1949.

Blackman, A. C., *Biblical Interpretation*. Philadelphia: The Westminster Press, 1957.

Blass, F., Debrunner, Albert, and Funk, Robert W., *A Greek Grammar of the New Testament and Other Early Christian Literature*. A translation and revision of the 9th-10th German edition incorporating supplementary notes of A. Debrunner. Chicago: The University of Chicago Press, 1961.

Bonsirven, Joseph, *Exégèse Rabbinique et Exégèse Paulinienne*. Paris: Beaushesne et Ses Fils, 1938.

Bowie, Walter Russell, "The Teaching of Jesus: III. The Parables." *The Interpreter's Bible*. Ed., George Arthur Buttrick. Vol. III. New York and Nashville: Abingdon Cokesbury Press, 1951.

Brown, Francis, Driver, Samuel R., and Briggs, Charles Augustus (eds.), *A Hebrew and English Lexicon of the Old Testament with an Appendix Containing the Biblical Aramaic*. Based on the Lexicon of William Gesenius as translated by Edward Robinson. Boston and New York: Houghton Mifflin Co., 1907.

Bruce, Alexander Balmain, *The Parabolic Teaching of Christ*. A Systematic and Critical Study of the Parables of Our Lord. 5th revised edition. New York: George H. Doran Co., 1884.

Bruce, F. F., "The Poetry of the Old Testament." *The New Bible Commentary*. Eds., F. Davidson, A. M. Stibbs, and E. F. Kevan. Grand Rapids: Wm. B. Eerdmans Publishing Co., 1956.

Bultmann, Rudolf, *Existence and Faith*. Shorter writings selected, translated, and introduced by Schubert M. Ogden. New York: Meridian Books, Inc., 1960.

————, *Jesus Christ and Mythology*. New York: Charles Scribner's Sons, 1958.

————, *Jesus and the Word*. Tr., Louise Pettibone Smith. New York: Charles Scribner's Sons, 1934, 1958.

————, *The Presence of Eternity*. History and Eschatology. The Gifford Lectures, 1955. New York: Harper and Brothers, 1957.

————, *Primitive Christianity in Its Contemporary Setting*. Tr., R. H. Fuller. New York: Meridian Books, Inc., 1956.

————, *Theology of the New Testament*. 2 vols. Tr., Kendrick Grobel. New York: Charles Scribner's Sons, 1954-55.

Bultmann, Rudolf; Lohmeyer, Ernst; Schniewind, Julius; Thielicke, Helmut; and Farrer, Austin, *Kerygma and Myth*. A Theological Debate. Ed., Hans Werner Bartsch. Revised edition of this translation by Reginald H. Fuller. New York: Harper and Brothers, 1961.

Burgon, John W. and Miller, Edward, *The Traditional Text of the Holy Gospels*. 1896.

Burrows, Millar, *The Dead Sea Scrolls*. With translations by the author. New York: The Viking Press, 1955.

———, *More Light on the Dead Sea Scrolls*. New Scrolls and New Interpretations with Translations of Important Recent Discoveries. New York: The Viking Press, 1958.

Burton, Ernest De Witt and Goodspeed, Edgar J., *A Harmony of the Synoptic Gospels in Greek*. Chicago: The University of Chicago Press, 1947.

Buttrick, George Arthur (ed.), *The Interpreter's Bible*. 12 vols. New York and Nashville: Abingdon Press, 1951-57.

Calvin, John, *Commentary on the Acts of the Apostles*. Tr., Henry Beveridge, 1844. Reprint, Grand Rapids: Wm. B. Eerdmans Publishing Co.

———, *Commentary on the Book of Psalms*. Tr., Rev. James Anderson. 1845. Reprint, Grand Rapids: Wm. B. Eerdmans Publishing Co.

———, *Commentary on a Harmony of the Evangelists: Matthew, Mark, and Luke*. Tr., William Pringle. 1845. Reprint: Grand Rapids: Wm. B. Eerdmans Publishing Co.

Charles, R. H. (ed.), *The Apocrypha and Pseudepigrapha of the Old Testament*. Oxford: At the Clarendon Press, 1913.

Childs, Brevard S., "Memory and History." *Memory and Tradition in Israel*. Studies in Biblical Theology series. Naperville, Illinois: Alec R. Allenson, 1962.

Clark, Gordon H., *Religion, Reason, and Revelation*. Philadelphia: Presbyterian and Reformed Publishing Company, 1961.

Coates, J. R. and Kingdon, H. P., *Bible Key Words*. Tr. and ed. from Kittel's *Theologisches Wörterbuch zum Neuen Testament*. New York: Harper and Brothers, 1958.

Cremer, Herman, *Biblico-Theological Lexicon of New Testament Greek*. Tr., William Urwick. 4th English edition with Supplement. Edinburgh: T. & T. Clark, 1895.

Cruden, Alexander, *Cruden's Complete Concordance to the Old and New Testaments*. Eds., A. D. Adams, C. H. Irwin, and S. A. Waters. Philadelphia: John C. Winston Company, 1930.

Cullmann, Oscar, *Christ and Time*. The Primitive Christian Conception of Time and History. Tr., Floyd V. Filson, Philadelphia: The Westminster Press, 1950.

Dana, H. E. and Mantey, Julius R., *A Manual Grammar of the Greek New Testament*. 2nd edition (only minor changes). New York: The Macmillan Co., 1957.

Danker, Frederick W., *Multipurpose Tools for Bible Study*. St. Louis: Concordia Publishing House, 1960.

Davidson, F., Stibbs, A. M., and Kevan, E. F. (eds.), *The New Bible Commentary*. Grand Rapids: Wm. B. Eerdmans Publishing Co., 1956.

Denzinger, Henry, *The Sources of Catholic Dogma*. Tr., Roy J. Deferrari from the 13th edition of Henry Denzinger's *Enchiridion Symbolorum*. St. Louis: B. Herder Book Co., 1957.

Dodd, Charles Harold, *The Parables of the Kingdom*. New York: Charles Scribner's Sons, 1936.

Duplacy, Jean, *Où en Est la Critique Textuelle du Nouveau Testament?* Paris: J. Gabalda et Cie., 1957.

Edersheim, Alfred, *The Life and Times of Jesus the Messiah*. 2 vols. 3rd edition, 1927. Reprint, Grand Rapids: Wm. B. Eerdmans Publishing Co.

Eichrodt, Walther, "Ist die typologische Exegese sachgemässe Exegese?" *Probleme alttestamentlicher Hermeneutik*. Ed., Claus Westermann. München: Chr. Kaiser Verlag, 1960.

Ellis, Earle. *Paul's Use of the Old Testament.* Grand Rapids: Wm. B. Eerdmans Publishing Co., 1957.

Englishman's Greek Concordance of the New Testament. 9th edition. London: Samuel Bagster and Sons, Ltd., 1903.

Englishman's Hebrew and Chaldee Concordance of the Old Testament. Being an Attempt at a Verbal Connexion between the Original and the English Translation with Indexes, A List of the Proper Names and Their Occurrences, etc. 2 vols. London: Longman, Green, Brown, and Longmans, 1843.

Enslin, Morton Scott, *Christian Beginnings.* New York and London: Harper and Brothers Publishers, 1938.

Epstein, I., *The Babylonian Talmud.* 35 vols. London: Soncino Press, 1948.

Fairweather, William, *The Background of the Gospels,* or Judaism in the Period Between the Old and New Testaments. 4th edition. Edinburgh: T. & T. Clark, 1926.

Farmer, H. H., "The Bible: Its Significance and Authority." *The Interpreter's Bible.* Ed., George Arthur Buttrick *et al.* Vol. I. New York and Nashville: Abingdon Press, 1951-57.

Farrar, F. W., *History of Interpretation.* Bampton Lectures, 1885. New York: E. P. Dutton and Co., 1886.

Feine, Paul, *Theologie des Neuen Testaments.* Achte, durchgesehene Auflage. Berlin: Evangelische Verlagsanstalt, 1951.

Filson, Floyd V., "The Gospel of Christ the Risen Lord." *The New Testament Against Its Environment.* Studies in Biblical Theology series. London: SCM Press, 1950.

Fuchs, D. Ernst, *Hermeneutik.* Stuttgart: F. R. Müllerschön Verlag, 1954.

———, *Zum hermeneutischen Problem in der Theologie.* Die existentiale Interpretation. Tübingen: J. C. B. Mohr (Paul Siebeck), 1959.

Gadamer, Hans-Georg, *Wahrheit und Methode.* Grundzüge einer philosophischen Hermeneutik. Tübingen: J. C. B. Mohr (Paul Siebeck), 1960.

Gilkey, Langdon B., "Cosmology, Ontology, and the Travail of Biblical Language." *The Journal of Religion.* Vol. XLI. No. 3 (July, 1961), pp. 194-204.

Goodspeed, Edgar J., *Problems of New Testament Translation.* Chicago: University of Chicago Press, 1945.

Goodwin, W. W. and Gulick, Charles Burton, *Greek Grammar.* Boston: Ginn and Co., 1930.

Goppelt, Leonhard, *Typos: Die Deutung des Alten Testaments im Neuen.* Gütersloh: 1939.

Gottwald, N. K., "Poetry, Hebrew." *The Interpreter's Dictionary of the Bible.* Ed., George Arthur Buttrick *et al.* 4 vols. New York and Nashville: Abingdon Press, 1962.

Grant, Robert M., *The Bible in the Church.* A Short History of Interpretation. New York: The Macmillan Co., 1948.

———, "History of the Interpretation of the Bible: I. Ancient Period." *The Interpreter's Bible.* Ed., George Arthur Buttrick *et al.* Vol. I. New York and Nashville: Abingdon Cokesbury Press, 1951-57.

Gray, George B., *The Forms of Hebrew Poetry.* London: Hodder and Stoughton, 1915.

Grundmann, Walter, "*dunamis/dunamai.*" *Theologisches Wörterbuch zum Neuen Testament.* Ed., Gerhard Kittel. Vol. II. Stuttgart: Verlag von W. Kohlhammer, 1935.

Gunkel, Hermann, *Die Psalmen. Göttinger Handkommentar zum Alten Testament.* Ed., W. Nowack. Göttingen: Vandenhoeck & Ruprecht, 1926.

Harrison, Everett F. and Pfeiffer, Charles (eds.), *The Wycliffe Bible Commentary*. Chicago: The Moody Press, 1962.

Hartmann, Benedict, *Hebräische Grammatik*. Wiesbaden: Otto Harrassowitz, 1961.

Hatch, Edwin and Redpath, Henry A., *A Concordance to the Septuagint and Other Greek Versions of the Old Testament* (Including the Apocryphal Books). 2 vols. Graz, Austria: Akademische Druck—U. Verlagsanstalt, 1954.

Hauck, Friedrich, *"parabole," Theologisches Wörterbuch zum Neuen Testament*. Ed., Gerhard Friedrich. Vol. V. Stuttgart: W. Kohlhammer Verlag, 1954.

Heine, G., *Synonyme des neutestamentlichen Griechisch*. 1898.

Hofmann, Johann Christian Konrad von, *Interpreting the Bible*. Tr., Christian Preus with a foreword by Otto A. Piper. Minneapolis: Augsburg Publishing House, 1959.

Holmes, Arthur F., "Three Ways of Doing Philosophy." *The Journal of Religion*. Vol. XLI. No. 3 (July, 1961), pp. 206-212.

————, "The Methodology of Christian Philosophy." *The Journal of Religion*. Vol. XLII. No. 3 (July, 1962), pp. 220-222.

Howes, Mary Ruth, "Jesus' Use of Comparative Imagery in the Gospel of Luke." Unpublished Master's Thesis, The Graduate School, Wheaton College, 1957.

Huck, Albert, *Synopsis of the First Three Gospels*. Revised by Hans Lietzmann. English edition by F. L. Cross. 9th edition. Oxford: B. H. Blackwell, 1949.

Hunter, Archibald M., *Interpreting the Parables*. Philadelphia: The Westminster Press, 1960.

Jastrow, Marcus (ed.), *A Dictionary of the Targumim, Talmud Babli and Yerushalmi, and the Other Midrashic Literature*. 2 vols. New York: Pardes Publishing House, 1959.

Jeremias, Joachim, *The Parables of Jesus*. Tr., S. H. Hooke. London: SCM Press, Ltd., 1954.

Jülicher, Adolf, *Die Gleichnisreden Jesu*. 2 vols. 2nd edition of Vol. I. Tübingen: J. C. B. Mohr, 1910.

Kantzer, Kenneth S., "The Authority of the Bible." *The Word for This Century*. Ed., Merrill C. Tenney. New York: Oxford University Press, 1960.

Kautzsch, H. and Cowley, A. H., *Gesenius' Hebrew Grammar*. 2nd English edition. Revised in accordance with the 28th German edition. Oxford: At the Clarendon Press, 1910.

Keil, Carl F., *Biblical Commentary on the Prophecies of Ezekiel*. Tr., James Martin. 2 vols., 1876. Reprint: Grand Rapids: Wm. B. Eerdmans Publishing Co.

Keil, C. F. and Delitzsch, F., *Biblical Commentary on the Old Testament*. Tr., James Martin. Vol. III: *The Pentateuch*, 1885. Reprint, Grand Rapids: Wm. B. Eerdmans Publishing Co.

Kittel, Gerhard and Friedrich, Gerhard (eds.), *Theologisches Wörterbuch zum Neuen Testament*. 8 vols. (when complete). Stuttgart: Verlag W. Kohlhammer, GMBH, 1933—. English tr., G. W. Bromiley. Grand Rapids: Wm. B. Eerdmans Publishing Co., 1963—.

Klassen, William and Snyder, Graydon F. (eds.), *Current Issues in New Testament Interpretation*. Essays in honor of Otto A. Piper. New York: Harper and Brothers, 1962.

Koehler, Ludwig and Baumgartner, Walter, *Lexicon in Veteris Testamenti Libros*. A Dictionary of the Hebrew Old Testament and Aramaic parts of the Old Testament. Grand Rapids: Wm. B. Eerdmans Publishing Co., 1957.

Kraeling, Emil G., *Rand McNally Bible Atlas*. New York: Rand McNally, 1956.

Kraft, Charles Franklin, *The Strophic Structure of Hebrew Poetry*. Chicago: The University of Chicago Press, 1938.

Krämer, Helmut; Rendtorff, Rudolf; Meyer, Rudolf; and Friedrich, Gerhard, *"Prophētēs," "prophētis," "prophēteuō," "prophēteia," "prophētikos," "pseudoprophētēs." Theologisches Wörterbuch zum Neuen Testament.* Ed., Gerhard Friedrich, Vol. VI. Stuttgart: Verlag von W. Kohlhammer, 1959.

Kroeber, Alfred Lewis, *Anthropology:* Race, Language, Culture, Psychology, Prehistory. New York: Harcourt, Brace, and Co., 1948.

Kümmel, Werner George, Third Chapter, Fifth Section: "Exegesis and Its Hermeneutical Foundation." *Das Neue Testament: Geschichte der Erforschung seiner Probleme.* Freiburg/München: Verlag Karl Alber, 1958.

Lampe, G. W. H. and Woolcombe, J. J., *Essays on Typology.* Studies in Biblical Theology series. London: SCM Press, 1957.

Lewis, C. S., *Reflections on the Psalms.* New York: Harcourt, Brace and Co., 1958.

Liddell, Henry George and Scott, Robert, *A Greek English Lexicon.* 2 vols. 9th edition. A new edition revised and augmented throughout by Henry S. Jones and Roderick McKenzie. Oxford: At the Clarendon Press, 1940.

Lisowsky, Gerhard, *Konkordanz zum Hebräischen Alten Testament.* Nach dem von Paul Kahle in der Biblia Hebraica. Ed., R. Kittel, Besorgten masoretischen Text. Unter verantwortlicher Mitwirkung, Prof. Leonhard Rost. Stuttgart: Privileg. Württ. Bibelanstalt, 1958.

Lowth, Robert, *Lectures on the Sacred Poetry of the Hebrews.* Ed. and tr., Calvin E. Stowe. Andover: 1829.

Lubac, Henri de, "Typologie et Allegorisme." *Recherches de Science Religieuse.* Vol. XXXIV. 1947, 180-226.

Mandelkern, Solomon, *Veteris Testamenti Concordantiae: Hebraicae Atque Chaldaicae.* ed. Altera Locupletissime Aucta et Emendata Cura F. Margolin. 2 vols. Graz: Akademische Druck-U. Verlagsanstalt, 1955.

Marti, D. Karl, *Kurzgefasste Grammatik des biblisch-aramäischen Sprache.* Dritte Verbesserte Auflage. Berlin: Verlag von Reuter und Reichard, 1925.

McKenzie, John L., "Problems of Hermeneutics in Roman Catholic Exegesis." *Journal of Biblical Literature.* Vol. LXXVII (Sept., 1958), pp. 197-204.

McNeill, John T., "History of the Interpretation of the Bible: II, Medieval and Reformation Period." *The Interpreter's Bible.* Ed., George Arthur Buttrick *et al.* Vol. I. New York and Nashville: Abingdon Cokesbury Press, 1951-57.

Metzger, Bruce M., "The Language of the New Testament." *The Interpreter's Bible.* Ed., George Arthur Buttrick *et al.* Vol. VII. New York and Nashville: Abingdon Cokesbury Press, 1951-57.

Milik, J. T., *Ten Years of Discovery in the Wilderness of Judea.* Tr., J. Strugnell. Studies in Biblical Theology series. Naperville, Illinois: Alec R. Allenson, 1959.

Minear, Paul Sevier, *Eyes of Faith.* A Study in the Biblical Point of View. London: Lutterworth Press, 1948.

Moreau, Jules Laurence, *Language and Religious Language.* A Study in the Dynamics of Translation. Philadelphia: The Westminster Press, 1961.

Moulton, James Hope and Milligan, George, *The Vocabulary of the Greek Testament*. Illustrated from the Papyri and Other Non-Literary Sources. Grand Rapids: Wm. B. Eerdmans Publishing Co., 1949.

Moulton, Richard G., *The Literary Study of the Bible*. An Account of the Leading Forms of Literature Represented in the Sacred Writings. Revised and partly re-written. Boston: D. C. Heath and Co., 1899.

Moulton, W. F. and Geden, A. S., *A Concordance to the Greek New Testament*. According to the text of Westcott and Hort, Tischendorf, and the English revisers. 2nd edition. New York: Charles Scribner's Sons, 1900.

Muilenburg, James, "Preface to Hermeneutics." *Journal of Biblical Literature*. Vol. LXXVII (March, 1958), pp. 18-26.

Nestle, D. Eberhard and Nestle, D. Erwin, *Novum Testamentum Graece*. 24th edition. Stuttgart: Privilegierte Württembergische Bibelanstalt, 1961.

Nida, Eugene A., *Message and Mission*. The Communication of the Christian Faith. New York: Harper and Brothers, 1960

Oesterley, W. O. E. and Robinson, Theodore H., "The Forms of Hebrew Poetry." *An Introduction to the Books of the Old Testament*. New York: The Macmillan Co., 1934.

Oxford Universal Dictionary on Historical Principles. Prepared by William Little, H. W. Fowler, J. Coulson. Revised and edited by C. T. Onions. 3rd edition, revised with Addenda. Oxford: At the Clarendon Press, 1955.

Parry, S. John, *The Pastoral Epistles with Introduction, Text, and Commentary*. Cambridge: The University Press, 1920.

Payne, J. Barton, *The Theology of the Older Testament*. Grand Rapids: Zondervan Publishing House, 1962.

Pfeiffer, Charles F. et al. (eds.), *Baker's Bible Atlas*. Grand Rapids: Baker Book House, 1961.

Pfeiffer, Robert H., *History of New Testament Times* with an Introduction to the Apocrypha. New York: Harper and Brothers Publishers, 1949.

———, *Introduction to the Old Testament*. New York: Harper and Brothers, 1941.

Pink, Arthur W., *Exposition of the Gospel of St. John*. Swengel, Pennsylvania: Bible Truth Depot, 1945.

Plummer, Alfred, *A Critical and Exegetical Commentary on the Gospel of Luke*. The International Critical Commentary. New York: Charles Scribner's Sons, 1914.

Procksch, Otto, " 'Wort Gottes' im AT," *Theologisches Wörterbuch zum Neuen Testament*. Ed., Gerhard Kittel. Vol. IV. Stuttgart: Verlag von W. Kohlhammer, 1942.

Ramm, Bernard, *Protestant Biblical Interpretation*. A Textbook of Hermeneutics for Conservative Protestants. Complete revised edition. Boston: W. A. Wilde Co., 1956.

Reese, Alexander, *The Approaching Advent of Christ*. London: Marshall, Morgan, and Scott, 1936.

Rengstorf, Karl Heinrich, "didaskalia." *Theologisches Wörterbuch zum Neuen Testament*. Ed., Gerhard Kittel. Vol. II. Stuttgart: Verlag von W. Kohlhammer, 1935.

———, "heterozugeō." *Theologisches Wörterbuch zum Neuen Testament*. Ed., Gerhard Kittel. Vol. II. Stuttgart: Verlag von W. Kohlhammer, 1935.

Richardson, Alan, *An Introduction to the Theology of the New Testament*. London: SCM Press, 1958.

Richardson, Alan and Schweitzer, Wolfgang (eds.), *Biblical Authority for Today*. A World Council of Churches Symposium on "The Biblical Authority for the Church's Social and Political Message Today." London: SCM Press, 1951.

Ristow, Helmut und Matthiae, Karl, *Der Historische Jesus und der Kerygmatische Christus*. Beitrage zum Christusverständnis im Forschung und Verkündigung. Berlin: Evangelische Verlagsanstalt, 1961.

Robertson, A. T. and Davis, W. Hersey, *A New Short Grammar of the Greek Testament*. For Students Familiar with the Elements of Greek. New York and London: Harper and Brothers, 1933.

Robertson, A. T., *A Grammar of the Greek New Testament in the Light of Historical Research*. 5th edition, 1931. Reprint, Nashville: Broadman Press.

Robinson, James M., *A New Quest of the Historical Jesus*. Studies in Biblical Theology series. London: SCM Press, 1959.

Robinson, Theodore Henry, *The Poetry of the Old Testament*. London: Gerald Duckworth and Co., 1947.

Rosenthal, Franz, *A Grammar of Biblical Aramaic*. Wiesbaden: Otto Harrassowitz, 1961.

Runes, Dagobert D., *Dictionary of Philosophy*. Paterson, New Jersey: Littlefield, Adams, and Co., 1961.

Rylaarsdam, J. Coert, "Exodus." *The Interpreter's Bible*. Ed., George Arthur Buttrick *et al.* Vol. I. New York and Nashville: Abingdon Press, 1951-57.

———, "The Problem of Faith and History in Biblical Interpretation," *Journal of Biblical Literature*. Vol. LXXVII (March, 1958), pp. 26-32.

Schmidt, Karl Ludwig, "Basileia." *Bible Key Words* from Gerhard Kittel's *Theologisches Wörterbuch zum Neuen Testament*. Tr. and ed., J. R. Coates and H. P. Kingdon. Vol. II. New York: Harper and Brothers, 1958.

———, "The Church." *Bible Key Words* from Gerhard Kittel's *Theologisches Wörterbuch zum Neuen Testament*. Tr. and ed., J. R. Coates. Vol. I. New York: Harper and Brothers, 1951.

Schmöller, Alfred, *Handkonkordanz zum griechischen Neuen Testament*. Text nach Nestle. Achte Auflage. Stuttgart: Privilegierte Würtembergische Bibelanstalt, 1949.

Schniewind, Julius, "A Reply to Bultmann." *Kerygma and Myth*. A Theological Debate. Ed., Hans Werner Bartsch. Revised edition of this translation by Reginald H. Fuller. New York: Harper and Brothers, 1961.

Schultz, Samuel J., *The Old Testament Speaks*. New York: Harper and Brothers, 1960.

Schürer, Emil, *A History of the Jewish People in the Time of Jesus Christ*. Tr., John Macpherson, Sophia Taylor, and Peter Christie. 2 divisions, 5 Vols. 2nd revised edition. Edinburgh, T & T Clark, 1890-93.

Schweitzer, Albert, *The Quest of the Historical Jesus*. Tr., W. Montgomery. 2nd edition. London: Black, 1911.

Scott, R. B. Y., "Isaiah: Chapters 1-39." *The Interpreter's Bible*. Ed., George Arthur Buttrick *et al.* Vol. V. New York and Nashville: Abingdon Press, 1951-57.

Shedd, Russell, *Man in Community*. A Study of St. Paul's Application of Old Testament and Early Jewish Conceptions of Human Solidarity. 1958. American section, Grand Rapids: Wm. B. Eerdmans Publishing Co., 1963.

Smart, James D., *The Interpretation of Scripture*. Philadelphia: The Westminster Press, 1961.

Snaith, Norman H., "The Language of the Old Testament." *The Interpreter's Bible*. Ed., George Arthur Buttrick *et al.* Vol. I. New York and Nashville: Abingdon Press, 1951-57.

Spicq, C., *Saint Paul: Les Épitres Pastorales*. Paris: J. Gabalda et Cie., 1947.

Stählin, Gustav, *"Muthos."* *Theologisches Wörterbuch zum Neuen Testament.* Ed., Gerhard Kittel. Vol. IV. Stuttgart: Verlag von W. Kohlhammer, 1942.

Stendahl, Krister, "Implication of Form Criticism and Tradition Criticism for Biblical Interpretation." *Journal of Biblical Literature.* Vol. LXXVII (March, 1958), pp. 23-28.

Strack, Herman L. and Billerbeck, Paul, *Kommentar zum Neuen Testament aus Talmud und Midrasch.* Vol. IV, Part 1: Neunzehnter Exkurs; "Der gute und der böse Trieb." München: C. H. Beck'sche Verlagsbuchhandlung, 1928.

Strong, Augustus Hopkins, *Systematic Theology.* Vol. III. Philadelphia: The Griffith and Rowland Press, 1907-09.

Strong, James, *The Exhaustive Concordance of the Bible.* New York: Abingdon Cokesbury Press, 1947.

Swete, Henry Barclay, *The Apocalypse of St. John.* The Greek Text with Introduction, Notes, and Indices. Reprint, Grand Rapids: Wm. B. Eerdmans Publishing Co., 1951.

Tasker, R. V. G. (ed.), *Tyndale Bible Commentaries.* Grand Rapids: Wm. B. Eerdmans Publishing Co., 1956—.

Taylor, Vincent, *The Text of the New Testament.* London: The Macmillan Company, 1961.

Tenney, Merrill C., *New Testament Survey.* Revised edition. Grand Rapids: Wm. B. Eerdmans Publishing Co., 1961.

Terrien, Samuel, "History of the Interpretation of the Bible: III, Modern Period." *The Interpreter's Bible.* Ed., George Arthur Buttrick *et al.* Vol. I. New York and Nashville: Abingdon Cokesbury Press, 1951-57.

Terry, Milton S., *Biblical Hermeneutics.* A Treatise on the Interpretation of the Old and New Testaments. Grand Rapids: Zondervan Publishing House, n.d.

Thompson, Samuel, "Philosophy and Theology: A Reply to Professor W. F. Zuurdeeg." *The Journal of Religion.* Vol. XL, No. 1 (January, 1960), pp. 9-18.

Tillich, Paul, *Systematic Theology.* Vol. I. Chicago: The University of Chicago Press, 1951.

Trench, R. C., *Synonyms of the New Testament.* 11th edition, 1890. Reprint, Grand Rapids: Wm. B. Eerdmans Publishing Co.

Trinquet, J., *"Abdias."* *La Sainte Bible.* Traduite en français sous la direction de l'École Biblique de Jerusalem. Paris: Les Édition Du Cerf, 1956.

Vos, Geerhardus, Chapter I: "The Nature and Method of Biblical Theology." *Biblical Theology: Old and New Testaments.* Grand Rapids: Wm. B. Eerdmans Publishing Co., 1948.

Vos, Howard, Harrison, Everett F., and Pfeiffer, Charles (eds.), *The Wycliffe Bible Commentary.* Chicago: The Moody Press, 1962.

Webster's New English Dictionary of the American Language. Cleveland and New York: The World Publishing Co., 1960.

Westcott, B. F., *The Gospel According to St. John.* The Greek Text with Introduction and Notes. 2 Vols. 1908. Reprint, Grand Rapids: Wm. B. Eerdmans Publishing Co.

Westcott, Brooke Foss and Hort, F. J. A., *The New Testament in the Original Greek.* Vol. II: *Introduction; Appendix.* Cambridge and London: Macmillan and Co., 1881.

Westermann, Claus (ed. and contributor), *Probleme alttestamentlicher Hermeneutik.* Aufsätze zum Verstehen des Alten Testaments. "Theologische Bücherei." Neudrucke und Berichte aus dem 20. Jahrhundert. Vol. II. München: Chr. Kaiser Verlag, 1960.

————, *Essays on Old Testament Hermeneutics.* Tr., James L. Mays. New York: John Knox Press, 1963. This is an English translation of the above German work.

White, R. E. O., *The Biblical Doctrine of Initiation.* A Theology of Baptism and Evangelism. Grand Rapids: Wm. B. Eerdmans Publishing Co., 1960.

Wieand, Albert C., *A New Harmony of the Gospels.* The Gospel Records of the Message and Mission of Christ. Revised edition. Grand Rapids: Wm. B. Eerdmans Publishing Co., 1950.

Wilder, Amos Niven, "The First, Second and Third Epistles of John," *The Interpreter's Bible.* Ed., George Arthur Buttrick *et al.* Vol. XII. New York and Nashville: Abingdon Press, 1951-57.

————, "New Testament Hermeneutics Today." *Current Issues in New Testament Interpretation.* Essays in honor of Otto A. Piper. Ed., William Klassen and Graydon F. Snyder. New York: Harper and Brothers, 1962.

Wolfson, Harry A., *Philo.* Foundations of Religious Philosophy in Judaism, Christianity, and Islam. 2 Vols. Cambridge, Massachusetts: Harvard University Press, 1948.

Wood, James D., *The Interpretation of the Bible: An Historical Introduction.* 1st edition. London: Duckworth, 1958.

Wolff, Hans Walter, "Zur Hermeneutik des Alten Testaments." *Probleme alttestamentlicher Hermeneutik.* Ed., Claus Westermann. München: Chr. Kaiser Verlag, 1960.

Wright, George Ernest, "Archaeology and Old Testament Studies." *Journal of Biblical Literature.* Vol. LXXVII (March, 1958), pp. 39-51.

————, *God Who Acts.* Biblical Theology as Recital. Studies in Biblical Theology series. London: SCM Press, 1952.

————, *The Old Testament Against Its Environment.* Studies in Biblical Theology series. London: SCM Press, 1950.

————, *The Rule of God.* Essays in Biblical Theology. New York: Doubleday and Co., 1960.

Wright, George Ernest and Filson, Floyd V., *The Westminster Historical Atlas to the Bible.* Revised edition. Philadelphia: The Westminster Press, 1956.

Wright, George Ernest and Fuller, Reginald., *The Book of the Acts of God.* Contemporary Scholarship Interprets the Bible. New York: Anchor Books, Doubleday and Co., 1960.

Würthwein, Ernst, *The Text of the Old Testament.* An Introduction to Kittel-Kahle's *Biblia Hebraica.* Tr., Peter R. Ackroyd. New York: The Macmillan Co., 1957.

Young, Edward J., *An Introduction to the Old Testament.* Grand Rapids: Wm. B. Eerdmans Publishing Co., 1949.

Young, Robert, *Analytical Concordance to the Bible.* 22nd American edition. Grand Rapids: Wm. B. Eerdmans Publishing Company, 1955.

Zuurdeeg, Willem F., *An Analytical Philosophy of Religion.* New York and Nashville: Abingdon Press, 1958.

————, "The Nature of Theological Language." *The Journal of Religion.* Vol. XL, No. 1 (January, 1960), pp. 1-8.

INDEX OF AUTHORS

Index of Subjects

Accidence, basic to linguistic interp., 13, 14, *see also* Morphology

Accusative absolute (Greek), use of part. in, 135

Acrostics, in Heb. poetry, 329, 330

Action, kinds of: in Grk. verb, 132-33; in Heb. verb, 137

Actions, emblematic, *see* emblematic symbols

Acts of God: importance of, 58-60; attitude of orthodoxy to, 58; nature of response to, 59; ambiguity of some theol. lang. about, 59; conviction of bib. writers that these were redemptive, 61; historically centered, 73, 78

Actualization, of historical reality, 175

Adjectives:
—Greek: followed by complementary inf., 134; one function of Grk. part., 135; modified by adv., 136; gen. with, 142-43; function in case relations, 144; function & position, 145
—Hebrew: classification, 147; usage, 148

'adonay, 81n

Adverbs:
—Greek: classification, 132; usage, 136; art. with, 146
—Hebrew: classification, 137; usage 140

Affirmation, Grk. particles of, 136

Agapē, agapētos, agapaō, 127

Aiōn, use in expressions of time & eternity, 111, 112n, 241n

'al, weaker neg., 141; in prohibition, 157

"al, prep. 147, 156

Alētheia, 123

Alexandria, school of: background, 31-32; expanded influence, 33

Allegorical method: reasons for use in Grk. lit., 28; use by Stoics, 28; in Alexandrian Judaism, 28-29; in patristic period, 30; Epistle of Barnabas, 31;

Origen, 32; Ambrose, 34; Augustine, 34; part of fourfold interp. of M. A., 35; period of prominence 600 to 1200, 36; obscures both lit. & fig. meaning, 37; rejection of in M. A. led to Ref., 38; "monkey tricks"—Luther, 39

Allegorizing: dangers in point by point comparison, 231; falsely identified with typology, 236

Allegory: discussed, 230-35; more extensive form of metaphor, 230; defined—charted characteristics of, 230; context for, 232; extent of use, focal point, 232-34; contrasted with typology, 237-38; principles for interp., 234-35

Alliteration: use in outlines, 105; in Heb. poetry, 330

Alphabetical poem, *see* Acrostics

'amar, stresses God's authority to speak, 81

Amoraim, interpreters of *Tannaim*, 27

Anabaptists, examples of post-Ref. zeal for Bible, 42-43

Anacrusis, in Heb. poetry, 329

Anagogical interp., part of fourfold interp. of M. A., 35

Analogical language: defined, 59; use in contemp. theol., 59-60; 73-74(note 51)

Analogy, in interp. and fulfillment of prophecy, 296, 297-98

Analytical philosophy, cited as example of philos. pre-understanding, 18

Anastasis, 304n

Anoigō, 319n

Anthropology: tool for interp. hist. & culture, 164; value of, 165

Anthropomorphism: opposed by Manichaeanism, 34; disliked by philosophers, 314

Antioch, school of, stress on hist. interp., 33

Antitupos, 239, 240

397

from lit., 197-98; opaque, 199-211; extended, 212-35; typology, 256; in prophecy, 303-05; developed from lit. lang., 304-05; objective reasons for classification, 304, 305; lit. m aning serves as base, 307; never to be judged by subjective labels, 307; employed to describe real event, 307; necessary in revelation, 308; blended with lit., 317-318; essential to convey truth of experiences beyond empirical observation, 322, 376; must have impact on our contemporaries, 322; in poetry, 331; in Proverbs, 334; to be observed in understanding prophetic poetry, 336; nature of shift from lit. illustrated, 350; awareness of brings new depth to doctrinal interp., 350; role in prophecy, 376; see also Literal

Fire, lake of: banishment of Death and Hades to this lake, 320-21; persons consigned to this place, 320-21

Flexibility in syst. theol., 354

Foretelling, see Prophecy

Form vs. content in formal logic, 76

Form, linguistic, very important in bib. lang., 116

Forms, see Morphology

Fourfold interpretation: in M. A., 35-36; Thomas Aquinas, 37; Nicholas of Lyra, 37; abandoned by Luther, 38

Freedom of agent does not invalidate inspiration, 94

Fullness of thought, fig. of speech involving this, 195-97

Functional linguistics, 131

Galah, meaning "to uncover," 192n

Gam, gam kiy, in concessive clauses, 156

Gameō, fig. use by Jesus, 229n

Gar, in coordinate causal clauses, 150

Geenna, as place of punishment, 320

Gemara, comments by Amoraim, 27

Genitive absolute (Grk.), part. used in, 135

Gentiles: object of God's interest in OT, 88; part of three orders of man, 88

Geography: one basic element in understanding of history, 165, 176

Geschichte, emphasis on subjective involvement with facts, 61

Gevurah, descriptive of God's mighty deeds, 58n

Ginesthai en, with noun = verb to be + adj., 217n

Glossa Ordinaria, use in M. A., 36

Gnosis, F. C. Baur's interest in, 46

God: as abstract idea in 20th cent. commentaries, 49; metaphorical language used to describe him, 73; both acts and speaks, 80; covenant name of, 81; action as Creator, 86; action

with Israel, factor of Bible's unity, 86-87; action in Christ, factor of Bible's unity, 87-88; action with those in Christ, 88-89; typology in connection with his people, 240-42; poet's basic convictions about essential for understanding his poetry, 333; revealed in history, 352; fellowship with through Scripture, 356-59; direction from, 359-61; counsel of in personal dialogue, 363-64

Grace, role of in parables, 226-27

Graf-Wellhausen hypothesis, see Wellhausen hypothesis

Grammatical-historical-contextual analysis: in Calvin, 40; need to keep proper perspective on background, 159; in interp. of prophecy, 299

Grammar: Grk., 43, 130-31; Heb. & Aram., 43, 130; revision of, 130-31; use in interp. syntax, 157; role in determination of lit. & fig. lang., 303; duty of bib. theol. to unfold significance of, 347; awareness of by syst. theol., 348

Greek language: koine a simplification of classical, 13; three main elements, 14; source for herm. principles, 13-14; materials in Grk. outside NT, 13-14; essential for the examination of the phenomena of inspiration, 93; pronunciation, 115; history of, 125; grammars, 130-31

Gregory I, end of patristic period, 30

Habits, how to correct bad ones, 377-78

Hades: in lang. of climax, 319-20; personified, 321

Haggadah: non-legal material in mishna and midrash, 25; in Talmud, 27

Hagios, term for people of God, 274, 297

Hakkol, the totality of which God is creator, 311-312 (n. 5)

Halakah, legal material in mishna and midrash, 25; in Talmud, 27

Hanoshek, example in assonance, 330

Harmony of Christians, commanded, 361

Harmony of the Gospels, tool for interp. 108

Hebrew grammars, see Grammar

Hebrew language: source for herm. principles, 10-13; struggle with Aram., 11-12; consonantal system, 13-13; main elements, 13; grammars & lexicons, 43, 117, 130; required for study of phenomena in inspiration, 93; pronunciation, 115; history of, 124-125

Hedraiōma, descriptive of Church, 302n

Hegel, background for Wellhausen hypothesis, 45

Helkuein, as synonym, 128
Hellenistic background, use in *TWNT* word studies, 52
Hellenists, Jews who spoke Greek, 125
Hēmera, eschatological term, 241n
Hēn, Heb. interjection, 141
Hermēneia, hermēneuō, 3
Hermeneutics: not peculiar to Scriptures, 3; definition, 3; importance of, 3-4; objective of, 5; two dimensions, 6; difficult because of time-barrier, 6; hist. of, 20-53; Jewish endeavors, 21-30; areas of general, 99; existentialist, 172-74; old historical approach to, 173; materials involved in special herm., 178; role of general herm. in interp. prophecy, 299; in doctrinal interp., 350-51; general herm. as area plagued by artificial assumptions, 371-72
Heterozugeō, fig. use, 259n
Hēykal, at Jerusalem in OT, 254
Hillel's seven rules of exegesis, 25
Hina: purpose, 151; substantival clauses, 152; variety of translations, 157; reason for parables, 217

Hinnēh, Heb. interjection, 141, coord. construction in temp. clauses, 155

History: methodology of hist. important for interp., 17; hist. crit. in 19th cent., 45; presuppositions of hist. crit., 46; *Historie* with its factual emphasis, 61; outward acts of God as basis for man's inner response, 59; m aning in, 61-64, 159-64; facts personally encountered, 61; three elements of, 62, *into* of God's action, 70; goal or destiny of, 72; framework for God's acts, 73, 78, 352; in bib. narrative begins with creation, 86; essential for study of phenomena of inspiration, 93; importance for school of Antioch, 33; for Calvin, 40; view of in 17th & 18th cent., 43; historicism in 19th cent., 44; danger of exaggerated emphasis upon, 159; essential to understanding of content, 159; as historical science, man-centered, 159-60; reconstruction of historical backgrounds difficult, 161; hist. situation more important than precise dates, 161, 176; complex hist. reconstructions as working hypotheses, 162; tools for study of, 164; works on hist. backgrounds, 165; geography, 165; politics, 166-67; knowledge of essential in cultural context studies, 171: current emphasis on in interp., 172-76; principles for interpreter, 176; influence of prior history on hearers & readers, 176; as background for typology, 237, 238-39; people of God therein, 240-42; no exact empirical demonstrations,

243; determinative of lit. & fig. lang., 303; importance for prophecy, 289-92, 376; occasion behind writing of Psalms, 332; necessary for understanding of prophetic poetry, 336; concern of bib. theol., 344; influence on presentation of theol., 346; theol. must show significance, 347; awareness of by syst. theol. essential, 348; syst. theol. brings into coherent whole strands from various hist. periods, 353; understanding of history useful for devotional study, 362; consummation of, 376
Historical theology, *see* Biblical theology
Hiphil stem, causative active, 138, 206n
Hithpael stem, intensive reflexive, 138
Hodous, in Prov., 4n
Holy Spirit: relation to herm. principles, 4; role in interp. 4, 39, 42; indispensable in interp. for Luther, 39; ignored by rationalistic historicists, 47; activity in inspiration, 92; content of OT promise, 110; relation to truth, 123; medium through whom Jesus speaks to disciples, 209; means of exorcising demons, 226; presence demonstrated in Church, 241; fruit of Spirit to be shown by doctrinal interpreters, 349; role in guidance, 361; role in devotional application, 361; not to be quenched, 362; vital fellowship with essential, 365; activity in the minister, 366; described as an anointing, 373; help in forming good interpretive habits, 378
Hophal stem, causative passive, 138
Hopōs, purpose, 151
hos, relative, 150
hōste, result, 151
hostis, relative, 150
hoti: object clause, 152; syntax help from Bauer's lexicon, 158
Humanism, related to rationalism, 43
hu', demonstrative pronoun, 148
huios, status of Christ, 301n
Hyperbole, discussed, 193-94

Iconoclasts in theology, attitude towards creeds, 354
Ideas, in creedal formulations, 354
Iēsous, numerical value of letters in name, 201
Ignatius, Christocentric interpretation, 31
'im, in conditional, concessive clauses, 156
Imagery, apocalyptic, 303; *see also* Figures of speech, figurative language
Imperative mood: usage testifies to authoritative character of NT, 85; ex-

18th cent., 43; *see also* Textual criticism

Marcion: threw out OT, had little regard for Gospels, 31

Mar'eh, descriptive of how God spoke to Moses, 207n

Marginal references, use in Bible study, source for parallels, 100, 101

Mashal, didactic poetic discourse, 207, 253

Massoretic text; Dead Sea Scrolls show LXX may be earlier in some readings, 16; not always reliable, 43

mē: Grk. neg. in questions, 136; as subjective neg. in Grk., 141

Meaning, *see* Interpretation, Hermeneutics

Meiosis, *see* Litotes

mē pote, neg. purpose, 217

Meros: use in connection with resurrection, 304n; in connection with tree of life, 274n

Meshol mashal, as descriptive of Ezekiel's fable, 204

Message: in cultural context of communication, 170; in existentialist herm., 174

Metaphor, metaphorical meaning: metaphorical vs. lit., 33, 211; designed, i.e., intentional metaphorical lang., 73, 79, 183-85, 317; undesigned, i.e., metaphorical lang. without full consciousness of fig. character, 73, 79, 183, 317; relation to mythical phraseology, 73; examples, 73, 79, 183-85; of the body, in Eph., 106; as figure emphasizing comparison, 183-85; in teachings of Jesus, 184; in OT, 184-85; less extensive form than allegory, 230; chart form of characteristics, 230; used by Paul, 234, 252; in creation of man, 309

Metals, emblematic, *see* Emblematic symbols

Metonymy: in writings of Paul, 186; in OT, 186; nature of, 185-86

Midrash, Midrashim: commentaries on OT, 24; Halakah (legal) and Haggadah (sermonic) matter therein, 25

Midrash pesher, explained by comment & example, 256-60

Min, Heb. prep., 147

Miracles: in controlled continuum, 9; rationalist's attitude toward in 19th cent., 44; eliminated in Baur, 46; place in ministry of (historical) Jesus, 49, 136; as act of God to produce immediate & later effect, 59; pointers to reign of God, 226; as symbols, 266-68

Mishna: topical interpretation of OT, topics contained therein, 25; rabbinical authorities for, 25; various collections of, 25; "canonical," 25; Halakah & Haggadah, 25; as background for understanding of Talmuds, 26-27; composers of, 27

Missionaries (modern), involvement in cultural contexts, 171

Moed, topical category of Mishna, 25

Mood:

—Greek: classification, 132; function & use, 133-34; part. used like indicative, 135; indicative in temp. clauses, 150; subjunctive in temp. clauses, 150; indic. in result clauses, 151; mood as crucial key to conditional sentences, 151; present imp. in prohibitions, 153; subjunctive in prohibitions, 153

—Hebrew: classification, 133; uses, 138

Moral interpretation, part of four-fold interp. of M.A., 35

Morphology: in linguistical analysis, 75; nature of, 115-17; analyzed in grammars, 130

"Multiple sense," *see* Fourfold interpretation

Murabba'at & Dead Sea Scrolls, 15

Mustērion: associated with revelation, 107n, 112n; content of, 111n; *see also* Mystery

Muthos: meaning in polytheism, 71n, 72; *see also* Myth

Mystical interpretation, *see* Allegorical method

Mystery: interp. of in Eph. 3:4-6, 102-04; illuminated by larger context of book of Eph., 106, 107; *see also* Mustērion

Mythology: and Scriptures, 68-73; Bultmann's definition, 69; centrality of myth in polytheistic society, 71; contrasted with truth in Grk. throught, 72; confusion of meaning with classical usage misleading, 71; status of in Bible, 71-72; current usage confuses explanation of fig. lang., 79; not characteristic of history in Israel, 175; *see also Muthos*

Nachash, use in assonance, 330

Names, emblematic, *see* Emblematic symbols

Naos, use of temple in Jerusalem, also fig., 254

Nashim, topic in Mishna, 25

Naviy, use in OT, 285n

nefesh chayyah, in Genesis 1, 2, 9, 316

Negation: in Grk., 136; in Heb., 141

Nestorian controversy, school of Antioch involved, 33

Ne'um yhwh, God communicating, 80-81

"Proof texts": used in 17th & 18th centuries, 43; in disrepute because of abuse, 351; rightly used, 351
Prophecy: alleged to be history written after event, 162, 289; lang. & content of, 178; sources of message from God to prophet, 280-85; nature of prophetic message, 285-295; past & present aspects, 287; future aspect as separate study, 287-88; aspects as part of unified message, 287-88; foret lling & forthtelling, 288; alleged to be history written beforehand, 289-92; enigmatic character of, 289; in apocalypticism, 289; progressive character of, 292-94; lang. of, 295-299; futuristic aspect, insistence on lit. fulfillment of all details, 296; symbolical interp., 296; analogy or equivalency in future aspect, 296; example of analogy or equivalency in particular prophecy, 297-299; didactic, 299-300; principles for interp., 299-305; typological, 300-01; direct prediction, 300-01; fulfillment of in NT, 300-01; Christological orientation, 301-03; attitude toward, 362; role of general & special herm. in, 376
Prophet: defined, 280, 286; not source of prophetic message but mediary, 281; restricted perspective of, 294-95
Prophetic perspective, 294-95
Prophētēs, scope & extent of ministry, 285n
Prophet's message, wholeness of, 287
Prophets, principles for interpreting poetry in, 336-37
Propositions, when attached to concrete event rather than abstract assertion, 58
Pros, with articular inf., 151
Prose: fig. lang. therein not so effective as in poetry, 331; in Job, 335
Protasis, conditional part of sentence, 151
Proverbs: little help from context in interp., 112; often grouped topically, 112; principles for interp., 334-35
Pual, intensive passive, Heb. st m, 138
Purpose, of a book: bearing upon study of genuine parallels, 105, 108; must be observed in connection with context, 113
Purpose (grammatical), as use of Greek inf., 134

Qahal; assembly use as background for ekklēsia, 121; frequency in various parts of OT, 124-25
Qal, simple Heb. stem, most frequently used, 138, 140
Qayitz, part of play on words, 268

Qehal yhwh, Christian Church as true congregation of Jehovah, 241
Qētz, part of play on words, 268
Qumran: locale of Dead Sea Scrolls, 15; kind of community life, products, 22; methods of interp., 22
Quotations: interp. of OT in NT, 255-62; lit. interp. of OT, 255-56; typological interp., 256; with interp. alterations, 256-60; used in new train of thought, 260-61; allegorical interp., 261-62

Rationalism: invalid principles, 4; ruled in theology in post-Ref. period, 42, 43; among interpreters, 47; relation to Bultmannian interp. of life of Christ, 64; explanation of future aspect of prophecy, 289; threat to theology, 338-39; see also History; historicism
Realism, in language, Arthur Holmes, 73n
Reason, final authority in post-Ref. period, 41
Receptor: terminal goal of communication, 170; cultural surroundings, 171
Redactor, assigned "source" of teachings on Holy Spirit in OT, 47
Redemptive history, in OT, 175
Referent, as object of thought, 76
Reign of God: presence of 224-26; parables of, 224-26; loyal adherence to, 227; crisis in, discussed, 227-29; central under both covenants for Eichrodt, 243-44; all details of Christ's earthly reign not spelled out, 306
Relationships (grammatical), see Syntax
Religious-social, see Social-religious situation
Result (grammatical), as use of inf. in Grk., 134
Resurrection: inconceivable as historic fact for Bultmann, 63; as example of interpreted event, 65
Revelation: relation to event, 64; equated with event, 64; relation to interpreted event, 65; davar, a pure expression of, 85; and inspiration, 94; binds two covenants together in vocabulary, 126; creativity thereof makes use of words already in use, 126; as source of prophecy, 283-84; progressive, 352
Rhēma, as synonym, 126
Rhetorical question, see Interrogation
Rhetorical style, in Grk. gives variety to indirect discourse, 152
Riddles: defined, 199; discussed, 199-202; secular, 199-200; sacred, discussed, 201-202; observe in religious purpose, content, outcome, 202; in

INDEX OF SCRIPTURES